South Asia 2060

South Asia 2060

Envisioning Regional Futures

Edited by
Adil Najam and Moeed Yusuf

A

ANTHEM PRESS
LONDON · NEW YORK · DELHI

Anthem Press
An imprint of Wimbledon Publishing Company
www.anthempress.com

This edition first published in UK and USA 2013
by ANTHEM PRESS
75–76 Blackfriars Road, London SE1 8HA, UK
or PO Box 9779, London SW19 7ZG, UK
and
244 Madison Ave #116, New York, NY 10016, USA

First published in hardback by Anthem Press in 2013

British Library Cataloguing-in-Publication Data
A catalogue record for this book is available from the British Library.

Library of Congress Cataloging-in-Publication Data
The Library of Congress has cataloged the hardcover edition as follows:
South Asia 2060 : envisioning regional futures /
edited by Adil Najam and Moeed Yusuf.
pages cm
Includes bibliographical references and index.
ISBN 978-0-85728-074-9 (hardback : alk. paper)
– ISBN 0-85728-074-0 (hardback : alk. paper)
1. South Asia–Forecasting. 2. South Asia–Politics and government–21st century.
3. South Asia–Foreign relations–21st century. 4. South Asia–Economic conditions–21st century.
5. South Asia–Social conditions–21st century. 6. Economic forecasting–South Asia.
7. Social prediction–South Asia.
I. Najam, Adil, editor of compilation. II. Yusuf, Moeed, editor of compilation.
DS341.S6354 2013
303.4954–dc23
2013019505

ISBN-13: 978 1 78308 035 9 (Pbk)
ISBN-10: 1 78308 035 3 (Pbk)

This title is also available as an eBook.

CONTENTS

ACKNOWLEDGMENTS

Conceived and implemented at the Frederick S. Pardee Center for the Study of the Longer-Range Future at Boston University, this book is part of a series of efforts undertaken by the center aimed at better understanding regional futures. Others in the series include conferences and reports on *Africa 2060* and *Latin America 2060*, published by the Pardee Center in 2010 and 2011 respectively (http://www.bu.edu/pardee/). These efforts further the Pardee Center's mission of facilitating research and "generating scholarly discourse and policy options on longer-range challenges and to seek to identify, anticipate and enhance the potential for human progress in the longer-range future."

At the time of putting this book together we were, respectively, director (Adil Najam) and research fellow (Moeed Yusuf) at the Pardee Center. We initiated this book four years ago and carried it along with us as our professional lives took us away from Boston while the manuscript was still being compiled. We are happy to have been able to pull together original essays by some of the most noted experts on South Asia and are highly indebted to each author who has contributed to this volume. We are grateful not only for their contributions but also for their patience and indulgence as we went through the rounds of revisions and edits. We are fully aware that all of them took up this assignment at our personal requests despite being overly committed.

We are deeply saddened to note that two of our contributors, Sir Hilary Synnott and Jalal Alamgir, will not be around to witness the publication of this volume. Both of them passed away before the manuscript went to print. Their chapters were however submitted and accepted before their unfortunate passing. We dedicate this collection to their memory.

As part of the effort, the Pardee Center supported three seminars meant to showcase the effort and to provide a chance for some of the contributors to present their essays. We are indebted to the Sustainable Development Policy Institute, Pakistan, the Singapore Institute of International Affairs, Singapore, the Institute of South Asian Studies at National University of Singapore, and Tufts University's Institute for Global Leadership for partnering with the Pardee Center to host these seminars.

As editors we would like to thank the entire team at Anthem Press. From the early encouragement and constant support of Tej P. S. Sood to the operational editorial hand holding of first Janka Romero and then Rob Reddick, we could not have wished for more supportive and professional assistance.

We are also deeply grateful to the Pardee Center staff who have organized and managed the project and kept both of us honest during the book's long journey to completion. In Theresa White and Elaine Tang we received excellent organizational assistance. A special note of thanks is due to Cynthia Barakatt who provided editorial support in the initial stages of the project and encouragement through all its phases. Invaluable editorial assistance came from two talented and dedicated research assistants: Faris Islam, then an undergraduate at Tufts University, during the very initial phase; and from Jennifer Mitchell, then a Babar Ali Fellow at the Lahore University of Management Sciences (LUMS), during the very final phase. We would also like to express our thanks to Dr Muhammad Ramzan, director library at the Lahore University of Management Sciences (LUMS) and his team for their valuable help in preparing the index.

Finally, and most important of all, we owe our gratitude to colleague, friend, and then Pardee Center research fellow, Ahmet Selim Tekelioglu without whom the process of reviewing, editing and finalizing the manuscript would have been impossible. His meticulous attention to detail, excellent organization, constant good humor and remarkable patience and persistence have been critical to the completion of this collection. Ahmet was the true backbone of this project and remained involved throughout the review process and also performed the thankless task of accumulating all submissions and copy editing the entire manuscript. We are sure that we are joined by all our authors in thanking Ahmet for his efforts and his constant good cheer.

LIST OF ABBREVIATIONS

AAA	Aam Aam Accords
ADB	Asian Development Bank
ASEAN	Association of Southeast Asian Nations
ASEM	Asia–Europe Meeting
AUW	Asian University for Women
BIMSTEC	Bay of Bengal Initiative for Multi-Sectoral Technical and Economic Cooperation
BJP	Bharatiya Janata Party
Bodo/NDFB	National Democratic Front of Bodoland
CBMs	Confidence-building measures
CDs	Communicable diseases
CE	Common Era
CEB	Ceylon Electricity Board
CNG	Compressed natural gas
CNPC	China National Petroleum Corporation
CPJ	Committee to Protect Journalists
CT	Compact township
CTBT	Comprehensive Test Ban Treaty
DALYs	Disability-adjusted life years
EU	European Union
FDI	Foreign direct investment
FSA	Film South Asia
FTA	Free trade agreement
GAP	Good Agricultural Practices
GDP	Gross domestic product
GM	Genetically modified
GMP	Good Manufacturing Practices
GNH	Gross national happiness
GNI	Gross national income
GW	Gigawatts
HDI	Human Development Index
HDL	High-density lipoprotein cholesterol
HDR	Human Development Report

HKH	Hindu Kush Himalaya
HYV	High yielding varieties
IAEA	International Atomic Energy Agency
IANS	Indo–Asian News Agency
ICT	Information communication technology
IFIs	International financial institutions
IIT	Indian Institute of Technology
IMR	Infant mortality rate
IPCC	Intergovernmental Panel on Climate Change
IPL	Indian Premier League
IPP	Independent power producer
ISAF	International Security Assistance Force
ISFTA	Indo–Sri Lanka Free Trade Agreement
kW	Kilowatts
LAMP	Literacy Assessment and Monitoring Programme
LNG	Liquefied natural gas
LoC	Line of Control
LTTE	Liberation Tigers of Tamil Eelam
MDG	Millennium Development Goals
MERCOSUR	Southern Common Market
MFN	Most-favored nation
MOOCs	Massive open online courses
MOUs	Memorandums of understanding
MW	Megawatts
NCDs	Noncommunicable diseases
NGO	Nongovernmental organization
NICs	Newly industrialized countries
NPT	Nuclear Non-Proliferation Treaty
NTBs	Nontariff barriers
ODI	One Day International
OECD	Organisation for Economic Co-operation and Development
OPP-RTI	Orangi Pilot Project's Research and Training Institute
OSCE	Organization for Security and Co-operation in Europe
PCB	Pakistan Cricket Board
PLF	Plant load factor
PPP	Purchasing power parity
PPP	Private power provider
R&D	Research and development
RMB	Renminbi
SAARC	South Asian Association for Regional Cooperation
SAC	South Asian countries
SADA	South Asia Dispatch Agency
SAEF	South Asian Editors' Forum

SAFMA	South Asia Free Media Association
SAFTA	South Asian Free Trade Area
SAMA	South Asia Media Association
SAMW	South Asia Media Wise
SANWFZ	South Asian Nuclear-Weapons-Free Zone
SAPTA	South Asia Preferential Trade Agreement
SATIS	South Asia Agreement on Trade in Services
SAU	South Asian University
SEWA	Self Employed Women's Association
SIPRI	Stockholm International Peace Research Institute
STIs	Sexually transmitted infections
TAPI	Turkmenistan–Afghanistan–Pakistan–India gas pipeline
TB	Tuberculosis
TFR	Total fertility rate
TRIPS	Trade-Related Aspects of International Property Rights
TTP	Tehrik-i-Taliban Pakistan
TVET	Technical and vocational education and training
TWh	Terawatt hour
ULFA	United Liberation Front of Assam
UNDP	United Nations Development Programme
UNESCO	United Nations Educational, Scientific and Cultural Organization
UNICEF	United Nations Children's Fund
UNIFEM	United Nations Development Fund for Women
USSA	United States of South Asia
WHO	World Health Organization

Introduction

IMAGINING SOUTH ASIAN FUTURES

Moeed Yusuf and Adil Najam

Regions, by definition, are artificial constructs. South Asia is no exception. By all the attributes used to define regional groupings – geography, shared history, cultural, political and linguistic commonalities, cost effectiveness of economic interaction and even historical tensions originating from a shared past – South Asia is not just any region, but an ancient, well-established and important one. Yet, despite libraries devoted to the study of all things South Asian, there is relatively less intellectual effort to define the South Asian regional identity, practice as it pertains to the region and the long-term future of the region and its implications for the world.

Consisting of eight geographically proximate but extremely diverse states, the region is home to over one-fifth of the world's population – by 2060, it will be the world's most populated region; it sits atop a globally strategic location, watching over key sea lanes and offering the most attractive transit route to some of the richest energy reserves in Central Asia; the region is rife with conflict, and with nuclear weapons and global terrorism in the mix, its future has profound security implications for the rest of the world; and more recently, its economic potential attracted great positive attention, principally in the case of India but also for the region in general.

Indeed, even as the region's importance and its potentially deep impacts, both negative and positive, on the rest of the world are well understood, this has drawn attention towards trying to understand the region's future trajectory and the opportunities and threats it poses, collectively, both within and outside its geographical expanse. This book focuses on future-oriented analyses of the region – as a region – and invites the authors and the readers to think about the same. What are the longer-range opportunities and challenges that face or emanate not from the individual countries that make up South Asia, but from South Asia as a region?

The dynamic, even turbulent, nature of South Asia today makes the inquiry of where it is heading even more interesting. What has been written about the subject tends to be (i) overly focused on security issues and (ii) shies away from tackling the region in its entirety, instead limiting attention either to the two larger countries, India and Pakistan, or conducting case studies of individual states. This collection is an attempt to look at a wide set of issues from a regional perspective and to begin painting a canvas of regional sensibilities about where South Asia as a region stands today, and where it is heading.

We posed broad, regionally oriented questions to our contributors as starting points: Is regional integration likely to advance or retreat even further? Will we even be talking about a "South Asian region" 50 years from now? How will the fates of individual countries within South Asia impact the region as a whole? Will the region still be seen as a threat to global stability? And how might the fate of the region impact the rest of the world? While the analyses contained herein have gone much beyond these concerns, they still provide a sense of the future without losing sight of these overarching themes. However, our enterprise is not predictive. Instead, current trends and structural realities are studied to produce authoritative, forward-looking analyses within specific sectors and topics. The intent is to project what the range of possible futures might be and, much more importantly, to identify the conditions that might determine which path the region will follow into the next half-century. By having covered a varied and broad array of subjects, we seek to present a holistic study of South Asia going forward, including what is happening within the region and how the region is likely to impact and be impacted by the rest of the world.

A half-century framework is a useful device to do so because it is long enough to shake people off the focus on the *immediate* and the *urgent* and yet short enough for them to imagine a world that would be different in what are the most *important* dimensions. This is because many people can think back to "what was" 50 years ago (grandparent views) and also imagine ahead to "what could be" different in 50 years (grandchildren views). More importantly, the most critical issues that confront this region – poverty, security, ecology, etc. – simply cannot be changed by short-term policy band-aids and require us to think of deeper structural change. A longer-range framework encourages this type of systemic thinking. It also moves us away from the conventional, in-the-moment analyses that have been in the forefront of the South Asian discourse: terrorism, extremism, conflict, fragility of states, fundamentalism, etc.

This book is a product of a two-year long effort of the Boston University Frederick S. Pardee Center for the Study of the Longer-Range Future and is the product of an ongoing dialogue amongst thought leaders from across South Asia and the world, and from various disciplines, on the likely longer-range trajectories of South Asia's future as a region. The 37 essays – thought pieces – in this book focus on a range of functional areas that impinge upon South Asia's future. We organize these functionally across four themes. We begin with five context-setting essays that discuss the "idea" and future of the South Asian region as a whole. The next section consists of ten essays dealing with the future of interstate relations and security aspects of South Asian ties. Contributors to the section discuss democracy, religion, conflict, the presence of nuclear weapons and regional integration issues. This is followed by a section tackling various aspects of the South Asian economy including macroeconomic prospects, globalization, trade, trends in urbanization, water security, energy and technology. Another eleven essays examine the well-being of its people, including the prospects of a South Asian population dividend, health, education, women empowerment and civil society forces such as media and sports. In inviting authors there has been a conscious attempt to broaden the canvas of the South Asian conversation and to make sure that the overbearing issues of security and conflict are given due emphasis but do not overwhelm and drown out issues pertaining to development and human well-being.

This volume brings together 44 experts with many centuries of collective expertise and experience in South Asia who were invited to write authoritatively and from their own disciplinary and professional perspectives on an array of issues relevant to the region's future. The authors bring a mix of practitioners and academics including former state officials, policymakers, academics, public intellectuals, as well as civil society activists. Authors were invited to ponder upon future possibilities, potentials and pitfalls for the region in their own "voice" but where the reader can also identify with the "conversation" that the book seeks to embody. There is no attempt to forge a consensus, but interestingly a number of common themes do organically emerge from this conversation.

Written by some of the leading scholars and practitioners working on South Asia and including experts from a variety of fields, from the region and beyond, each essay is a stand-alone testament and it is neither useful nor possible to summarize all of the chapters here. However, in reading all of them together we as editors have identified five key overarching and related themes that come across as central to understanding and shaping the future of South Asia as a region.

#1: The Idea of South Asia

South Asians tend to instinctively recognize and connect with each other as South Asians, but the idea of South Asia does not come naturally to citizens of the region. Yet the chapters in this volume suggest that it is not an idea that South Asians are willing, or able, to let go of. The essays in this book demonstrate that for reasons of geography, of history and of geopolitics it is hard to talk about the region as a region without quickly turning it into a problematique around one or a few of the major powers in South Asia. Yet, we as editors are ourselves surprised that none of our authors is ready to seriously question the idea of South Asia or propose that the regional identity would or should wither away soon. Interestingly, the weakness of our collective "Southasianness" only highlights the strength of our aspiration for such an identity.

The dilemma is portrayed, for example, in the editorial policy of the journal *Himal* – whose editor, Kanak Mani Dixit, is a contributor to this volume – which chooses to speak of "Southasia" as one word rather than of "South Asia," which it believes is an "aloof geographical term" that does not capture the sense of "historical unity of our common living space." While the primacy of the existing nation-states in the region is nowhere questioned, the desire to eventually supplement it with a strong sense of regional identity remains evident in the region and in many of our essays. However, South Asia remains far from becoming Southasia just yet.

Just what does it mean to be Southasian, or even South Asian? Are regional states inclined to view themselves as part of the larger region, and is there reason enough for the world to look at the region as a whole that can be dealt with at a regional level? Are shared – but contested – histories and geographies enough to craft and hold a regional identity? These and other such questions remain open. While they are sometimes raised in this volume, they have yet to be answered. They can ultimately only be answered by the realities in the region itself, including the shape of regional institutions but not limited to just that. The politics of these realities does not seem to be changing anytime soon. But, as we shall note later, other realities – including those related to economic, social, cultural and even sports interaction – intervene to keep the idea of South Asia alive and kicking. Technology, trade, politics, even cricket, could ferment the imagination into reality in ways that cannot be easily imagined right now. Our reading of the essays in this volume suggests that the future of the geography we know as South Asia will depend, at least in part, on what happens to the idea of Southasia. We are not in a position to say what that will be just yet, but it is clear that the aspiration of Southasianness is entrenched more deeply in the South Asian mind than we had imagined. It is an idea that our regional politics has often rejected and fought against. But the resilience of the aspiration suggests regional politics may eventually have to embrace it.

#2: Regionalism: Practice and Institutions

Competitiveness – not cooperation – defines today's South Asia; regional institutions remain nascent and weak. Multiple efforts at institutionalizing regional cooperation have stalled. In fact, the South Asian states were so hesitant in undertaking substantive regional initiatives that failure of regionalism was scripted in the tentativeness with which these attempts were made. It is hardly surprising then that the desire to treat the present as the South Asian moment – to underscore the compulsions that must push South Asia towards regionalism – among several of the authors is often overwhelmed by the reality that South Asian entities seldom conceive of themselves, or behave, as part of a regional framework.

The future of arrangements such as the South Asian Association for Regional Cooperation (SAARC) and other truly regional endeavors hangs in the balance but a collective read of the chapters highlights a discernible sense that South Asia represents, first and foremost, an unfulfilled potential. That a successful South Asian future lies in a stronger SAARC and greater regional efforts all round is accepted across the board. Yet, the concern that the challenges South Asia faces are immense is unmistakable; the ability of South Asian states and citizens to overcome these cannot be taken for granted. The irony is that while several authors point to regionalism as being key to overcoming the region's principal challenges, they also point out that the presence of these very challenges undermines any drive towards regionalism to begin with.

At the heart of South Asia's failure to implement regional solutions is the long-standing dispute between India, the central actor in terms of size, geography, economy, and military might, and Pakistan, the largest among the rest of the South Asian states.

The propensity of the two largest states to view each other as inherently competitive has been overbearing: the smaller neighbors, otherwise well placed and eager to piggyback on a cooperative spirit and action from their larger neighbors, have instead been frustrated by the intransigence in New Delhi and Islamabad.

The future of the praxis of cooperation in the region then remains uncertain. Some argue that there is a real danger of these countries settling for the suboptimal: going for extraregional and subregional arrangements in pursuit of their individual priorities. Shall this happen, and there is already some evidence of it, this new reality could undermine societal strength of the "Idea of South Asia." Others however still see compelling reasons why these countries could overcome their differences and move ahead as a regional grouping. Indeed, there is some evidence that this may even be happening as efforts like the opening of India–Pakistan trade begin to bear some early fruits. One thing is clear to all our authors and to us: no positive scenario for South Asia as a region is plausible if India and Pakistan remain locked in their decades old rivalry.

#3: The South Asian State

The South Asian state is, simultaneously, real and imagined, strong and weak, and a potential stumbling block and a hopeful prospect for future of the region. Perhaps owing to the colonial legacy of the region, the South Asian state has been a key actor in almost all aspects of the life of South Asians; it has had a rather overbearing presence. Its performance, varied as it is across cases, has for the most part fallen short of expectations of the average South Asian's demands on the state.

What is clear is this: neither can the South Asian state continue to make excuses for its poor performance without altering its ways, nor will populations – whose own demands on the state have grown over time – continue to accept such arguments at face value. From individual security to economic development to education, the South Asian state has been weak to deliver on its social contract with its citizens. And this expectation–reality disconnect on the part of the people of South Asia shows no immediate sign of narrowing. And yet, our contributors are both skeptical and hopeful when it comes to the future role of the South Asian state – skeptical, because of the past, and hopeful because of the growing awareness among rulers that the status quo is becoming more and more difficult to maintain.

A collective reading of the volume will also underline the need for a regional learning curve. South Asian states have a lot to learn from each other. Problems, challenges, and potential solutions that the South Asian states face are not identical, but they have deep similarities. As much as people-to-people relations signal the birth of a new perspective for the future of the region, state-to-state relations can garner a similar perspective. It would have been easier to achieve this with stronger regional institutions and mechanisms, but as many of our contributors argue, the lack of existing mechanisms can give us open and fruitful ground for cooperation along more innovative lines.

The South Asian state, despite all its weaknesses, is here to stay. It may not deserve the imagined glory many in the region attribute to it, but as an institution it will be key for the future of the region. Interestingly, a collective lesson from the chapters in this book suggests that the nature of government is very varied in the region, but the nature of the state is not. The South Asian state may have old habits but it is not a static construct. When pushed by forces of internal or external reform, it has changed, reformed and weathered with amazing agility. A future South Asia with a diminished state is unlikely, but one with a still dominant but a more inclusive one is highly possible, even likely. People of South Asia will be better served if our energies are directed to constructively forcing it to play a positive role in the future. Our contributors, while different in their degrees of optimism, form a collective voice towards this goal.

#4: Security and Development

To many, South Asia represents an overpopulated region riddled with conflict. It is. But it is also much more than that. The multitude of internal, interstate and international conflicts in South Asia have led to a disproportionate focus on the region's security challenges. A "securitized" discourse and an assumption that there is an inevitable trade-off between security and development are often considered foregone conclusions for the South Asian region. A collective read of this volume confirms the impossibility of talking of either security or development in the South Asian context without drawing a link with the other. However, it also highlights the need to consider security and development, not as trade-offs but as two pillars of progress that must be pursued in tandem.

Does security come before development, or does it work the other way? This question has preoccupied many regional experts on the subject. A number of essays in this volume allude to it as well. The conventional wisdom holds that security has trumped development. Indeed, given the region's numerous and serious security problems, one cannot ignore the fact that South Asian security is marred by a grim past and present, and that the region is grossly underdeveloped in terms of human well-being. Empirics seem to support the assumption that improved security would have to precede better development outcomes. In regional terms, the overbearing presence of India and Pakistan's troubled relationship and their policy to hold back a truly regional development focus to prevent the other from gaining in the process has been all too obvious. But also within each major regional state, sustained conflict and political upheavals have led to resource utilization that has been heavily skewed towards strong security rather than development.

There is the other view as well. Increasingly, development gains, especially ones that create economic interdependence within the region, are being seen as a pathway to improved security. For proponents of this narrative, the way to break the "securitization" of the South Asian narrative is to produce tangible economic gains which will naturally reduce the hold of security-centric premises and generate greater support for a focus on development outcomes.

A close read of the volume at hand hints at no such clear-cut directionality or ordering. The tension that emerges from coexistence of both security and development challenges is not one that will be solved through a focus on one at the expense of the other.

Quite to the contrary, the tone that emerges from this volume is that just like the problems are intertwined and synchronized, the way out of the security-development impasse is a concerted effort in addressing both issues. Indeed, there is desperation in the narrative that seems to suggest that *because* security and development are so closely connected in South Asia it is irrelevant which one we start with. The benefits of tangible advances in either are so very real and so very profound that they do not need to be justified beyond their own self. A related undertone to the narrative is the sense across the region that their governments have now grown accustomed to and quite adept at using the arguments of insecurity and a lack of development as excuses for their ability to better deliver development or security.

A key message of this volume, then, is to break the viciousness of the circularity of the conventional arguments. This is so because unlike conventional thinking, the relationship between security and development is not one of a trade-off, but rather codependence. In other words, both security and development are needed, and they are needed at the same time in order to provide South Asians with a brighter future. Parallel, synergetic tracks must be pursued – this requires more focus on people and less on militaries and weapons than at present.

#5: South Asia and Its People

Our authors invest the greatest hope in a fundamental people-centric transformation as the drivers of South Asia's destiny in the years to come. While recognizing the enormity of the challenge – it entails a fundamental departure from traditional governance in the region – a sense of confidence in the South Asian citizen as an agent of positive change comes across clearly throughout the volume. The earlier discussion on the South Asian state notwithstanding, quite clearly our authors repose far more faith in the change ability of the South Asian citizen – as an economic agent, as a social agent and ultimately as a political agent – than of the South Asian state. The preference is strong and candid.

A sense of opportunity flows from the belief that South Asia is moving – perhaps too slowly for many, but it is – towards a model where a people are willing and able to shift systems. At the heart of this shift are the very powerful forces of demography, technology and globalization. The population is young, restless and impatient. But also idealistic and willing to bet on change. It is also increasingly connected – even at the lowest economic strata – with technology and with the possibility of technology. And because of that it is very acutely aware of what is happening elsewhere in the world and it is determining its aspirations as well as its action strategies from that awareness.

On the one hand, standards of education and healthcare are set to rise and democratic institutions, however broken, are also increasingly becoming the norm. These bring greater awareness and enhanced capacities to claim individual and collective rights and demand better social sector outcomes. On the other hand, South Asia's young population is unlikely to have all its needs met notwithstanding better state performance. It is likely, therefore, to not only push for change but also become agents of that change in an increasingly connected world where the young South Asian is as connected – and often more – than most.

Most important here are the regional implications of this cross-region shift. In a region that is likely to continue providing more than enough legitimate reasons for alienation, disenfranchisement and disgruntlement, the discontented, especially with greater awareness of rights, are certain to run up against the traditional model. Then there are remarkable efforts by civil society actors that are already putting shared interests and passions up front and setting the stage for a paradigm shift in favor of the common man and woman in South Asia. Initiatives such as "Hands Across the Borders" and "Aman ki Asha" are already looking to increase contact and understanding among peoples and providing alternate forums to envision regional futures.

Greater voice for the citizens and a reoriented focus on human well-being is beginning to compel states to explore obvious complementarities among South Asian states. Once this process generates momentum, the multiple compulsions for South Asian states to work together could become the principal lens through which leaders of states are forced to approach cross-border interactions. There is already growing recognition, highlighted by our contributors, that much of South Asia's challenges and opportunities are common. Issues ranging from natural resources (climate change, water, energy), to basic requirements like education, health and poverty alleviation, to security issues such as terrorism all lend themselves to greater cross-border cooperation. The most optimistic among the authors see these compulsions and the nascent movements to craft a new equilibrium in favor of the average South Asian as progressing to their logical conclusions.

The new South Asia will affect South Asian citizens born today. In the best case, they will find an environment conducive to cooperation across South Asia; one that allows every South Asian to look at his or her regional identity proudly and with a sense of purpose and conviction.

* * *

We did not go out to seek an optimistic verdict from our authors. Indeed, we did not expect one. We are surprised, but quite happy, to get one. Maybe the biggest surprise for us was that even with such a large contingent of such experienced and diverse authors, no one is willing to give up on South Asia; many because they see the overwhelming potential of the region as a region, some because they think it is too important to let go of and will only become more important. Maybe it was in pushing the time horizon that the conversation shifted. While the analysis rooted in today's South Asia – sometimes from the very same authors – is predominantly (and justifiably) rooted in the problems to be surmounted, the tone of the chapters that follow often stems from the realization of the possibilities. In the road that leads from here to tomorrow, it is critical that South Asia addresses those problems – and as best as we can at whatever scale – but it is equally important that the aspiration of the possible is also forever kept in sight.

Section I

SOUTH ASIA AS A REGION

Chapter 1

PRISONERS OR MASTERS OF DESTINY?

Ramesh Thakur

Global govern*ance* for a world without *world* govern*ment* faces a fundamental paradox. The policy authority for tackling global problems and mobilizing the necessary resources is principally vested at country level, in states, while the source and scale of the problems and potential solutions to them are transnational, regional and global. One result of this situation is that states have the capacity to disable decision making and policy implementation by global bodies like the United Nations, but generally lack the vision and will to empower and enable their own global problem solving on issues such as human rights abuses, gender discrimination, environmental degradation, human trafficking, terrorism and nuclear weapons.

Could regionalization, by inserting an additional level of governance between the state and the world, provide a satisfactory resolution of this paradox? What are the implications of regionalism and interregionalism for global governance and world order? And what might a regionally integrated South Asia look like in 50 years' time? In this essay, I will first comment on the rise of regionalism in recent decades and then describe how South Asia has bucked the trend, before concluding with a personal, highly idealized vision of the South Asian region in the year 2060.

The Rise of Regionalism[1]

Regional integration refers to a process in which a group of countries, usually contiguous, move from a condition of disconnected isolation to one of partial or complete unification. The shift involves a progressive lowering of internal boundaries within the integrating zone and a de facto rise of external boundaries vis-à-vis countries outside the region for the flow of goods, services, capital, labor, people and even ideas. Although regional integration does not have to involve the construction of permanent intergovernmental structures of mutual cooperation, usually it does.

Regional organizations have proliferated across the world since 1945. Some have argued that the nation-state has become an unnatural, perhaps even dysfunctional,

---

1 This section draws on R. Thakur and L. V. Langenhove. "Enhancing Global Governance through Regional Integration," *Global Governance* 12, no. 3 (July–September 2006): 233–40.

unit for organizing human activity and economic interactions in a borderless world and that it does not represent any genuine community of economic interests. Instead, the natural economic zones are "region states" whose boundaries are drawn not by politicians but by the invisible hand of the global market for goods and services. And their primary links are not with host countries but with the global economy (Ohmae 1993).

The growth in the number and geographical coverage of regional organizations is accompanied by increased diversity in the "substance" or "content" of integration. For example, some regional integration projects are limited to the achievement of economic integration among the countries concerned. Others extend integration beyond purely economic concerns in a so-called "new regionalism" (Hettne et al. 1999; and Söderbaum and Shaw 2003), which holds that trade and economy cannot be isolated from the rest of society. In this approach, integration can also encompass matters of law, security and culture.

The European Union (EU), the first and most advanced instance of "new regionalism," incorporates explicit political elements in a deep economic integration. The EU requires that would-be member states meet certain standards of behavior in public and foreign policy before they can be considered to be truly "European." The new regionalism has also spread to other continents, both through the creation of new organizations (like the Southern Common Market, MERCOSUR, in Latin America) and through the upgrading of previously existing regional and subregional economic bodies (as with the reinvention of the Organization of African Unity as the African Union). Nevertheless, regionalism remains uneven across the world and in Europe itself; there were major setbacks in 2010 as several countries in the eurozone were hit by major economic crises, raising questions of the viability of economic integration without fiscal and even political union.

In parallel with spreading and deepening regional integration, recent decades have also seen the gradual emergence of interregionalism, or relations among different regions, which interact with one another as regions. Initially the EU dominated in this area, building formal relations with the Association of Southeast Asian Nations (ASEAN) as early as 1980. Regular Asia–Europe Meetings (ASEM) and the EU–MERCOSUR agreement followed in the 1990s. Now regional organizations from all continents have become more active in pursuing interregional connections.

Thus regionalism has become an integral part of contemporary multilayered and multiactor governance. Neither states by themselves nor the United Nations (UN) as their universal collective forum can substitute for regional governance. Whether in Africa, the Americas, Asia or Europe, countries share certain policy problems and approaches on a regional scale that they do not hold in common with all countries on a global scale. At the same time, however, regional governance cannot substitute for the UN, particularly in promoting security and development in the world. The task is therefore to build effective partnerships among states and regional and global agencies, and also among governmental and nongovernmental actors.

South Asia: A Region *Sans* the Sense of Regionalism

Among the world's inhabited continents, Asia has the least sense of pancontinental identity. It is an essentially geographical construct developed by the Europeans to differentiate themselves from the "Other." In the UN system, for example, which functions ubiquitously and pervasively on the basis of geographical groupings, Asians are the least united. Even on the sporting field, Europeans, Africans, Latin Americans and North Americans have a sense of shared bonds that is missing in action in Asia.

Within Asia, South Asia is marked by its own paradox. It is one of the sharpest natural regions of the world, with clearly defined physical characteristics, shared histories and considerable economic and administrative coherence inherited from the British Raj. Yet regionalism was progressively weakened after the departure of the British as the independent countries went their separate ways politically, economically and in their foreign policies. To date, interstate tensions have inhibited the rise of South Asian regional identity, institutions and interactions. Can the direction of causality be reversed: is it possible to envisage better relations among South Asian countries as a consequence of the creation of regional institutions? After all, the primary original motivation behind European economic integration after 1945 was geopolitical, to prevent another war between Europe's great historic enemies. Today, war between Britain, France and Germany is indeed unthinkable.

The South Asian region comprises Bangladesh, Bhutan, India, the Maldives, Nepal, Pakistan and Sri Lanka. Although Afghanistan joined the South Asian Association for Regional Cooperation (SAARC 1985) in 2007, for most practical purposes, because of the Western military intervention that has neglected the country's history being rooted in its geography (Thakur 2012), it has been largely disconnected from regional cross-currents. South Asia's combined population represents one-fifth of the world's people. It is also a population characterized by poverty, illiteracy, and low life expectancy. South Asian countries do not fare well on these measures even by developing-country standards, let alone by world or industrial-country standards. In addition, most of them are wracked with problems of internal security and economic scarcities which threaten them with political destabilization and territorial disintegration. The region is home to one of the most concentrated grouping of fragile and failing states. Yet, on the positive side, South Asia too has been infected by the worldwide movement toward greater democratization and market freedoms.

India by itself accounts for around three-quarters of South Asia's total population, land area and economic product. This has a triple consequence. Most obviously, India is the natural hegemon of South Asia. Second, other countries find it difficult to imagine existential threats to India. And yet thirdly, if India were to suffer from state failure and breakup, the consequences for all other countries in the neighborhood would be horrific as well.

India's position in the region is distinctive also for the fact that all other states, save the Maldives, share a border with India but not with any other. This has three important consequences for India. First, all other states have every prospect of strained relations with India but little chance to develop friction in sparse relations with each other. Second, having India as a common problematic neighbor encourages the others to team up against the regional giant. Third, India is open to major social and political forces sweeping any of its neighbors. Whether it be civil war in Afghanistan, Maoist insurgency in Nepal, Islamic fundamentalism in Bangladesh and Pakistan or Tamil insurgency in Sri Lanka, the turmoil will spill over into India.

By size, location and power India is and will ever be the principal actor in South Asian international relations. Geopolitics ensures too that India is the hub with spokes running to all the other states in the region, so that South Asian international relations revolve around India. India has not been free of difficulties in bilateral relations with any of its neighbors: demographic overspills from Bangladesh (while the latter itself can be flooded by refugees from Myanmar), the flow of goods across India from landlocked Nepal, the use of water from shared river systems with Pakistan, the spillover effects of ethnic warfare in Sri Lanka, the demarcation of maritime boundaries with the two large neighbors of Bangladesh and Pakistan and the perennial problems in relations with Pakistan.

India has a considerable military capacity to influence the outcomes of varying levels of conflict in South Asia. But it lacks the economic underpinning and diplomatic finesse to bend regional affairs to its political will. Consequently, its self-appointed managerial role in the region remains flawed. Its aspirations to regional leadership are continually thwarted by the stubborn refusal of other South Asian countries to learn the art of "followership" (for a discussion of this evocative concept, see Cooper, Higgott and Nossal 1991). The smaller countries were especially emboldened to challenge India's preeminence by the humiliation inflicted on it by China in 1962.

The fact that India has sometimes had disputes with all its neighbors simultaneously suggests that India itself might be the center and cause of some regional disputes. Anxious to project itself on the world stage, India has appeared irritated at regional obstacles in its path to the status of a world power. In a remarkable tribute to a fatally flawed foreign policy, India finds itself without a network of useful friendships in its own region. India's potential lies first and foremost in its neighborhood. Instead of realizing this potential, India has frightened all its neighbors at one time or another. They have tended to view India as overarmed, overweening and "over here."

The search for a regional security structure remains as elusive today as it was in 1947. The pivot of South Asian regional geopolitics is the India–Pakistan rivalry. On the one hand, Pakistan is everyone's favorite basket case on the brink of state failure and collapse as well as being suspected of state complicity in cross-border terrorism. Its bloody birth, the history of unremitting hostility with India, the bitter legacy of the loss of its eastern half to India-assisted secession in 1971, the decades of civil war with international entrapments in Afghanistan, the military capture of the commanding heights of the nation's polity, the rise of Islamism as a global phenomenon, and the stranglehold of corruption on the country's institutions have left it fractured as a society and broken as a polity. On the other hand, Pakistan has a middle class that is as well educated as India's, a vigorous and inquisitive print and electronic media, an independent and assertive judiciary, and per capita income comparable to India's.

The World of 2060

South Asia's diffidence in moving towards open economic regionalism is in marked contrast to the evident trend toward free trade agreements in several parts of the world. For all South Asian countries, prosperity will require the flattening of regional borders, price-driven competition, free markets, the state limited to its elemental functions and an abandonment of dirigisme.

In November 2011, Pakistan caused a frisson of excitement in India by announcing the grant of most-favored-nation (MFN) status, something that India had granted to Pakistan back in 1996. The excitement faded as Islamabad, facing opposition from sections of the business community and religious organizations, "clarified" that it was merely considering whether to do so. In early 2012, Pakistan did confirm that it was moving to a negative list for trade with India, whereby anything that was not on a proscribed list would be tradable. Although India had wanted a 600-item negative list, Pakistan approved a list of 1,209 items. This would still open up an estimated 6,850 commodities for trade against the existing 1,900 and pave the way for MFN status in a year or so (Joshua 2012). Quick calculations showed that this would increase the volume of bilateral trade from the existing $2.7 billion to an estimated $6 billion by 2014 (TOI 2012). In effect Pakistan emulated the strategy adopted by India vis-à-vis China in the 1980s not to hold bilateral trade hostage to the boundary dispute. For such efficiency – and trade – promoting gains to accrue, both countries would need improved infrastructure, additional trading points on the border, better customs facilities and financial services, and further dismantling of nontariff barriers to trade.

One goodwill gesture that India could make is to comply fully with the provisions of the Indus Waters Treaty in order to assuage some real fears that Pakistan has with respect to water flows (Iyer 2012). Conversely, should the Arab Spring spread eastward, Pakistan's educated middle class reclaim ownership and control of the nation's destiny, and civilian rule and secular democracy take hold there, other than Pakistanis themselves, Indians will be the happiest in the world and ready to embrace their neighbors most warmly.

If the implications of the above analysis are understood, internalized and embedded in practices and institutions over the course of the next 50 years, what might South Asia look like in 2060, both in the region itself, and in the mode of articulation of the region with the rest of the world?

First and most obviously, there will be a complete economic union: a single market with no tariff or nontariff barriers to the movement of goods, services, capital and labor; a customs union with a common external tariff whose height will have been progressively lowered as well anyway; South Asia–wide regulatory norms, instruments, and institutions to ensure a level playing field for producers, manufacturers, and consumers alike; cross-recognition of qualifications, skills, and certifications with common professional governing bodies for tradesmen, engineers, doctors, lawyers, etc.; domestic supplier status for businesses for procurement tenders in all countries regardless of the country of origin of the firms bidding for contracts, except perhaps in such sensitive sectors as defense; comparable labor and industrial laws and policies to facilitate entry and exit of workers and firms, with market forces and price mechanisms determining business decisions and the role of government being to provide the public goods like law and order and infrastructure; and so on. There will be a common currency, most likely called the rupee. A powerful and independent South Asian Central Bank will have the responsibility to ensure that member countries' monetary and fiscal policies do not stray outside agreed bands. There will also be tough enforcements of competition and anticorruption laws and norms and common prudential and surveillance instruments to stop the market running amok as it did in the USA and Europe in 2008–2009.

Economic integration will spur market efficiencies, scale economies, specialization based on factor and other comparative advantages, and a shift to more productive, innovative and balanced economies. By 2060 therefore all South Asian countries will fare very well in the World Bank's ease of doing business rankings. The size of the market will attract considerable investment capital; and the advanced infrastructure, good governance norms and institutions, and highly skilled, educated and mobile labor force will underpin rising prosperity. Pakistan will have become "the great trading crossroads of the world" (Rashid 2012): a hub for commerce, trade and energy transportation networks between the Middle East, South Asia and China. At the same time, government policies will have kept a watch and check on inequalities between individuals (bottom and top 10 percentiles), groups (castes, religions, regions) and countries. That is, South Asia will have a region-wide free market combined with a social welfare ethos that provides affordable social security safety nets for the poor and the underprivileged. Consequently, South Asia will have climbed dramatically up the human development ladder as well.

The advances in human security will be matched by a highly progressive human rights machinery that seamlessly integrates national with regional norms and institutions, including a South Asian Human Rights Commission to advocate and defend human rights and a South Asian Human Rights Court to enforce human rights laws and check that national laws and practices comply with regional norms. Few Asians are amused at being lectured on universal human values by those who failed to practice the same during European colonialism, and now urge them to cooperate in promoting "global" human rights norms. The solution is to focus on human rights at the regional level. In the South Asian context, economic, social and religious rights are as critical as civil and political rights to safeguard the rights of the poor, the marginalized, the tribals, the illiterate, the migrant and itinerant workers, the outcastes and of course women. South Asian values and sensibilities are also better attuned to a balance between rights and responsibilities rather than a privileging of the former at the cost of neglecting the latter.

There will be an appropriately mandated and adequately resourced High Commissioner for National Minorities and Tribal Peoples who will ensure that the rights and interests of Tamils in Sri Lanka, Muslims in India, Hindus in Pakistan, *adivasis* and tribal peoples across South Asia and so on are properly protected in law and are enforced by the civil service, police, and judiciary. Other regional institutions will include variations of a South Asian parliament, commission, president and foreign minister. The South Asian regional university will be reinforced by 2060 with a network of applied science, technology, social science, strategic studies and peace research institutes.

To be poor and a female in South Asia is to be doubly cursed. Women can confront insecurity that is direct (for example honor killing), or rooted in structural and cultural violence. While men suffer from the public violence of criminality and wars, the violence inflicted on women is mainly in the private realm of the household and is mostly suffered in silence. In the words of an eminent Sri Lankan:

> Even before birth women suffer from sex selective abortion, at infancy they may face female infanticide, as young children they will have to put up with incest and son preference, as adolescents they may be sexually abused or trafficked, as young women they may suffer rape, sexual harassment, acid attacks; as wives they may experience domestic violence, dowry related violence, marital rape or honour killings, and as widows they may be required to self immolate or be deprived of property or dignity. The vulnerability to violence at every stage of their life-cycle makes VAW [violence against women] a terrible south Asian legacy that requires concerted regional, national and local level action. (Coomaraswamy 2005, 4730)

Her analysis proved tragically prescient in 2012 with regard to Malala Yousafzai, the Pakistani schoolgirl shot (but not fatally) to stop her campaign for girls' education; and "Nirbhaya,"[2] the young university student raped and killed in New Delhi. Policy measures in response, by 2060, include strengthened state capacity to monitor and enforce laws against women-specific violence like rape, national implementation machinery for international commitments signed by states, and regional compacts to protect women and promote their empowerment and welfare.

Like women, children are acutely vulnerable to abuse. They are forcibly recruited as child soldiers or sex slaves. They are more vulnerable to death caused by disease and starvation, especially when access to medical help and food aid become deliberate tactics of war. They have the right to be protected by their own government. Where national governments fail, the regional community cannot abdicate from its responsibility to protect them. The national, regional and global machinery for enforcing laws and norms for protecting the rights of children will have been strengthened still further by 2060.

Children and women are trafficked for sexual purposes across South Asian borders – for example from Nepal to India – and from South Asia to other regions. In 2010,

---

2 The word means "without fear." Although her identity was revealed in the international media, this is in breach of Indian law and so the pseudonym is used here.

around 800,000 people were trafficked internationally every year and large numbers were trafficked internally, to service the sex trade, the adoption industry, the begging for alms industry, the market for domestic and industrial servitude or trafficking in brides and organs. Amnesty International believes that "the trafficking of women into forced prostitution is one of the most widespread and pervasive forms of violence against women" (Amnesty International 2004, 1). Even after they have been rescued by the authorities, trafficked women are vulnerable to violations by law enforcement, criminal justice and other agencies.

Human trafficking is a problem in almost every South Asian country, with children being its biggest victims. National performance lags behind international law making in combating the threat. The dominant national security paradigm in 2010 tends to treat the problem as a crime against the state. In 2060, this will be considered to be a crime against the individual person within the framework of human security. The trafficked persons will be treated by the police, immigration and criminal justice system as victims and the focus of prosecution will have shifted to where it really belongs: the buyers and sellers and the corrupt officials who collude with them. The requisite policy responses include ratification of global protocols against human trafficking, its incorporation into domestic legislation and the criminalization of trafficking in national law, and robust regional machinery to police and enforce antitrafficking laws through active cooperation among border control, intelligence, and law enforcement authorities.

There is another dimension. South Asia is a major source for migrant workers to many Middle Eastern countries; these people migrate to work as domestic help, for example as maids, as well as casual laborers. Often these are precisely the groups that lack legislative and police safeguards in countries of destination and are very vulnerable to abuse. In 2060 South Asian countries should have common norms and pooled investigative and advisory services to protect the rights and ensure the welfare of one another's citizens working and traveling abroad.

They should also have common environmental norms, laws and institutions backed by a South Asian Environmental Protection Agency. In addition, precisely because South Asia is so sharply integrated in its physical features, there will be South Asian regional bodies to regulate waterways, manage river systems, establish water usage and distribution norms, monitor water tables and pollution indices, control deforestation and oversee reforestation, encourage biodiversity, preserve ecosystems and so on. Similarly, there will be a powerful, active and highly visible regional body to safeguard and patent traditional knowledge, including with respect to medicinal plants and health exercises, and protect and promote these as public goods beyond the grasp of rapacious individuals and firms out to appropriate intellectual property rights.

Progress on South Asian regionalism has been held hostage for over six decades by the India–Pakistan dispute over Kashmir. The ceasefire line/Line of Control (LoC) – that is, the de facto border between India and Pakistan running through the spine of Kashmir – has barely moved between 1947 and 2010. But the conflict has exacted huge costs from both countries and even more from Kashmiris. Sensibly, all sides will agree that in the modern age, what matters is not who formally controls a territory but how free all people are to move within and in and out of any territory. They will work hard and successfully to make the line separating Indian from Pakistan-administered Kashmir irrelevant for all practical purposes as a daily reality.

With the Kashmir logjam broken by 2060, both countries' regional role will have acquired enhanced credibility. India and Pakistan will be able to engage in normal relations and reduce defense expenditures by a considerable sum without any security derogation. Their defense forces will be engaged primarily in the tertiary sector of national, regional and global constabulary, peacekeeping and disaster relief operations. South Asian countries – especially Pakistan, Bangladesh, India and Nepal – will be major contributors to UN peace operations. In 2060 there will be thriving South Asian institutions for training and educating both regional and international soldiers, police officers, civilian personnel and even NGOs in the skills, requirements and obligations of international peacekeeping. South Asia will be a major node of peacekeeping best practices and lessons learnt.

A universal Nuclear Weapons Convention is signed in 2030 and comes into effect in 2040. By 2050, the world's nuclear weapons stockpiles are verifiably destroyed and the peaceful nuclear energy programs are being overseen by the International Atomic Energy Agency (IAEA) which is in charge of an international nuclear fuel bank. The South Asian Atomic Energy Commission works in close collaboration with the IAEA to ensure that the energy needs of South Asia are met within global safety, security and nonproliferation standards.

South Asian countries will also accept the compulsory jurisdiction clause of the Statute of the International Court of Justice and habitually refer any outstanding interstate disputes among themselves for adjudication to the World Court. They will be among the leading exemplars of the rule of law in international affairs.

South Asian countries will also have stopped being the haven for basing, financing or arming one another's terrorists, and instead will have initiated measures of regional cooperation against terrorism and drug trafficking. India will suffer blowback from Tamil terrorists in Sri Lanka and Sikh terrorists in the Punjab. Pakistan will be consumed by Islamist terrorists it had nurtured as potent weapons against India. Sometime between 2010 and 2060, South Asian countries will conclude that it is better for them to cooperate against the common menace of cross-border terrorism than to use it as a weapon against one another. Their antiterrorism collaboration will embrace the full range of responses, from social and economic to political and security.

They will all be party to bilateral, regional and multilateral regimes for regulating and controlling the in-border production and storage, and the cross-border transfer, of terrorism-related materials, skills and technology. They will collaborate also in tackling the underlying or root causes of terrorism: lack of democratic institutions and practices, political freedoms and civil liberties; group grievance based on collective injustice; intractable conflicts; poverty; and intercivilization suspicions. They will have learnt from bitter experience that terrorism flourishes amidst repressive, inept, unresponsive and dynastic regimes that spawn angry and twisted young men taking recourse to lethal violence. Consequently their antiterrorism campaign will be anchored in the norms of accountability, the rule of law and nonderogation of core human rights and civil liberties, including life, liberty and due process.

The retreat of the threat of terrorism will have led to a boom in South Asian tourism by 2060. No other region in the world will compare or compete with South Asia – with its wealth of natural wonders and historical legacies, architectural monuments, diversity of authentic experiences – for internal and international tourism. By 2060 there will be an active and highly visible South Asian Tourism Development and Marketing Board to promote joint tourism with enticing package deals that give people memorable experiences based on historical, religious, musical, archeological, architectural or other interests spanning all South Asian countries. One such package could take them to all the major sites of interest with respect to the Mughal dynasty. Another could include travel to all the major points of interest with respect to the rise and spread of Buddhism. A third could visit the sites of the major Hindu temples, while a fourth could expose tourists to the wonders of the Himalayas in Pakistan, Nepal and India. Yet another package could be organized to sample the delights of the varied cuisine across South Asia. The possibilities are endless. All of this, as indeed commercial activities, will be greatly facilitated by the South Asian Association for Regional Cooperation (SAARC) adopting a regional equivalent of the Schengen Agreement in Europe to usher in passport-free travel the length and breadth of South Asia.

Tourists from within South Asia will also flock to the annual regional sporting competitions where performance standards will have risen to world class by 2060. The importance of sports to fostering national and regional identity has been seriously underestimated by South Asian countries. Their per capita performance until 2010 in the summer and winter Olympics, in world soccer, and in most world sporting championships is scandalous. This will have been addressed and rectified by 2060, not the least owing to the rising standards of sports performance in intraregional competitions.

Regional integration needs more active participation of civil society organizations. In an increasingly diverse, complex and interdependent world, solutions to collective action problems are attainable less and less at any one level or by just state actors. Under contemporary conditions of complex civilization, governments can satisfy only a small and diminishing proportion of the needs of human beings as social animals. Citizens look more and more to civic associations to channel a growing range and variety of social interactions. Civil society organizations play increasingly active roles in shaping norms, laws and policies. These activities need to be enhanced vis-à-vis regional bodies, as they have been upgraded in relation to the UN and other global governance agencies. Increased participation of civil society can be critical to enhance the legitimacy of regional institutions. At the same time, civil society organizations must also attend to their own legitimacy, so that they are not seen to be unaccountable, unrepresentative, self-serving and irresponsible.

Conclusion

Thus South Asian regional institutions could be the conduit for "domesticating" global norms in South Asia but also shaping global norms with South Asia–sourced values and worldviews on relations between individuals, groups, society, markets and public authorities. Amitav Acharya calls the two distinct processes norm localization and norm subsidiarity (Acharya 2004 and 2011, see also Acharya 2009).

If regionalism is elevated to the status of a major plank of the SAARC countries' foreign policies, it would enhance their global importance, influence and role; enable other South Asian states to exercise a moderating influence on India as the regional hegemon; and promote the economic development of all states in the region.

For such a bold and ambitious vision to be realized by 2060, South Asia will require a quality of national leadership that was missing until 2010. Leadership consists of outlining a bold vision for the community as a whole and then inspiring individuals and groups to transcend their immediate self-interest in identifying both intellectually and emotionally with the shared vision. It calls for the capacity to set standards of conduct and benchmarks of progress, explain why these matter, and coax everyone into striving for and achieving these standards and goals. Unfortunately, leadership cannot be produced to order. Faced with a dystopian regional reality, we can but dream of a South Asian utopia.

Chapter 2

SOUTH ASIAN FUTURES: THREE SCENARIOS

Stephen P. Cohen and Jacob Friedman

Political instability and domestic disorder in India, Nepal, Sri Lanka and Pakistan have drawn further continuing international attention to South Asia. In the two biggest states, creeping domestic militancy jeopardizes security in major Pakistani cities while India struggles with Naxalite activity in its north and east. These instabilities, plus the continuing prospect of an India–Pakistan crisis, make South Asia's future very hard to predict. However, instability also presents opportunities – the future is not rigidly path-dependent. With the caveat that all long-range predictions are guesses, here are three plausible but very different scenarios. The real future could see the region go down one, two or even all three of these paths, perhaps at different times, and it will be shaped by processes that we only partially understand.

Scenario #1: The United States of South Asia (USSA)

In 2013, reconciliation between India and Pakistan looked to be a tenuous prospect, at best. A new crisis over alleged beheadings, and the suspension of progress on economic normalization, led to gloomy predictions about the future. Despite the fact that Pakistan and India had returned to the negotiating table, Hawkish voices on both sides of the process called India–Pakistan normalization improbable, if not if not impossible. However, there were small steps that, in retrospect, were forerunners of a promising future.

Groups in favor of normalization included not only liberals and peaceniks, but the business community and even the Pakistan army, which was hard pressed at home and on Pakistan's western border.

The first major break with past psychological pathologies was the spontaneous extended applause given to the Pakistani team at the opening of the Pakistan Cricket Board (PCB) Test match series between the two nations in Mohali in August 2013, almost on par with the welcome extended to the Indian team itself. This reception may have been the pretext for politicians on both sides to revive plans for deeper economic cooperation.

The fruits of these labors would not be seen until 2017, when India and Pakistan convened a conference on the preservation of South Asian agriculture.

This conference led to the 2020 Aam Aam Accords (AAA), setting a common standard for South Asian mangoes. Indian and Pakistani mango farmers had seen their crops challenged by lower-quality Mexican and South American fruit in the international marketplace. This step began the process of transforming South Asia from one of the world's least economically integrated regions to one where there was strong economic cooperation within and between its states. The two countries, along with Bangladesh, formed a common AAA branding and established definitive standards for South Asian mangoes. Combined with a rigorous marketing campaign in the West, the AAA brand was a huge economic success for the three countries. Despite the fact that the price fixing and regional standards clearly violated free market principles, they ensured the highest quality in the global marketplace; it was only a matter of time before the AAA products displaced their imitators.

Emboldened by this successful cooperative enterprise, the countries decided to extend cooperation to another common interest, cricket. The Indian Premier League (IPL) had long been regarded as the best cricketing league in the world, drawing audiences across India and the English-speaking world through their simulcasting deal with the US video titan YouTube. The league had strong popularity in Pakistan, Sri Lanka and Bangladesh, and despite the fact that Pakistani players had been barred since the league's second season in 2009, audiences for IPL games numbered in the tens of millions in Pakistan. Indeed, when Rohit Sharma achieved the impossible, hitting for his first double century to lead the Deccan Chargers over the Rajasthan Royals in the 2021 IPL finals, over 70 million watched in Pakistan. As a result, in 2024 the IPL opened expansion teams in Pakistan, Bangladesh and Sri Lanka, transforming the IPL into the Asian Premier League. Audiences continued to blossom, culminating in the 2030 APL final between the Pakistani franchise Lahore Lions and the Indian Delhi Daredevils, which drew over 500 million viewers across the Subcontinent.

Buoyed by the success of these matches, border controls were relaxed in an effort to stimulate cross-border tourism. The flow of South Asian tourists between the nations suggested new prospects for regional peace, as the trips across the border had a humanizing effect on the once-warring states and their citizens. Kashmiris benefited the most from cross-border tourism, and conflict in the region stopped nearly overnight. Indeed, Kashmir underwent a drastic transformation from warzone to tourist haven, making the Kashmiri people fabulously wealthy in the process.

Yet, the relaxed borders did not have the same effect in terms of attracting tourists from beyond South Asia's borders. Reflecting on the success of the AAA mango advertising campaign, the tourism boards of the several South Asian states teamed up for what would prove to be a fateful advertising campaign. Tourism to South Asia was advertised by promoting "the United States of South Asia," a campaign emphasizing the new ties between the nations and the region's newfound security. The campaign was so successful that all future economic cooperation between the nations took place under the banner of the United States of South Asia, including the 2040 USSA

Economic Community plan, the establishment of the USSA parliament in 2047, the establishment of a USSA peacekeeping force in 2053 and the establishment of the USSA rupee as a standard currency across the region in 2058. A lot of this cooperation was a response to a change in American policy that came out forthrightly for the Line of Control as a permanent international border between India and Pakistan – a policy that triggered a debate in both countries (and among Kashmiris) about the futility of the 90-year-old deadlock.

While the USSA was initially a tricky prospect for all politicians in the region, eventually the peace dividend made the plan quite popular among citizens of the new USSA. While each nation maintained autonomy within the new system, internal borders were effectively abolished, in favor of a Schengen-style border regime. This move allowed politicians on all sides to quiet malcontents in their countries, who claimed that the arrangement would ruin each nation's independence. At the same time, though, it allowed for the free passage of people and goods, which allowed the economies of the USSA nations to flourish.

Scenario #2: Globalization and Its Discontents

Many outside observers, seeing the rise of India's outsourcing empire, believed that globalization was a rising tide that would lift all boats in South Asia. This assumption, often made without a perfect understanding of the region, proved to be incorrect. While globalization had some negative effects on every nation in the region, it proved to be, on balance, a positive thing for India's economy.

Globalization turned out to be a malign force for Pakistan, though. The floods of 2010, widespread sectarian violence, and the rise of the Pakistan Taliban demonstrated the weakness of the Pakistani state. Then, as international investment flowed into India, the two nations began to inch apart in terms of prosperity. Pakistan found itself choking on India's dust, and its leaders – civilian and military alike – resolved that it had to do something to catch up with India's booming economy. Unfortunately for them, by the time they resolved to take action in 2031, it was far too late. Years of ineffective leadership had weakened the central government's grip on the state. By 2031, Pakistan had lost control over most of Khyber-Pakhtunkhwa or Balochistan, as well as large chunks of Sindh, which hampered the government's efforts to minimize Islamic extremism and improve education. When government workers tried to enter these areas to establish schools, hospitals and other public services, they were often run out of town or worse.

At the same time, Indian relations with Pakistan stagnated. As a result, India turned away from its western border, strengthening trade and military bonds with the other South Asian nations. As a result, a sharp contrast between the Subcontinent's east and west quickly emerged. East of the India–Pakistan border, nations flourished as India's success helped bring prosperity to Bangladesh, Nepal and Sri Lanka. West of the border, the picture was far grimmer. Afghanistan and Pakistan were in a deep state of dysfunction, brought on by this dismal governance. This slow decay of the

Pakistani state, inadvertently propagated by corrupt and ineffective politicians, became a serious security concern, even for China, which had established itself as Pakistan's strongest and most influential ally – yet the Chinese only understood the importance of force in maintaining order, not the importance of building state institutions, let alone democratic ones. Nor did their exploitation of Pakistani resources do much to rebuild state integrity.

The severity of the governance and law and order problems became readily apparent to the rest of the world in 2034, when militants again laid siege to the Pakistan Air Force Base at Sargodha. The site, one of many where nuclear weapons were stored, was besieged for nearly four days by a contingent of militants numbering in the thousands. It was only with a great deal of luck and the timely intervention of troops from the Jhelum Cantonment that the siege was lifted and the militants' attempt to capture nuclear material was foiled. A quickly convened session of the UN Security Council led to communist-style self-criticism between the council and Pakistani representatives. It was made quite clear to the Pakistani leadership that the lack of security around their nuclear devices could not be tolerated and that they must relinquish control of the devices the easy way or the hard way. The easy way entailed that Pakistan give up the weapons willingly in exchange for a big payoff of foreign aid and development money. If Pakistan had resisted, the UN Security Council had drawn up plans for a multilateral force to seize the weapons or, failing that, permanently crash the Pakistan economy.

The problem of Pakistan's internal security issues only compounded the growing gap between Pakistan and India. Pakistan's society, which had always been strong, began to experience serious cognitive dissonance. It found itself twisted one direction by the influential nonresident Pakistanis (NRP) community, which had considerable influence and which agitated for liberalization. However, it was also pulled in the other direction by the most hard-line Islamist elements in the country, as an eminent Pakistan journalist, Ahmad Rashid, feared in a prophetic interview with *Der Spiegel* in 2010. In the end, the hard-liners won out, finally answering definitively the debate between moderate and extreme Islamists within Pakistan. The resolution of this debate, however, only sparked further conflict among and between the country's Islamic sects. Eventually, they sought out international ideological allies and found them in Iran and Saudi Arabia. While the ideological makeup of both nations had drastically shifted since the beginning of the twenty-first century, due to the restoration of democratic rule in the Republic of Iran, which dropped the "Islamic" from its name after the Supreme Islamic Council went into exile upon Ayatollah Khamenei's death in 2017 – and the rise of a UK-style constitutional monarchy in Saudi Arabia, both nations still held important stakes in the ideological scrap between Sunni and Shi'a in Pakistan.

At the core of Pakistan's downward slide was the ongoing debate, still unresolved, as to the idea and purpose of Pakistan. The debate involved India, indirectly, as New Delhi had missed many opportunities to rebuild its relations with a sagging Pakistan. While Pakistan's ideological balance had been settled, the fundamental issues of governance was still unresolved. The judiciary, emboldened by the Lawyers' Movement of the early twenty-first century, attempted to seize an outsized role in the power structure of Pakistan starting around 2012. While the courts had once been weak and flimsy, bending to the will of Pakistan's army, the judiciary dug in its heels, overturning laws it believed were counter to the best interests of the nation. However, the Pakistani parliament, president and prime minister broke the back of the judiciary. Instead of resolving the power struggle that had plagued Pakistan since its founding, this just left the parliament, prime minister, president and the army to fight over who would hold the country's reins. As of today, the battle still rages.

With this power struggle paralyzing the country, international eyes have turned away from Pakistan. But then again, since Pakistan was relieved of its nuclear weapons in 2034, it had become little more than just another problem state – a Nigeria without oil. Without a formidable nuclear problem to deal with, the international community largely lost interest in Pakistan in favor of its much more powerful and secure neighbor, although India's developments were hampered by its nonrelationship with Pakistan. While Iran and Saudi Arabia maintained a stake in the Pakistani state due to ongoing sectarian tensions fueled by these outside nations, the rest of the international community was content to banish Pakistan to the back of their minds. Even India, once Pakistan's fiercest rival, maintained little interest in its neighbor's situation beyond keeping Pakistani refugees from spilling over the border. In 50 years, Pakistan had slid from a major regional player into complete obscurity and South Asia itself remained a backwater. Despite India's valiant attempt to pose as an Asian power, it still had to cope with its neighbors, and they in turn still regarded India with suspicion. India had discovered the hard way the difference between regional dominance – which it had – and regional leadership – which evaded it still.

Scenario #3: "Let Me Explain Why This Was Inevitable"

The trajectory of South Asia was irrevocably altered on the morning of 20 August 2030. A team of Lashkar-e-Taiba terrorists, flying an explosives-laden, ultralight aircraft, slammed into the Indian prime minister's residence at 7 Race Course Road in New Delhi, killing the prime minister instantly. The Indian government demanded an apology from the Pakistani government and sent a squadron of Sukhoi Su-30 MKI fighter-bombers to attack Lashkar-e-Taiba camps in Muzaffarabad. As might have been expected, the Pakistani military did not accept this violation of Pakistani airspace. There were Pakistani reprisals across the Line of Control (LoC) in Kashmir by Pakistan's special commando forces. One incursion led to another, and soon a small-scale war between the two nations was underway. Both nations ignored every possible chance to de-escalate the conflict and their forces were soon engaged in fierce fighting along the whole length of the border as well as the LoC.

Indian generals, who had sought and received authority to use nuclear weapons as part of an extended "Cold Start" military doctrine, sought to decapitate the Pakistani army with a tactical nuclear strike at garrisons near Rawalpindi. Unfortunately for the entire Subcontinent, the Indian military greatly underestimated Pakistani resolve.

The strikes did cripple some army units, but rather than bringing an end to war, it led to its final escalation. Pakistan retaliated with overwhelming force and blinding speed, launching the vast majority of its arsenal at India, hitting targets across the country. In the blink of an eye, Delhi, Mumbai, Bangalore, Chennai, Kanpur, Ahmedabad, Jaipur, Chandigarh and Amritsar ceased to exist as organized cities. Millions of lives were snuffed out as surely as one blows out a candle. Making matters worse, although that was scarcely possible, errand warheads caused the destruction of the Bhakra Nangal and Pong Dams in Himachal Pradesh, sending a torrent of irradiated water rushing down the Sutlej and Beas rivers. The remnants of the Indian government were determined to strike back, and launched an equally overwhelming counterattack, leveling Karachi, Islamabad, Lahore, Multan, Faisalabad, Gujranwala, Peshawar, Quetta and Muzaffarabad.

As the dust settled, and the levels of Punjab's rivers receded, the extent of the catastrophe was apparent. For all intents and purposes, Punjab was in ruins. Whatever hadn't been hit directly with a nuclear attack was either submerged in irradiated mire, covered in fallout or both. Even the interiors of both countries, which had largely escaped the worst of the blasts, found themselves in danger from the more durable radioisotopes present in fallout, most notably strontium-90 and cesium-137. These radioisotopes, shot into the atmosphere by the blasts, rained out over unaffected areas and irradiated what little clean land remained in Pakistan, and western and central India. Upon hearing reports of these deadly rains, Indians of all backgrounds streamed east, hoping to outrun death falling from the sky. As hundreds of thousands crossed into Bangladesh, the government in Dhaka sensed an opportunity, and annexed much of West Bengal and Tripura. The northeastern states of India also chose to break away from what remained of India, forming a loose confederation of independent states with the easternmost parts of Nepal and Bhutan. South India, while certainly affected by the strikes, managed to avoid the worst of the disaster. Setting up a capital in Mysore, the newborn Dravidian Republic attempted to salvage what remained of the region's industry. Sri Lanka, unaffected by the blasts, acted quickly to establish relations with the Dravidian Republic.

As a result of the events of 20 August 2030, South Asia's once-promising development was completely derailed. The remains of India and Pakistan found themselves in a situation where they desperately needed international assistance. However, few countries were willing to take the risks implicit in running an aid operation in an irradiated wasteland. The two states did receive token assistance from some countries, the International Red Cross and the United Nations, but it was not nearly enough given the severity of this historic disaster. Much of the Subcontinent was quite literally bombed back to the Stone Age. Subsistence farming became the preferred method of survival, as nearly all light and heavy industry was destroyed. The devastation did produce one unexpected success story, however. Bangladesh quickly rose from relative obscurity to a position of regional power. It stitched up trade agreements with China, the United States, and other world powers. Similarly, the Dravidian Republic salvaged much of South India's industry, and was able to gain a large export role, despite being forced to establish wide exclusion zones around the remains of Bangalore and Chennai. For the large part, though, the Subcontinent had faded into obscurity, where it remains today.

Conclusions: The Future Outlook Remains Cloudy

The conclusion that can be drawn from these scenarios is that the future of South Asia remains largely unwritten, and events that might determine its 2060 future may not have yet occurred. While a combination of factors will shape the next ten years in South Asia, these factors may not prove as durable as some have projected. Creeping domestic militancy has jeopardized security in major Pakistani cities, but efforts at reconciliation with India could undermine the role that militant groups have played in Pakistani foreign policy. Positive developments in the India–Pakistan relationship would have a knock-on effect for growth and stability that would be felt across South Asia, but growing instability has put the future of the region in doubt. The three scenarios are guesses, but they are emblematic of the three broad futures that South Asia might follow.

Scenario one envisions a South Asia at peace because of reconciliation. This scenario is not beyond the realm of the possible. Recent high-level dialogues between Pakistan and India have rekindled the hopes of a peace and reconciliation process, and such a practice will likely take the form of an acknowledgement of common interests for both nations. The relationship between India and Pakistan will be the crucial relationship in the region, as a thaw in relations between the two nations will have positive socioeconomic consequences across the region.

Scenario two envisions a South Asia characterized by an ascendant world power, India, and a failed state, Pakistan. This scenario is emblematic of Jonathan Paris's belief that Pakistan will continue on a roughly flat trajectory and "muddle through," or slightly worse. While muddling through would seem to be an optimistic projection, given Pakistan's current problems, it could also lead to this scenario.

The last scenario envisions a shattered South Asia. Such a future is now technically and politically plausible as the weapons and the miscalculations are there in abundance, as are the militant groups with their eyes on obtaining nuclear weapons. Given Lashkar-e-Taiba's record of cross-border attacks, the conditions that would precipitate the beginnings of such a scenario are not so farfetched. Indeed, the Mumbai attacks of 2008 could have easily started such a conflict if not for sane, competent leadership on both sides.

In the end, though, the real-world outcome is likely to be a function of one, two or even all three of these scenarios, the product of factors that we cannot predict with certainty today. We are sure, however, that once it happens there will be experts who will explain why it was inevitable.

Chapter 3

FEDERALISM ON THE ROAD: REGION AND REGIONALISM

Kanak Mani Dixit

A critical dysfunction was created as the British sun set on the Subcontinent, for it left two countries trying to develop competitive nationalist sensibilities in the bitter aftermath of Partition. Each new country required a manufactured nationalism, with its mix of symbolism and an exclusive if not customized history. Before long, one of the partitioned countries had broken into two, each requiring its own nationalist narrative, and that is how South Asia has developed centrifugally these last six decades, time spent defining the distance between the power elites of Dhaka, New Delhi, Kathmandu, Colombo and Islamabad. This agenda has affected the possibilities of an economically productive, socially inclusive South Asian regionalism on the one hand, and, on the other, diverted focus from representative, accountable democracies at the provincial and district levels. The capital establishment in each country has sought to consolidate itself by force-feeding the populace with conspiracy-laden xenophobia to be called up at will, all the while keeping at bay the demand for devolution of power to states and provinces.

The brittle capital-centric evolution of the countries of South Asia is tailor-made for egotistic, exclusivist nationalism. This type of nationalism not only regards its neighbors with suspicion, but also fails to embrace even those it claims to be its own – where New Delhi does not countenance flexibility on Kashmir, Islamabad on Sindh or Balochistan, Dhaka on the Chittagong Hill Tracts, Colombo on the north and east, and so on. At the start of the second decade of the twenty-first century, we are still in the process of evolving as Pakistanis, Indians, Bangladeshis and Sri Lankans. This is of course not a bad thing, but in acquiring the exclusive identity of the nation-state we have lost touch with the overarching value of empathy – external and internal. This has left us with a South Asia battered by animosities, where a united front has failed to develop to check the blundering or malevolent overseas players. The animosities have, most importantly, affected economic advancement in the poorest, most densely populated parts of the region.

The nationalist urge among people can be an effective tool for cultural unity, to develop a sense of belonging amidst a diverse, competitive and confusing world. But when developed into chauvinist ultranationalism, as seems to be the requirement of newborn nation-states, it creates suspicions against countries and communities outside one's own pedigree, and affects societies in numerous ways. Ultranationalism becomes the whip used by the right-wing and radical-left demagogues. By and large, civil society stalwarts fail the test of public intellectualism in standing up to ultranationalism, and get converted into cowering conspiracy theorists themselves. Ultranationalism is what renders us heartless when horrors happen across the border, generating an empathy deficit that prevents a response when floods or earthquakes ravage contiguous regions. It forces us to look at the neighbor with binoculars tinted with New Delhi, Dhaka or Islamabad shades rather than take in the unaided view from Amritsar, Multan, Lahore, Guwahati or Calcutta. It stops us from looking into our own weaknesses, turning us into demagogues ourselves, hell bent on blaming someone else for all ill that visits our territory and people. Part of the reason South Asia has the largest proportion of the world's poor and unhealthy children, women and men – concentrated in the northern half of the Subcontinent – is because we fight, we prepare to fight and we put our money into the military machine. We do not trade while we allow smuggling. Nationalism alone, without the balm of Subcontinental regionalism, leaves us materially poorer by diverting rupees and takas from investment and development.

Indus–Ganga Plain

South Asia's people as a whole were robbed of sensitivity and sensibility by the act of Partition and the arraigning of the two largest South Asian countries against each other. This helped push ultranationalism into the agenda all over. Six decades on, it is time to confront the need to identify the hidden aspects of our identities above and below the level of nationalism. The people of the region by and large already have a series of self-ascriptions which include the clan-community identity, the district identity, the provincial-state identity and the national identity. As the capital elites entrench national identities, it will become harder to devolve power to the state and to provinces within the nation-state, as well as reach for consolidation of the South Asian identity.

South Asia must rise together to achieve what the "genius" of the people making up nearly a fourth of the world population can deliver, but the formula to achieve regional unity is not yet clear. If being South Asian is advantageous for all the societies of the Subcontinent, including that of India as the largest entity, we must first understand the challenges to developing the regional identity. The countries of the region are a varied group in terms of size and diversity surmounted by the asymmetric presence of India. Six decades have been enough to destroy the earlier loose "Indian" identity and deliver new identities along nationalist lines. When one colonial power departed, "historical India" got subsumed into India the nation-state, while the others had to strive to create their own *raison d'être*. In Pakistan, in particular, attempts were made to create a separate past based on a compartmentalized Indus historicity, even though the Ganga and Indus plains, while two catchments, have had a continuity throughout history.

The Indus–Ganga *maidaan*, as the name implies, is one continuous plain flatland without a ridgeline dividing the catchments of the Jamuna in the east and the Sutlej in the west. The two river systems have two marginally differentiated species of the fresh water dolphin, the Indus variety known as the *bhulan*, with the creature in the Ganga and its tributaries called the *sonse* or *susu*. As the clash of the Subcontinental geological plate partitioned the catchment, the two species came to acquire separate names and marginally different anatomies. This separate evolution in geological time represents the present-day condition of the India–Pakistan relationship, one that holds all South Asia hostage. The people of the two countries remain identical in heritage, yet pulling apart on the sand. To take the symbolism further, the problem child of South Asia is its populated, cantankerous northern half that lives off of the Indus and Ganga. The people who are most alike each other – from Bangladesh across the expanse of North India to Pakistan – harbour the most animus against each other.

In the Indus–Ganga region, only Nepal evolved differently, evading direct colonization and therefore existing two-and-a-half centuries as a nation-state. Experience of "continuous nationalism" should have given modern-day Nepalis a sense of confidence that tempered the ultranationalism of the newborn states, but this has not happened. The xenophobia of the highlander vis-à-vis the plains *raja* or *nawab* was transferred to the East India Company, then to the viceroy, and today Nepali ultranationalism can be read as synonymous with New Delhi–focused anti-Indianism.

The other countries of South Asia were all born after 1947: India and Pakistan in the August of that year, Sri Lanka in 1948 and Bangladesh in 1971. Even though India had it all in terms of heritage and identity, it too fell for heightened nationalism. The first six decades after 1947 have thus been spent in defining the nation-state all over South Asia, each country and capital trying to project an image to the world even while trying to deal with the subidentities within.

India Know Thyself

What used to be known as British India is largely what makes up South Asia today, although you will have to add Nepal and Afghanistan to that mix, and even Burma and Tibet. The Subcontinent was a vast empire holdout kept together to serve the colonialist's needs, a two-century interlude that ended in the exhilaration of independence subdued by the bloodletting of Partition. India inherited the imperial mantle, including the name "India," a massive country at the center of the region. India's size and clout gives South Asia an asymmetry that requires a definition of regionalism here that cannot be borrowed from Europe, Southeast Asia or Latin America. India is South Asia in only a slightly truncated form, with competing identities and divisions, including the northeast vis-à-vis the mainland, the north–south divide, and rivalries between languages and religions, aboriginal versus mainstream, caste divides, class divides and so on.

India, some claim, does not need Subcontinental regionalism because by itself it already incorporates much of South Asia by size, economic strength, geopolitical prowess and miscellany. The country borders all the other original members of the South Asian Association for Regional Cooperation (SAARC), while none of them so much as touch each other at the border. Only with Afghanistan entering SAARC is there an exception to this rule. The satellite imagery of South Asia itself delivers up the coastline of India. True, India can chart its own course in the world, seeking world power status on par with the United States, European Union and the People's Republic of China. But the establishment in New Delhi will realize yet that India cannot be complete without the company of the rest of South Asia. It is true that the Indian citizen feels less of a tug to reach out to the larger Subcontinental identity because the country already encompasses the larger part of South Asia by geographical area and diversity, population size and even access to history. But modern India cannot really spin off from what was historical India, which of course is what we now call South Asia for want of a better proper noun. Others may want "South Asia" more, but India needs South Asian regionalism to buttress its own place in the world, to have a sense of historical worth and – most importantly – to promote economic growth of its populated Ganga heartland.

India thus holds the key to the South Asian evolution because, as the most populous country, its political evolution would deliver the formula for the rest. The fact that India has a longer democratic experience than its neighbors allows it to face up to the challenges of ultranationalism and required state restructuring, which will make it easier for the others to follow suit. We await the day, therefore, when India sees the advantages for itself of South Asian regionalism, which requires a release from the New Delhi–centric nationalism, which has defined itself in contradistinction to Pakistan, the much smaller neighbor. Indian nationalism defined vis-à-vis Pakistan is also why the matter of Kashmir and cross-border militancy becomes such an overwhelming national security issue in India. For perspective, New Delhi policymakers must try and compare what India's 1.2 billion population faces against the militancy and terror to what the 180 million Pakistani citizens face from sectarianism, political extremism, suicide bombings and external intervention. India is a country the size of a continent, but its internal discourse tends to be parochially narrow when it comes to geopolitics and national security – the bane of newborn nation-state nationalism.

Federal Traction

Geopolitically, India is a gigantic country with a small-state mindset – thanks in large part to its opinion-making elites in the media and academia. The rest of South Asia awaits a liberal-minded national polity to evolve in India, which would provide its politicians and diplomats the space to exhibit neighborly empathy based not on magnanimity but proactive self-interest. The task of redefining South Asia should begin not in Islamabad or Dhaka, but in the minds of the hubris-laden opinion makers of New Delhi. And what these opinion makers are asked to do is merely to reorient their personal vision vis-à-vis their own nation-state, as one that must devolve power from the center to the states. Ipso facto, this modified vision will lead to the evolution of South Asia as a regional entity defined according to the modern specificities and historical continuities of the Subcontinent. The devolution within India will have an immediate and salutary impact on the neighboring societies.

The search for a formula for South Asian regionalism coincides with what India needs for the sake of its own population, that is, the putting up of a more energetic federal structure providing more autonomy to the country's smaller units – which happen to be states. Since the 28 states of India already exist, devolving additional powers to them in principle and in practice would generate more ownership and involvement of people in governance. Taking more items from the "Union List" of the constitution and placing them in the "States List" would help in governance internally, which would temper nationalism at the nation-state level without really weakening it. A "proper federalism" could go one step further – recognizing the historical interlinkages within the Subcontinent, the individual states would be allowed to deal more easily with neighboring provinces of another country or the entire neighboring nation-state itself. While federalizing India, one would be simultaneously helping create the format for South Asian regionalism, a format that is presently bogged down in the marsh. It is important for India to start this trend because its democracy, one would hope, has the flexibility to take leaps of imagination, such as allowing its states the right to interact with the neighboring provinces and even national capitals.

The ideal of enhanced federalism would be the energizing of individual entities within India and Pakistan as the two largest countries, and creating conditions for better interactions between Bangladesh and Nepal vis-à-vis the contiguous neighboring state units of India. Given the logjam created by the capital establishments, it is only by going "federal" that there can be regionalism, reflecting as it would a natural evolution of the Subcontinent beyond the nation-state. Of course, the national elites of each of the neighboring countries would like to remain sovereign equals to New Delhi, as they should, and that *de jure* reality would not be affected. In the meantime, a federalizing of India would mean that there would be more connection and efficiency in the Subcontinental economy due to closer contact between sovereign and nonsovereign entities of similar demographic size and economic power, such as Nepal–Bihar, Bangladesh–Northeast, Sindh–Rajasthan and so on. Over time, the citizens of India's states will understand that true federal autonomy or devolution is almost as good as national sovereignty, in terms of the flexibility to plan for economic viability and growth.

South Asia beyond SAARC

The concept of South Asia has become important because, while the nation-state model inherited from Europe has proved viable and is here to stay, another complementing layer is seen as necessary. We must revive the temporal linkage of the region to history as well as the contemporary geographical connections with fellow economies and peoples. The attempt to establish South Asian regionalism from the top has continued now for two decades – through the track-two efforts pushed by the English-speaking vanguard of South Asia, through efforts at grassroots people-to-people linkages, and by the governments who established SAARC. Because of these efforts, a South Asian sensibility is emerging slowly, promoted by the world's acceptance of this region as "South Asia" in lieu of the "Indian subcontinent." Increasingly, the collection of socioeconomic data, the focus of international organizations, as well as academic studies look at South Asia as one unit.

However, there have been numerous weaknesses in the attempts to promote a South Asian regionalism. One of them has to do with the inability to address the primary asymmetry of the region, viz. India's size and importance vis-à-vis the rest. Another challenge for conceptualizing South Asia is the need felt by many to consider the entire SAARC region at one go, having to include all eight member countries when carrying out any activity. Including each and every country for each and every forum, discussion and resolution is impractical and robs the respective efforts of vitality. One sees therefore a need to "loosen up" the definition of any South Asian action or activity, and there is no reason why bilateral or trilateral matters should not be considered "South Asian" – such as when Bhutan collaborates with Bangladesh and Nepal, or Pakistan with Sri Lanka.

The way to construct a practical, sustainable, self-regenerating regionalism in South Asia is therefore not through the SAARC organization, which is a collaboration among the eight governments of South Asia. The existence of SAARC is itself a welcome matter, if only because it signifies ideational buy-in by the eight members of the idea of regional cooperation. But SAARC is a top-down, interforeign ministry enterprise whose goals and agenda are necessarily limited because the organization represents the individual capital establishments and bureaucracies. The people-to-people efforts at developing contact and empathy are crucial, but they are affected by the downright hostile visa regimes and closed borders. The timid efforts also tend to get swamped by media overkill the moment there is a terrorist blast with cross-border implications, for example. The suggestion therefore is for a simultaneous third track, that of developing federalism within the individual countries of South Asia, and most importantly within India and Pakistan. This would be considered an imperative within each country in any case, because the "breakup" of large state/provinces into smaller units, with proper devolution of governance power, is urgent. Such federalism also would lead as a matter-of-course to a uniquely South Asian regionalism, as the federal units interact with each other and with neighboring nation-states.

The Quality of Empathy

"South Asia" should be seen more as a sensibility than a geographical region, with empathy residing as the value at its core. The tendency to equate SAARC with South Asia, as if they were synonymous, limits us to the restricted governmental visions for South Asia. Also, beyond the founding countries of SAARC and the new addition of Afghanistan, the larger vision of South Asia must include Burma and the Tibet Autonomous Region of China, which lie in the penumbra between South Asia and other parts of Asia.

Even as we consider the different ways to conceptualize South Asia, and as the top-down efforts of the national establishments and elite society have continued, there have been people-to-people efforts to bring together the peasantry, the labor, the fisherfolk and other communities together on the regional platform. However, the distance, costs and the obstructions in cross-border travel has meant that these efforts have not sparked and grown exponentially as they should have. The failure in cooperation at the people's level is seen, for example, in the lack of a South Asian people's movement for denuclearization, on human rights, on climate change or on disaster preparedness. Many of the relevant region-wide efforts of the past have been supported by Western donor organizations which see regionalism as promoting peace and socioeconomic progress, but these efforts wither and eventually die the moment the funding stops. Nor have people's movements been able to start a campaign to prevent the absolute closure of the borders of South Asia, and the thousands of miles of barbed wires erected by India along the frontiers with Pakistan and Bangladesh are a poignant reminder of how South Asia is growing apart even while there is talk of regionalism in seminar halls and workshops. Only the Nepal–India open border stands today as open as it was, indicating the ideal border regime for all South Asian frontiers. But even the Nepal–India frontier regime is coming under threat due to the lackadaisical intelligentsia of Kathmandu and its inability to confront the growing national security mindset in New Delhi, which has begun to murmur about restrictions on the open border.

While South Asia's people at large are not able to travel to each other's countries as pilgrims or tourists, the frontier porosity which had allowed the border communities to interact is also now largely a thing of the past. This has added to the regional distancing. Meanwhile, the idea of South Asian regionalism has failed largely to jump the language divide in the two largest countries of the region, and English remains the language of promoting the concept of South Asia. It is only when the Urdu press in Pakistan and the Hindi press of North India begin to buy into the imperative of South Asian regionalism that there will be a change at the political level. Such a demand for regionalism must be based not on romantic "*bhai-bhai*" notions but on economic logic and historical continuity, helping to change mindsets and giving politicians the courage to sally forth. Until there is a political ownership of the idea of South Asia among the "vernacular middle class," which can only be realized through the "language" media and scholarship, it does not seem possible that regionalism will sink roots other than in the elite discourse.

With the intergovernmental efforts of SAARC having limited success, the track-two efforts stalled and the mass public unable to interact across borders and unable to activate the idea of South Asian regionalism, there is clearly a need for another formula – as long as we believe that South Asian regionalism is important for the economic and social progress of the mass public. This is where one arrives at the conclusion that promotion of federalism within the countries of South Asia is a sensible path for the development of regionalism. Devolution of power would be done within each country for the sake of the individual provincial populations, but the bonus would be that it would foster regionalism in South Asia as a whole. This would also be the way to tackle the asymmetry of India's presence without challenging any nation-state nationalism, including that of India.

The idea, obviously, is not a South Asian federation of SAARC, but an internal federalizing of the organization's member states. This will create units that are good for local governance but will also create units of relatively the same size with converging interests that can talk and work more easily across the international frontiers. What is required today therefore is momentum in the individual countries to federalize further, as a natural demand of the times within those nation-states. A "federal South Asia" would thus emerge as an ancillary product, a flexible nonthreatening outcome which would complement the SAARC structure without compromising the national sovereignty of the individual countries.

More autonomous, self-confident federal units would create a more even playing field for all participants. India would remain the regional behemoth, but its federal units would naturally have more cause for and confidence in reaching out across the international frontiers. The specific advantage of federalism is that it would not take away the external sovereignty of any one country, but only make the individual states more devolved and autonomous within. With a South Asian evolution on the basis of internal federalism, the existing animosities in one part of South Asia would not necessarily impact another part of South Asia. There would be less tension and more economic synergy between contiguous federal units, or between federal units and contiguous nation-states. This, of course, presupposes that the center-state/province division of powers in the federated states would allow the federal units to develop cross-border relationships. Not allowing this facility would defeat the purpose.

A more rapid evolution of South Asian regionalism via other means seems urgent given the many issues coming to the fore which neither SAARC nor other efforts have been effective in addressing thus far. The poverty in areas contiguous to neighboring countries has to be tackled using the logic of economic good sense. As people become more aware, the irrationality of the Indian Northeast not being able to take advantage of the Chittagong port or for raw cotton from Pakistani Punjab to have to arrive in Indian Punjab factories via Mumbai will seem obvious.

Once South Asia–specific regionalism gains traction, so many imponderables of today could become possible tomorrow. India seeks a seat in the UN Security Council, whereas obviously a formula has to be devised for regional representation at the roundtable in New York City. Such a situation is only conceivable when interstate South Asian tensions subside. A federated South Asia would be one where the question of Kashmir would seem incongruous, and there would be moves to resolving it without much more dithering. The Indian Ocean is presently seen as a maritime region where only the littorals with power will access and exploit, in line with how the great powers exploited the world commons. The same is true for Antarctica, which lies at the southernmost tip of the Indian Ocean. Only a confident South Asian regionalism would allow an organized and coordinated response to Indian Ocean security and natural resources, or the Subcontinental access to Antarctica. As China rises as a world power, should the cooperation from the south of the Himalayas be defined through the fractured nation-states? It is obvious that a better construct and regional response would be to see China's counterpart – and competitor in the world marketplace – as South Asia rather than India alone. The present-day South Asian interstate relationships are defined in such a way that the neighbors will take actions on the basis of nationalist positioning, which may not always be to the advantage of the economies and the peoples of those very countries.

It is obvious that all of South Asia must coalesce into one loose entity for the purpose of confronting and countenancing the world, and to respond to evolving internal realities. Given the difficulties in people-to-people contact, and the limited impact of elite collaboration, the answer to South Asian regionalism seems to rest in the rise of federalism within, at least, the two larger countries of the region. This would provide a win–win formula internally and regionally, a strong platform for South Asian cooperation between federal units, as well as between these units and nation-states. While continuing with the parallel efforts, the federalist idea for South Asia is probably one whose time has arrived.

Chapter 4

DIVERSITY IN SOUTH ASIA

John Thomson

Is diversity of population, belief or culture good or bad? There is no consensus on this point, nor has there ever been. Almost by definition, diversity is implicit in empire. Yet empires tend to fall in pieces because of disunity. For nationalists, diversity is generally undesirable and has sometimes been persecuted. If moral issues bulk so large as to make intolerance a virtue, diversity appears evil. But if cultural, particularly artistic, fertility is the objective, the evidence is overwhelmingly in favor of diversity. Diversity implies compromise. Compromise is good if it resolves disputes but is of dubious value if it merely papers over divisions, which later break forth more strongly.

In the South Asia of the twenty-first century it is not useful and might indeed be dangerous to promote diversity or alternatively to seek to reduce it. So much depends upon what sort of diversity is at stake and upon the quality of the ideas supporting it. This essay deals with a few of the diversities, particularly economic, cultural and religious, as they affect India and Pakistan. A brighter South Asian future requires, foremost, a deal between these two primary parties. Yet, the inevitable political difficulties involved could be reduced if both parties know that they will be able to present a compromise in the context of a wider South Asian plan for the future.

At first sight it seems remarkable that a parcel of land nearly cut off from the rest of the Asian continent by uniquely massive mountain chains – the Pamirs, Hindu Kush, Karakorams and Himalayas – should contain so many and such various diversities. But the Subcontinent's long coastline gives it easy access to foreign ports and opens it to influences from abroad. The latter, especially in modern times British and American, have been far greater than anything emanating from China. This will probably persist for the next 50 years but with Anglo-American influences increasingly subsumed in those epitomized in the word globalization. Such influences will have a more or less equal impact across the gamut of South Asian countries but within each country their influence will be uneven. For instance, the English-speaking professional elite will be considerably influenced and will have a lot in common with each other whereas the socioeconomic groups at the lower end of the scale such as industrial workers and the poorer peasantry will be less open to foreign influences and less affected directly by them.

Although external influences are likely to be more influential than ever, the traditional distinctions such as caste, tribe, religion, custom, language, music and culture will persist strongly even if progressively more affected by global influences, especially those with economic consequences. As people move up the ladder towards prosperity their outlook and lifestyle tend to change, but so great is the number currently living in poverty and so important are the declining yet relatively high fertility rates that in 2060, it is reasonable to suppose, South Asia will not be much less diverse than it is now.

Nevertheless, conscious policy decisions will bring significant changes and it is mainly to that area that I direct my remarks. Change will come not only, as I have said, from outside influences but also from improving education, from growing prosperity (or the reverse), from the evolving contribution of women, from increasing exposure through teaching and improved communications to new and varied ideas, from reactions to the breakdown of traditional ways of behavior and especially from the consequences of a growing gap between the privileged and the poor. Whether these changes produce a net improvement in well-being and contentment or the reverse remains to be seen.

All this will have an impact on the existing disparities between India and Pakistan. Defining differences between these two countries is always difficult. No sooner is a distinction identified than it has to be qualified by exceptions. Yet it is worth noting their distinct attitudes towards diversity. In India, the most diverse of countries there are persuasive policy reasons, largely lacking in Pakistan, for maintaining diversity.

With a population well in excess of one billion, there will always be tensions and troubles in India with some group or another feeling aggrieved or believing that agitation will open the road to greater prosperity. The jostling – or worse – between groups is traditional and for that reason is usually met with some understanding and a readiness for limited accommodation. Diversity and accommodation are strongly characteristic of Hinduism and so the politics and the culture of India go somewhat hand in hand. This is important because otherwise India might come apart. Its very diversity is a protection. If the tensions were all along one great fault line, such as Hindu versus Muslim or Hindi speakers versus non-Hindi speakers, the prospects would be dire. As it is, the variety and complexity of divisions within the Indian population, with many people belonging to more than one group, promotes flexibility and adjustment. Pakistan is different. Islam calls for unity and clarity. Without those characteristics Pakistan may not permanently overcome its natural disabilities – five very unevenly balanced provinces with Punjab dominating the rest, a geography strung out along the Indus rather than held together by it, little effective depth in relation to its length and its most prestigious city, Lahore, within a few minutes' drive of an adversary. Unity does not necessarily mean uniformity and it should not mean the dilution of local or ethnic identities. For instance, collaboration for the good of Pakistan as a whole involves substantial recognition of minority interests such as those of the Baloch and the Pashtuns as well as the advancement of minority members to positions of influence. But Pakistan cannot afford the relative laxity of Indian central control. The Pakistan army is both the guardian and the symbol of unity to an extent that is not true in India. The great parade down Raj Path in Delhi on Republic Day is more notable for the variety of people, clothing, music and dancing than for tanks and guns.

The Growing Gap between the Privileged and the Poor

I want to draw attention to a particular aspect of the interaction between global and traditional influences that will certainly affect both India and Pakistan, though probably with different outcomes. I suggest policymakers need to focus on the growing gap between the privileged and the poor. This phrase is of course simple shorthand for a complicated issue that has varied manifestations in different parts of the world. It is as much a global issue as climate change. The consequences in developed countries may become no less important than those in developing nations, especially since several of the latter are managing their economies better than the former.

In the past, the disparity between the privileged and the poor was largely tolerable by virtue of custom, a slow pace of change and the relative paucity of the privileged. All these conditions are already undermined, and none will last for long. The expansion of the privileged classes, the rapidity of change and consequent shocks to traditional assumptions, taken together with the increasing awareness by the poor of the possibilities of change as well as the slow rise in their standard of living are causing tensions with potentially grave effects.

The issue involves three sets of figures. Table 1 sets out some illustrative figures for population size and growth. Table 2 sketches some predictions for the growth and size of gross domestic product. Table 3 gives illustrative figures for disparities in recent years.[1]

Disparities in the future are a matter for speculation and policy; to predict them is merely to guess. The most important consideration for policymakers, public perception, escapes the three tables and indeed all mathematical computation, and it may or may not closely track the data.

Already in India the so-called Maoist or Naxalite insurgency is a large-scale populist movement. It has been predictable for many years and yet it seems, at least in its scale and seriousness, to have taken the authorities by surprise. It is likely to grow. Nevertheless, I do not expect India to be overwhelmed by this or similar movements. As indicated above, the diversity of the country will help to cushion the effects of populist discontent.

Pakistan, however, is in a more risky position. The elite are more prominent, the middle class proportionately smaller, the contrasts, for example, in literacy more obvious and the prospects for national development less rosy. There are exceptions, of course. For instance, in the better agricultural lands of Punjab the prospects are every bit as good as on the other side of the border. But as already suggested Pakistan is a more fragile state and is beset by bigger problems than India faces. The gap between privileged and poor could therefore be more serious.

---

1 I am grateful to Danielle Mancini for help in collecting and presenting this data.

Table 1. Population figures for South Asia

	Population in 1950 (in thousands)	Population in 2000 (in thousands)	Fertility rate in 1950–1955 (children per woman)	Current fertility Rate 2005–2010	Population projection for 2050 (in thousands)
Afghanistan	8,151	22,856	7.70	6.63	76,250
Bangladesh	37,895	129,592	6.70	2.36	194,353
Bhutan	168	571	6.67	2.68	962
India	371,857	1,053,898	5.91	2.76	1,692,008
Maldives	74	273	7.00	2.06	405
Nepal	8,231	24,401	6.15	2.94	46,495
Pakistan	37,542	144,522	6.60	4.00	274,875
Sri Lanka	8,241	18,745	5.80	2.33	23,193

Source: This section draws on United Nations Population Division, "World Population Prospects: The 2008 Revision," Working Paper no. ESA/P/WP.210 (2009) and UNDESA, Population Division Data Bank, available online at http://bit.ly/6bu54 (accessed 20 March 2013).

Table 2. GDP per capita in South Asia

	GDP per capita in 1960 (in USD)	GDP per capita in 2000 (in USD)	GDP per capita in 2050 (projection in USD)
Afghanistan	$126	N/A	N/A
Bangladesh	$79	$335	$5,235
Bhutan	N/A	$762	N/A
India	$84	$453	$20,836
Maldives	N/A	$2,294	N/A
Nepal	$53	$225	N/A
Pakistan	$81	$536	$7,066
Sri Lanka	$146	$873	N/A

Source: Complied through World Bank, World Development Indicators, available online at http://bit.ly/gLzg6s (accessed 25 March 2011).

While it would be foolish to make a firm prediction for 2060, it is already high time to take careful account of the disparities between the privileged and the poor and of the rate at which they are increasing. Probably they have a good deal to do with the growth of the Pakistani Taliban. The risks need to be assessed not only in mathematical terms but crucially, as already suggested, in relation to differing perceptions by various groups. And these groups extend way beyond the broad socioeconomic categories of rich and poor; allowance must be made for various discontented groups latching on to the privileged/poor resentments as a way to increase and broaden their appeal.

Table 3. Lowest and highest income shares in South Asia

	Income share held by lowest 10% (in year indicated)	Income share held by highest 10% (in year indicated)
Afghanistan	N/A	N/A
Bangladesh	8.8% (2005)	26.6% (2005)
Bhutan	2.3% (N/A)	37.6% (N/A)
India	3.6% (2005)	31.1% (2005)
Maldives	N/A	N/A
Nepal	6.0% (2008)	40.6% (2008)
Pakistan	3.9% (2005)	26.5% (2005)
Sri Lanka	1.1% (2004)	39.7% (2004)

Source: Complied through World Bank, World Development Indicators, available online at http://bit.ly/gLzg6s (accessed 25 March 2011), and CIA, *The World Factbook*, available online at http://1.usa.gov/luviOP (accessed 26 May 2011).

Careful analysis is necessary but is not a substitute for action. Timely corrective policies applied in a politically acceptable manner will always be difficult but delay will be damaging. This is true throughout the region. The difficulties being what they are, there will be a tendency to postpone action and governments being what they are, it is probable that some will fail to act.

If either India or Pakistan is slow or negligent – and worse, if both fail to act – the consequences could be particularly serious because of the interaction between them. Effective action to this end might in some respects, for example in issues of energy, water and trade, bring them closer together. However if one or both allow the resentments of the privileged/poor gap to become associated with nationalistic or religious differences, the consequences, it can be said confidently, will be ugly.

Religious Influences

One risk barely faced by India is an insurgency rooted in economic and social discrimination acquiring a religious dimension. In Pakistan, this may already be happening – the Pakistani Taliban looks like an anti-Western, anti-elite, populist movement, especially of young men with an economic grudge who find solace in affirming their Islamic identity in ways largely different from their social superiors. Besides, a religious cloak adds respectability and attracts foreign funds. Whatever the rationale for an Islamically tinged insurrection – and there will be some in the middle classes with their own special reasons – an event of this sort whether in Pakistan or Bangladesh will cast a pall over South Asia. Such an event in non-Pashtun Afghanistan will have a lesser effect because it's more closely connected with Central than South Asia;

Herat and Mazaar-e-Sharif are of the Silk Road rather than the Grand Trunk Road. Any Pashtun movement, including of course the current war between the Taliban and the West, sadly cannot avoid being highly relevant to developments in Pakistan and in the Indo–Pak relationship. This war, essentially about control of Pashtun lands and dominance in Afghanistan, is one from which the West should swiftly disengage. But they will find it difficult to do so as long as the Westerners continue to see it as part of a great struggle against Muslim extremists, a struggle which Western public opinion is prone to turning into a war against Islam.

On the issue of Islam, in both global and local aspects, Pakistan is in a swing position. The evolution of Islamic thought in Pakistan and developments in the Muslim Umma together with non-Muslim reactions to it could rock South Asia or promote a diverse culture of tolerance in the Subcontinent. The issue extends way beyond the confines of this essay but is relevant to it. At the time of independence, it seemed that Pakistan, reflecting the attitude of its creator, Jinnah, would become a truly modern Islamic state. Had it done so, Pakistan would have had a global influence parallel to India's influence in the nonaligned movement. Even now it is not out of the question that a powerful strain of Islamic thinking might arise in South Asia stressing the tolerant and peaceful elements of the Prophet's message. The essential equality of all Muslims fits well with Pakistani nationalism and democracy. Were Pakistan to lead the Muslim world in a modernist direction, which might well happen in the course of the next 50 years, it would have positive effects in South Asia and beyond. But the chances of that happening are linked not only to Pakistan's internal conditions but also to a resolution of the rivalry with India. The latter unfortunately seems to put a premium on conservative thought and aggressiveness.

A principal reason for some optimism about the emergence of modernist Islamic thought arises from the gradual emancipation of women. Apart from issues of justice between the genders (on which Shi'a Islam is perhaps more likely to be progressive than Sunni Islam) there is such clear economic disadvantage to holding back female education and employment that it becomes progressively harder to maintain that Islam intended that Muslims should be poorer and less intellectually capable than other people, Hindus, for example.

As things stand, the tendency is in the reverse direction. As Pakistan (and Bangladesh) fail to match up in one field after another with modernizing India, the temptation grows to view Islam as the great equalizer, the means to intensify national will to counter India and to attract foreign money and support. In short, Islam becomes the moral equivalent of a nuclear weapon. The insurgency in Kashmir hints at what could happen. And now the rivalry is also manifest in Afghanistan.

Conclusions

If Pakistan continues along this path and India continues to react as it has done, there is no strong reason to suppose any change in their rivalry over the next 50 years.

After all, in the early days of independence, no one on either side conceived that the rivalry would be unresolved after 60 tough and contentious years. It is clearly possible that it will get worse. In that case, one cannot exclude a further war and possibly the use of a nuclear weapon. Assuming the outcome of such a war will be in favor of India, the balance of power and interest throughout South Asia would tip decisively towards Indian dominance, which some will probably perceive as dictatorial.

It is thoughts such as these and what has been said above about the possibility and significance of modernist Islam that lead plausibly to the conclusion that the future of all of South Asia depends critically upon the Indo–Pak relationship. Of course this is not the only consideration to impact South Asia's future and it may not prove to be the most important. But however that may be, it is hard not to believe two things.

The first is that it is clearly in the interest of South Asian countries including India and Pakistan to have the quarrels between them peacefully resolved. The second is, the sooner they achieve this, the better it will be for the two countries and for the whole region. The potential for events turning uglier is certainly alive and once that happens there may be no going back. Sixty years of failure is long enough to reveal what does not work. In such circumstances, to compromise the future of one-fifth of the human race requires an obstinacy that suggests moral obtuseness.

The broad requirements for an Indo–Pak settlement are well known; in this brief essay what remains to be stressed is the role that South Asian countries as a whole might play in easing a settlement. The main elements could be:

- undertakings to respect the independence and sovereignty of all members of the South Asian Association for Regional Cooperation (SAARC);
- undertakings to promote good relations, and cultural as well as commercial exchanges between all members;
- undertakings to settle all disputes amicably and, in that context, to support and respect the Indo–Pak settlement;
- if any member is attacked, undertakings to consult immediately with the object of rendering assistance to the victim;
- agreement that India and Pakistan will consult forthwith with the object of (i) limiting their nuclear arsenals, (ii) in due course eliminating them and establishing a nuclear free zone in South Asia;
- agreement to consult regularly on improving their negotiating positions in international commercial affairs, such as on removing tariffs on their textile exports
- and agreement to make a joint approach to the World Bank to support a long-term program of energy development in South Asia.

Thus, I see an interaction between the Indo–Pak relationship and the dynamics in the rest of South Asia. Regional stability, prosperity and the protection of sovereign independence will be promoted by an amicable settlement of the differences between the two rivals while for their part the other members of SAARC can provide a politically helpful framework for a bilateral agreement. Conversely, failure to reach an agreement heightens all risks throughout South Asia, political, security and economic. And this will be especially true in case of a failure to deal adequately with the problems arising from the growing gap between the privileged and the poor. It is essentially a matter of managing the different kinds of diversity in South Asia.

Chapter 5

FUTURE'S PAST

Manan Ahmed Asif

Introduction

Prophets are best at predicting the future – though, they tend towards the dystopic and the apocalyptic. The more philosophically inclined among us, when asked to imagine the future, create utopias secluded in the woods or contained on an island – in other words, by clearing away the accretions of the past and the unseemly present. Everyone else tends to read the best or the worst of the present moment and write it into the future – cars replaced by flying cars, cities replaced by mega cities, wars replaced by greater wars and so on. Such is the grasp that the present has on us – it is always natural, progressive, rational and *just so*. Historians, being neither prophets nor philosophers, usually have no thoughts on the future. We are busy figuring out what happened, why it did not happen some other way and why we should care it happened the way it did. But we do have a charge to unsettle whatever "truths" seem above reproach in our presents, to question basic assumptions of how things appear *now* and to argue for an imagination that ponders all possible futures, not just the ones that seem predestined.

My claim, as a historian, is simple: The "South Asia" we inhabit is a recent construct. It is a limited and restrictive political space as compared to more than a thousand years of textual history and thousands more in material and cultural memory. The stories it currently tells are themselves limited, the imaginations it cultivates are themselves rigid. The geographies that seem so indelible, so permanent, are mere shadows upon regional perspectives that are still legible movement and life patterns, in languages, in customs, and in cultural imaginations. Taking this *longue dureé* look at the Indic peninsula compels us to imagine varied configurations for the future 60 years, hence. I also take this as an opportunity to be fundamentally optimistic – that we can collectively realign our political memory to look at the past in a new light and, hence, imagine other futures.

Conceptions of the Past, Realities of the Present

We have a very limited, highly prejudiced, imagination when it comes to comprehending the premodern in South Asia. This is so because our evidences are often fragmentary, malleable or encoded in political and social tropes that are overtly determined. But the fault doesn't lie there. It lies, I would argue, in our overtly presentist vocabulary within which we chose to frame the past. The words we use, informed by our immediate past, are already encoded with incomprehensible difference – *coercion, submission, conversion, conflict.* The categories we construct are already hegemonic – "Hindu," "Muslim," "invader," "indigenous." We take these ahistoricized words and categories and proceed to give them universality that they don't deserve even for the here and the now. What is produced are deeply pessimistic formulations, of clashes and conquests, which suggest only intractable fault lines etched into the sites and spaces of South Asia. There is a terrible conflation at work in our historiography when it reads a mosque destruction in 1992 or the political tension between India and Pakistan in 2005 as a necessarily transparent rerendering of a temple destruction in 1024 or the military conflict between the Mughals and the Marathas in 1682. That past, unmoored from its historical specificity, overshadows the contexts of the present. That particular past is used to explain, uncritically, or to justify, unambiguously, that which is left unexamined and unassimilated in the present.

Such a reading of the past is itself historically situated. Already from the late eighteenth century, the British efforts to narrate a history of India assumed "difference" within its inhabitants. When James Mill, in 1817, argued for a demarcation of Indian pasts into Ancient/Hindu, Mohammadan and British India, he was codifying as fact what the East India Company was engaged in as practice. The Uprising of 1857, the birth of nationalist politics in the 1880s, the splintering of public space as Hindu or Muslim in the 1890s along with the partition of Hindavi language as Urdu/Hindi created new representations of the past, all charged with explaining communal difference to a politics which was rapidly coagulating along religious lines. The *Arya Samaj* or *Anjuman Himayat-e Islam* were communal answers to political problems, which took as granted the idea of a unitary community. Hence, by the time Muhammad Ali Jinnah declared in 1940 that " [...] the Hindus and Muslims belong to two different religious philosophies, social customs and literatures. They neither intermarry nor interdine together, and indeed they belong to two different civilizations, which are based mainly on conflicting ideas and conceptions," he was echoing an established understanding of incommensurate difference. Jinnah did see the political danger in ascribing difference only to the realm of religion and hence offered a 1000-year-old history of cultural practices as evidence of both scriptural and practical difference. Yet, articulated as such, difference remained paramount – in policy, in historiography and in the everyday political realm. The sixty odd years since 1947 have cemented difference, as only shed blood can. Given such renderings, we can only imagine dystopic futures for 2060 – 1947 gives us 1992, which gives us 2002, which in turn gives us 2009 and so on and so forth. The best minded among us can just hope for temperance.

Let me briefly offer a slightly lesser acknowledged history of the last millennium. However, I want to draw teleology away from the linear, progressive and ask you to imagine three concentric circles, each encoded with deliberately imprecise dates. The innermost circle, labeled 750–1250 CE, is where a specific dialogue of political theology is mostly concentrated, though it emanates outwards. The second circle, labeled 1220–1850 CE, is the site of development of a new political language, administrative and localized. The third circle, labeled 1480–1947 CE, is the space of a distinctly visible vernacular culture, though it permeates back towards the center. The point of these concentric formulations is very basic: each of the processes I mention are visible (alongside other processes I do *not* mention) throughout this past, but at varied levels, and with varied emphasis. Into these contained, overlapping zones, we can sketch out both a history of South Asia and a sense of the regionalities that neither make difference as the *raison d'être* nor banish it from view. What follows is idiosyncratic and sketchy, so I urge the readers to seek greater details in the appended reading list.

An Alternative History

The Indian Ocean trade routes linking the coastal cities in western India to Sri Lanka and the East China Sea on the one end and to Yemen and the Red Sea on the other give us a clue to the regional foci of the first millennium. The Greek accounts, dating back to the fourth and third century BCE veer between utilitarian accounts of sea currents and ports to the fantastic and the marvelous descriptions of creatures and inhabitants. There is not much to suggest that these merchants and sailors ever inhabited the space or constituted a lived community. For that, we go to the Arab geographers and their accounts dating from the mid-ninth century, which tell of pivotal ports like Sarandip (then Ceylon, now Sri Lanka) that connected cities such as al-Mansura, Multan, Lahore, Aror or Indian states such as Kerala and Gujarat. In these accounts we begin to see how various sectarian and religious communities coexisted in mutually understandable political and cultural balance. I use the word "understandable" to highlight that it wasn't the absence of strife (since there were near constant battles), nor the logic of hegemony (the Arab accounts routinely praise "great" kings of al-Hind) which enabled coexistence. Rather it was the mutual recognition of dueling interests, balanced for the sake of building communities – the Arab frontier city-states were inconsequential in relation to the Deccan-centered Rashtrakuta rajas or the Kanuaj-based Gurjara-Praritharas. This is most visible in the political theology which developed in this frontier region – treaties with the bordering Rashtrakutas and the Gurjara-Paritharas, coinage with dual Arabic–Sanskrit legends (some bearing the inscription *śrī madhumadī* – the blessed Muhammad) built to Indic weight and protection for the pilgrims to the Sun Temple in Multan. To give a concrete example, *Hudud al-Alam* (Limits of the World), a geography compiled in late tenth century lists Lahore as a bustling city, with almost no Muslim population, under an Isma'ili governor. It notes, with approval, the security provided by the city to the traveler and the trader but it also carefully encodes sectarian difference into the description. Similarly, the accounts that specify the reusage of sacral space (e.g., building a mosque at the site of a temple, a Sunni mosque at the site of an Isma'ili mosque, reusing temple corpora) situate these acts as frontier practices which were inherently multivalued – legible as political and as religious acts, and as such, negotiable. The early thirteenth-century Persian *Chachnama* narrates several accounts of sacred sites being protected specifically for their sacral and political value after a dialogue with the attendants and the community.

The "Muslim" empires that followed in the eleventh and twelfth century were based not in Damascus or Baghdad but in Ghazna and Ghur (Afghanistan), situating them specifically as Indic polities – the Ashokan Empire from the third millennium BCE stretched to Kandahar, after all. Hence, they need to be contextualized in much the same way as the Chola dynasties in the south – belonging to a mutually intelligible political theology in the Indic peninsular. Evidences for such a framing are abundant. Mahmud of Ghazna (d. 1030), that foremost iconoclast, employed Hindavi commanders and battalions. Tilak, the commander of the Hindavi troops, first got a job as a translator with the Mahmud court and then rose up the ranks, eventually having his own quarter in the city of Ghazna. Some accounts of that city, as well as surviving architecture, reveals a multiethnic space where artisans, trades and craft communities from the Sindh and Rajasthan thrived. The regional specificity of Mahmud's court is also visible in Buddhist temple paintings in Ladakh, which show the royal family clothed in textile patterns and a style recognizable from Ghazna to Baghdad.

As we enter the thirteenth and fourteenth centuries, we can now talk directly about the development of a new political language – Persian, and later Hindavi. The rapid rise of the Mongol Empire across central and western Asia prompted mass migrations to cities across southern Asia – especially where pre-existing networks of patronage and habitation were the strongest. These new migrants leveraged a networked globe where scriptural and scribal qualifications could enable someone to move across the cities of India and beyond (one can use the life of Ibn Battuta as exemplar of such a network). The capacity of the Delhi and Deccani courts to absorb such immigrants was possible only because of greater and tighter integration between the throne-city and its environ. I am, however, not referring simply to the Persian language, but to an Indo–Persianate literary culture, which sustained itself through deeply heterodox political communities – scribal, bureaucratic, martial, artisanal and governing. These knowledge brokers (*munshi, vakil, `amil* to name just a few categories) were just as likely to be Brahmin or Kathari as Sunni or Shi'a. They acted as translators of custom, practice and law across the wide swaths of bordered empires and imperial practices, making possible the many transitions between the political entities from the Delhi Sultanates in the thirteenth century to Vijayanagar to the Mughal – and the Rajput, the Maratha and then the Sikh, the Nizam and the British. It was also in this realm that official acts of translations were conducted – in texts (of *Yoga-vasishta* or *Ramayana*), in architecture, in painting, cuisine and royal clothing.

The largest circle belongs to the vernacular culture. We can use the emergence of Hindavi vernacular, from the fourteenth century forward, to best contextualize this realm. However this isn't a scriptural tradition, rather one that combines orality, practice and daily rituals where various strands of spiritual knowledge make new forms – deeply rooted in the local, from Punjab to Awadh to Deccan to Bengal. The clearest we can access it for the premodern is in the poetic and literary culture – the Hindavi riddles of Amir Khusrau (d. 1325), Khawaja Nakhshabi's *Tuti Nama* (c. 1350),

Maulana Daud's *Cāndayān* (1379), the *Padmavat* of Malik Muhammad Jayasi (d. 1542), the *Madhumalati* of Shaikh Manjhan Shattari, the Panth of Kabir (early sixteenth century), the *kafiyyan* of Shah Hussain (d. 1599) and Bulleh Shah (d. 1757), the *Heer* of Waris Shah (d. 1798). The short list is merely to sketch a literary culture that translated sacral and mystical sentiments within communities across the vast plains of north India and dipping down to the Deccan. Hence, these names and texts reflect everyday life in living communities (whether "Hindu" or "Muslim") where such narratives, stories, and songs found daily practice and were sustenance.

These processes were never mutually exclusive nor were they sequential. One way to imagine them is to see the circles radiate out from the various royal cities which dotted the geography of the premodern India peninsular – where the political theology was most visible in the courts, among the nobility, the political language of everyday governance tied the court to that city and others beyond via a diverse and vast bureaucratic class, and the vernacular cultural practices entwined the millions of inhabitants across the regions.

Making a Community through Bollywood?

Read against this long history – of intersectarian, interreligious politics, rooted languages, nested stories, entangled everyday lives – civilizational difference seems impossible to argue. Yet, ethnic and religious strife, whether intercommunal or intersectarian, is now the norm. The regional connectors such Kashmir, Kabul-Peshawar, Sri Lanka and Dhaka are decoupled. The centers of power, and consequently, access to development, is cordoned off for the vast majority and the various demagogues from the radical right continue to have unfettered access to the mainstream. Except for a few restricted exercises (cricket), the states have been careful to keep the segregation intact.

Clearly, the work of the various states in demonizing the other is well documented through these decades (not just Hindu–Muslim but the linguistic and ethnic "Others") resulting in bloodsheds across South Asia. The bloody scars of the various partitions (those of 1905, 1947 and 1971) themselves constitute a radical history of violence and grievances that rewrites the everyday. Clearly, the states are active agents in constituting the cultural landscape – either directly or indirectly. Given all that, what can we say about those three concentric circles, constituting nearly 1,300 years of historical time? Is that world of mutually comprehensible difference vanished, taking along with it, the vernacular culture?

However, I started writing this piece with an optimistic mindset. I gave you that long history to assert that what I hope to see is neither impossible nor improbable. To imagine a South Asia where cultural comprehension exists despite difference is to remember the life of the Lahori *munshi* Chandar Bhan Brahmin (d. 1662) who was cherished by three successive Mughal emperors for his eloquence, his service and his intelligence. To imagine a South Asia with porous borders is to realize the cultural network of poets and texts that stretched from Kabul to Dhaka to Sri Lanka. To imagine a South Asia where difference is mutually comprehensible is also to look at the *desi* diaspora around the world.

I think that the Bombay-based Hindi film industry (Bollywood) does create a public, and a vernacular culture that is legible across western and southern Asia – a rarely discussed facet of this global juggernaut – there is, of course, substantial academic attention paid to the ways in which audiences from Egypt and Morocco to Hong Kong and Singapore consume Bollywood. Within South Asia, Bollywood enables the creation of new cultural referents, and provides a common vocabulary; most crucially it keeps long-standing historical and cultural themes within living memory – the particular view of love, of jealousy, of friendship, of the beloved that we can easily trace to the vernacular epics of the seventeenth century. Most of this is not a surprise considering that from the very beginnings of Indian cinema, the epics (from the *Mahabharata* to *Laila Majnun*) have been a popular source, and that the film industry has remained far more agnostic on the faiths of its workers than the surrounding society.

To be precise, in arguing Bollywood's role in sustaining a particular vernacular culture, I am referring largely to its aural effect – the embedding of cultural markers within songs. I am less keen to argue the role of the movies themselves – even those as disparate as *Jodha Akhbar* (2008) or *Mission Kashmir* (2000) – which do create the capacity to imagine the Other, by presenting both the syncretic and the demonic, mainly due to the limitation of space. The dominance of radio *sangeet* programs from the 50s, 60s and 70s, which popularized the vocals of Kishore Kumar, Mohammad Rafi and Lata Mangeshkar with the words of Majrooh Sultanpuri and Sahir Ludhianvi, to this day in secondary and tertiary markets across South Asia is no accident. There is a wonderful sequence in Kabir Khan's *Kabul Express* (2006) where the Indian, Pakistani and Afghan characters (journalists, army officers and suspected terrorist) break out into a Sahir Ludhianvi song from the 1962 film *Hum Dono*. This modern rendition of a verse creating a community of listeners is not too far removed from one that informed the listeners of *Heer Ranjha* of Waris Shah. A more recent phenomenon is the surprising popularity of the *Coke Studio Music Sessions* in Pakistan, which pairs folk songs and singers with more contemporary arrangements – the intense emotive capacity displayed by the Pakistani audiences enraptured in Balochi or Seraiki or Punjabi lyrics echoes my sense of "making a community/" The purpose was mainly to give bathos to the idea of the Other – the capacity and the possibility to imagine, and to know.

It is the viewer/listener's engagement with the motifs, the sounds, the looks, the dialogues, the lyrics of Bollywood that writes a very different type of narrative. It creates an everyday poetics and disseminates it across a broadly varied ethnolinguistic terrain. So, to imagine that group from *Kabul Express* singing Sahir Ludhianvi's lyrics (through Dev Anand, of course) is to recognize that there already exists a cultural space where such a translation can happen effortlessly. This is, then, the most significant point – that despite the political and religious jaggedness, the cultural terrain of South Asia remains broadly ecumenical and diverse.

Asserting comprehensible difference does not mean negating difference or reverting to some Nehruvian secularity or some Ayubian militarized communalism. Neither does it mean to ignore the internal contradictions and inequities of each polity in South Asia. Further, an argument for the role of Bollywood poetics in sustaining a conversation does not reduce the complexity of Bollywood itself – a commercial product appealing to the broadest possible demographic at the lowest common denominator. Those readings remain valid. I am positing a narrower, third reading that focuses primarily on the role of the song as it combines the various genres, inhabits various linguistic registers, yet "speaks" in a cultural vernacular that continues to hold valence. It is this capacity that allows us to connect not only the past, but also the many implicated presents – e.g., the role of AM and FM radio, especially Radio Ceylon, All India Radio and Radio Pakistan in constituting this shared listenership. Similar is the case of cultural blogs, YouTube and Twitter in maintaining an audience, a repository of cultural memories.

Present as Future?

I am reminded of the late Kashmiri-American poet Agha Shahid Ali's poem, "Farewell":

> At a certain point I lost track of you.
> You needed me. You needed to perfect me.
> In your absence you polished me into the Enemy.
> Your history gets in the way of my memory.
> I am everything you lost. You can't forgive me.
> I am everything you lost. Your perfect Enemy.
> Your memory gets in the way of my memory.
>   (Ali 1998)

Cultural memory is not a salvation, and culture, however defined, is not a project. Yet, imagining our Other as a sympathetic interlocutor, against the immediate political and social past is a necessary act of disruption. Owning up to a history that undermines the rigidities of the presence is a shared responsibility. The long past of South Asia offers concrete ways of imagining mutually comprehendible difference, and the specificities of regional polities and economies demonstrates interconnectedness. That it once was doesn't mean that it will be – it simply shows that what *is* is only one possible future among many.

Section II

STATE RELATIONS

Chapter 6

THE FUTURE OF DEMOCRACY

Jalal Alamgir

This paper forecasts the future of democracy in South Asia. It applies a four-step methodology: baseline definition, detection of first-order trends, identification of certainties and uncertainties and finally the construction of scenarios. The essay accordingly is divided into four main sections: each section begins with a brief description of the task, followed by an analysis of the South Asian situation. The final section provides an overall interpretation on the possible state of democracy in South Asia in 2060.

Baseline

By democracy I imply a minimalist notion – an electoral political system which gives the opposition a fair chance to win. Because our focus is on South Asia as a region, we have to "deprioritize" differences across national boundaries and distill commonalities that might form the basis of a future system. Through most of the past 50 years, the common platform across South Asia has been a Westminster-style parliamentary system, with single-member constituencies and first past the post voting. Periodic challenges to this, either presidential – in Pakistan, Sri Lanka, and the Maldives – or military-autocratic as in Bangladesh and Pakistan, or one-party rule like India and the Maldives have been precisely that: temporary challenges, which eventually gave way. Even monarchies like Nepal and Bhutan have moved toward greater parliamentary legislation.

Aside from this system and a common susceptibility to dynasties, democratic performance has varied widely across South Asia. The violation of civil and political liberties is widespread across the region. Financial abuse of public trust is common; South Asian countries have consistently ranked in the bottom half of the world's corruption indices. Insurgency rages in the region's periphery across Pakistan's tribal areas, Kashmir, Nepal, until recently Sri Lanka, Bangladesh's southeast, the Indian northeast and more than a third of rural India. Additionally, terrorism has increased since the late 1990s and the current states of South Asia have built large security forces, which, combined with a decay of civil service – except in India – continue to threaten civilian political leadership.

It will be erroneous to blame democracy per se for these problems of political performance, for these challenges have been more acute during periods of weak or no democracy. There is increased acceptance among political elites in the region that fair competitive systems offer them the best chance to exercise power, whether for the public good or in an abusive capacity. In other words, democracy, at least formally, has become "the only game in town." At the intermediate level, within parties and political organizations, South Asian political leadership has been by and large authoritarian. Leaders have not displayed, in Larry Diamond's words, a "deep, unquestioned, routinized commitment to democracy" (Diamond 1999, 65). At the mass level, however, all survey data indicate strong support for democracy. The word democracy has a positive connotation among people across South Asia. Except for Pakistan, where results have varied, South Asians overwhelmingly favor the rule of "leaders elected by the people." Taken together, "for every one South Asian response that endorses dictatorship, there are six South Asian responses that prefer democracy" (deSouza et al. 2008, 86).

Looking Back: First-Order Trends

The baseline indicates strong support for democracy despite weak performance, but we cannot assume that democracy will continue by default. In fact, a significant share of the population, while they support democracy, is open to alternatives, such as "strong leaders" or "military rule." This was on display, for example, after a military-backed takeover in Bangladesh in 2007.

So what trends might influence the strengthening of democracy? Among the many factors debated in the literature on democratic consolidation, three are viewed as common and positive: income and wealth, economic growth, and literacy and education level. In consistence, a recent survey of South Asia found that formal education is the single biggest factor in determining support for democracy. "In South Asia, someone with a graduate degree is seven times more likely to support democracy than is a nonliterate person" (deSouza et al. 2008, 92).

The combined positive influence of these factors on democracy was predicted back in 1959 by Seymour Martin Lipset who wrote that "the factors of industrialization, urbanization, wealth and education, are so closely interrelated as to form one common factor" (Lipset 1959, 80). Lipset termed these factors together "the economic development complex." Within these, however, a negative association exists between income inequality and democratic consolidation.

According to another strain of research, cultural factors matter. Cross-national research has found that democratic viability in a given country is positively correlated with whether that country had been a British colony, whether English (as opposed to French) was spoken more widely, and whether Muslims were a minority (Clague et al. 2001). Obviously, these are correlations, not causations. South Asia–focused research, however, finds that religious differences matter less, but that ethnic diversity helps, especially because minorities in any given area are stronger promoters of democracy (deSouza et al. 2008).

Outside these domestic factors of consolidation, we need to consider extraneous forces – sourced primarily outside South Asia – that may constrain region-wide democratic politics. Gasiorowski and Power (1998), for instance, find the political environment of the neighborhood to be a major predictor of democratic consolidation. In addition, we need to consider a number of other significant factors such as international terrorism, American foreign policy and climate change.

Looking Forward: Certainties and Uncertainties

The aforementioned influences are all derived from past data, which are predictors but do not form a forecast. To move towards a forecast, we need to first classify predictions into relative certainties and uncertainties, and then pick the most significant of these to build scenarios. This section focuses on the first task.

In South Asia, the influence of all factors correlated with democratic consolidation will be affected by one certainty: climate change. Environmental degradation associated with climate change will have two major impacts. Due to climate change, sea-level rises in the south will combine with floods from glacial melting in the north to drive hundreds of millions of people into forced migration. This will not only create a region-wide humanitarian disaster but also change the boundaries of South Asian states. Boundaries and nation-states have changed in the region relatively frequently, from the early Hindu kingdoms through the Mughals, the British and as recently as 1971. Thus it is not hard to imagine that they will change again – this time driven by the environment. However, it is uncertain whether this will lead to fragmentation or a unified South Asia.

The second major impact of climate change will be on food. Climate change will put access to freshwater under such strain that, according to United Nations Development Programme (UNDP), 2.5 billion people will be affected by water scarcity by the year 2050. Since 85 percent of freshwater in the region is used for irrigation, this will jeopardize the breadbaskets of the Indus and Ganges river systems. By 2060, a food crisis is a relative certainty, mitigated only partially by technological advances.

Of the factors positively correlated with democracy, an increase in income and literacy across the region is a certainty. Regardless of cyclical downturns, we can be fairly sure that Lipset's "complex of economic development," mentioned earlier, will improve further in the next 50 years. By 2050, South Asia as a region is projected to become the second largest economy in the world, after China. Additionally, the gross domestic product per capita is projected to increase between 10 to 20 times across the region (Goldman Sachs 2007). While significant economic inequality will exist, its extent is uncertain. Overall wealth will grow, increasing the influence of the top quartile of income earners. Toward the bottom however, climate change will render the most vulnerable parts of the population into a poverty cycle, with a loss of land, food shortages, disease and forced refugee status. The gap between the richest and poorest quartile will increase. The relationship between inequality and democracy however is not straightforward according

Table 1. Ordered list of relative certainties and uncertainties

Key certainties	Key uncertainties
Climate change → Humanitarian and food crisis	Border changes (fragmentation vs. unity)
	Extent of domestic violence
Increase in income and literacy	Extent of economic inequality
Presence of large security forces	Target of mass-destructive terrorism
	Incidence of international war
	Direction of US foreign policy
	Political environment in the wider neighborhood
	Extent of government social spending
	Democracy at the party level

to Barro (1999), it is not the two extremes, but the middle-class share of income that influences democracy the most; the overall trajectory of the middle class's relative share of income remains uncertain despite a huge projected swell in its ranks.

Inequality has engendered violence in South Asia, and given the impact of climate change, such violence may continue. However, it may be mitigated by large governmental social spending to help people cope. The future direction of religious tension and ethno-nationalism is also uncertain as regional/local collapses (like warlordism), strains from climate change, reactions to terrorism, unequal economic growth and other factors might lead to greater fragmentation. On the other hand, shared crises such as climate change or common positive trends, such as region-wide economic growth and the establishment of a common market might reduce the political – but not cultural – importance of ethnic groups. It is certain, however, that large security forces will continue to remain across South Asia, which will keep the likelihood of human rights violations fairly high.

What about terrorism? One analyst notes, in a narrowly based forecast, "for any Pakistani revolutionary, India is a convenient enemy and a fifth Indo–Pakistani war in 62 years a desirable goal" (Kaminski 2009). Access to technology may place mass-destruction capabilities within the reach of terrorist groups. The targets of future terrorism are uncertain and terrorism may stay largely confined to the geographic fringes of the region without disrupting overall democratic consolidation. However, international terrorism would be of concern since it may trigger an international war as demonstrated by the discourse after the 2008 Mumbai attacks.

The success of US foreign policy in Afghanistan will obviously be an influence in anti-establishment violence in the Af–Pak region. The overall grounds for violence however will also be influenced by whether America is able to achieve, in the coming decades, greater balance in its uneven foreign policy position with regard to the Arab–Israel conflict. The oppression of Palestinians has been central to the narrative, rationale and recruitment strategy of major militant groups in the region. It is also uncertain whether China will decide to engage itself in mediating international conflicts as its power increases.

A fairer state of affairs in the Middle East will help strengthen democracy in South Asia. Greater political openness in China may also help. However, it is uncertain

Table 2. Democracy in 2060: Scenario grid

Key uncertainties	Regional fragmentation	South Asian unity
Low levels of violence	Likely outcome 1: Federal democracy	Likely outcome 2: Centralized democracy
High levels of violence	Likely outcome 3: Breakup of South Asia	Likely outcome 4: Illiberal democracy

whether China will continue its "string of pearls" approach aggressively in South Asia. This approach envisions an encirclement of the Indian Ocean by states favorably disposed to China. Such containment of India will extend distrust between India and her neighbors. This would contribute toward fragmentation, which may be in China's interest, for a unified South Asia would be a greater competitive threat for China. Its policy will likely be to encourage a level of fragmentation but not so much that it would threaten regional stability.

Future Scenarios

We are now in a position to construct a scenario grid, shown in Table 2, by juxtaposing the two most significant uncertainties – "significant" here implies the capacity of these factors to alter regional political institutions. This yields four scenarios, each of which is theoretically equally likely to develop. While the mix of uncertainties varies in each scenario, the three relative certainties we identified remain constant – crises bred by climate change, increase in income and literacy, and existence of large security forces.

In scenario one, ethnonationalism or religious tension combined with the effects of climate change, have led to regional fragmentation by 2060. However, timely intervention, large social spending by governments, and effective use of security forces have mitigated the eruption of violence between the groups. Although borders have changed, the fragmented regions have become largely self-governing and externally peaceful, arranged in a loose federation akin to the political structure of current-day India. Under this scenario, democracy persists well.

In the second scenario, a region-wide increase in income and literacy has created a common market and a common humanitarian catastrophe has further promoted the notion of One South Asia. In view of the billions of people needing help, citizens and governments have combined to create some form of a political union. Large security forces remain present, but a strong central government oversees rehabilitation and keeps peace. The powers of local government, while visible, are less significant than in the first scenario. Again, democracy persists well.

Scenario three is the breakup of South Asia – despite an increase in education and income, large-scale human movements have erased the viability of inclusive politics. Political violence has increased as terrorist incidents have involved the use of chemical and biological weapons in urban areas. Regions of what was formerly Afghanistan and Pakistan have broken off and communal violence and insurgencies fed by inequality, food crises and migration have torn India apart. One-quarter of Bengal is lost under water. The region is composed of smaller political units, with varying forms of government. They compete intensely with each other, and a few conventional wars have been fought along the way.

In scenario four, pro-unity political parties and leaders have together created a form of political union to deal with common crises, but have been unable to persuade significant portions of the population. Some South Asian cities are among the richest in the world, but in the poorer, rural and less-educated areas, ethnonationalist insurgencies have flared up. The secular central government has increased the powers of its security forces. Central power rotates by democratic elections, and elections reflect majority opinion, but human rights violations are frequent and flagrant, due to the license to use force and the existence of intolerant sentiments in various regions. Democracy persists, but it is an illiberal democracy.

What do these four scenarios say about the future of democracy? In only one scenario have we projected a complete breakdown of democracy in South Asia. Some form of democracy continues in the other three scenarios. This does not readily translate to a 75 percent probability in favor of the persistence of democracy, but it does mean qualitatively that South Asia's long-range future has a greater likelihood for the existence of democracy than its absence. This democracy might be centralized or federal. It may be liberal or illiberal. Certain baseline conditions also augur well for the persistence of democracy. The region by now has experience with parliamentary politics, its political institutions are broadly comparable – thanks to a common British colonial experience, which, as mentioned before, has been found to be positively correlated with democratic persistence. Also, South Asia's ethnic, linguistic and cultural diversity and complexity mean that democracy may be the only viable political system.

The system in 2060 however will be different than today's democracy. The recent region-wide survey of political attitudes revealed a strong distrust for politicians (deSouza et al. 2008). Four out of five respondents preferred decision making by experts rather than politicians. While they value the political choice that democracy brings, South Asians also value the army, strong leaders, experts and religious traditions. They do not want to replace democracy with authoritarianism, but they want to redefine democracy so that it is not an empty electoral exercise, but a model that combines other virtues, namely "discipline (as exemplified by the army), order (as personified by a strong leader), wisdom (as embodied by experts) and values (as represented by religious leaders)" (deSouza et al. 2008, 95). A change in the region's future boundaries will offer opportunities to undertake institutional reforms that can incorporate these traits. Technologies, such as voting from mobile communications devices will change the nature of elections, while technological and geographic changes together will automatically shift the content of politics in South Asia. Chances are good that such politics will be exercised democratically in 2060, regardless of the institutional specifics.

Chapter 7

CONFLICT AND RECONCILIATION: THREE SCENARIOS

Amitabh Mattoo

There are few regions in the international system whose future seems to have been as difficult to predict as South Asia. Almost all the writings that looked at South Asia, say 50 years ago, were way off the mark. That is true even of the assessments of individual countries. There are several reasons for these inaccurate predictions. Forecasting the future, as we know, is a small industry in the West. Thinking long term is, of course, important, as is identifying the main drivers of change. But most Western analyses of South Asia have suffered from a clear ethnocentric bias. Analysts have predictably, if unfortunately, sought to capsule the region into a preconceived Western mould. "Occidental" attempts at forcing an Eastern intellectual puzzle into preconceived categories have just not worked.

Take the case of the India–Pakistan relationship, arguably the single most critical factor for the region. The conflict between India and Pakistan is easy to describe, but painfully difficult to understand. We have witnessed how apparently well-thought-out prescriptions have failed, even as policy analysts have invented catchy titles for the troubled relationship. "Enduring rivalry," "sustained conflict," and "ugly stability," are terms that form the standard lexicon of South Asia watchers particularly in the United States. But this really is *reductio ad absurdum* as is evident to almost anyone with more than just a passing sense of history of the region. The reality is that the India–Pakistan relationship is, and has been, about almost everything that matters: history, memory, prejudice, territory, identity, religion, sovereignty, ideology, insecurity, trust, betrayal and much, much more, in a very *desi way*. And yet there are few, almost none in the field of international relations – a discipline that I am most familiar with – who have attempted to develop a comprehensive analytical framework to engage with these multiple overlapping variables.

The case with South Asian scholars is only a little different. Many South Asian scholars – being almost participant-observers, as it were – have injected their writings with their national prejudices and forced their analysis through the narrow sleeve of misplaced patriotism. We get thus an Indian view, a Pakistani view or a Nepali view but rarely a South Asian view. This essay attempts to be different – recognizing, of course, that the biases of a Kashmir-born, Western- educated, middle-class Indian may be less evident to the author than to a discerning reader who may discover the idiosyncrasies born out of these multiple identities and influences.

This essay, in essence, seeks to ask one fundamental question: how secure will South Asia be by 2060? Security here is defined as freedom from fear, in its most comprehensive sense. Comprehensive security would thus mean that citizens of the region would be free from fear in the economic, political, cultural and social realms. In 2006, Indian prime minister Manmohan Singh described his vision for peace and empowerment in Jammu and Kashmir. This vision can easily be extrapolated for the entire region. He said:

> Real empowerment, my friends, is not about slogans. Only when every man, woman and child from Ladakh to Lakhanpur and from Kargil to Kathua through Kashmir feels secure, in every sense of the word, can we truly say that people have been empowered. Security is freedom from fear and this is what we want to achieve. We want the people of Jammu and Kashmir to be free from all fears about their future. It is only this sense of comprehensive security, within a framework of good governance that can really empower the people. We want the people to be physically secure and this can only happen if violence and terrorism ends permanently. We want the people to be economically secure and this can only happen if the tremendous potential of the state is channelized and every citizen has access to quality education and healthcare. We want every group to be politically secure and this can only happen once power is decentralized to the villages. Finally, we want every community to be culturally and socially secure. This means that we value the cultural distinctiveness of every community and create conditions for the flowering of their languages, their lifestyles and their arts and crafts. And we have to ensure that those who have been displaced can return to their homes. This vision of empowerment and comprehensive security is related to good governance and people's active participation in formulating policies and monitoring their implementation. (Prime Minister's Office India 2006)

This essay identifies five drivers that will be the critical forces of change over the next half a century, builds three scenarios around them and makes three tentative conclusions.

The Drivers: The Five Ds

Demography

By 2060 South Asia will have a population of close to two billion, and the largest pool of young people in the world. While most of the rest of the world is aging, South Asia is comparatively youthful. In India alone, there will be over 600 million people under the age of 25. This youth bulge could potentially be the region's greatest asset or it could become its worst nightmare. South Asia could become a major source of the global workforce, or it could witness heightened and often violent social unrest.

Reaping the benefits of this enormous demographic dividend requires massive public investment in education, health, delivery of essential services and in other aspects of social infrastructure. While there are improvements of individual countries in their standing, for instance, in the human development index, the overall picture remains dismal particularly in the western part of South Asia. In India, the National Knowledge Commission (of which the author was a part) made radical recommendations that it believed could transform the country into a "knowledge society" by 2020. The recommendations include those on implementing the right to education, schooling, vocational education, distance learning, higher education and research. Clearly, for South Asia, in its entirety, to become a major knowledge hub – even by 2060 – will require an immediate change of focus and priorities and a massive infusion of funds. The alternative is greater extremism, further radicalization and violent conflict, which could overwhelm the entire region.

Democracy and devolution

There is, at present, a so-called "democratic" moment in South Asia. All South Asian countries can claim, with varying degrees of justification, to be democracies. And yet most of these are fragile and incipient democracies, at best. On the other hand, the chances that the democratic process could be reversed, in at least some of these countries, are not negligible. In almost all countries, there is widespread public cynicism about politicians, political parties and, in the wider sense of the word, about politics in general.

In addition, corruption is rampant and public perception of corruption is even higher. Transparency International, in its 2010 public perception survey of corruption lists India as the 87th most corrupt amongst 178 countries surveyed. Pakistan ranks much lower at 143, while Bangladesh is ranked at 134, Sri Lanka 91, Maldives 143, Nepal 146 and Afghanistan 176. Only Bhutan, ranked 36, is amongst the first 50 least corrupt countries.

The immediate challenge in this aspect is threefold: to stabilize democracy in all its formal aspects, increase the accountability of public institutions and improve the delivery of public services. But for democracies to become truly inclusive and stable requires a devolution and decentralization of power. Devolution is about empowering people, making people feel that they belong to the polity they live in, and about increasing the accountability of public institutions and services. Alienation grows when people feel disconnected from the structures of power and the process of policy formulation; in contrast, devolution ensures popular participation in the running of the polity.

The internal benefits of a strong decentralized democratic polity are far too great to need elucidation here, but there is strong evidence also of the spin-offs in terms of interstate relations. Mature democracies rarely go to war with each other, and the chances of building sustainable peace are greater between states that are bound by a common democratic tradition. On the other hand, the collapse of the democratic moment could create conditions for not just greater internal instability but also be instrumental in heightening interstate tensions in the region.

Dialogue and reconciliation

It is clear, beyond doubt, that the conflict between India and Pakistan – the two largest countries of the region – and the manner in which this relationship is crafted will greatly impact on the future of the region.

At what level does one analyze the India–Pakistan relationship: at the level of the international system or in interstate terms, or does one address the intersociety dimension or focus at the human level? And where does one look for remedies? Perhaps the only way that this relationship can move forward is by systematically beginning a process of reconciliation at *every* level. Only through such a "grand" reconciliation will it be possible for India and Pakistan to live comfortably next to each other and for communal relations in the Subcontinent to heal, well and truly. Given the nature of South Asian polities, this process of reconciliation could perhaps only be state driven initially, but once there is enough backing, push and momentum, the process can accelerate and move on, into an auto mode. Most importantly, leadership and public perception of the process in India and Pakistan will be of paramount importance. Without determined leadership on both sides that is ready to shoulder the domestic political backlash it will be extremely difficult to carry the process to success. Preparing and convincing the populace in both countries for the benefits of reconciliation will probably be the most daunting task that awaits leaders on both sides of the border. Without a doubt, this process will be affected by factors both within and outside. Not only will the reactions of the states in the region impact the process but also worldwide reaction, and most importantly that of great powers that have stakes in the region, such as the United States and China, will play a crucial role in determining where the reconciliation process goes. The reconciliation, were it to happen, would, arguably, be grand in its design and vision, but incremental in its process and execution: several flakes that would come together and snowball into an unstoppable avalanche of peace. And yet a failure of a process of dialogue and reconciliation will continue to cast a huge shadow over the region. And whatever becomes of the India–Pakistan relationship going forward will reflect in the overall health of interstate relations in the South Asian regions.

Development and integration

Much has been written about uneven and noninclusive pattern of development in South Asia. Even the economic success of India hides huge pockets of deprivation which are one important cause for the Maoist insurgencies that have assumed the proportion of being the most serious challenge to India's stability. The other countries of the region have fared even worse. The internal insurgencies in Pakistan (driven partly by religious extremism), the Maoist insurgency in Nepal, the Tamil rebellion in Sri Lanka, and the anarchy in Afghanistan can be correlated to flawed development policies and massive economic marginalization of huge sections of the population across South Asia. In the absence of a more inclusive developmental agenda, which delivers on the ground, these "million mutinies" will further undermine stability in the region.

It is also clear that the region will be able to exercise its full potential only if there is increased integration, greater connectivity and the growth of regional institutions. The vision of a common south economic space where there is a free movement of capital, trade, goods, services, ideas and people has been articulated by political leaders in the past, but only if there is a clearly laid out blueprint which is translated into reality on the ground can we truly hope to realize the great economic and social dividends that could be realized from a region where borders will become irrelevant and be reduced to being just lines on a map. While institutions such as the South Asian Association for Regional Cooperation (SAARC) have taken considerable steps in this regard, a lot is left to be desired to accomplish a truly integrated South Asia.

Diversity

South Asia is not just one of the most populated regions in the world, but also one of the most heterogeneous parts of the world. This diversity has occasionally been celebrated and has been viewed as a source of strength. And yet there have been strong exclusivist tendencies in many parts of the region. Attacks against minorities, marginalization of linguistic and cultural groups, and the rise of radical homogenizing tendencies are a source of both internal instability and external tensions. The manner in which South Asian countries are able to moderate these tendencies and ensure that cultural, linguistic, religious and other minorities are empowered will play a critical role in the future of the region.

The Scenarios

South Asia as a secure community: The jannat scenario

In this scenario, South Asia after 50 years will be characterized by at least the following:

- A recognition that war, the use of force and large-scale violence will not be used to resolve interstate or intrastate conflicts;
- A convergence on common goals and shared values, including a commitment to democracy, fundamental freedoms, rights of minorities and multiculturalism;
- A growing irrelevance of borders, with the region becoming an open space for the free flow of ideas, goods, services and people;

- A transition to a knowledge region that will harness the enormous demographic dividend of its youthful population and emerge as the global knowledge hub that provides one-fourth of the workforce to the rest of the world;
- A politically decentralized region that recognizes the sovereignty of its members but is increasingly functionally dependent on common institutions;
- A region that will harness its renewable and nonrenewable resources in an environmentally conscious manner and addresses the concerns of marginal communities.

This might sound too rosy for some, yet not enough for others. Will South Asia ever be able to reach this point? The answer lies in part in to what extent we are able to avoid the next two scenarios.

Security anarchy: The barzakh scenario

In this scenario, South Asia will be characterized by anarchy, which is defined as the absence of any supranational legitimate authority and where self-interest is the prime determinant of the policies of the states in the region. South Asia would resemble what it is today:

- Increased intrastate violence and asymmetric warfare;
- Deep political, societal and economic instability in many states;
- Fragile democratic structures;
- Increasing internal unrest especially amongst the youth;
- Low levels of physical, environmental or economic security;
- Growing marginalization of minorities and traditionally deprived communities.

Security nightmare: The jahannnum scenario

In this scenario, we could potentially witness the following:

- Pandemics that spread across the region and beyond;
- Environmental catastrophes plaguing the natural resources;
- Civil wars in several states with a high risk to spill over into the entire region;
- An end to the "no-nuclear-weapons-in-fighting" game between India and Pakistan;
- Exacerbated interstate conflicts fuelled by resource competition and sense of insecurity;
- Deep cleavages at every level exacerbating already problematic sociopolitical inequalities;
- Collapse of at least one state resulting in increased outside interventionism.

Needless to say, this doomsday scenario is what we have managed to escape so far. On the other hand, one would, without much trouble, find many in the region who think that this is precisely where we are headed. While this may seem overly pessimistic, without necessary steps, South Asia may well descend towards the second, and ultimately the third scenario.

Three Conclusions

First, South Asia is at a tipping point today. The decisions taken by the leaders of South Asia over the next five to ten years will largely determine whether South Asia will become a *jannat*, a *jahannnum* or continues to be in the "twilight" zone of *barzakh*.

Second, only a determined political leadership – displaying extraordinary foresight, creativity and imagination – and radically departing from the policies of the past can change the course of the region's future. A leadership that relies only on the bureaucratic and military establishment for "policies" will sadly only reinforce the status quo. The people of South Asia must be brought on board; they must support positive change and become drivers of it at the same time. This is the only route that has a real chance to avoid the *jahannnum* or a perpetuated *barzakh* scenario.

Third, the young people of South Asia are its greatest potential asset. If there is one single policy that can make a significant difference to the future of this region, it is an investment in the growth of this new generation. This will, as earlier stated, require a dramatic shift in priorities and an unprecedented investment in education. There is no other option if we want South Asia not just to survive but to realize the great civilizational potential of this region.

Chapter 8

RELIGION AND STATE FORMATION

Najeeb Jung

South Asia is one of the most diverse regions in terms of religion, ethnicity, language and cultural practices. It includes believers of all Semitic and Oriental religions. The history of state formation in South Asia is an interesting interplay of religion and politics. All states, except India and, more recently, Nepal, have their own declared state religions. While in Afghanistan, Pakistan, Bangladesh and the Maldives Islam is the state religion, Sri Lanka and Bhutan have declared Buddhism as their state religion. India and lately Nepal are declared secular states and have made provision for equal treatment of all religions in their constitutions.

Religions in South Asia: Precolonial Period

Oriental religions like Hinduism, Jainism and Buddhism originated in South Asia. Semitic religions arrived in South Asia very early due to the vibrant trade relations between South Asia and West Asia. Christianity reached the region as far back as the first century CE (Fernando and Gispert-Sauch 2004, 59). Before the European colonial powers established their predominance in the western coast of India, Christianity was already established as a major religion there.

Islam arrived in South Asia in the seventh century. It was brought to the Malabar Coast as part of the trade and cultural interactions with the Arabs (Rantattani 2007, 24). Later, Islam spread to northern India as part of the interactions between Persia, Central Asia and South Asia. Religion and religious interpretations functioned as ideological cover and justification for kingdoms and empires. In the "ancient" period, Brahmanical Hinduism and Buddhism provided the necessary legitimacy for various power centers in the vast land mass of South Asia. The Gupta, Chalukya and Chola empires used Brahmanical Hinduism as a legitimizing ideology of their respective empires. The Mauryas, especially Ashoka, the Kushan Empire and King Harshvardhana used Buddhism for the same purpose.

In the "medieval" period, Islam spread over to the Indo–Gangetic Plain and established itself as the religion of the ruling elite. The sultanate period witnessed many a tussle between the orthodox version of Islam and its more popular Sufi traditions.

Many a time, the rulers took sides in this tussle according to the context and compulsions of political power. Under Mughal rule, Islam gained even more prominence but the efforts of the Mughal kings to ensure a kind of judicious balancing of both Hinduism and Islam exacerbated the tensions between traditional Islam and the demand for a syncretistic tradition. The debate finally settled in favor of traditional orthodox Sunni Islam under the regime of Aurangazeb (1618–1707), the last of the great Mughals (Avari 2013, 103). Throughout, Islam played an important role in the ideological state apparatus of the Mughal Empire.

Religions in South Asia: Colonial Period

Till the colonial period, the diverse religious traditions coexisted on the South Asian land mass in a more or less peaceful manner. Empires and state formations emerged and disappeared in South Asia in the precolonial period and largely kept themselves away from intervening in the religio-cultural life of the people. This status quo underwent radical change under colonialism.

While the limited interests of the early colonialists never demanded a serious intervention in the politico-cultural life of the people, whenever they attempted to do that, it resulted in stiff resistance. A joint Hindu–Muslim effort against the Portuguese attempts in the sixteenth century to mould the polity is one such example.[1] Nonetheless, this scenario changed under British colonialism. Unlike other colonial powers, the British wanted to establish their political power in South Asia. For this they used all means at their disposal – from brute force to the construction of ideological cover to legitimize their presence and hegemony over the politico-administrative structures in various parts of South Asia. Communalism based on segregating religious communities as exclusive entities became their major tool in dividing the unity of the people. The invention of communalism played a major role in creating the gulf between Hindus and Muslims in South Asia.

British colonialism used the discipline of history and the conduct of census to develop a communal ideology. The classification of the history of the Indian subcontinent in religious terms; i.e. the ancient (Hindu) period, the medieval (Muslim) period and the modern (British/Christian) period and the writing of text books based on this classification created divisions along communal lines (Misra 2004, 194). The juxtaposition of the "glorious period" of ancient/Hindu India and the period of "subjugation" under the medieval/Muslim rule created the expected effect. The implied logic in this historical narrative was that the British provided the balance between the distinct warring categories of Hindus and Muslims. This was projected as a justification for their claim to rule the Indian subcontinent.

The rise of the National Movement in India since the launching of the Indian National Congress in 1885 was an attempt by the Indian elites to confront the colonial authorities.

---

1 The Arabic text *Tuhfat-ul Mujahidin* written by Sheikh Zainud-Din Makhdum in 1583 exhorts the people of Malabar to wage a holy war against the Portuguese colonizers (Makhdum 2006).

The overt display and use of Hindu symbols as part of the National Movement alienated the Muslims from it. The formation of the All India Muslim League in 1906 (Gould 2012, 48) was in a way a reaction to the pro-Hindu tilt of the National Movement under the militant Hindu nationalists. The colonial authorities within no time used the suspicion between the Muslims and Hindus to divide the National Movement. The prejudices and suspicion between the Hindus and Muslims led to the formulation of the idea of "Muslim nationalism" in South Asia and the demand for the creation of Pakistan – the homeland of the Muslims in the Indian subcontinent and finally resulted in the partition of the Indian subcontinent into India and Pakistan in 1947. Since then the conflict between two religious communities in the pre-independence period transformed into a conflict between two postcolonial nation-states.

Religion and Conflict in South Asia: Postcolonial Period

Pakistan was created as a state for the Muslims of the Subcontinent. Its founding fathers envisioned a secular state even though Muhammad Ali Jinnah, the founder, used religion to mobilize the Muslims and fight for a separate state. But the tussle between secular leaders and those who wanted an Islamic state reflected in constitution making in the early stages. After the formation of Pakistan, the founding fathers realized that the only unifying factor in the otherwise diverse and plural Pakistan was Islam and Islam alone.

The assumption that Islam would ensure the unity of a diverse country like Pakistan crumbled when the country got dismembered into Pakistan and Bangladesh in 1971. The formation of Bangladesh underlined the fact that religion could not be the basis of nation building. Instead of making this realization a fact of nation building in the modern world, the ruling elite of Pakistan moved further towards Islam, which later led to the Islamization of the state. The push towards Islamization was stronger under General Zia-ul-Haq during the 1980s. It ended up rendering Islam into a divisive force, pitting secular against religious forces, Sunni and Shi'a, Muslim and non-Muslims against each other.

Today, the religious right and the Jihadis have become the biggest challenger to the state in Pakistan. The ultraright does not have much electoral support but its influence and reach over the state apparatus is enormous. In Pakistan's political culture, Islam will continue to be used in manifold ways for political ends.

The rise of the Taliban since 1994 in Afghanistan and subsequently their increasing spread within Pakistan is a grave cause of concern. Their establishment of an Islamic Emirate in Afghanistan from 1996 till the end of 2001 was the manifestation of the kind of Islamic state they had to offer. The Taliban espouse a violent and intolerant interpretation of Islam. Their anomalous interpretation of Islam has emerged from an extreme and perverse interpretation of Deobandism.

The interplay of religion and politics has led to adverse consequences for the other states of South Asia as well. In India, Partition left a bitter legacy of a communal divide between the Hindus and Muslims. The rise of Hindu nationalist sentiments communalized politics since the late 1960s. The Jana Sangh and its later *avatar* the Bharatiya Janata Party (BJP) built on an ideology based on Hindu nationhood called Hindutva. It's an exclusivist ideology and at its extreme, demands the Indianization of the Muslims in India, implying that Muslims in India were aliens and had not adapted to Indian culture. During the 1980s, the Hindu right gained in strength. Mobilization revolved around an old mosque called Babri Masjid, which the Hindus claimed was actually the birthplace of Lord Ram, one of their important deities. In December 1992, the Babri Masjid was brought down by Hindu radicals (Stern 2003, 188). This was followed by some of the worst rioting that India has witnessed. The Gujarat riots of 2002 were one of the worst forms of communal violence that Muslims have faced in independent India. Many Hindu groups through their aggressive militant brand of Hindutva have made political inroads and continue to promote an ideology of Indian nationalism based on Hindu nationhood. This has resulted in the insecurity and alienation of Muslims in India.

The Sikhs, the other major religious group in India, also passed through a troubled phase. In pursuit of political power, some Sikh political parties appealed to Sikh religious sentiments. What started as a moderate movement for greater autonomy changed course to demand a separate state called Khalistan, a Sikh-dominated state. The movement acquired a militant stance and launched a violent campaign for an independent state. The violence that was to follow was brutal and indiscriminate. Highly communal and selective mass killings were carried out to create a communal divide in the well-integrated Hindu–Sikh communities. On one hand the government dealt with the problem through a political package to address the Sikh demands of autonomy and political power, but on the other hand used strong counterinsurgency measures to deal with the violent militant groups. Though there was an intense period of violence in the Indian Punjab, the healing has been quick and religion is no longer a source of tension between the Sikhs and the Hindus.

Sri Lanka's devastating ethnic conflict also has strong undercurrents of the interplay of religion and politics. It has historical roots. The colonial administration gave privileged treatment to the minority Sri Lankan Tamils (Hindus) concentrated in northern Sri Lanka over a period of time. This led to tremendous discontent among the majority Sinhala (Buddhist) population. In the postcolonial phase of Sri Lankan history, through the process of the indigenization of political power, the majority Sinhalas established firm control on the administration and started discriminating against the Tamils. They created a historical narrative in which Sri Lanka is depicted as a Sinhala–Buddhist nation always in conflict with Tamils – the outsiders (Obeyesekere 2004). The perpetuation of the Sinhala–Buddhist communal ideology by the Sri Lankan state and the civil society led to the ethnoreligious conflict between the Sri Lankan state and the Tamils. The communal ideology also led to the victimization of the Sri Lankan Muslims by both the Tamils and the Sinhalas. Religion, thus, has been a major factor in the destabilization of the polity and social fabric of Sri Lanka.

The modernization process in Bhutan led to the precipitation of ethnoreligious conflict in a massive manner. The conflict between the Bhutanese state dominated by the Ngalongs (Mahayana Buddhists) and the Lhotshampas (people of Nepali origin who are mainly Hindus). The state-sponsored ethnoreligious conflict led to the expulsion of more than one hundred thousand Lhotshampas from Bhutan (Acharya 2011, 48).

The situation in Bangladesh is also reflective of the general South Asian pattern of majority–minority conflict. The religious minorities in Bangladesh, mainly Hindus and Buddhists residing in the Chittagong Hill areas have encountered many problems due to the radicalization of Islam. For long, the tribals of Chittagong waged an armed struggle against the Bangladeshi state in order to protect their culture and religion.

Islamization, assertive Hindu nationalism and now Talibanization stand in the way of the creation of modern South Asian states in search of peace, progress and prosperity. The promotion of exclusive religious nationalism has divided the people and states of the region and it has retarded growth and development, inhibiting its people from achieving their full potential. South Asia's religious diversity and its pluralist nature of society needs to be protected. Religions can coexist harmoniously, as they had done historically. But the politicization and radicalization of religion is leading to greater communalization of society and increasing the divide among religious communities. This has only weakened the state- and nation-building process in South Asia.

Looking Ahead: Some Thoughts for the Future

Will South Asia be mired in continuing religious conflicts? Or like the European nation-states primordial identities will be subsumed under cosmopolitan identities? In the short term, the situation in South Asia doesn't look too bright, particularly in the Af–Pak region. And it is difficult to predict the long term, as social transformations can generate forces that are conflictual or consensual. However, the role religion will play in politics will be conditioned by several factors.

Political elites will have to play an important role. The democratic space for political mobilization has to increase. Power has to be diffused as more and more social groups feel that the power structures can be changed through political mobility. People have to develop stakes in their states and their ruling elites. The state has to be viewed as the provider of both development and security. States that are weak in their welfare functions cannot take for granted the allegiance of their citizens to the idea of the state. The institutional legitimacy of the state will have to come about from the ability of the state to create consensus in society. In the absence of these, religion is sure to feature as one of the forms in which political mobilization against the state will be carried out.

In the current context of globalization where all South Asian states are actively following neoliberal policies, there are immense possibilities of the emergence of divisiveness, which may also create conditions for religious conflicts. The neoliberal policies pursued by the South Asian states are increasing wealth and income disparities.

Some indigenous groups feel that their right over their natural resources is under threat as multinational corporations are making inroads. The disproportionate access to resources by various groups and classes in society in turn may compel people to mobilize themselves around tangible identities. Among the identities available, the most potent would be religion. As a cultural system religion has many qualities like symbols, rituals, faith/practices and peculiar categories of dos and do nots readily available for the construction of communities that have strong internal bonding. Essentially, a political conflict in the absence of ideologies can take the form of religious conflict.

On the other hand, globalization also has the potential to erode divisiveness. Political and economic liberalization can open spaces for democratic political mobilization. The rational for the Sikh agitation based on their religious identity eroded the moment India embarked on economic liberalization. Similarly, as India notches up impressive growth rates, Hindu nationalist parties are finding it hard to mobilize on the basis of Hindu religious identity. The surge of the BJP in the last decade has been arrested in the last two general elections held in India. This may last as long as the Indian state is able to maintain a high growth rate and also the equitable distribution of wealth.

South Asia also has to take hope from the experiences of other regions in the world. The surge of fundamentalism in religious communities has sometimes led to its opposite current. The possibility of the appearance of "liberation theology" in various religions cannot be completely ruled out. Afflicted with the burdens of religious bigotry and violence, it is possible that the believers may take recourse to a completely different interpretation of religion and move away from the tide of fundamentalism.

The Latin American experience of the 1970s is a classic example in this regard. When the official church (Catholic Church) sided with the military regimes in the Latin American countries, believers and a section of the clergy came out and started cooperating with secular and sometimes atheistic political ideologies like Marxism. The emergence of "liberation theology" was the result of this cooperation. Prominent liberation theologians like Father Ernesto Cardenal even took part in active politics and became a minister in the revolutionary government of Daniel Ortega in Nicaragua (Sabia 1997, 82). The "liberation theologians" interpreted the Bible in the context of Marxism and other secular ideologies and led to the creation of a body of literature pertaining to faith and social action in the context of Christianity, which still inspires many people (Smith 1991).

One can only hope that the trajectory in South Asian politics also has this possibility, not in a dogmatic way but in a manner that is liberating. The Dalit assertion in India has this potential. Lately, the Dalit activists have started talking about a kind of "Dalit spirituality," which is far removed from the hierarchical Brahmanical Hindu theology and way of life. Similarly, the assertion of various Muslim groups against the conservative interpretation of Islamic tradition and "Fatwa culture" is a welcome sign in this direction. If religion, instead of anchoring people in their faiths, becomes a constant source of conflict and violence – that brand of politics may face rejection. But the battle has to be at the ideological level. For instance, the Taliban cannot be fought with force only. To undermine the growing influence of the Taliban, there is a need for an ideological battle. South Asia's indigenous and rich tradition of Islamic spiritualism popularized by great Sufi saints needs to be popularized again. Religion needs to remain personal faith and not used in statecraft or as a means to bring political change. The world is not bereft of political ideologies to bring political change.

Chapter 9

WILL SOUTH ASIA STILL BE TERRORISM'S CENTER OF GRAVITY?

William Milam

Terrorism, in this essay, equates with violence; it involves the use of violence to achieve what are essentially political goals. In this context, terrorism becomes almost synonymous with extremism from which springs the frequent sectarian violence that is also, sadly, a characteristic of most of South Asia, as well as the frequent social and gender violence. Terrorism is only one source then, though the major one, of the violence that is a constant factor and threat in the life of most South Asians.

Terrorist violence comes in many varieties in South Asia, and no country of the region but for the ministates of Bhutan and Maldives has escaped its ravages. In several of the region's countries it seems to emanate as much from exterior forces as from domestic ones. In others, its genesis is primarily from indigenous grievances and/or deficiencies of domestic governance. While it clearly is the product of distinct political and social toxicities in each of the various countries of the region, there are many common threads. The most important of these is its almost automatic resort to violence – often a preference for violence. This defines terrorism/extremism, no matter what the goals are.

These goals differ from country to country. In some they are cloaked in millenarian garb, i.e., they promise a period of general righteousness and happiness in the indefinite future – an egalitarian world of shared prosperity or a return to a purer world of a mythological past. Or they can be more worldly and practical – a share of power, and/or of the national pie, an end to class discrimination and/or an ethnic feeling of dispossession or an unquenchable yearning to run their own affairs.

In each country, there can be no doubt that poverty and illiteracy, and the alienation that accompanies them, is a backdrop to the more country-specific causes of terrorism. But in each country, poverty and alienation are almost always catalysts to a more toxic combination of social pathologies that drive numbers of people, primarily young people, to violence as the way to achieve country-specific political goals.

The path to a region that is free from terrorist violence is, in a nutshell, through improved governance, which includes higher sustainable economic growth, a more inclusive political process, and when necessary, measured military force (enough to win, not so much as to alienate noninvolved populations) to resist terrorist encroachment on the writ of the states. This is not as simple as it sounds; some of the toxicities are lethal, fired by religious extremist ideology or radical revolutionary rhetoric, often imported from outside.

There is, at present, an almost region-wide struggle against the various forces of terrorism/extremism in South Asia countries. But not all the countries of the region are equally affected and the outlook varies depending on the country in question. In the following section, the trends in each of the region's countries that are affected by terrorism are summarized as succinctly as possible. Taxonomic descriptions are not necessary. Current readers will be familiar with them, and readers in the medium and far term will only need the sketchiest of summaries in order to understand what the trends of their time evolved from.

Trends in South Asian Terrorism – What Do They Portend?[1]

Pakistan is, these days, the hub of our discontent. It has traded places with Afghanistan as the crucible of terrorist outreach and the primary exporter of terrorism to the region as well as the world. It has been customary to view the conflicts in Pakistan and Afghanistan, both involving the heavy use of terrorist violence, and both having ultimately similar interests in stopping that violence, as inextricably linked, and they are usually treated, both analytically and politically, as two halves of the same problem. Until recently, it seemed that, despite the similarities, the two countries were moving slowly in different directions, but events and behavior of the past year – to be described below – make that conclusion less tenable.

Pakistan, long known as an exporter of terrorism to Afghanistan and Kashmir, has since the early 2000s also become the main site for training terrorists who plan attacks in the West. Adding to the complexity of terrorism's pernicious growth in Pakistan is the fact that the country is also now the scene of a full-scale Islamist extremist insurgency against the Pakistani state. That conflict is not close to resolution, and the country teeters in the balance.

The interconnections in Pakistan between the groups that export violence, and those who use it domestically against the state, are as complex as a cobweb and as strong as steel mesh. In the middle of that mesh, somewhere, is Al-Qaeda to which they are all linked in one way or another. Mixed into this grim picture also is increasingly frequent and larger-scale sectarian violence than seen before, often committed by extremist groups that interpolate political and sectarian goals. The current scale is such that it is now claimed by many that there is underway a full-scale genocidal attack on the Shi'a minority of the country (which accounts for about 20 percent of the population). Al-Qaeda itself has, of course, a harsh sectarian – anti-Shi'a – element.

---

1 The discussion in this section is based primarily on US Department of State, "Country Reports on Terrorism 2009," 147–63. Available online at http://1.usa.gov/kdwjbx (accessed 15 May 2010).

Several strands of that mesh lead back to the state. A number of the extremist organizations were actually created by the Pakistani state, which has used them as tools (proxy armies), both to defend its interests in Afghanistan and in its 66-year effort to wrest Kashmir away from India. The extent of continuing connections between some of these organizations and the Pakistani military is the subject of intense debate (as was the case in the November 2008 Lashkar-e-Tayyaba raid on Mumbai).

These creations of the state have, in some cases, turned against their creator, and may act on their own to accomplish a political agenda the state now has somewhat less taste for, though clearly cannot abandon (i.e., challenging India). In addition, some of these proxy armies' agendas have grown more ideological and radical over the decades and these groups now seek, in addition to a Pakistani Kashmir and/or fundamentalist Afghanistan, to transform the Pakistani state, which they consider "apostate," into one that meets their definition of a truly Islamic state.

The primary extremist group that has turned on the state is the Tehrik-i-Taliban Pakistan (TTP), better known as the Pakistani Taliban. Beginning in about 2004, this group, an amalgam of former Taliban from the Pakistani tribal areas and a number of groups of Islamist jihadist warriors that share its objectives, became increasingly aggressive in using violence against the state and its citizens – the TTP was, for example, responsible for the assassination of Benazir Bhutto. Using violence, or the threat of it, and intimidation, the TTP took control of some parts of the tribal areas and some of the settled areas such as Swat. Before 2009, the Pakistan army sought mainly to deal with the TTP encroachment by arranging "peace agreements," but it proved impossible to hold the TTP to such agreements. Public revulsion at TTP actions in Swat finally forced the army to fight, and since then it has taken the offensive to some of the Taliban's home areas.

The dangers of this extremist challenge to the Pakistani state from militant groups located in the tribal areas of Northwest Pakistan, and the high cost of the Pakistani army's efforts to dislodge them, or in most cases to contain them, remain politically sensitive, with ambiguous public support because of their connection to the US drone program. On the other hand, the rapidly growing threat of militancy and extremist action in Pakistan's largest province, Punjab, are less well understood. At this point, this remains a potential third rail in Pakistan's politics, and seems to have become a "no-go" area for the Pakistani army (see Ayesha Siddiqa's worrisome recent paper, 2013).

Thus, the present prognosis for Pakistan is worrisome, to say the least. The newly elected government talks of "conciliation" with the Taliban but has produced no coherent strategy as to how it will do this. The Taliban show little interest at this point. The continuation of escalating Sunni extremist attacks against the Shi'a would weaken public support for any such strategy. It has produced, however, no coherent strategy as to how it intends to push back terrorism. The onus falls on the army, which controls security policy anyway, but finds itself enmeshed in the steel mesh that characterizes the Pakistani situation. It is challenged directly by the TTP and its allies, and indirectly by a plethora of powerful terrorist groups, with starkly different political agendas, whose links with it are obscure, and, except for the TTP, with most of whom it lives in an uneasy informal truce.

Political stability in Pakistan is also challenged by the escalating sectarian strife and killings perpetrated by some of these same groups. The constraints in responding to these multiple challenges are several, but its India-centric phobia that has always been at the core of Pakistan's national identity and strategy is key to whether Pakistan can find a way out of this dilemma or whether it will at best muddle along in perpetual struggle against extremists while its economy and society continue to unravel.

In Afghanistan, terrorist violence has been a feature of the landscape for almost thirty years and is the major tool in the Taliban kit as it wages an asymmetric guerilla war of insurgency against the current Afghan government and its – mainly – Western allies. This violence has been on a steady upward trajectory for the past several years as the Taliban and its allies make continued inroads against government forces and against the International Security Assistance Force (ISAF), the alliance of the government's allies.

The insurgent Afghan Taliban fight under an Islamist banner although it is made up of an array of groups that range from virulently extremist to xenophobic nationalist, and to mainly mercenary. The two major Afghan Taliban groupings are headquartered in Pakistan; so the connection of the insurgent conflicts in Afghanistan and Pakistan could not be clearer. The Afghan Taliban, however, also draws upon the traditional Afghan nationalist aversion to foreign occupation, and this helps them bring in allies that are not necessarily motivated by Islamist political objectives, but also accept the use of terrorist violence as legitimate in an insurgency.

The hope for a smooth political solution in the near term have, however, faded, but one still seems possible in the longer term as there are visible signs of war weariness in general and of a feeling on all sides that no-one can win outright. A political solution would clearly involve a political role for parts of the Taliban in some sort of national government. One strong signal in this direction came when Taliban spiritual leader Mullah Omar renounced one of the principal tenets of Al-Qaeda's *weltanschauung*, the objective of striking out against the West.

There are many more political bridges that remain to be crossed, and there remain many doubts on both sides that such a solution is possible. So, the trends that shape the future of this conflict with an opposition using terrorist violence, and that will have much resonance elsewhere in the region, are still to be determined. We must be cautious, however, since a political solution in Afghanistan without one in Pakistan leads to the question as to whether the former is sustainable if Pakistan remains unstable, or if it and/or the terrorist groups in it are unhappy with the outcome.

But recent events, since this was first written, make this conundrum perhaps more hopeful. At a minimum, the Pakistan army may have relocated its India-phobia to Afghanistan. It is even possible that India-phobia has been replaced by fear of a return of political instability and military fragmentation in Afghanistan as the US/NATO departure plans come to fruition in 2014. Recently, the Pakistan army has shown strong signs of a reversal of strategy and is ostensibly trying to establish a working relationship with the Afghan government, as well as with the US and NATO, in a renewed effort to bring about reconciliation between the Afghan central government, the various other competing power centers in

Afghanistan, and the Taliban. At the time of this writing, the tangible results of this effort are near zero, and there are many who doubt both Pakistani intentions, and the sincerity of the Taliban, even if they join a "peace process," fearing they may be just playing a waiting game until all but a minimal US/NATO remains and an ill-prepared, underfunded, underequipped Afghan army is all that is between them and complete power.

India's indigenous terrorism problem is of a very different variety than in the two countries to its west, but it remains a persistent, if less well recognized, hindrance to the country's otherwise rapid growth and modernization. In addition to the homegrown terrorist problem, India has, of course, also suffered from terrorist acts committed by Pakistani jihadists, primarily in Kashmir, but also in New Delhi and Mumbai.

From a regional point of view, the Kashmir insurgency is the most important and critical. Much has already been written on this 63-year year dispute, but despite all that attention and many worthy efforts, a solution seems as far away as ever. There is among Kashmir's Muslims a residual desire for independence, which New Delhi has sometimes damped down by inclusive policies and flexibility, and has sometimes stirred up by heavy-handed punitive policy and the maintenance of an enormous military presence. But, particularly since 1989, the problem has been further complicated by Pakistan's interference, through its proxy fighters which, *inter alia*, stir up and/or assist indigenous insurgents. Kashmir is the core problem between the two countries that must be settled before terrorism in the region can be overcome.

India faces domestic insurgencies in its far northeast that are less dangerous and have always been contained through a combination of force and political outreach. In this region, ethnic minorities have never felt a part of greater India, and believe that they are left out of the country's mainstream. They seek greater autonomy or even independence for their region. Almost all of the seven northeast states have had, over the years since independence, their own insurgencies, but fortunately for New Delhi, at different times. India's response has traditionally been to use measured force to suppress insurgent groups, joining this with an offer to the insurgents to join the political process, if they accept the principle of Indian unity. That these problems keep popping up indicates a need for recalibration.

A far more difficult insurgency, driven probably by feelings of economic and social dispossession, is found in parts of India's most economically backward (often tribal) areas of its eastern regions, West Bengal, Orissa, Andhra Pradesh and Jarkhand. In these regions a revolutionary communist/Maoist insurgency waxes and wanes, which at times may involve as many as 20,000 to 40,000 armed fighters. This insurgency began in West Bengal almost forty years ago, was crushed, but has reappeared in recent years. It has resorted to serious violence in recent years, aimed at inflicting terror on the local population and sending signals to the central government of its continuing challenge.

One of the problems in handling this insurgency is that, in India, law and order remain a state prerogative, not a federal one. In some of the states where the insurgency is strongest, law enforcement has been uneven, at best, and corrupt. More importantly, the insurgency is exacerbated by the influx of outsiders, primarily resource extraction companies, that cut deals with corrupt local officials and return little, if anything, to the indigenous inhabitants who are mainly tribal and subject to the discrimination that tribal people face throughout the country. The central government has promised a large influx of resources for economic and social development of these areas. However, whether that will be followed up with action remains to be seen.

It is not very likely that, given the overwhelming strength of the Indian state's military, paramilitary, and police power, any or all of these insurgencies together would put the Indian state in any danger. Clearly, however, failure to deal with them effectively reduces and retards India's political modernization and economic advance toward the ranks of great powers.

Bangladesh and Sri Lanka appear to have succeeded in turning the tide forcefully against terrorism/extremism. The Bangladesh government that came to office in early 2009 with an overwhelming majority in the parliament took strict action to crackdown on both domestic and foreign terrorists groups. It improved its counterterrorism cooperation with India in doing this. Bangladesh is, however, a country in which all these gains can disappear because of bad governance – much offset by active and beneficial NGOs – or with a change of government to the party that is traditionally allied with, and soft on, Islamists.

In Sri Lanka, the government used overwhelming force to finally put an end to the Liberation Tigers of Tamil Eelam (LTTE) insurgency that had lasted over twenty-five years and because of much effective terrorist violence by the insurgents had led to thousands of deaths. This does not seem to have made the government more democratic, but, in fact, has likely contributed to the drift of Sri Lanka toward a police state. At the end of the long insurgency, there was hope that the government would reach out effectively to those insurgents left alive, and to the broader Tamil community, and begin a necessary healing process. So far, such efforts have been, at best, half-hearted, and the price may be a persistence of repression of the Tamil minority and failure to establish genuine ethnic peace – in other words, possibly a resurgence of the insurgency.

In the case of Nepal, the political violence has been almost entirely over local issues. The Maoist revolutionaries shifted from terrorist violence to democratic politics through a peace accord negotiated several years ago. The Maoists emerged as the largest party in the constituent assembly in the subsequent elections and formed a government. The arrangement has, however, broken down, primarily over the contentious issue of integrating the Maoist fighters into the army. Even though the Maoist government was voted out of power, they do not seem to have gone back to their former ways. The situation remains unstable and a return to civil war is possible. Nepal's only connection to international terrorism seems to be through its serious deficiencies of governance, which offers terrorists from other parts of the region a place to hide and/or to transit.

Terrorism: The End of Hope or the Catalyst for a New Beginning?

It is not beyond imagination that increasing waves of terrorist/extremist violence emanating from Pakistan could impede, perhaps undercut, progress in Afghanistan and that terrorism could spread beyond their borders, infecting again those countries of the region in which the balance remains uncertain. That is the worst case scenario – a future in which the terrorism now virulently extant in Afghanistan and Pakistan cannot be contained and spreads throughout the region, using the many, various local discontents and grievances, including those in India, for its fuel.

The best-case scenario starts with a political solution in Afghanistan which meets Pakistan's needs there, and a Pakistan–India rapprochement that would lead to a bilateral agreement on Kashmir. These would encourage the Pakistani state to renounce – and mean it – the use of nonstate proxy warriors to achieve its foreign policy goals, and perhaps to undertake the grindingly difficult task of taking down – not uniquely by force – its own creations, the Pakistani jihadist groups devoted to terrorist violence.

It is likely that the reality will lie somewhere in between, but it is impossible to forecast just where at present. A more probable scenario – with several variations – is that India, which has clearly opted for rapid modernization and set its course to join the major powers of the world, will be the balloon that pulls Bangladesh, Sri Lanka and Nepal upward toward higher growth and faster modernization. In other words, India could be the catalyst for a growing and modernizing east subregion of South Asia. Whether, in the end, the western anchor of Pakistan and Afghanistan would also be pulled along by the force of this example, and perhaps by an India that could relax its inhibitions about settling issues that a great power should not let fester and hold back the region it so dominates, is only a hope, not a certainty.

It is not clear whether the region's political culture is strong enough and its political systems coherent enough, its politicians tough enough and wise enough, to act forcefully over the next few decades to move all its countries in the direction of growth and modernization and away from terrorism. If not, some sort of intraregional, east–west split is likely, with India and Pakistan at the center of it. Those countries that have not succeeded in quenching the use of terrorism as a political tool and/or have become instead launching pads for terrorists to the rest of the region, to say nothing of the rest of the world, will certainly be at odds with those that have quelled terrorism and want to concentrate on regional modernization and growth. Intraregional conflict, obviously, also has a nuclear implication.

The upshot is that India and Pakistan are right where they have always been since South Asia gained its independence in the mid-twentieth century – at the heart of the divide over whether the region will move forward or remain static. India has not always been the lodestar of regional progress in this equation, but that is its role now. Pakistan has not always been the harbinger of regional failure, but it certainly is now.

Chapter 10

SPECULATIONS ON NUCLEAR SOUTH ASIA

Pervez A. Hoodbhoy and Zia Mian

The conflict between India and Pakistan may be the most serious and imminent danger to the South Asian region and to humanity over the next 50 years. During this period, India and China will continue their rise as great powers and rivals, even if they do not become peers of the United States. This will ensure that Pakistan remains at the heart of regional and global politics for decades to come.

We examine the dynamics of the India–Pakistan nuclear relationship and how it may evolve, especially as it becomes increasingly part of a larger set of strategic relationships involving the United States and China. At the same time, Islamist politics in Pakistan, which may gather strength in coming decades, seeks to more directly confront India and the West. We look in particular at the risk of nuclear war and of nuclear terrorism. We consider also how India and Pakistan might respond to the renewed global effort to eliminate nuclear weapons.

There is another nuclear danger growing in South Asia. India and Pakistan have relied on nuclear energy for electricity production on a small scale for decades and have ambitious plans for expanding their respective programs. Other countries in the region have been seeking to start their own programs. This is part of a renewed worldwide interest in nuclear energy. But the March 2011 Fukushima nuclear disaster in Japan offers a stark reminder of the ever-present danger of nuclear accidents. We explore the implications for South Asia of a catastrophic nuclear accident.

Nuclear Dynamics

The nuclear arms race between Pakistan and India is an expression of a deeper conflict that has shaped the national narratives of the two countries. The wars of 1948 and 1965 over the status of Kashmir and the 1971 war over East Pakistan – which saw India intervene and inflict a decisive defeat on Pakistan – entrenched the idea, especially in Pakistan, of the threat from across the border. India's first test of a nuclear weapon in 1974 drove Pakistan to press ahead with its own nuclear capability. Six decades of almost unremitting hostility have both limited their economic, political and cultural ties as well as prevented any substantial process of South Asian regional integration from gaining hold.

Nuclear weapon policies have hardened in recent years and the South Asian confrontation seems set to endure, with limited prospects for any kind of long-term restraint or détente. Today these two South Asian countries are locked in an open-ended hostile competition to continuously upgrade and expand their nuclear arsenals.

India clearly seeks to become a major nuclear power. In July 2009, it launched its first nuclear-powered submarine and plans eventually to deploy several of these submarines. India is also developing an array of missiles from the 5,000 kilometer-range Agni-V missile to cruise missiles and submarine-launched ballistic missiles.

With far fewer resources, both technical and economic, Pakistan has been seeking to increase the size of its nuclear arsenal and to maintain some kind of parity with India. It completed its second plutonium production reactor in 2010, and is building two more, while expanding associated fuel and processing facilities. The nuclear arsenals held by Pakistan and India are widely believed to be about one hundred weapons each. It is possible that these arsenals will increase in the next two or three decades to several hundred weapons on both sides.

All this is possible because making nuclear weapons and their delivery systems is becoming easier with time, and cheaper. Modern technology is highly modular and detailed knowledge of scientific principles is no longer vital. Scientists are only marginally necessary; engineers suffice to make working nuclear weapons. Computer-controlled precision lathes and other machines have made reverse engineering of mechanical parts easy. No longer is "rocket science" a correct expression for indicating scientific complexity. This, along with help from China, is why Pakistan – with no other examples of technical achievement – has succeeded in building up its nuclear arsenal and missile fleet (Hoodbhoy 2009).

Contrary to claims made by nuclearization advocates on both sides, nuclear weapons have not displaced conventional arms. India was the largest arms importer in the world for 2006–2010 (SIPRI 2011). It is planning to spend as much as $55 billion on weapons over the next five years (Misquita 2009). India's military spending will continue to expand with its economy; it already has the eighth largest military budget in the world.

For Pakistan, defense spending for 2010–11 was set at almost $8 billion, a 30 percent increase over 2009, and amounting to 21 percent of the total budget. A further 18 percent increase in military funding was announced in the 2011–12 budget. It has signed arms sales agreements worth over $6 billion since 2001, including for new US-built F-16 jetfighters. China, an old ally, is also supplying the country with jet fighters and other weapons.

In both India and Pakistan, which are still very poor countries, the very large commitment of funds to nuclear and conventional arms suggests that the nuclear–military–industrial complex is likely to grow stronger. This will make it more difficult to restrain military competition and associated spending in coming decades in either country.

A continuing India–Pakistan arms race, episodic crises and the nuclear shadow will ensure that South Asia as a whole will remain unstable. For 25 years the India–Pakistan conflict has frustrated the hopes underlying the creation of the South Asian Association for Regional Cooperation (SAARC). The SAARC charter declares that "the objectives of peace, freedom, social justice and economic prosperity are best achieved in the South Asian region by fostering mutual understanding, good neighborly relations and meaningful cooperation among the Member States." Without ending the India–Pakistan conflict, these goals will be unattainable.

Regional and Global Dynamics

The future of nuclear South Asia is increasingly wrapped up in great power politics. For six decades, the United States has sought to have India become part of its strategic and economic plans for Asia especially as a counter to China. In the early years, the US hoped that India could serve as a pro-Western capitalist democracy able to compete with communist China, which had its revolution in 1949, two years after India won independence.

In recent years, as China's economy has boomed, it has emerged as a potential great power competitor to the United States. Thus the US has pressed again to recruit India. Indian leaders, for their part, have seen an opportunity to use a new relationship with the US as a way to drive India's rise as a major power. The new US–India relationship was formalized in the "Next Steps in Strategic Partnership" agreement of January 2004. A senior American official announced that "its goal is to help India become a major world power in the 21st century [...] We understand fully the implications, including military implications, of that statement" (Reuters 2005).

The relationship between India and China, however, differs fundamentally from India's relationship with Pakistan. It is less hostile, less visceral and free from the kind of tension that makes a Pakistan–India confrontation an ever-present possibility. Trade and investment ties between India and China have boomed in recent years as the economies have grown. A part of the Indian establishment, however, sees China as a convenient bogeyman for boosting Indian defense efforts. General Deepak Kapoor, India's army chief and chairman of its chiefs of staff, said he wanted to be able to mobilize and deploy for war very quickly, and to be able to fight a two-front war, against Pakistan and China (*Times of India* 2009). India also wants to be able to project military power from the Persian Gulf to the Malacca Strait (which connects the Indian Ocean to the Pacific) and seeks, among other things, to have ballistic missile defenses and space-based capabilities.

This has obvious consequences for Pakistan. As India builds up its military capacity, with US help, Pakistan will rely even more on China for military assistance. This four-cornered arms race can probably be sustained at a very high level in the decades ahead. The Goldman Sachs BRICs projections of the future growth of the economies of Brazil, Russia, India and China suggest that by 2050, India will have a gross domestic product (GDP) comparable to that expected for the United States (over $37 trillion), and half of that expected for China. Pakistan is projected to have a GDP in 2050 that is fourteenfold greater than in 2010.

An additional regional factor in the nuclear dynamic is the possibility that Iran may decide to turn its search for a nuclear weapon capability into a fully-fledged nuclear weapon program. It is worth recalling that both India and Pakistan acquired the capability many years before they made the decision to build an actual nuclear arsenal.

Nuclear Risks and Consequences

Pakistan's leaders have made it clear that they are prepared to use nuclear weapons first in any conflict; they hope this threat will prevent war, because they fear being overwhelmed by India's conventional military might if war should happen. While India has offered an agreement for no-first use of nuclear weapons, its armed forces seem prepared to try to destroy Pakistan's nuclear capability before it is used, and seek their own capability to launch a nuclear attack if they believe that enemy nuclear missiles are armed and ready for launch. Pakistan, in turn, may seek to preempt such a situation by using its nuclear weapons even earlier in a conflict rather than risk losing them in a massive, rapid Indian conventional assault.

The experience of Hiroshima and Nagasaki showed that a single nuclear weapon can devastate a modern city. About a hundred thousand people died in each city, but people living a few miles away from these cities were not affected directly and so were able to shelter refugees and provide some assistance to the injured. It is unlikely that nuclear war between India and Pakistan would involve only the use of a single weapon. If each side used only five weapons each, and targeted cities, they would kill on the order of three million people and injure at least as many (McKinzie, Mian, Nayyar and Ramana 2001). Relief and recovery from such destruction would be beyond the capacities of either country. The other countries in the region have few resources they could divert. The broader international community would be stretched thin to manage the recovery effort.

A larger India–Pakistan nuclear war would devastate South Asia and affect much of the world. Recent studies by Alan Robock and others looking at an India–Pakistan nuclear conflict, in which these countries used 50 weapons each, found that the smoke produced by burning cities would spread to cover the South Asian region within five days; in nine days it would begin to encircle the world and cover the Earth in less than two months. The smoke would darken the sun for as long as a decade, cooling the Earth's surface and causing drought that would devastate global agriculture. This possibility should give new urgency to South Asian regional efforts and broader international efforts to have India and Pakistan restrain their arms race.

The other grave nuclear danger facing Pakistan and India is nuclear terrorism. Today, with about one hundred nuclear weapons spread across Pakistan and fissile materials for many more already stockpiled and still being produced or processed at a growing number of locations, the threat from religious extremists – both from outside as well as inside the nuclear establishment – is also very real, albeit unquantifiable. It is known that the Al-Qaeda leadership met with sympathetic former senior scientists in Pakistan's nuclear weapons program. By engineering a nuclear catastrophe in some Western city, Osama bin Laden's disciples may dream of provoking a nuclear response from the US that would rally new supporters to their cause and unleash a final showdown between the West and the Muslim world.

It is not just the United States but also India – and Pakistan even more – that need to fear nuclear terrorism. London or New York may be the preferred targets for Al-Qaeda militants but Islamabad and Delhi may be much easier. If a retaliatory nuclear response from India on Pakistan's cities is triggered, this would be the fulfillment of a dream to ignite the ultimate conflict that would destroy both *kafirs* (unbelievers) and *munafiqs* (Muslim hypocrites). Along with India and the West, the radical Sunni interpretation of Islam that drives the Islamist militancy in Pakistan treats Shi'a Muslims as an enemy. A radical Islamist takeover in nuclear Pakistan could push Iran into a deadly corner.

The origin and nature of the Islamist militancy in Pakistan ensures that it will be an intergenerational process and will shape Pakistan and the region's future for at least the next 50 years. In the 1980s, the military regime of General Zia, Pakistan's Islamist parties, Saudi Arabia and the United States created a generation of radical young Afghans and Pakistanis committed to jihad. The *madrassas* that trained these militants continue to operate and are the only schools for many hundreds of thousands of boys and girls still in their teens. The militant worldview they learn will guide their thinking for decades.

Towards Nuclear Disarmament: Implications for South Asia

Pakistan is at the heart of nuclear fears for much of the international community. The September 11, 2001, attacks on the United States raised fears of nuclear terrorism by Al-Qaeda. The beginnings of the twenty-first century also brought new concerns about the spread of nuclear weapons materials and knowledge on the black market. In 2003, A. Q. Khan, the head of Pakistan's program to produce highly enriched uranium for nuclear weapons, admitted to having trafficked key nuclear weapons technologies and weapon designs from this program to Iran, Libya and North Korea, and possibly others. These developments have added new urgency to the long-standing goal of eliminating nuclear weapons.

These concerns are shared by all the great powers. In September 2009 a unanimous United Nations Security Council Resolution 1887 declared "We are all committed to seeking a safer world for all and to creating the conditions for a world without nuclear weapons" (UN Security Council 2009). But the abolition of nuclear weapons may not come soon. Even the most ambitious nuclear disarmament effort, led by the international campaign known as Global Zero, imagines the final elimination of nuclear weapons only by 2030.

A South Asian Nuclear-Weapons-Free Zone (SANWFZ) offers one way to pressure Pakistan and India to restrain their nuclear ambitions and build a stronger South Asian regional community. Initially such a treaty might include only Sri Lanka, Bangladesh,

Nepal, Afghanistan, the Maldives and Bhutan. A treaty would permit these countries to exert official and popular pressure on Pakistan and India to disarm, strengthen nuclear-disarmament movements in these countries and offer the two governments a path back from the nuclear abyss if political circumstances improve. There are already nuclear-weapons-free zones in Latin America, the South Pacific, Southeast Asia, Africa and Central Asia, which commit countries in these regions not to acquire nuclear weapons.

Nuclear Energy

Along with nuclear weapons, India and Pakistan have nuclear energy programs that date back over four decades. These programs have performed poorly, in part because the two countries have chosen to develop nuclear weapons rather than sign the 1970 Nuclear Non-Proliferation Treaty (NPT) as nonweapon states. This has largely cut them off from the international trade in nuclear materials and technology, especially nuclear reactors. It has not restrained the ambitions of their nuclear energy establishments, however.

In September 2009, Prime Minister Manmohan Singh stated that India planned to have a nuclear capacity in 2050 of 470 GW, more than one hundred times the current nuclear capacity (which is based on 20 operating nuclear power plants). Under this plan, by 2050, India would have a larger nuclear energy capacity than the total global nuclear electricity capacity today. To realize this goal, India would need over four hundred large modern nuclear reactors, about as many as the total number now operating in the world (Ramana 2009). India hopes to import a large fraction of these new reactors. This has been made possible by the special exemption for India from international rules governing nuclear trade that the US pushed through in 2008.

Pakistan has somewhat more modest nuclear ambitions – but may have more difficulty realizing them. It has three operating nuclear power reactors, one was imported from Canada over forty years ago and two were bought from China, and plans to increase its nuclear capacity over tenfold by 2030. Pakistan would have to import these reactors from China since other suppliers continue to abide by international rules banning such sales. It has sought an exemption like the one granted to India. But there is particular international concern about nuclear sales to Pakistan because of still unresolved questions over the A. Q. Khan network. It is possible, however, that the sanctions against Pakistan will be lifted eventually.

Other countries in the region also have plans for nuclear energy, but on a much smaller scale. Bangladesh has signed a cooperation deal with Russia for two 1,000 MW nuclear plants. As part of a 20 year plan to develop nuclear energy, Sri Lanka is seeking to acquire nuclear reactors from India. As the number of nuclear power plants increases so will the risk of accidents. This concern is likely to become more important in the wake of the nuclear disaster that destroyed four reactors at Fukushima in Japan, contaminating areas out to several hundred km from the site, and releasing radiation that was detected over 6,000 km away in Pakistan and over 8,000 km across the Pacific Ocean in the United States (Nayyar, Ramana and Mian 2011).

A simple model of the consequences of an accident at one of Pakistan's two 300 MW Chinese-supplied reactors at Chashma, located on the bank of the Indus River, suggests that there could be 12,000–23,000 cancer deaths, and perhaps three times as many cases of cancer, over distances of about 300 km from the reactor (about the distance to the border with India) (Mian and Nayyar 1999). Significant areas extending to 70 km from the nuclear power plant would have to be evacuated because of the high levels of radioactive contamination. Surface and groundwater could be contaminated perhaps to distances of 100 km. Another two Chinese reactors are planned for this site.

It is hard to imagine how Pakistan or India could cope with a major nuclear accident (Hoodbhoy 2011). The scale of catastrophic nuclear power plant accidents, especially involving large nuclear reactors, means that any such accident in South Asia, where population densities are much higher than in Japan or the former Soviet Union, would likely have consequences for millions of people, and could easily cross state borders. It would also impose enormous economic costs on the country in which the accident took place and, depending on the wind direction and weather, neighboring countries.

The benefits of nuclear energy in South Asia are questionable. In all the countries of the region, there is a growing divide between the increasing demands for electricity and petroleum from cities and continuing dependence on wood and dung by the majority who live in the villages. Nuclear energy will do little to meet the basic energy needs of the rural majority, who are not connected to the grid, and even if they were connected they could not afford to buy the high-cost nuclear electricity. Rather than nuclear energy, South Asia needs to develop and provide small-scale, local, sustainable, affordable and safe energy systems.

Reading a Cracked Crystal Ball

It would have been impossible in 1947 to imagine the South Asia of today. It is an exercise in grand speculation to imagine in any detail what South Asia may be like 50 years hence, in 2060. Nonetheless, it seems likely that the struggle between India and Pakistan will continue. Elites in both countries, for different reasons, seem determined to build up their nuclear arsenals and conventional forces and accept the high economic, political and social costs of their confrontation, and live with the risk of nuclear war.

The geopolitics will be complex and unstable. The United States and India may together seek to balance and contain Chinese power and influence. China may increase its support to Pakistan to help offset India. The United States may be compelled to aid Pakistan to prevent it from being overwhelmed by Islamist forces. The arms race could be fierce, and given rapidly growing economies in China and India, involve massive expenditures especially in high-tech conventional weapons. Less likely perhaps is that America and Russia move decisively towards abolishing nuclear weapons. Britain, France and China would join them, and India and Pakistan may have no choice but to go along.

The India–China economic rivalry may become the most important concern for India. Knowing that Pakistan, aided by China, will be a thorn in its side, India could make significant concessions to Pakistan on Kashmir and the increasingly charged issue of allocation of Indus River water. If Pakistan is able to end the Islamist militancy, détente could change into the long-awaited rapprochement between Pakistan and India. This could open the door for a process of South Asian regional integration finally to take hold.

It is as likely, however, that the Pakistan army's narrow interests will keep it committed to the struggle against India, regardless of cost and consequence. In a replay of the US–Soviet race, Pakistan could break its back trying to keep up with India. The South Asian region would fester as the two countries wrestle for advantage in every forum. Left unchecked, it would result in the economic, political and social collapse of Pakistan, which would unleash chaos. Under such circumstances, it is possible to imagine that the jihadis may capture a nuclear weapon. A fearful India and United States would intervene, raising concerns in China. The prospect of great power conflict would loom.

The nightmare scenario is that Pakistan's generals, faced with collapse, decide to threaten nuclear war. As the Cuban Missile Crisis showed 50 years ago, in the midst of crisis, there is fear, miscalculation, errors of judgment, flaws in command and control, and simple bad luck, and any of them could trigger a nuclear war. The Subcontinent's cities would become radioactive ruins. Tens of millions would die. The pall of smoke would darken the world; it would be a global calamity.

Chapter 11

NUCLEAR RISK: OVERSTATED OR UNDERRATED?

Hilary Synnott

Few manmade events would change the nature of South Asia more than the use of nuclear weapons in anger. In 40 years of bitter rivalry the United States and the Soviet Union never used their nuclear weapons against each other. India and Pakistan have similarly not been drawn into full blown conflict in the 12 years since they declared their nuclear weapons capability, despite multiple aggravations. Have the risks been overstated and has nuclear deterrence made South Asia safer than before? Or should more be done to reduce the risks, however small they may be, because of the dire consequences of any use of nuclear weapons? And are these consequences adequately appreciated by other countries in the South Asian region?

Many South Asians regard India and Pakistan's possession of nuclear weapons as primarily a bilateral matter between those two countries. The issue is tied up with the complexities surrounding the birth pangs of those two nations, the Kashmir dispute and the several wars and alarms which have arisen over the last six decades. The other six member countries of the South Asian Association for Regional Cooperation (SAARC) are ready for the Association to be used as a vehicle for alleviating tensions so far as might be possible and without investing too much hope in the prospect. But experience has shown that there is little to be gained from volunteering opinions about the differences between India and Pakistan, still less from assuming a proactive role in attempting to resolve them. There is therefore no debate within SAARC or, it seems, on a bilateral basis about the possible consequences of the possession of nuclear weapons by two of its members.

More generally, debate about such matters often arouses strong emotions. The effects of the intentional detonation of a nuclear weapon are so horrific that some people take refuge in a conviction that they can never be used. A former Indian defense minister reflected such a view in suggesting that nuclear weapons were "not really useable" (Singh 1999, 336). Even to posit the prospect of actual use or war-game scenarios that allow for such a possibility implies, in the eyes of some, a dangerous and unrealistic ruthlessness that should not be tolerated. Cool-headed analysis can become equated with cold-hearted inhumanity. On 10 August 2010, one prominent British politician who deals with such matters was described in the British daily *The Times* as a cross between Donald Rumsfeld and Dr Strangelove, which was not meant as a compliment.

But nuclear weapons do exist. They cannot be uninvented. And there is sadly no early prospect of them being eliminated, either on the part of the five Nuclear Weapons States as designated by the Nuclear Non-Proliferation Treaty (NPT) or by Israel, or within South Asia. Rather, there are increasing signs that they are proliferating beyond these countries. Nor can there be grounds for consolation that human reason will ensure that they will not in practice be used, since the very basis of the concept of deterrence is that they *could* be. The deterrence strategy of both India and Pakistan makes this quite clear. The fact that there has been no aggressive nuclear weapon detonation since 1945 is no basis for concluding that there will be none in the future.

Exaggerated Fears?

Within South Asia, however, there are special, South Asia–specific sets of argumentation that reinforce the more sanguine viewpoint. Accounts of the views of South Asian "nuclear optimists" have been well-documented elsewhere (Krepon 2003). In addition to carefully argued reasons for relative optimism, the writer encountered other attitudes in the same direction, voiced by senior South Asian officials soon after the nuclear tests in 1998. These took the line that the West had nothing to teach South Asia over such matters: in contrast to the twentieth-century wars in the West, which caused tens of millions of deaths, those in the Subcontinent had been far less damaging. India and Pakistan understood each other well and knew better than to overstep certain limits; East and West had managed their nuclear deterrents without using them for decades, and to imply that South Asia would fail to do so was "racist." Such reactions reflected the deep resentment at that time caused by the perhaps unrealistic demands made on India and Pakistan in United Nations Security Council Resolution 1172 which insisted that both countries cease their development of nuclear weapons and become parties to the NPT and the Comprehensive Test Ban Treaty (CTBT) (Synnott 1999, 28).

At a less emotional level, the reactions to two serious incidents have been interpreted as demonstrating how reciprocal nuclear deterrence affects political behavior. In 1999 Pakistani military forces crossed the Line of Control (LoC) in Kashmir, near Kargil, in a premeditated, albeit ill-conceived, act of aggression. And in 2001–2002, following a terrorist attack on the Indian parliament and another on an Indian army camp in Jammu, both countries' armies were mobilized for ten months, which gave rise to international concern that an ensuing conflict could lead to nuclear conflagration. Nuclear deterrence may have helped prevent the escalation of these incidents. In any event, they will have encouraged caution, as was the case between East and West over the Berlin crisis of 1961 and that over Soviet missiles in Cuba in 1962. And to some extent they alerted countries further afield about the implications for them of the Indo–Pakistan nuclear relationship (Quinlan 2009, 135).

Other developments, too, may have assuaged fears about the presence of nuclear arsenals within the heavily populated South Asian region. There seems little prospect that the number of warheads in the Subcontinent – between 50–100 in each of the two countries – will approach even the declining numbers held in Russia and the West, currently standing at about 2,500. Initial Western concerns about the possibility of accidental or unauthorized nuclear detonation have been eased by evidence that, with the passage of time, warheads have been made more safe and elaborate control mechanisms have been put in place. While mindful of strictures in Article 1 of the NPT relating to assistance in control over nuclear weapons, the United States has in practice offered advice on safety issues to both countries, including by providing technology and funding to Pakistan (see for example, Kerr and Nikitin 2010, 14).

In the case of India, international confidence has been enhanced by the fact that overall control of nuclear weapons and other strategic issues has remained firmly in the hands of the central civilian government, to which Indian military authorities are clearly subservient. The supremacy of civilian control was demonstrated both in the 1999 Kargil crisis and in the 2001–2002 military standoff. In the former case, the Indian army was mortified at the accusation of having been caught napping; a body of opinion favored "hot pursuit" back over the LoC into Pakistan-administered Kashmir. The government however resisted this temptation and the crisis was brought to a conclusion with the help of US president Bill Clinton. The terrorist attack on the Indian parliament in December 2001 aroused a deep and widespread anger in India, directed primarily at Pakistan. But when an overzealous general overstepped the mark in the border area in the Thar Desert, he was swiftly relieved of his command.

Confidence in Pakistani arrangements rests on opposite considerations. Although nominally under the direction of a committee headed by the prime minister, it is the Pakistani military which controls nuclear policy and practice. For all the wider disadvantages of army dominance over Pakistani strategy and other aspects of political affairs, the army is de facto the country's most effective institution. The Strategic Plans Division, headed by a retired three star general, has done much to publicize its many-faceted control systems, to the extent that then chairman of the US Joint Chiefs of Staff, Admiral Michael Mullen, felt able to declare in September 2008: "To the best of my ability to understand it – and that is with some ability – the weapons there are secure" (Kerr and Nikitin 2010, 1–10). There can be no doubt, sad though it is, that there would be greater grounds for concern if such matters rested exclusively with the civilian administration, which has proved so chronically weak.

Underrated Risks?

Progress in managing South Asia's nuclear arsenals may have been swifter than that of the North Atlantic Treaty Organization during the Cold War with the Soviet Union when, in the course of several decades the doctrine of "Mutual Assured Unacceptable Destruction" was modified to one of "Flexible Response." The main effect of such doctrinal changes was to reduce the usage of nuclear weapons to a minimum in the event of a particular situation. In South Asia, a realization of the effects of nuclear use may have moderated political behavior in the interests of avoiding any such usage during recent crises.

But as Neil Joeck has argued, India and Pakistan's nuclear capabilities have not in practice created strategic stability and do not reduce or eliminate factors that contributed to past conflict (1997, 12). And continued moderation can by no means be relied upon. Following the 2001–2002 crises both countries were swift to develop narratives that best served their cases. As Michael Krepon points out, when both Indian and Pakistani leaders claim to have succeeded at brinksmanship, they may be inclined to continue such practices, and this could lead to consequential misjudgment. The initiation of war could again come as a surprise to one side. Since both military establishments express confidence in achieving their objectives in the event of another war relating to Kashmir, one would be proven wrong if this occurred. Nuclear capabilities that are in a high state of readiness or are in motion to reduce their vulnerability could become more susceptible to accidents or misuse. Deterrence optimists tend to discount accidents and inadvertence as contributing factors in crossing the nuclear threshold, but accidents happened during the Cold War, although none involved a major detonation. And decisions made by local commanders during deep crisis could have led to misjudgments and worse. Accidents, inadvertent steps, and misjudgments during crisis could also occur in South Asia. Nor can domestic turmoil and its impact on command and control be ignored (Krepon 2003, 13–15).

Furthermore, both during the Cold War and in the South Asian context, there was and is little that can be done to reduce the effects of aggressive nuclear detonations if they were to occur. Even if the risk of use is low, the effects would be catastrophic, not just for the two counties involved but for the wider region and beyond; so much so, that the risk cannot be run. Every effort should therefore be made to eliminate as many sources of risk as possible. And yet political relations between India and Pakistan, which all too frequently erupt into crisis, remain fraught with tension. It may be true that the rationale for India's nuclear capability does not rest solely on issues surrounding Pakistan. But this adds to, rather than detracts from, reasons for concern since there are more theoretical circumstances in which it might be used.

This is not the place to explore how, in an effort to reduce risk, relations between India and Pakistan might be improved: the issues are familiar enough. There is however much less familiarity with the likely and possible consequences within the South Asian context of nuclear detonations were they actually to take place. Organizations such as the US Office of Technology Assessment have examined the effects of a nuclear war on the civilian population, economies and societies of the US and Soviet Union, and their reports make chilling reading (Office of Technology Assessment 1979). If similar studies have addressed South Asia, they are not widely known. Indeed the perception on the part of some representatives of major British commercial companies in Pakistan in 2002, when British nationals were officially advised to leave India and Pakistan during the period of tension at that time, was that the risks were overdrawn, and that a tactical nuclear weapon seemed to be little more than a larger version of the "Daisy Cutter"

1500-pound BLU-82 bombs which the US Air Force were then using in Afghanistan. Discussion with senior Pakistani officials at that time suggested a level of knowledge which was scarcely more developed than that of the nonofficial "amateurs." This is scarcely surprising, since general public perception about nuclear warfare has been colored largely by accounts of Hiroshima and Nagasaki and by heavily censored official advice conveyed in the 1950s and 1960s in the context of a possible East–West conflict. It is only recently that authors such as Professor Peter Hennessy have been able to describe more secret information about what might actually happen across a broad spectrum of society. No such material is available in relation to South Asia.

Possible Consequences

Existing studies may be able to quantify the direct destructive effects of nuclear blasts and of thermal and nuclear radiation. But other consequential effects are harder to quantify with any precision since much would depend upon the conditions at the time and the nature of the explosion. Radioactive fallout reaching the troposphere, for instance, would be brought to Earth in a matter of weeks while that which entered the stratosphere might carry great distances and descend over a period of years. But it is certain that, beyond the severe damage caused by the immediate blast, there would be additional deaths arising from injuries and the unavailability of medical care. Contaminated water would lead to intestinal infections, which could in such circumstances prove fatal, as well as cause further spread of disease. Disruption of administration and general disorganization would exacerbate the direct economic damage. Food production and distribution would be diminished. Longer-term effects would include a higher incidence of cancer and of genetic disorders.

These sorts of effects, horrific as they are, would be broadly if not exactly similar in nature to those predicted in other possible theaters of conflict. But South Asia differs from other such theaters in its dependency on the Himalayan watershed. The Hindu Kush Himalaya (HKH) region, referred to by some as the "Third Pole" because it contains the largest area of frozen water outside the polar regions, provides irrigation, power and drinking water for 1.3 billion people – over 20 percent of the world's population. From Afghanistan in the west, through Pakistan, India, Nepal, Bangladesh and Bhutan to Myanmar and China in the east, the HKH region extends 3,500 km over eight countries and is the source of ten major Asian river systems, including the Ganges, the Brahmaputra and the Yangtze, Mekong and Yellow rivers (Humanitarian Futures Programme 2010, 2). This region is already regarded as under stress as a result of climate change, the degradation of ecosystems, water management issues and the effects of natural phenomena. The effects of nuclear contamination of this crucial support of life can only be imagined.

The inexorable conclusion from such facts is that all South Asian countries would be profoundly affected by any use of nuclear weapons in their region. Radioactive fallout would most likely contaminate rivers, drinking water supplies, irrigation systems and the water table over vast areas, impinging on the lives of tens if not hundreds of millions of people over extended periods of time. Victims would not of course be limited by international borders. More immediate effects are difficult to quantify but, quite apart from the deaths, injuries and other consequences of the direct blast, could include widespread flooding as rivers break their banks as a result of sudden snowmelt. The tragic flooding in Pakistan in the summer of 2010 is illustrative of the sort of devastation, albeit in that case over a relatively limited region.

Short of actual use of such weapons, the risk of usage, the fear of such a risk and the cost of whatever efforts may be made to deal with possible consequences will remain so long as the weapons themselves remain in being.

South Asian countries, China, and whoever else has any stake in that region – which in practice means humankind in general – therefore have a direct interest in the implications of the possession by India and Pakistan of nuclear weapons. Differences between those two countries can no longer be left to be handled only bilaterally by the two parties or by major international powers. Left to their own devices, there seems little prospect that India or Pakistan will resolve them on their own. Indeed, new frictions have arisen over Baluchistan; and Afghanistan seems to be in danger of replacing Kashmir as the main battleground. It is not necessary for other countries to take sides over the substance of such differences. But there is surely a case for doing more to ensure that both long-standing and more recent real or perceived grievances are managed in a manner which keeps risk to an absolute minimum and, above all, does not make matters worse. South Asian countries, from Afghanistan in the west to Bangladesh in the east, would bear the brunt of the destruction that would ensue from a nuclear conflict in South Asia. The challenge for South Asia is to try, with others, to forge a collective approach that makes a greater impact than its current peripheral influence.

Editors' Note:

Unfortunately, US president Bill Clinton's characterization of South Asia as the "most dangerous place" in 2000 remains accurate even today. While India and Pakistan have avoided the temptation to move towards active deployment of their nuclear arsenals like the Cold War rivals, their major disputes remain outstanding and continue to thrust them into crises periodically. The two countries have lagged in instituting bilateral risk reduction and escalation control measures and in fact seem to be flirting with the possibility of a nuclear arms race. All this when South Asia must live with the undesirable reality that nonstate actors continue to have the ability – and will – to force the two sides into heightened crises.

Current trends leave little room for optimism. India's economic rise has bolstered its ability to spend appreciably more on defense than Pakistan and this differential will only increase in the coming years. Pakistan's conventional deficit may well force it to rely even more on its nuclear deterrent; it is already believed to possess the fastest growing nuclear program. Moreover, introduction of new technologies is likely to challenge crisis stability further. Both sides are tipped to develop a sea-based deterrent, India has expressed interest in developing a ballistic missile defense capability and Pakistan has already introduced tactical nuclear weapons into the mix. Until outstanding disputes between the two sides are resolved, crises will remain a reality, as will the likelihood of escalation. Without proactive efforts at developing risk-reduction and crisis-prevention mechanisms, current and projected nuclear developments will make South Asia less, not more, secure in times to come.

Chapter 12

THE SHADOW OF THE INDIA–PAKISTAN STALEMATE

Maleeha Lodhi

South Asia today is among the few regions in the world moving at a snail's speed towards greater regional cooperation that can empower its constituent nations with the means to address common challenges and benefit from opportunities offered by globalization. One of the principal factors for the lack of progress towards an integrated and cooperative South Asia is the decades-old state of unresolved tensions between the region's two largest countries and economies: India and Pakistan.

South Asia is unique because it includes three of the world's ten most populated countries with all the complex challenges these demographics mean for fighting poverty and fostering prosperity. But it is India and Pakistan that account for much of the region's population, economic output, military strength and of course nuclear capability. Between them they overshadow the rest of the region. In many crucial respects the fate and fortunes of South Asia depends on the future trajectory of the India–Pakistan relationship that will likely define the destiny of the region as a whole.

If these two countries are able to break from their troubled past, South Asia will move towards greater integration with peace dividends for all the member states of the South Asian Association for Regional Cooperation (SAARC). Should they fail to escape their past, individual countries will perform differently – some will still do better than others – but the region as a whole will be unable to realize its vast and promising potential.

Indo–Pakistani Divide

The roots and contours of the Indo–Pakistani history of hostility and conflict are well known. The bitterness and animosity spawned by the partition of the Subcontinent were reinforced by the developments following independence and crystallized into an early conflict over Kashmir, seen by Pakistan as the centerpiece of the unfinished business of Partition.

The two countries went to war three times, twice over Kashmir while the third culminated in the breakup of Pakistan. There have been several near-wars and frequent flare ups of tensions as well as border clashes. The induction of the nuclear factor qualitatively transformed the region's security environment by imparting a nuclear dimension to the Indo–Pakistani confrontation. India's "peaceful" nuclear test of May 1974 drove the region inescapably on to the path of nuclear competition that was to see both India and Pakistan acquire nuclear weapon capabilities and then test them to become declared nuclear powers in 1998.

India–Pakistan confrontation and tensions came at a high cost, not only for the people of these two states, but also for South Asia in general. Not only did their adversarial relationship distract the two countries from addressing and directing resources to their pressing and common challenges of alleviating poverty and promoting rapid economic development but it hobbled evolution of regional economic cooperation that could have worked to the benefit of all regional countries.

Even though South Asian countries formed a forum for regional cooperation, SAARC, its potential has been stymied by continuing tensions between the two nuclear neighbors. The development of trade and economic ties has suffered as informal trade flows have dwarfed formal trade, at least between India and Pakistan. Moreover, with travel restrictions, stringent visa regimes and multiple barriers on communication, the people of South Asia have been unable to build mutually beneficial economic ties or capitalize on trading opportunities in the neighborhood. Recent efforts to liberalize trade between India and Pakistan have marked an important step forward but movement is slow, fragile and much below potential.

The advantages of mutual trade between South Asia's two largest economies have long been compelling. Even if all that happens to start with is the bilateralization of current indirect trade – which takes place through third countries or other "informal" ways – the dollar volume of the present level of $2.6 billion in annual trade could quadruple. But tentative steps taken so far have not given the normalization process enough momentum to make the embryonic economic relationship irreversible.

Lack of progress in resolving political differences between the two countries continues to cast a shadow on prospects for regional economic integration and collaboration on critical issues ranging from poverty to terrorism. The key to South Asia's destiny lies principally in the hands of the leadership in New Delhi and Islamabad. There is reason for cautious optimism as increasingly both countries acknowledge the imperative for a rapprochement, long evident to those outside government.

There are at least four factors that should urge the two countries towards greater cooperation rather than confrontation:

- Pakistan cannot attain its critical goal of economic recovery and stability and India cannot achieve its full economic potential if the two states are locked in tensions that routinely flare up because their disputes remain unresolved.
- Pakistan's ability to surmount the threat posed by violent extremism and militancy requires stabilizing relations with Delhi and addressing its security concerns that

arise from its troubled relationship with India. While the militant threat is a clear and present danger, Islamabad cannot fully focus on this when the strategic environment with India remains fraught. This requires resolving their political disputes through meaningful talks that can help mitigate Pakistan's security concerns.

• There is a manifest sense in both countries that there is no military solution to the Kashmir dispute or to other problems. The conflict in Kargil, military stand-off in 2001–2002 and the inflamed situation that followed the Mumbai terrorist incident served to confirm this for both sides.

• The two countries need to carefully manage their relations in a nuclearized environment. The strategic relationship between them remains undefined and potentially unstable. There is no substitute for mutual accommodation to stabilize the nuclear and conventional military relationship.

Conditions for Durable Peace

Durable peace in South Asia will need result-oriented engagement between India and Pakistan to establish an architecture of strategic stability in three critical dimensions: finding an acceptable and just solution to the key source of bilateral contention, Kashmir, and institutionalizing both nuclear and conventional military restraint.

Ultimately forging "normal" ties will depend on whether the two countries can: (a) address and overcome their differences on Kashmir, nuclear-military issues and their more recent sources of contention: sharing of waters and their respective interests in Afghanistan and (b) identify and build on the areas of convergence including trade, regional economic cooperation and North–South issues.

Talks between the two during 2011–12 through a broad-based peace process called the "Composite Dialogue" raised hopes that progress would be made on several of the issues on the eight-point agenda. While the tone of bilateral relations improved in this period and several confidence-building steps were taken, no progress was made on resolving any of the disputes, all of which remain in a state of deadlock.

The peace process that had gone off the rails in 2008 after the terrorist attack in Mumbai resumed in 2011. By the middle of 2012 two full rounds had been completed. The mélange of diplomatic engagement at various levels and across ministries helped to inject some energy into the diplomatic process. Trade liberalization became the centerpiece of efforts to normalize ties. This got underway in February 2012 when a "negative" list replaced the so-called "positive" one, significantly increasing the items that could be traded between the two countries. The aim was for Pakistan to confer most-favored-nation status to India by the end of 2012 once Islamabad's concerns about tariff and nontariff barriers (NTBs) maintained by India's more restrictive regime were removed.

Towards this end three memorandums of understanding (MOUs) were signed between the two countries in September 2012, which sought to address the NTBs issue. The three MOUs dealt with (a) redressing trade grievances, (b) customs streamlining and (c) "mutual recognition" that covered the area of harmonizing standards.

A new visa agreement was also signed in September 2012 to liberalize the regime that had been in operation since in 1974. A necessary accompaniment to the expansion of economic relations between the two countries, this aimed to make it easier for people in five categories to travel across the border, including businessmen, senior citizens and divided families. For the rest of the applicants the regime remained quite restrictive.

These moves improved the business environment and the atmospherics between the two countries. Both countries also began to explore cooperation in several energy and infrastructure projects including what is commonly known as Turkmenistan–Afghanistan–Pakistan–India (TAPI), the multi-billion dollar gas pipeline involving Turkmenistan, Afghanistan, Pakistan and India. In May 2012 a gas sale purchase agreement was signed in Delhi among them, marking progress in taking this project forward. All four countries characterized this as a step towards peace.

But while this signified movement in the dialogue process there was no progress on the many disputes that divide the two countries and that have been the cause of past conflict and confrontation. Similarly little headway was made in launching new or expanding old conventional military and nuclear confidence-building measures (CBMs). Pakistan delinked trade from other aspects of the dialogue in the hope that moving first on issues long India's priorities – trade/economic and people-to-people contacts – would elicit reciprocity and Indian willingness to tackle disputes. So far this has not happened.

Impasse continued on all the old disputes and on new irritants. On Kashmir little changed. Both countries used the dialogue to reiterate their long-standing positions. On Siachen, Pakistan perceived a hardening in India's position. Islamabad's offers to settle the dispute went unreciprocated. Pakistan had made these overtures in the wake of the avalanche that struck the Pakistani part of the glacier in early 2012 and claimed the lives of many of its soldiers. A statement by the Indian army chief in September 2012 indicating unwillingness to solve this dispute reinforced Pakistan's perception.

There was no movement in talks on the dispute over Sir Creek. On water disputes too gridlock persisted. India continued to block financing for the Daimer–Bhasa Dam in multilateral institutions like the Asian Development Bank, to the disappointment of Pakistan that faced a growing energy crisis. All this suggested that even issues that seemed on the face of it to be noncontentious or previously regarded as low hanging fruit, such as Siachen, did not seem amenable to compromise.

In a strategic environment unaltered by the improvement in trade and political ties the flare up of tensions along the Line of Control (LoC) in Kashmir in January 2013 came as a reminder of how easily or quickly unresolved issues could set back the peace process. This highlighted the fragility of the LoC even though the 2003 ceasefire has by and large held here. The outbreak of tensions in early January 2013 saw the familiar exchange of diplomatic demarches and accusations between the two countries. Tensions dissipated a few weeks later but not without affecting the peace process. Prime Minister Manmohan Singh declared on 19 January that it would no longer be "business as usual" with Islamabad. This was followed by a number of steps by Delhi to make good on this declaration.

India cancelled a meeting on water issues between the water secretaries of the two countries and stalled the third round of the composite dialogue. It also suspended an important part of the visa liberalization agreement and declined to set any new date for its implementation. While trade and travel across the LoC, halted by India on 10 January 2013 was later revived, the cooling in relations was perceptible.

For its part Pakistan delayed conferring MFN status to India. The main reason for this lay at home – opposition from agriculture, textile and a number of other industry groups who said they had neither been consulted by the government nor had their concerns been met over India's restrictive trade practices. As general elections were approaching at the time the government did not want to risk alienating key economic sectors or provoke political controversy by pressing ahead on this front. The MFN move stalled, reinforcing the slackened pace of the rest of the peace process. This also reinforced the start-stumble-stop pattern of diplomatic engagement that has long characterized their relations.

But the elephant in the room or the dialogue process was Afghanistan. With no formal discussion ever held on an issue that has poisoned relations in recent years, suspicions of each other's strategic intentions could intensify rather than ease in the future. As the 2014 deadline for an end to the American and NATO combat mission approaches this could inject greater uncertainty in the Pakistan–India relationship. In the likely complex posturing by regional powers for influence in post-NATO Afghanistan, Pakistan and India can again become mired in a tense, action–reaction cycle.

Three Scenarios for the Future

Against this backdrop the near-term outlook for Pakistan–India relations as also for the future of South Asia is marked by uncertainty. Ties between the two largest countries remain prone to crisis as the trust deficit persists. Three scenarios can be postulated for these relations in the near term.

The first is a diplomatic standoff with little mitigation of mutual suspicion and mistrust remaining high. In this scenario erratic or sporadic dialogue becomes just a means to restate positions, not reduce tensions or engage in problem solving. This is the most volatile scenario for its potential to relapse into an escalation of tensions, heightening the risk of an uncontrollable crisis. This scenario could unwittingly end up handing militant groups the ability to call the shots by igniting fresh rounds of tensions between the two countries.

The second scenario is one of managed tensions. In this, differences and disputes continue in a no-war, no-peace situation but where both political will and diplomatic means are available to insure that tensions do not spin out of control. This helps to avoid a confrontation or breakdown in the relationship. This scenario provides space for normalization of some aspects of the relationship. For part of their troubled history Pakistan and India were able to evolve such a regime but this has always alternated with periods of heightened tensions, confrontation and conflict. This offers no assurance of a stable relationship. Instead it would leave it accident prone.

The third is the most desirable scenario and one that both countries should aspire to work toward. In this case, both countries adopt a problem-solving approach and engage purposefully to find a negotiated resolution of their disputes while identifying and building on areas of convergence in an effort to achieve a strategic equilibrium. Efforts are directed at confronting and addressing the causes, not just the symptoms, of their tensions. In this scenario trade ties are built and people-to-people contact is encouraged to establish peace constituencies that serve as the foundation for longer-term rapprochement. This is seen as necessary but not sufficient to build durable détente. Settlement of disputes in fact becomes the engine that powers a sustainable peace process. This is the only model of relations that can deliver lasting peace and stability.

It is the realization of the third scenario on which the region's progress hinges. But for now, Pakistan–India relations seem stuck in the less-promising, second scenario with all its attendant risks while the cost of nonresolution of disputes continues to mount for both nations as indeed for all of South Asia. This not only means retarding prospects for more rewarding regional cooperation but also SAARC's ability to emerge as a mechanism to help address common challenges and capitalize on opportunities in trade, investment and economic development.

The stakes for the region are high. The alternative to meaningful progress in building peace between New Delhi and Islamabad is the perpetuation of a cycle of tensions and confrontation, which risks putting South Asia at odds with the dramatic changes sweeping the world and unable to take advantage of the multiple opportunities peace offers to a region that can benefit much from greater integration.

Chapter 13

REGIONAL INTEGRATION

Lhaba Tshering

It has been almost three decades since the South Asian Association for Regional Cooperation (SAARC) was founded as an economic and political organization with lofty vision and far-reaching objectives. Unfortunately, little has been achieved through this body ever since. Today, South Asia is possibly the least integrated region in the world. The failure is neither because of the lack of potential nor because the countries are unable to recognize the vast opportunities that regional integration offers. Rather, this failure can be attributed to the lack of willingness on the part of the regional states to strive for the collective good of the region as a whole. Instead, they have unduly focused on bilateral differences created as a result of conflicts amongst specific countries, and, more recently, on the lack of collective efforts to combat terrorist movements. This chapter makes the argument that SAARC needs to shift its focus on the collective good of the region as a whole and lays out some of the ways in which it can do so.

Capitalizing on the Opportunities

The challenge, in many ways, is to turn South Asia into a cohesive region that identifies with and works towards collective regional prosperity. Recent economic and social developments in the SAARC region present an opportunity that the leaders of the region need to tap if they are serious about improving the lives of its 1.5 billion people. South Asia has experienced a period of robust economic growth of about 6 percent annually since 2000 resulting in significant progress in human development. The concern lies in the fact that this growth has not been a balanced regional growth.

Conflict between the two largest states, India and Pakistan, and its overbearing effect on the rest of the region has meant that efforts required to bring South Asia together have been constrained. Efforts to enhance regional trade have also not made headways. There are few signs that even the introduction of regional trading agreements, the South Asia Free Trade Agreement (SAFTA) being the last one, has had any positive impact. In fact, for some countries, regional exports have been declining as a percentage of overall trade.

This is a pity since with a population of 1.5 billion, the region presents within itself a huge domestic market that has the potential for tremendous trade creation and diversion of external trade currently being carried out with countries outside the region. A quick analysis of the individual trade of the member countries will confirm the potential and the importance of regional trade integration. However, harnessing the vast resources and potential of each country and engaging in meaningful and productive regional trade that benefits the region remains a challenge.

The good news is that the biggest country in the region, India, is fast rising as an economic power and it is no secret that it is competing with its traditional rival China for regional as well as global prominence. It is imperative for India to continue growing not only to keep pace with China and improve the economic conditions of its peoples but also to remain relevant in the region, and more so the world. Ironically, while its stature depends on its rise, its ascendance will also depend, in no small part, on its ability to foster greater regional cooperation and economic integration with its South Asian neighbors. Not only India, but the region as a whole, will have to benefit and move forward collectively. Too huge a differential would imply instability and resentment in other regional countries, and this will impose a political burden on India sooner or later.

The Indian economy growing at a steady rate of 6–8 percent presents a vast opportunity for the region. South Asia's smaller states have a lot to gain from the Indian rise and will thus be eager to tap into this opportunity. To cite Bhutan as an example, the country is well on its track to reap the best out of its geographical advantage of bordering India on three sides. Trade with India accounts for 90 percent of Bhutan's external trade and there is huge potential for additional growth in its volume. Mutually beneficial partnership projects such as the hydropower projects are already slated for accelerated development. India needs power to fuel its growing economy and Bhutan's swift rivers have the potential to generate about 30,000 MW of power. The earlier Bhutan can tap into this potential, the better off it will be. The revenue from the export of power will help reduce its dependence on external aid and provide the needed resources for many development projects. Other regional states are also as likely to gain from an integrated South Asia; if they could align their economies as well, the region could become an economic hub with India providing the stimulus that is needed. Should this happen, the disparity in the region will be reduced and this will provide a better opportunity for peace and sustained economic development in the region.

Discussion on increased trade and its economic benefits is incomplete without highlighting the importance of equity, both across the region and within individual countries. South Asia's inequality of economic distribution remains one of the most alarming in the world; it is imperative that economic growth is sustainable ensuring that the benefits that the states draw from their resources are spread out and not at the cost of the livelihoods of future generations. The need, more than ever before, is to redefine South Asian development to be more inclusive and people oriented.

Incidentally, the 16th SAARC Summit held in Thimphu in April 2010 proposed that SAARC consider adopting Bhutan's gross national happiness (GNH) Index as a benchmark for development. The GNH development policy propounded by Bhutan presents an alternative development objective for nations to follow. GNH advocates tolerance and harmony among people and rests very strongly on peace and tranquility. Most importantly, it places people at the center of development. The relevance and need for a new development paradigm based on the Bhutanese development philosophy is already gaining international recognition. At the core of this is why and how mankind should and can work towards the collective well-being of all beings. This is relevant in the context of regional integration. If the leaders of the region sincerely recognize the collective good of and as a region, opportunities are plentiful.

The need to center development around people in an integrated South Asia presupposes trust and confidence among citizens of this region. The current ground reality is that many of the citizens especially in India and Pakistan tend to view their countries as foes rather than friends. Institutions in these countries perpetuate this sense of enmity. For example, the political history school curriculum in India and Pakistan reinforces this sense and students grow up learning to hold the other responsible for conflict between the two. Even the supposedly independent and unbiased media tends to play a role in deepening this hatred amongst the people. In such an environment, any political decision that is perceived as a "giving in" to the other has a severe political fallout and so the politicians are, for understandable reasons, wary of taking decisions seen as being favorable to the "other" country even if they are best for overall regional peace and security. Similar problems, though to a lesser degree, can be highlighted in other states of the region.

This underlines the importance of people-to-people interactions and trust building. Steps are being undertaken in this direction. Plans to build a SAARC highway to overcome transport hurdles are already there. Discussions on removing visa constraints for free movement for the SAARC citizens are also underway. These would lead to more contact and in turn ease the cost of doing business, increase regional tourism and generate better understanding and appreciation of each other's culture. The SAARC regional tourism initiative is also a good step towards enhancing interaction. Of course, by no means enough and yet positive, regional leaders have declared 2011 as the year of "SAARC Tourism." This needs to be backed by a consistent and sustained program complemented with political will and resources to make the program a success. To be noted, annual events like the SAARC Motor Rally are already seen to make a significant impact in creating greater awareness of the region. Personally, this writer recalls the 1999 initiative by Sushil Bakshi and the late Sunil Dutt, "Hands Across the Borders," which brought together 16 youth leaders from South Asia in an expedition through India, Sri Lanka, Bangladesh, Bhutan and Nepal to build an environment of peace and development via greater interregional interaction. About a thousand public meetings were held with ordinary citizens as the group journeyed through both urban and rural areas. The expedition presented the heads of the states with an agenda for friendship entitled "Together Towards Tomorrow." This initiative brought about better understanding between the peoples involved. More of such citizen initiatives should be encouraged and supported. The rapid expansion of information technology in the region is another positive development, and it provides an obvious avenue to fast-track much of what is suggested here, especially including people-to-people contacts.

Bringing the discussion full circle, as people's trust and confidence amongst the region grows, it will lead to increased regional interaction and tourism, bringing about significant economic gains for the region and the people. In turn, this will contribute towards helping alleviate poverty, and, one hopes, better distribution.

Conflict in the Region

The question arises why even after decades of its formation SAARC has not been able to make any significant progress in realizing its goals. This is largely because of the lingering – and, in some cases, growing – conflicts in the region. Conflict is the single most important obstacle keeping this region from making the headways that it should have given all of its potential. The India–Pakistan cross-border conflict is the most prominent, but it is by no means the only one. In fact, most countries in the region are beset with serious cross-border or internal conflicts. If the region is serious about making progress, it has to address this issue as no other effort will be able to unlock the path to a truly integrated and progressive South Asia.

The regional conflicts can be attributed to a certain extent to the colonial legacy where the British adopted the "divide and rule" policy in what today are Pakistan, Bangladesh and India. When the British left, they left behind a purposefully "divided" region. Ever since then, India and Pakistan have been at odds and have gone to war several times, forgetting in the process the commonality between them and rather further underscoring the differences. The other countries in the region have not been free from bilateral and internal conflicts either. Sri Lanka was confronted with one of the world's most dreaded militant outfits, the Liberation Tigers of Tamil Eelam (LTTE), for decades, which prevented its economic progress as a nation despite its vast resources as well as the advantage of having open access to the sea. Likewise, Nepal has had its own political problems for decades and even today continues to suffer from severe political instability. Bangladesh has had its share of internal problems as well as constant bilateral tensions with India.

Even Bhutan, the smallest country, was not free from the menaces of terrorism. It was not only confronted with some serious terrorist movements from within but also had to deal with Indian outfits that had illegally occupied the thick jungles along the Indo–Bhutan border, posing great risk to the nation's sovereignty as well as its relations with India. Of course, the newest member of SAARC – Afghanistan – is also the one most deeply beset with conflict, internal as well as international. A new dimension has been added to the South Asian conflict with the addition of Afghanistan to the mix. Until now, it has mostly been the Indo–Pakistani factor that defined the fate of the region as a whole; now Afghanistan has become a central battlefield against terrorism. Any significant regional stability will now have to include bringing stability to Afghanistan. Just as terrorism is a truly global problem, in the region of South Asia it is also truly a regional problem.

In terms of militancy, while much of the attention has been focused on the fight against the Taliban and militancy in Kashmir, other militant movements – including the Maoist movements – have long plagued the region and continue to bleed its stability. It is certainly an issue that needs affirmative regional actions now. While some would argue that the Maoist group in Nepal is more of a political movement/group rather than a militant group based on its recent participation in the political process and the results of the last election, there are others who feel that they are otherwise. There are also those who suggest that there are strong ties between the Maoist groups in Nepal and those in India and the ones that operate across the borders into Bhutan, which have caused significant instability there. Even if the Maoists are not successful, their presence and activities will divert energy and resources that could be better spent in improving the lives of the people, as for example was the case in Nepal when it was battling against the Maoist insurgencies.

On a positive note, even in the conflict sphere, developments over the last few years have shown that if the countries and leaders are committed, even the most difficult challenges can be overcome. This is true even for the smaller countries. To cite Bhutan's case, militant groups like the United Liberation Front of Assam (ULFA) and National Democratic Front of Bodoland (Bodo/NDFB) had been using Bhutanese territory to launch attacks against India. Despite years of negotiations to convince the militants to leave Bhutanese territory, it made no headway. The Bhutanese government then had to choose between leaving the militants alone or flush them out by force. Both carried risks, the former meant that anti-India activities would continue from Bhutanese soil as well as living with constant fear of future uncertainty, and the latter meant that the national security would be threatened as militants were far greater in number and better trained and equipped than the Bhutanese armed forces. In 2003, a decisive operation was led personally by the fourth king, His Majesty Jigme Singye Wangchuk, who not only successfully drove the militants out of Bhutan but also ensured that the entire operation caused only minimum collateral damage on both sides. The operation proves that if political will is present, the militancy problem in the region can be brought to an end. In much of South Asia unfortunately, states, rather than taking decisive actions, have often supported militants against their neighbors.

The Sri Lankan government's military operation that put an end to the decades-old LTTE-led insurgency is further evidence of the importance of true political will in eliminating terrorism. While the credit for the success of the operation goes primarily to the Sri Lankan government, the noninterference from New Delhi at the critical point of the operation despite pressure from some of the political parties itself had an important role in seeing the operation through to a successful conclusion.

If the regional conflicts have to end, each member state of SAARC must make a firm commitment of zero tolerance against militants of all kinds. The Bhutanese and Lankan examples have important lessons for the rest of the countries. While the context of different countries can be different, the principle that all countries should take concrete and sincere steps to eliminate conflict between and within South Asian states is central to ensuring peace and stability in the region.

Finally, courtesy of the situation in Afghanistan and the spillover into Pakistan, international geopolitics have changed in favor of the region, which provides another avenue of hope. The then British foreign secretary David Miliband, while addressing the Kennedy Library Forums during a visit to the US about six months before the 2010 elections in Afghanistan, said that the war in Afghanistan cannot be won if India–Pakistan relations do not improve. He suggested that the foreign influences see it as imperative that the Indo–Pakistani relationship improve so that Pakistan can focus better on fighting the Taliban. This is clear evidence then that key foreign influences that perhaps propagated continued conflicts between Pakistan and India are beginning to change in favor of peace. It would be a pity if the leaders of the region fail to capitalize on this window of opportunity and build a stronger, more vibrant and integrated region. Internally, the individual states must begin to divert their resources and energy from supporting antistate elements in the other states to building confidence and peace. If both India and Pakistan were to devote a fraction of resources that each spend on proxy war and border security to building better relations between each other and on developmental programs, the impact would be tremendous. SAARC members should learn from the European Union experience, where some of the most dreaded enemies during the World Wars have come together into a regional block, bringing about far-reaching benefits to the region and its citizens.

Conclusion

The prospects for the South Asian countries to emerge as a strong, robust and integrated regional block with improved economic conditions and better lives for its peoples are real. However, the challenges and the hurdles to realizing this potential are equally compelling. Whether the region will remain as one of the least integrated and impoverished ones or emerge as the next regional power block will depend on the policy decisions that the leaders of today take as well as on how its citizens can harness the opportunities before them.

The key factor will be the willingness of leaders to put regional interests ahead of short-term political gains and to take affirmative action to end decades of conflict in favor of supporting each other in fighting terrorism, the principal regional threat. The political leaders must also create a conducive environment for its citizens and businesses to integrate. This will help enhance interaction and trade, in turn helping to build trust and confidence as well as generate economic opportunities for the people of the region.

The citizens must play their part in tapping the regional potential as well as demanding from their leadership, and supporting the political leaders that work towards better regional cooperation and peace building. If leaders and citizens work together, and if SAARC is used as a vehicle and platform for meaningful regional integration, there is no reason why South Asia cannot emerge as the next regional power block.

Chapter 14

THE FUTURE OF INTEGRATION

Nihal Rodrigo

Looking ahead towards the South Asia of 2060 would necessitate a close analysis of the historical, religious and ethnic factors that bind the region across contemporary borders; the depth, reach and pace of regional economic integration; the asymmetries in South Asia's human and social development; its security architecture and the impact on South Asia of the extraregional relations it seeks, as well as that of unsolicited interventions.

A report by the United States National Intelligence Council, entitled *Global Trends 2025: A Transformed World*, released in November 2008, envisaged the contemporary world moving into a period of historic changes, including what it described as a transfer of "global wealth and economic power [...] roughly from West to East" (National Intelligence Council 2008). It anticipated the rise of China and India as powers that could transform the geopolitical scenario. *Newsweek* magazine moved the assessment's currency well beyond the field of strategic studies, into the wider public domain, reporting what it called "the Post-American world" and the onset of "the Asian Century" (Foroohar 2009). I would prefer to describe it all, with apologies to the music composer Dvorak, as "the New World Symphony." India, the largest South Asian state, and China, a keen observer in the South Asian Association for Regional Cooperation (SAARC) could function as joint composers or conductors of the symphony, with every nation, including the United States – whose performance should not be downgraded – playing in harmony. The "Shared Vision for the 21st Century," a joint statement signed by Indian prime minister Manmohan Singh and Chinese premier Wen Jiabao on January 14, 2008, voiced a common theme, extolling "a harmonious world of durable peace and common prosperity" and trumpeting "the right of each country to choose its own path of social, economic and political development" without "drawing lines on the grounds of ideologies and values, or of geographic criteria" (Embassy of the People's Republic of China in India 2008). In practical terms, a press release issued on 8 August 2009 following the 13th meeting between special representatives of India and China on the boundary question stated that "for the questions left over from history," the two countries should seek "a fair and reasonable mutually acceptable solution" and that "China and India have no other option than living in peace and developing side by side" (Chinese and Indian Special Representatives 2009).

Assessing the Future of SAARC

Against this pragmatic background at the regional level, a number of evolving factors need to be taken into account when assessing the future of economic development and integration in South Asia. South Asian states will continue to assert a collective identity in SAARC which brings together Afghanistan, Bangladesh, Bhutan, India, Maldives, Nepal, Pakistan and Sri Lanka. There is much sarcasm about SAARC's pace of economic progress, yet the regional organization, established in 1985, plays an essential role in providing a multifaceted institutional forum and framework for advancing, at its own pace, deeper economic integration in South Asia. In addition, it provides opportunities for continuous dialogue among its eight member states on political, social, strategic and security issues – including behind-closed-doors dialogue when needed – during times when bilateral complications may pose impediments to closer regional cooperation.

Two safety clauses introduced into the SAARC Charter at the outset are that decisions need to be taken on the basis of unanimity and that bilateral and contentious issues shall be excluded from the deliberations of the association; these clauses reflected early apprehensions about what was seen as the "towering" presence of India dominating other members (SAARC Charter 1985). Equally, at SAARC's inception there were also some Indian qualms that the other South Asian states might gang up against it. India's current economic advances and its projected global role, including its equation with China and the United States, have given it greater self-confidence. All this is now expected to provide a more productive and conducive environment within the South Asian neighborhood for closer integration, though unruly aspects will remain.

An officially mandated group of eminent South Asian diplomats, economists and scholars presented a report in 1998 proposing a road map to drive the region forward from being a free trade agreement (FTA) area, to a customs union by 2015, towards the ultimate destination of an economic union and integration by 2020. The FTA has been in place since 2006 but progress towards the economic union has been slow, due to asymmetries among South Asian states. Indeed, the Asian Development Bank (ADB) describes South Asia as the least integrated region in the world with its intraregional trade at 5.5 percent of total global trade in 2008, in contrast to Southeast Asia's intraregional trade at over 25 percent of its global trade. Among the causes identified by the ADB for the situation in South Asia are poor land; sea and air connectivity; complicated procedures at border crossings, which stifle business; limited state–public partnerships; high protection and long exclusion lists in the FTA. Disparities of scale and in systems of economic management constitute another handicap. These aspects, however, are being gradually addressed.

Advancing the "Gujral Doctrine" relating to asymmetric responsibility incumbent on the stronger South Asian states towards their weaker neighbors, Indian external affairs minister S. M. Krishna has reiterated that India is "committed to fulfilling its responsibilities in an asymmetric and nonreciprocal manner" (Krishna 2009). India has reduced the number of items on its own negative list and provided zero-duty access for select exports from the least developed countries in the region. India's intraregional trade in 2008 totaled $109 million. It has risen considerably since.

A South Asian agreement relating to the services sector was completed at the 16th SAARC Summit held in April 2010 in Thimpu, Bhutan, covering transport, travel and tourism, insurance, investment and financial services, migration and medical services. Progress in these areas will help bridge and balance regional asymmetries. Already in the travel and tourism sector, for example, Indian–Sri Lankan asymmetries have been mitigated, if not fully balanced. Sri Lankan airlines have more entry points into Indian airports than any other airline in the world and the largest number of tourists visiting Sri Lanka is from India. India's economic strength is being gradually seen as an opportunity rather than as an obstacle in the region. At the United Nations in New York, Dr Sheel Kant Sharma, SAARC secretary general, on September 26, 2009 was optimistic that the proposed agreement on trade in services could "unlock strong regional synergies and lead to greater intra–South Asian flow of capital, people, goods and services and open up new vistas of economic cooperation." Additionally, South Asian cinema, music, media and sports – particularly cricket – could also help cultural synergies spread.

Overcoming Hurdles to Regional Cooperation

Colonial legacies and lingering border disputes on the other hand have constricted trade flows within South Asia. Much Indo–Pakistani trade has, for example, been transited through third countries, including some outside the region, bloating costs and prolonging delays. The importance of an efficient regional multimodal transport system has been realized. India and Pakistan are currently in an in-principle agreement on the movement of "all permissible trade items" through the Wagha–Attari road link as well as the Khokrapar–Munabao railroad across the Line of Control (LoC) on the Srinagar–Muzzaffarabad and Poonch–Rawalakot routes. Pakistani president Asif Zardari at the United Nations General Assembly in 2009 said that India and Pakistan must "accommodate each other's concerns and interests [...] [we should] peacefully resolve our problems and build South Asia into a common market of trade and technology" (Zardari 2009). Indian prime minister Manmohan Singh commented that "economics, technology and travel are altering older mind sets of suspicion, fear and hostility" (Singh 2008). The potential benefits of efficient trade movement would also serve to muffle, to an extent, bilateral confrontations, or at least to move them behind closed doors for negotiations.

Beyond the state, also of considerable institutional significance in the future development of the region's integration, is the role played by the corporate sectors, chambers of commerce and industry, research organizations and think tanks. There are also a number of professional groupings with region-wide membership designated as Apex organizations or SAARC-recognized bodies, which effectively support specialized integration processes; they include associations of accountants, architects, engineers, surgeons, management development institutes, members of the legal profession, writers, artists and even election commissioners. These networks provide valuable professional and technical inputs to the government sectors concerned, helping them more efficiently integrate activities relating to their specialized areas of competence. They have all continued their activities even when the movement of interstate official processes has been grounded due to bilateral or political turbulence.

The 2nd South Asian Economic Summit held in New Delhi on 11–12 December 2009 – following on its inaugural session held the previous year in Colombo – was an initiative largely developed by the Research and Information Service for Developing Countries in India and the Institute of Policy Studies in Sri Lanka, undertaken in collaboration with the ADB, the United Nations Development Programme (UNDP) and South Asian governments. The collaborative initiative has helped maintain continuity and consistency in the integration process. Xiaoyu Zhao, vice president of the ADB, stated that the ADB would help the process through "technical and financial support by facilitating dialogue and cross learning" and promoting the policy, regulatory and institutional reforms that are required to develop public–private partnerships (Zao 2009). A cooperative functional nexus is thus developing between the state sectors, the corporate sectors and research organizations in South Asia, which is being assisted by the UNDP and the ADB; this will be a positive factor in the future.

In the South Asian integration process, apart from economic asymmetries between states, the asymmetries within the states need also to be bridged. It is the poorest of the poor, the most desperate, who have the least connectivity with the regional processes that are gradually integrating and developing in South Asia. Statistics denoting high national and regional growth rates could sometimes induce official complacency and lead to the neglect of those who lack, and indeed need, growth the most. Connectivity between economic growth and inclusive human development in parts of the region is lacking. The theme of the 2008 SAARC Summit in Colombo, "Partnership for the Growth of Our People," was welcomed by the Pakistani prime minister "as a reminder of our joint responsibility to place people at the centre of the SAARC process. No country can realize its full potential without improving the socio-economic conditions of the people" (Gilani 2008). Poverty alleviation, for example, has proceeded well in Sri Lanka, where textile factories have been long located in relatively less-developed rural areas to integrate them into the overall development process bringing greater relief to the rural population.

Speaking at the Inauguration of the 92nd Conference of the Indian Economic Association in December 2009, the Indian prime minister conceded that to achieve the objectives of inclusive growth, it was necessary "to pay much greater attention to education, healthcare and rural development, focusing on the needs of the poor – the scheduled castes, scheduled tribes and religious minorities" (Singh 2009).

South Asian democracy has a plethora of political parties and the Indian prime minister recently declared that "competitive politics must not be allowed to divide our people on the basis of religion, caste or region." Events in Telangana, Gorkhaland, Bodoland and such areas in India indicate the nature of the difficulties that can also arise in other countries. Feelings of exclusion, uneven development and secessionist tendencies have been descending into violence and terrorism, whether motivated by political, ethnic, economic, social or religious lines, and have had serious domestic, regional and indeed international implications. Nuclear weapons capabilities and festering bilateral disputes could aggravate the situation. Foreign troops, deployed primarily to protect their own homeland security, have come to be deployed in Afghanistan. An article by Pakistani president Asif Ali Zardari in the *New York Times* in 2009 concluded that "it is an economically viable and socially robust democratic Pakistan that will be the most effective long-term weapon against terrorism, extremism and fanaticism" (Zardari 2009a).

US president Barack Obama, in his speech while accepting the Nobel Peace Prize in Oslo in December 2009, referred to Pakistan and Afghanistan, arguing that American operations were morally just and strategically necessary to defend the United States and others from future terrorist attacks. He invoked the exemplary peaceful approaches of Mahatma Gandhi and Martin Luther King but added, "make no mistake. Evil does exist in the world. A nonviolent movement could not have halted Hitler's armies."

By then, Sri Lanka, under President Mahinda Rajapaksa, had halted and defeated the terrorist armies of the Liberation Tigers of Tamil Eelam (LTTE), which the US Federal Bureau of Investigation described as the deadliest terrorist group in the world. Beyond the military defeat of the LTTE – which ruthlessly forced innocent civilians, including women and children, to serve as human shields – the victory also significantly represents a triumph against monoethnic terrorism. Free of the LTTE, members of the Tamil community can now freely engage, peacefully and without violence or duress, in addressing their grievances and negotiating their political role. It has ended one of South Asia's longest fought battles against racism and terrorism – one which has had linkages with and an impact on other South Asian countries and beyond.

Addressing South Asian foreign ministers in Colombo in February 2009, shortly before the defeat of the LTTE, Sri Lankan president Rajapaksa called for concerted efforts to defeat terrorism in South Asia through regional cooperation, as well as internationally through the United Nations Committee chaired by Sri Lankan diplomat Rohan Perera, which was working on a Comprehensive Convention on International Terrorism. Firmer implementation is required at the regional level on the South Asian Conventions and Protocols on the Suppression of Terrorism, respectively adopted in 1987 and 2004. Given the wider ramifications of terrorism within South Asia, and its linkages with and sponsorship of drug and human trafficking, regional agreements have also been signed on Narcotics and Drugs (1990), on the Trafficking of Women and Children (2002), and on Mutual Assistance in Criminal Matters (2008). Terrorism and its poison seeping across borders has been a major obstacle to the establishment of the stable security architecture that is so essential for closer economic integration in South Asia. To this end, in February 2009, South Asian foreign ministers signed a Ministerial Declaration on Cooperation in Combating Terrorism in Colombo.

The Wider Picture: Geostrategic Compulsions

Apart from ongoing developments in Afghanistan and Pakistan, South Asia is also seen as a vital geostrategically important region because of the Indian Ocean area, where maritime security has become a major international concern. Sri Lanka is located virtually at the center of this strategic area and Shyam Saran, special envoy of Indian prime minister Manmohan Singh, in an address at Port Blair on 5 September 2009, noted that around 70 percent of shipping to and from Indian ports is handled through the port of Colombo; a considerable amount of break bulk is also handled in Colombo before dispersal to other destinations. Colombo has been a major hub for intra–South Asian trade transfers. Sri Lanka is also a convenient link point between Europe, the Middle East and West Africa on the one hand, and Southeast and East Asia on the other hand – a position for which it has been known even before Christopher Columbus arrived in the Americas. The port of Hambantota, in the Southern Province of the island, is located a few nautical miles north of the busiest sea lanes in the Indian Ocean. Hambantota is currently being developed, with Chinese assistance, to facilitate East–West shipping and commerce – which would also benefit South Asia.

The United States Senate Committee on Foreign Relations in its report "Sri Lanka: Recharting US Strategy after the War" dated 7 December 2009 describes Sri Lanka as being "at the nexus of crucial maritime trading routes in the Indian Ocean connecting Europe and the Middle East to China and the rest of Asia" and that "the US, India and China all share an interest in deterring terrorist activity and curbing piracy that could disrupt maritime trade" (US Senate 2009). Sri Lanka and indeed South Asia, wedged between the East and West, get to be involved deeply in the security architecture of a broader pan-Asian, even global, paradigm.

International interest in cooperating with South Asia, as a region, beyond the purely bilateral equations with individual South Asian states, is growing. When the 15th SAARC Summit took place in Colombo in August 2009, countries and regional groups formally being associated as observers included Australia, China, Iran, Japan, the Republic of Korea, Mauritius, Myanmar, the United States and the European Union. Guidelines for cooperation with these observers were approved at the Colombo summit. An important aspect agreed on by South Asian countries is that observers can now contribute to the SAARC Development Fund to finance mutually acceptable projects. This is a major step for SAARC, which earlier had major reservations on the question of outside financial involvement in regional projects. China, the second largest economy in the world, held two conferences with South Asian countries, in Beijing (2008) and Chengdu (2009), which I attended, to seek clarity on the nature and extent of permissible Chinese involvement in regional projects. Klaus Swab, at the World Economic Forum held in Dalian, China, has projected that it would be China leading the world out of the global economic and financial crisis. Despite some bilateral border and other issues that continue to exist among the two economic giants India and China could be expected to work closer together in the future, which augurs well for the South Asian region as well.

Chapter 15

THE GIANT NEIGHBOR: WHY IS CHINA IMPORTANT?

Manu Bhaskaran

Introduction

In a nutshell, by 2060, we should see South Asia and China loom large in each other's eyes, with a thicket of relations tying each to the other despite inevitable stresses. Three projections are in place: first, China will be a South Asian political, military and economic power whether India and the rest of the region like it or not; second, the simultaneous rise of India will inevitably lead to tensions between China and India; and, third, there will be elements of complementariness and competitiveness in the economic relations between South Asia and China – but we suspect it will be more complementary than competitive.

What Will the World, China and South Asia Look Like in 2060?

Forecasting 50 years ahead is hazardous of course but there are some factors such as demographics, strategic national interests and cultural attitudes that either change very slowly or whose main trends are clear even over long periods of time. So, we can use such factors to map out a likely scenario. Rather than work out multiple scenarios, we will focus on what we believe to be the most likely one:

i. The global economy will be much bigger by 2060, with some key features standing out.

- The United States, major European nations and Japan will have a smaller weight in the global gross domestic product (GDP) but will almost certainly still dominate the top 15 economies of the world. In per capita terms, they will probably still remain much richer than high-growth economies such as China and India. Although their educational institutions, research laboratories, cultural icons and corporate brands will have to compete against those that will emerge from what is now the developing world, our view is that these Western institutions will still be leaders in many fields. We also believe that the next one to two decades will see huge economic restructuring in the United States, Europe and Japan – which will make these economies much more competitive and dynamic. The rise of China and India will not see the decline of these developed economies, except in a relative sense.

- The rise of the "laggards": a number of forces will help currently lagging economies to accelerate their growth processes. Aging trends in the West and many parts of East Asia as well as in India would by 2060 have opened the way for manufacturing and many services to be supplied by currently underperforming economies, particularly those with favorable demographics such as the Philippines. The simultaneous rise of China, India, Brazil, Turkey, Vietnam and others would have spurred the underperformers on while also expanding the demand for natural resources and low-priced consumer goods that these economies can excel in.

- The trajectory of the global economy from today to 2060 is likely to be marked by formidable challenges – among many others are accommodating climate change; shifting away from fossil fuels as the dominant source of energy; managing water shortages, which are likely to be serious in many developing countries; finding ways to adapt to higher prices and/or increased scarcity of many natural resources. It is likely that not all these challenges can be resolved by 2060. So the global economy in 2060 will most probably remain a challenging one.

ii. China in 2060 will probably be the largest economy in the world.

- While its per capita income will likely have risen to developed economy status, it will probably still lag the per capita income levels of the United States, Japan and the more advanced European countries.

- By 2060, its population will probably have been outstripped by India's but China will still be the second largest population in the world.

- China's vast size and prosperity will make it the world's largest consumer market, probably the world's largest market for tourists, the biggest source of foreign direct investment, among the world's largest sources of portfolio investment (investment in bonds, equities and other financial assets as well as real estate) and the world's largest consumer of energy and raw materials.

- Its companies will have a substantial presence in the global market, with homegrown Chinese brands gaining global stature not just in consumer goods but also in financial services and other service areas.

- And Chinese investment in R&D will have paid off, making China probably the second largest source of new technology after the United States.

- China's substantial investment in defense capability will continue in coming decades. By 2060, the cumulative impact of this defense spending will be to make it the second most powerful military force in the world, with a fully-fledged blue-water navy and state-of-the-art military technology for air, naval, land and space warfare. Its capacity to project force far beyond its immediate vicinity would be second only to that of the United States. China will also have emerged as a nation with considerable soft power by 2060 as its economic success allows its popular culture to blossom and reach out to the rest of the world, as its already good educational institutions become world leaders and attract talented students from all over the world and as it becomes more of a creator of technology than just an imitator.

iii. By 2060 South Asia will also have changed substantially.

- We see India growing by more than 8 percent a year for the next 30 years and then slowing moderately but still expanding at a dynamic pace. This will make India the second largest economy in the world by around 2040 and by 2060 it will have narrowed the gap with China in total GDP but will still lag behind materially in terms of per capita incomes. Still, like China, India will have become a massive consumer market, huge source of tourists, portfolio capital and direct investment. Its companies will make their presence felt globally, with Indian brands competing with American, European, Japanese, Chinese and other brands. India will also be a large source of innovation but its late start and relatively smaller government support will probably mean that Indian innovation will be driven much more by its private sector and be focused on a few niches. Because India is starting later to build its military capacity and is more fiscally constrained than China, India's capacity to project military force will probably be substantially less than that of China.

- We are reasonably confident that Bangladesh, Sri Lanka, Bhutan and the Maldives will have sustained rapid economic growth and emerged as more prosperous and dynamic economies with a materially greater presence in the global economic landscape than their current stature.

- We are less confident of the same degree of success occurring as quickly in Afghanistan, Pakistan and Nepal. We do not believe that Pakistan will be a failed state as some forecast but resolving the current political stresses to the point where Pakistan's economy can expand as rapidly as it did in the 1960s (when it was one of the fastest growing economies in the world) will be a challenge. Eventually we are sure that Pakistan will resolve these challenges and resume high growth but it would have lost considerable time compared to its other neighbors. Similarly, we see political schisms and potential violence continuing to plague Afghanistan and Nepal – for the simple reason that there are no easy solutions to their crises.

- Despite the often tense bilateral relationships in South Asia, we see economic integration in the region – which has lagged in most other regions – intensify over the next few decades. The demonstration effect of successful integration in Europe and Southeast Asia will probably persuade South Asians to put aside their differences to some extent and work harder at economic integration. The critical challenge to enhanced integration will be political – as the economic arguments become more compelling, we believe the political resistance can be gradually reduced.

- In population terms, South Asia will have become the most populous region on Earth. Not only will India have the largest population but Pakistan and

Bangladesh are likely to see more than a doubling of their populations, making them the next populous countries in the world after China and India.

As above projections point out, both South Asia and China are likely to keep opening their economies to the international economy and each other. Trade is already being liberalized but we are likely to see capital flows burgeon – especially as capital accounts in China and India open up. Tourist flows from these two regions to each other and other countries will probably grow rapidly.

How Will China and South Asia Impact Each Other?

i.   China will emerge as a South Asian power in addition to being an East Asian power. There are several reasons for this:
  • China's massive hunger for energy and raw materials and its huge dependence on international trade will make the Indian Ocean a legitimate sphere of interest for China. Many littoral states such as those in East Africa as well as Australia and Indonesia will become key suppliers to China. Critical sea lanes of communication will pass through the Indian Ocean.
  • Moreover, South Asia's likely economic and demographic trajectory will have made the countries in the region too large as a market to avoid. It is likely that China's exports to these countries will have grown exponentially, giving it a strong interest in the region.
  • Within South Asia as well, India's neighbors could well see it in their interest to ally with China in order to contain potential risks emanating from India whose massive size and likely military capabilities will make it a far more formidable adversary than now. Since Pakistan will have been slower to grow its economy and resolve its problems as argued above, it will need China as an ally to deter India.
  • Given its population size by 2060, the likely size of its economy and the probable technological capacity it would have developed by then, India will probably be the only nation besides the United States to have the potential to match or outmatch China in military power. That in itself would require China having at least some form of precautionary strategy to contain India – part of that strategy must necessarily involve alliances of some kind with India's neighbors.

In other words, by 2060, China will have a sizeable economic, diplomatic and cultural presence in South Asia. It will also have military relationships of various kinds with India's South Asian neighbors. And this will give it tremendous scope to influence domestic developments in South Asia outside India.

This relationship with South Asia (ex-India) will have an important effect on China's global power: having a strong political and military position in the world's most populous region will help China as it strives to achieve a global position in relation to the United States.

ii. We believe that China's relationship with India over the next few decades and in 2060 will be a difficult one. Many argue that since China and India lived peaceably with each other through the millennia and until the 1962 war, that conflict was an aberration and that a good relationship is the natural order of things. This is simply not the case.

- In history, the periods when Chinese empires and Indian empires actually bordered on each other in accessible locations where large armies could amass and where strategic and economic interests might have clashed were rare. While China for long periods of time had suzerainty over Tibet and Yunnan regions bordering on what is now India, the technology of transportation did not allow these to be easily accessible. These regions were distant and peripheral to the Chinese empires of those days – which meant that there was little reason for China and the then states and empires of India to rub against each other in a hostile manner.

- It is an entirely different situation now. Memories of the 1962 war remain in the psyches of the Indian intelligentsia. Tibet is strategic in controlling the headwaters of virtually all the major rivers that flow into India. China has built railways into Tibet and Han Chinese migration has swelled – Tibet is no longer a peripheral region. India's giving refuge to the Dalai Lama causes considerable dismay to China.

- Tibet also has a long border with Kashmir – which Pakistan asserts a claim over in opposition to India's. China's military and diplomatic alliance with Pakistan, India's major strategic opponent, is not likely to change (as argued above) and will continue to hurt Sino–Indian relations.

- China and India have also yet to settle the dispute over Arunachal Pradesh, which India occupies and asserts is its sovereign territory but which China claims as South Tibet. Recently, China has adopted a more proactive stand on Arunachal Pradesh, causing stress in relations with India, which had been improving until a few years ago.

- India has also reacted with discomfort to China's emergence as a South Asian power. Some of its strategic thinkers liken China's efforts to help India's neighbors build ports to a string of pearls strategy designed to eventually strangle India.

- China has also reacted with suspicion to a newly resurgent India's expanding strategic relationships. In particular, it has viewed India's substantially improved ties with the United States with deep suspicion.

- As China and India grow, their hunger for energy and raw materials is also likely to lead them to compete more intensively against each other to gain control over these resources. This has begun to some extent with Chinese and Indian companies scouring the world for raw materials and sometimes bidding against each other.

- One major area of contention will be water. Both China and India have looming water shortages. China's construction of dams in the upper reaches of rivers such as the Brahmaputra could be a cause for disagreements.

- More importantly, the Chinese and Indian political and intellectual elites appear to have too little an understanding or sense of empathy with each other. Philosophically and culturally the worldviews of these two civilizations are very different.

This is not to say that we are predicting an extreme scenario of military conflict or prolonged tensions, which make for gridlock in their diplomatic exchanges. Both countries' political elites do not want military conflict – unlike in 1962, today both sides have nuclear weapons, which makes the downside risks of war much more unpalatable. Unlike in 1962 both sides are making economic development the highest priority and do not want military distractions. Neither does India or China want to be used by external powers as a tool to contain the other. The burgeoning trade relationship between the two economies also gives the elites in both countries an added incentive to avoid war and to work hard to develop a healthy relationship.

Nevertheless, the strategic interests of each country and the legacy of the border disputes will probably lead to a relationship marked by increasing stresses interspersed by efforts to contain these tensions from spilling over into outright hostilities.

iii. The economic relationship between China and South Asia will be marked by elements of competition as well as complementariness – but we think the latter will dominate. Complementary economic ties will tend to grow as a result of:

- Differential paths of economic development: China is ahead of the game in moving up the value chain for two reasons. First, in the course of this decade, China will reach its "Lewisian" turning point – the point at which surplus labor from the rural sector moving to urban areas is no longer available at a low wage to the modern sector, forcing real wages to rise sharply. There is some evidence of this already happening in some parts of China such as Guangdong Province. Given China's aging population, the size of the cohort of youths joining the workforce will start to diminish as this decade progresses. Second, its supercompetitive position as a global exporter of manufactured goods is forcing it to allow an appreciation of its currency, the Renminbi (RMB). With both wages and the currency rising, China will have to move up the value chain, away from industries such as garments, toys, footwear and other labor-intensive activities, activities that remain areas of competitive advantage for India, Bangladesh and Sri Lanka for example. Given that China will probably maintain an edge over South Asia because of its head start in economic reforms, this pattern of China vacating certain activities as it moves up the value chain will continue benefiting South Asian economies.

- Moreover, we are also likely to see the manufacturing sectors in India and Bangladesh first (and Pakistan later) become more globally competitive as reforms continue and constraints such as infrastructure and unsupportive policy regimes are improved. Also, as South Asian integration improves economies of scale over time in South Asia, there will be more activities in the region that become globally competitive. We believe that Chinese companies will increasingly build supply chains that include South Asian economies as well.

- In global economic negotiations, China and South Asia currently have many common positions in areas as diverse as combating protectionism, creating a new global trade agreement and setting up a new international regime to manage climate change.

But there are bound to be competitive elements as well in the South Asia–China relationship:

- As discussed above, there is likely to be some degree of competition for water, energy and natural resources.
- There will be very large corporate sectors in China and India and within those there are bound to be some very large corporations that will compete against each other – such as for market share of key products or in making key acquisitions in different parts of the world.

Conclusion

China and South Asia will become much more tied together economically and politically as we move towards 2060. China's considerable interests in South Asia will make it a South Asian power as much as it is an East Asian one. The relationship between China and India will be key not just for the South Asian region but for the world as a whole – but here, we feel that the relationship will not be an easy one. Despite this negative factor, overall we see the China–South Asia economic relationship likely to be more complementary than competitive.

Section III

DEVELOPMENT

Chapter 16

SOUTH ASIAN ECONOMY IN 2060

Ishrat Husain

South Asian economies have grown rapidly during the last two decades recording an average growth rate of 6 percent annually. Incidence of poverty has been reduced although the absolute number of poor has increased in the last two years because of the external shocks and internal turbulence in some countries. The private sector has been the principal driver of the economic turnaround as increased competition resulted in improved efficiency with productivity growth accounting for half of overall growth. Structural reforms in trade, taxation, investment and foreign exchange regimes over more than a decade have contributed to this growth in productivity. Integration in the global economy through trade, investment, technology transfer and movement of labor picked up speed since 1991 and has begun to pay dividends. The scope for further gains remains vast as both trade/gross domestic product (GDP) and foreign direct investment (FDI)/ GDP ratios are low. Despite these favorable outcomes and a resilience to face external shocks, the region has the highest number of poor in the world, human development indicators place it in the lowest category, income and regional inequalities are on the rise and social cohesion is still an elusive goal. This paper argues that the growth and poverty reduction record could have been better if the potential of regional economic cooperation had been exploited, bilateral relations among neighboring countries were warmer and hostilities and trust deficits between countries were absent. An expanded market with economies of scale in production, better connectivity through infrastructure, trade facilitation and communications and an ease of movement for people and ideas offered enormous opportunities that were missed over a long period of six decades.

Intraregional Trade: Failure and Future Prospects

South Asia historically had high intraregional trade. In 1948 as much as one-fifth of the trade took place within the region but at 6 percent today it is the least integrated region in the world. In contrast, East Asia and the Pacific's intraregional trade has risen to 52 percent. Even Sub-Saharan Africa carries out twice as much intraregional trade as South Asia. Cross-border investment is negligible and while there is an overall liberal environment for foreign investment flows, there are a host of formal and informal restrictions on flows originating from within the region. Common historical and cultural heritage would – in other parts of the world – have eased the movement of the people, educational exchanges, access to each other's media and cultural resources, the sharing of scientific and technological knowledge and other forms of cooperation but none of this has happened. For example, Indian and Pakistani Punjab, Assam, and Sylhet, and Northern Sri Lanka and Tamil Nadu despite being geographically contiguous have not derived any benefits from their proximity to each other and drifted apart during the six decades following independence.

Trade facilitation with other regions and hubs such as Dubai has been a consistent policy goal of each of the South Asian countries individually, yet when it comes to trade across borders within the region, all kind of hurdles have been imposed. Issues of phytosanitary, health and environmental standards, quality testing and adherence to specifications are raised, causing considerable delays, lengthened travel times and higher transaction costs. Truck crossings, where allowed, take several days and allegations of harassment by the border officials are rampant. Nontariff barriers on India–Pakistan trade have therefore diverted normal trade flows to informal networks or border trade or are routed through third parties such as Dubai and Singapore, which raise costs for end-users. There is another compelling reason for promoting regional economic cooperation. All the countries in South Asia are characterized by leading and lagging regions. Growth poles extending to contiguous areas across national borders will expand markets of goods and services, facilitate larger capital flows, improve infrastructure and generate additional opportunities for earnings in the lagging regions. This strategy would force the respective national governments to invest in regional public goods and expansion of productive capacities in intraindustry goods and services.

Demography: Positive and Negative

Looking to the future, particularly the long term, South Asia's challenges are many but at least four of them will make a material difference to the social and economic outcomes in the next 50 years. The first challenge is the demographic – South Asia will be the only region of a sizeable population with more than 50 percent of its population in the productive employable age bracket. The flip side is that this region can ease its unemployment problem by supplying young workers to the rest of the world in an environment of aging populations and the rise in dependence ratios. Whether this challenge can be transformed into a dividend will depend upon the priorities, policies and programs that the governments of these countries are able to conceptualize and implement.

South Asia can be well positioned to reap the benefits of favorable demographics. To the extent that these countries invest in education, particularly technical and vocational education, expand access to higher and professional education and upgrade the quality and relevance of instruction, there is a strong likelihood of this demographic transition paying dividend. This dividend may elude us however, if South Asia fails to meet the goal of educating a growing younger population, equipping them with marketable skills and facilitating their mobility across the borders. The challenge is quite daunting as two thirds of the world's illiterate population resides in South Asia and the addition of new entrants to the labor force every year equals the entire population of a midsize country. A study by Goldman Sachs shows that with the continued movement of labor from rural agriculture to urban industry and services, India will earn an "urbanization bonus" (Goldman Sachs 2007a). Based on current trends, a massive 700 million people – roughly equivalent to the entire current population of Europe – will move to cities by 2050. This will have significant implications on demand for urban infrastructure, real estate and services. The movement of surplus labor from low productivity to high productivity and services contributes about one percentage point to annual GDP growth. Productivity in industry and services is more than four times that in agriculture, which employs nearly 60 percent of the labor force. A turnaround in manufacturing productivity has been central to the ratcheting up of productivity growth.

The dependency ratio is forecast to decline to below 50 by 2020. Savings rates tend to increase with falling dependency ratios, rising incomes and greater financial sector development. Empirical estimates for India indicate that savings tend to increase about 0.8 percent for every 1 percent fall in dependency. Assuming that the response is lower in other South Asian countries, the falling dependency ratio should be able to raise the savings rate by at least 6 to 7 percent by 2020. To the extent that investment rates rise *pari passu* the structural shift in growth paths could produce a rise of around 2 percent.

Climate Change: Tough Choices

The second challenge is coping with climate change and its consequences for agriculture, food production and energy supplies. Over 500 million people in South Asia have no access to electricity while growth is typically associated with carbon emissions. How South Asia can balance its energy needs and growth while addressing global warming is a serious dilemma for policymakers. A recent World Bank study on the impact of climate change on South Asian countries provides an authoritative account of what we can expect in the coming decades.

The study postulates that the imperatives of climate change and policies adapted to contain carbon emissions may slow progress toward many development goals, such as eradicating poverty, combating communicable diseases and ensuring environmental sustainability. Geography coupled with high levels of poverty and population density has rendered South Asia especially vulnerable to the impacts of climate change. High population levels translate into increased resource demands on an already stressed and largely degraded natural resource base. With an estimated 600 million people subsisting on less than $1.25 per person a day, even small climate variations can cause irreversible losses and tip a large number of people into destitution.

The region spans a variety of climate zones, including arid deserts, parched rangelands, freezing alpine mountains and humid tropical islands. The projected impact of climate change will be heterogeneous, suggesting that there can be no one-size-fits-all approach to building climate resilience across South Asia. Responses will need to be customized to specific risks and circumstances. Indeed, over 50 percent of South Asians – more than 750 million people – have been affected by at least one natural disaster in the past two decades. The human and economic toll has been high, with almost 230,000 deaths and about $45 billion in damages. The region shares common geological formations and river basins, leading natural hazards to frequently transcend national boundaries. With climate change the frequency and incidence of such natural disasters is projected to increase.

The monsoon is the most significant climate event in the region's economic calendar. It carries over 70 percent of South Asia's annual precipitation in a brief four-month period. A buoyant monsoon heralds bountiful harvests and financial security, yet when monsoons fail – or are excessive – suffering and economic loss are widespread. If climate projections are indicative of future trends, the risks associated with water-related climate variability are likely to worsen. The Himalayas are a vital life-sustaining resource for South Asia, supporting the approximately 1.5 billion people who live directly in the floodplains of its many rivers – the Indus, Ganges, Brahmaputra and Meghna. With rising temperatures, the ice mass of the Himalayas and Hindu Kush is retreating more rapidly than the global average, posing an unprecedented threat to water supplies, lives and economies in the region. With melting glaciers, flood risks would increase in the near future. The floods in Pakistan in August 2010 that caused a major devastation to human lives and property are a preview of the damage that extreme climatic events can bring about. In the long term, in absence of replacement for the water provided by glaciers, water shortages could result at an unparalleled scale. Reduction of yields for major crops by as much as 20 percent and an even sharper decline in agricultural incomes are part of the worst-case climate scenarios for the region as well as a growing scarcity of water. Avoiding this future will necessitate balancing more variable water supplies with the accelerating demand for water and would require significant adjustment to the region's agriculture.

South Asia also has long and densely populated coastlines with many low-lying islands. In the severe climate-change scenarios, sea-level changes could pose an existential threat, potentially submerging much of the Maldives and inundating 18 percent of Bangladesh's total land – directly impacting 11 percent of the country's population. Saltwater intrusion from sea-level rises in low-lying agricultural plains could lead to food insecurity, further increase the prevalence of water-related diseases and reduce freshwater supplies. Many of the region's primary cities, such as Chennai, Cochin, Karachi, Kolkata and Mumbai – the engines of regional growth – are located on the coast and threatened by rises in sea levels. The immediate impact of sea-level rises would be felt in coastal communities and ecosystems but the ripple effects could be felt beyond borders if there is a large-scale displacement of populations in the densely inhabited coastal areas and erosion of protective coastal ecosystems.

Reaping the Benefits of Technology: The Sooner the Better

The third challenge facing the region in the future is the speed with which South Asia is able to reap the benefits of technology and to use this as an engine of growth and human development. Recent economic theory and the related empirical evidence suggest that one of the major reasons why some countries find themselves in poverty traps are differences in the endowment of knowledge and the capability of poor countries to absorb new knowledge. The only way to break out of these poverty traps is the successful absorption of technology through a technically trained and highly educated manpower.

The capacity of South Asian countries to assimilate, adapt and widely diffuse emerging technologies is constrained by the shortages of skilled, technical and vocational manpower, outdated educational systems and neglect of research and development (R&D). A highly competitive world has raised the demand for skilled workers and professionals, yet the record of many South Asian countries in terms of meeting this demand is not very encouraging and the deficit in skills remains one of the major obstacles to successful technological diffusion. While the global average for technical and vocational education and training (TVET) enrollment is 10 percent, in South Asia this rate is only 1 percent. In addition to poor enrollment, the TVET system in South Asia also suffers from other constraints such as a gender gap.

The gross tertiary enrollment in South Asia is one of the lowest in the world, second only to Sub-Saharan Africa. East Asia has managed to raise the enrollment threefold from 7 to 24 percent in four decades while South Asia's ratio went up from 4.2 percent to 10.5 percent. The region is also characterized by disparities in access to higher education by females and the choice of disciplines by the enrolled students is also a matter of concern – only one-fifth of the tertiary level students in South Asia go for science and technology subjects compared to 40 percent in East Asia. Not only is access limited, but quality and relevance are also not up to mark. A low availability of well-qualified and competent teachers is amongst serious constraints hindering the expansion of quality higher education in the region. Additionally, the curriculum is outdated and has poor linkages with industry. As a result, the majority of graduates face difficulty in finding decent productive jobs.

Wage inequality has risen in South Asia and is a powerful contributor to rising total inequality. The skilled labor force and professionals are enjoying a huge premium, with the wage dispersion much wider than ever before and likely to grow further. Empirical estimates show that between one-third and one-half of overall income inequality can be accounted for by sharp differentials in wages at both ends. These inequalities have been wrongly attributed to liberalization policies pursued in the South Asian countries since 1991, but the real culprit is the premium skilled labor fetches in the market relative to the unskilled. Economic theory suggests that the rising premium earned by skilled manpower would attract investment in supply of these skills, but flawed public policies and capital market failure have not yet produced the desired response.

The domestic economies of South Asia are suffering from a mismatch between the supply of university and college graduates produced and the current and prospective demands of their employers. A study of fresh university graduates in India shows that only 10 percent of them were as good as those produced in any world-class institution, while about 50 percent of them were simply unemployable in their own country for the jobs for which they had been trained. The proliferation of institutions of higher education with poor academic standards, assessments based on rote memory and teachers of dubious quality are producing armies of unemployable youth. Industries, including agribusiness and services in contrast continue advertising for jobs that remain unfilled. As a result, unemployed youth have become an attractive source of recruitment by terrorists, extremists, narcotic agents, war lords, criminal syndicates and mafias of all sorts.

Information communication technology (ICT) tools can help South Asian countries leapfrog the literacy and skills gap by augmenting the delivery of innovatively designed, learner-focused contents and enable masses to read and write within a short period of time and for others to acquire marketable skills. As teachers always need to update their knowledge and skills to transfer them, online resources provide audiences with excellent opportunities to learn through a rich resource base. There are several examples of innovative approaches being practiced in South Asia – transforming the illiterate to semi-literate or functionally literate. Their coverage and outreach are limited however as they are run by nongovernmental organizations (NGOs) and civil society organizations and the replication of successful models and experiments can only be undertaken with the active involvement of the government.

R&D activities in South Asia – both by the public and private sectors – are negligible in scale and lackluster. South Asia spends only 0.65 percent of its GDP in R&D, which is less than half of what the East Asia and Pacific region spends and the private-sector contribution in this effort is quite insignificant. Universities and institutions of higher learning have very little links with the industry or other economic sectors and as a result the stock of R&D personnel in South Asia is the lowest among developing regions. The location of R&D centers by many Fortune 500 companies in India would definitely give this a boost, but the inclusion of the countries of the region as the feedstock for these companies would assure persistent and reliable supply of a larger pool of low-cost, highly skilled scientists, researchers and technologists.

Overcoming Bilateral Problems: Prospects for Regional Integration

The fourth challenge is the nature of bilateral political relations between the states of South Asia and the interrelated security concerns. If – and that is a big if – the perpetually adverse bilateral relations are normalized and all the countries manage to live in peace and harmony, without attempting to covertly or overtly destabilize the other, the prospects offered by regional economic cooperation are highly attractive. South Asia's geography has the potential to accelerate growth, as it has the world's second largest proportion of populations living in border areas, second only to Europe. High population density and better access to markets can facilitate growth by allowing South Asia to take advantage of agglomeration economies. Empirical studies using gravity model and simulations show that there is a significant trade creation effect under South Asia Preferential Trade Agreement (SAPTA) with little or no evidence of trade diversion effects on the rest of the world.

A removal of trade barriers by opening up access to larger regional markets stimulates competition, which could help boost allocation and productive efficiency by facilitating industrial restructuring. A regionally integrated South Asia would attract many global firms to locate their capacities within the region to meet the demand from South Asia's burgeoning middle class. These capacities can be used as the platform for these firms to supply their global requirements as economies of scale are exploited and average cost declines. Regional integration should not be construed narrowly in trade and economic terms, but must extend to travel and tourism – as Nepal and Sri Lanka are benefiting presently from integrated tours destined for India; educational and scientific collaboration; think tanks and joint research projects and the sharing and dissemination of practices and innovations in agriculture, biotechnology and ICT. In this regard, professional associations organized at the regional level can play a critical role.

An Asian Development Bank (ADB) study in regional economic integration argues that India, with 80 percent of the region's GDP and 75 percent of the population, would find it in its national interest to take a proactive role in promoting regional trade and investment integration and should take on principal responsibility for leading the effort. Confidence-building measures, a less condescending attitude by Indians and display of leadership qualities by the Indian government, businesses, media and opinion makers will gradually nurture a political climate in which the other countries feel confident and respond positively. This hasn't happened to date because narrow, parochial political considerations have dominated the course of events. Hopefully a rising influential civil society in the countries of the region could tip the balance in favor of this endeavor and act as a countervailing force to politicians in these countries.

Three Scenarios for the Future

It would be foolhardy to speculate as to what the world would look like in 2060. After all we failed to predict the timing, intensity and spread of the global financial crisis of 2007–2008. Only two decades ago, China and India were considered by the rest of the world as objects of pity for the poverty and misery of their population with development economists struggling to find prescriptions that could help these countries overcome what seemed at the time like intractable and insurmountable problems. Nobody had predicted at that time that China would overtake Germany and the US to become the world's top exporter.

With these strong caveats in mind let me speculate three scenarios for South Asia in 2060. Under the first "win–win" scenario, countries get their act together; develop mutual trust and confidence; act in concert on external threats; invest in regional public goods, infrastructure, education and skill formation; mitigate and adapt to climate changes and pursue sensible macroeconomic policies with a clear emphasis on equity. The outcomes of this scenario are quite obvious: rapid economic growth rates will raise the living standards across the region; reduce the incidences of poverty below 10 percent; contain income inequalities across geography, gender and classes;

push over half a billion people to the level of the Southern European middle class and achieve food and energy security with alternate renewable sources playing a leading role. Millions of skilled and technically qualified Indians, Pakistanis and Bangladeshis will be sought after and find productive employment in North America, Europe, Japan, Korea, Australia, the Middle East and elsewhere.

The second "lose–lose" scenario is the polar opposite of the first. If income inequalities – whether leading/lagging regions, urban/rural, male/female and top decile/bottom decile – continue to persist, dissatisfaction and despair will spawn widespread political discontent and disenchantment and institutions of governance become dysfunctional and discredited. Under this scenario, conflicts, terrorism, wars and local insurgencies supported by rival regional countries will transform South Asia into the laggard of the world and an area of highest risk to global peace and stability. Hordes of unemployed and unskilled youth will join the ranks of antisocial, antistate elements creating a clear and present danger to the established governments in the region. It is unclear whether these would be Naxalites, Maoists, Taliban, Al-Qaeda, Jihadis or Tamil Tigers, but in some form and shape worse than what we are confronted today, they would loom large on the horizon. Additionally, the highly educated and skilled men and women of South Asia will migrate to other parts of the world, depriving the countries in South Asia of talent and investment. Political instability, internal security conditions and perpetual external threats will have serious repercussions on the economic conditions in these countries. Incidence of poverty and income inequalities will take a turn for the worse and dependence on foreign assistance and charity will increase. Unstable economic conditions will be exacerbated by the food and energy shortages caused by climate change as governments would be unable to cope.

The third or "muddling through" scenario is based on the assumption that conditions will neither be as sanguine as the win–win scenario nor as bleak as depicted in the lose–lose scenario. The countries in South Asia will continue to make modest progress as they have done in the past and even if their share in global trade and investment will not be significant, workers' remittances will become a substantial part of foreign capital inflows. Interstate rivalries and intrastate tensions would not pose major disruptive shocks, but keep simmering. The potential benefits from globalization would, by and large, remain unrealized – South Asian intellectual capital would thrive and augment, not in the service of the region but in the extraregional environment. Environmental degradation and climate change effects would be managed without causing serious economic dislocations but the demand for income-elastic food, commodities and energy would be lower due to greatly limited additions to the ranks of middle income groups. The pressure therefore on food, water and energy resources would be mitigated to some extent.

Which of the three scenarios actually materializes by 2060 will depend upon the series of policy decisions, institutional changes, resource preservation or accretion and choices made by society at large. If good sense prevails, the past vitriolic narrative is swept away, and the external environment remains benign, the probability of the win–win scenario is reasonably high. On the other hand, the game of blaming each other for one's own weaknesses and deficiencies, finding scapegoats for failures, and keeping doors to each other shut will further vitiate the atmosphere and increase the likelihood of the lose–lose scenario.

As the structural, cyclical and behavioral variables in the above equation are too many and their future interactions not clearly known, it may be safe to bet on the "muddling through" scenario, combining some elements of the optimistic and pessimistic scenarios and in some way offsetting some of the incongruities inherent in them. This conclusion may be open to criticism in that it does not add much to our existing knowledge, but given the shortcomings of the human mind, poor understanding of human ingenuity and my own limited mental horizon, this is the best contribution I can make at this juncture.

Chapter 17

ECONOMIC FUTURES: CHALLENGES AHEAD

A. K. Enamul Haque

With a population of more than 1.5 billion and with a population growth rate of nearly 2 percent per year, South Asia will soon become the most densely populated region in the world. The economy of South Asia as a region had been growing at a rate of 9 percent per annum, according to the World Bank, but has slowed down to around 6 percent in recent years due to the global recession. The economic performance of all the South Asian Association for Regional Cooperation (SAARC) countries is not, however, the same but they all, with the exception of Afghanistan and Nepal, have accomplished more than many other countries in the world (World Bank 2009). For example, in 2009, the rate of growth for export was registered around 21 percent and that of imports about 36 percent, indicating that the region has been strongly integrating with the world. Simultaneously however, the integration of South Asian economies among themselves is minimal; internally South Asia is the least integrated region of the world. Additionally, the growth rate of energy consumption is currently around 5 percent, while growth rate of energy demand is about 6 percent meaning that there is a persistent shortage of energy in the region.

On the flip side, South Asian social indicators remain abysmal. The region has managed a primary completion rate of roughly 80 percent. In terms of literacy rates, that except for Sri Lanka and Maldives, South Asian countries are trailing behind (Figure 1). Bangladesh, Pakistan, Nepal and Bhutan have around the same level of literacy while India is slightly higher. Overall though, literacy levels of these countries left much to be desired.

The region has an under-5 mortality rate of around 83 per 1,000 children and a maternal mortality rate of 500 per 100,000 live births. Life expectancy at birth is around 64 years, and infant mortality is at 62 per 1,000 live births (UNSTAT n.d.). Also, access to improved water is around 87 percent for the region as a whole.

Poverty has been one of South Asia's greatest challenges. Nearly 28 percent of the South Asian population or more than 400 million people live below the poverty line with Bangladesh having the largest percentage of poor and Sri Lanka having

Figure 1. Adult literacy rate in South Asia

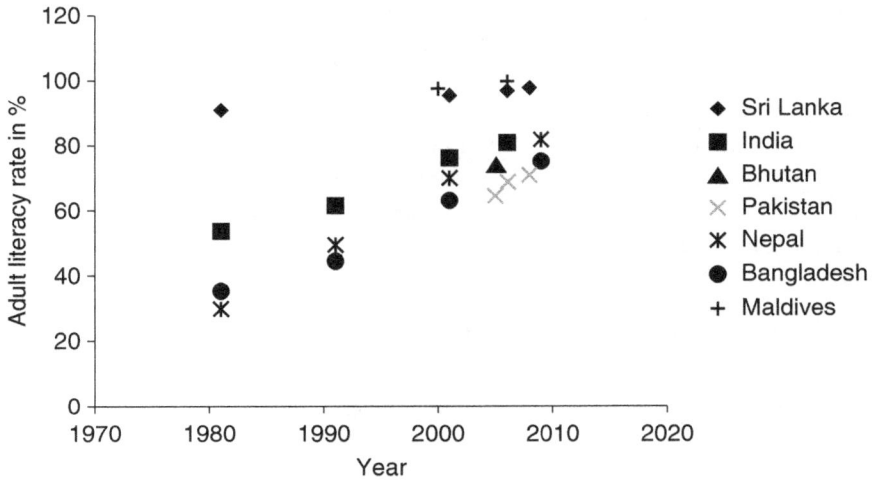

Source: World Bank (2011).

Figure 2. Per capita GDP in South Asia in 1965–2008

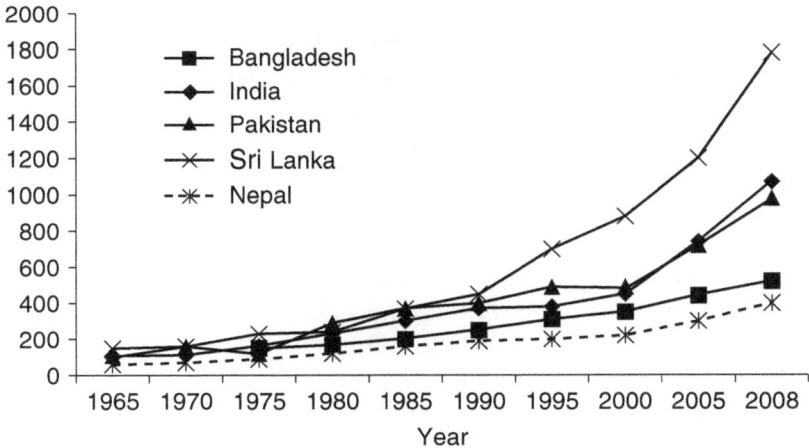

Source: World Bank (2009).

the smallest (Alpha Wolfram 2009). Researchers working on poverty literature have not been fully successful in explaining the prevailing high level of poverty in these economies – natural disasters remain one major culprit; they may explain why countries like Bangladesh could not reduce their poverty level despite significant progress in other social indicators. Even on per capita income, there is great variation among South Asian countries with only Sri Lanka posting respectable figures (Figure 2).

Finally, in terms of governance, except for India, South Asian countries are still unstable. We are yet to embrace the notion of tolerance not only towards our regional brethren, but also towards small ethnic groups living within a particular country. Today, conflicts of varying intensity and consequences between ethnic and religious minorities are present in virtually all regional countries and present a major problem for the overall progress of South Asia.

To be sure, it is the region's poor social indicators that have led thinkers and policymakers to view South Asia as a region of conflicts, hunger and disasters. The challenge ahead for South Asia is, therefore, enormous. While the region is set on a path of high economic growth, the disparity between rich and poor, and the degree of poverty, will be the major hurdles it faces.

The "Why" of South Asia's Present

Before positing the future, it may be worthwhile to highlight the underlying causes for South Asia's abysmal socioeconomic performance and the growing gap between countries within the region. A hunt for explanations shall take you to the colonial period.

Interestingly, South Asia's early development was rather impressive. As far back as 300 BCE, South Asia under the Mauryan Empire had already introduced silver coins, established trade routes, roads, military forces and introduced an elaborate tax system to be collected by representatives of the king. By the end of the fifteenth century, even as political tussles continued, South Asia had paved the way for a more prosperous economy with written rules and regulations guiding the principles of trade and commerce as well as public safety and security. Indian products like muslin from Dhaka, calicos from Bengal (Bengal Cat), Kashmiri shawls, steel and iron works, silk, handicrafts, spices like pepper and cinnamon, as well as opium and indigo were exported to Europe, the Middle East and South East Asia as well as China.

The prosperity of the region, however, came to a halt due to conflicts between rulers within India, the weakness of the central government in controlling dissident kings and rulers, and due to European intrusion into the political affairs of South Asia. Gradually, South Asia fell apart, divided and fragmented, and a process of colonization began. This led to deinstitutionalizing South Asia with new institutions and a culture that was alien to its population and whose essence the English educated population could only grasp. Figure 3 shows the relative position of India and China since 1 CE until 1913. It clearly shows that Indian economy stagnated since the early nineteenth century.

In 1947, when "British India" achieved its independence, it was divided into the "Muslim" state of Pakistan, and the secular but "Hindu" dominated state of India. Nepal and Bhutan, the two landlocked countries, remained heavily dependent on India to access ports but were never under a pure British rule. Sri Lanka got its independence in 1950. The legacy of colonization is a South Asia where great mistrust among states prevails and where political regimes in each of these countries emphasize these tensions and perceived threats of cultural, military and religious invasion – no one can clearly specify which threat is "real" and which is "imaginary" – to justify and strengthen their hold on national politics. No wonder then that it is even difficult for

Figure 3. Comparison of historical GDP of selected countries

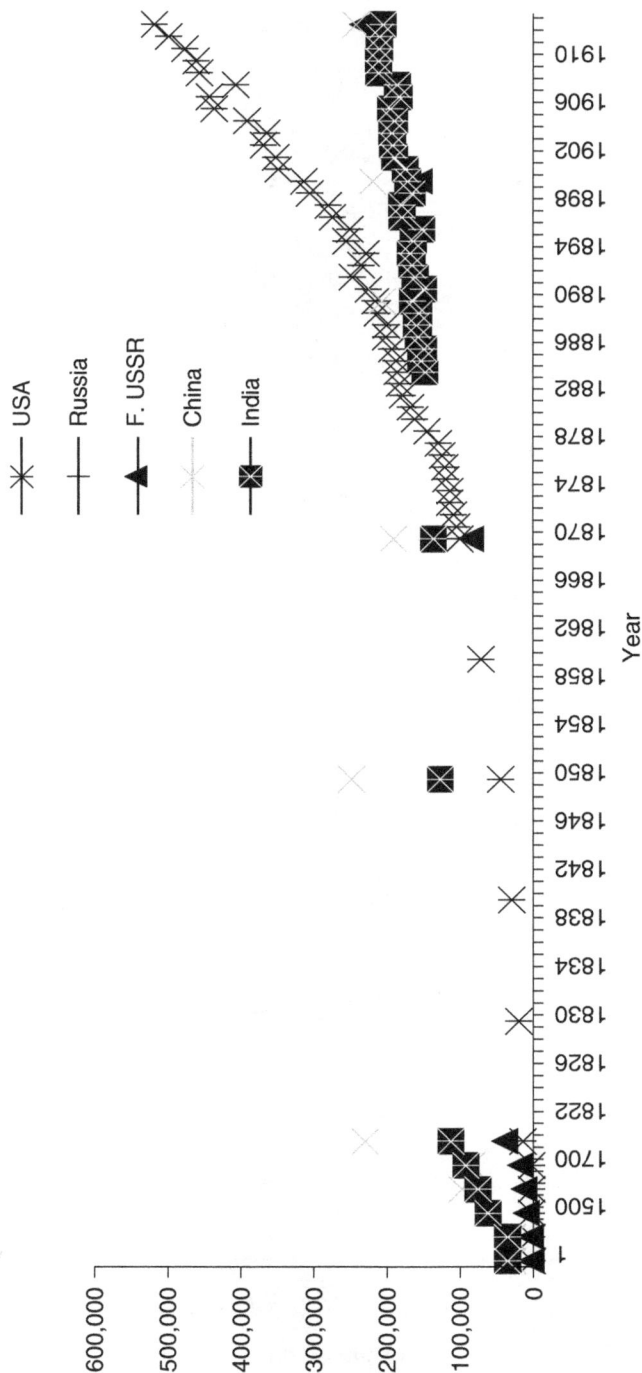

Source: Maddison (2003b).

Figure 4. Per capita income of India (1857–1900)

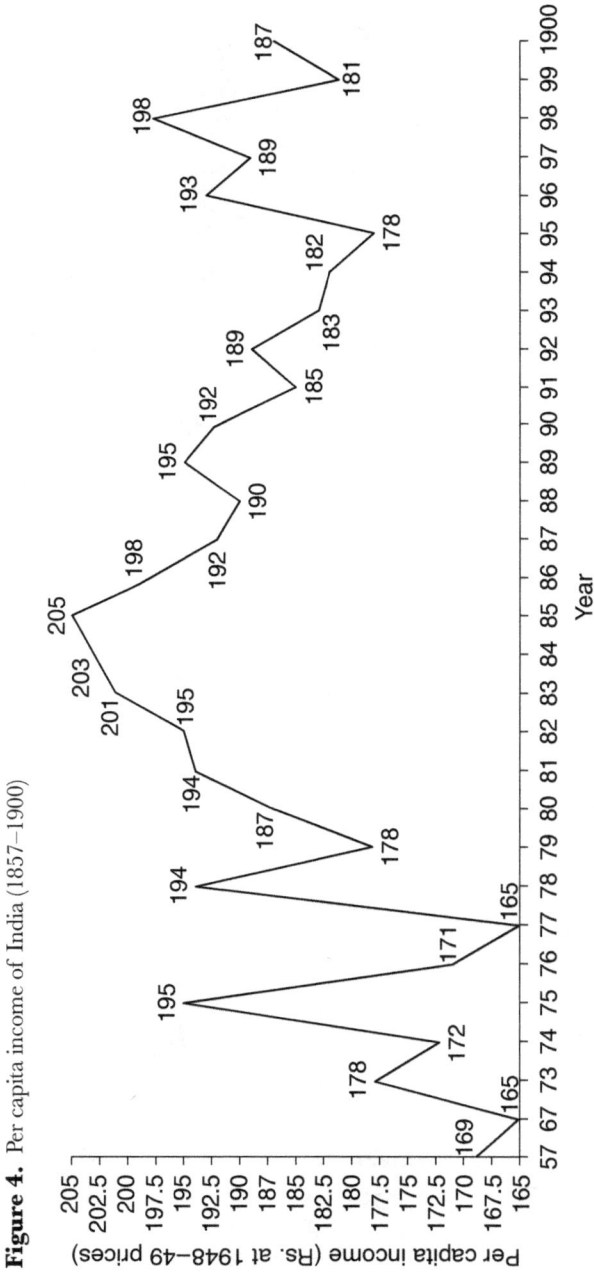

Source: Wolfram Alpha (2009), quoted from the work of Angus Maddison.

South Asians to have a meeting within South Asia except in smaller countries like Nepal and Sri Lanka – courtesy of the stringent visa restrictions and travel security rules imposed upon fellow South Asians.

The decline of South Asian brotherhood, once a real and tangible fact of life, has its roots in the colonial era when the Portuguese, the British and the French used Muslims and Hindus against each other in order to gain political power. On the economic front, Figure 4 shows how India's per capita income declined after 1885. The reasons were complex and not always easy to decipher but one can easily attribute them to its colonial rule when the economy was stagnant.

Such a decline fuelled into the already-existing dissatisfaction against the colonial rule and at the same time deepened the division between Muslims and Hindus. It triggered a wave of mistrust among Muslims leaders because they thought a Hindu-dominated India would simply crush their faith. The partition of British India in 1947 was a crystallization of these tensions. Later, other countries gained their independence, Sri Lanka in 1950, Maldives in 1965 and Bangladesh – from Pakistan – in 1971. Afghanistan and Nepal for most of their history remained independent countries but did sign treaties with the British in 1919 and 1816 respectively. In doing so, they had to suffer a great degree of social and economic humiliation from the British. The net result was that by the time all South Asians gained independence, they had already lost a large part of their wealth to the colonial powers. Add to that the lingering mistrust in the postcolonial era – with its roots also being in the colonization period – and it is rather easy to understand how South Asia has become one of the most impoverished regions of the world, with its economies largely dependent on outside powers.

Within a few years after independence both Pakistan and India lost their top leaders. By the 1960s, it was evident that South Asia had become fragmented with a deep division of mistrust, which prevailed even after the withdrawal of the British Empire. While the overall level of income, poverty, literacy and other social indicators remained very similar in most South Asian countries except Afghanistan and the Maldives, the current level of these indicators shows a significant difference between them even though they had started at almost the same point in terms of per capita income.

Challenges in the Twenty-first Century

Moving ahead, South Asian nations will continue to struggle to shed any anomalies still lingering from the colonial period. The new institutions governing the countries are yet to take root in the sociopolitical life of these nations. We must take note of the fact that some countries have done better than others. This implies that improvement at a relatively fast pace is possible. The challenge, of course, is to direct the improvement towards the ordinary peoples, the deprived and marginalized, of South Asia and to integrate better as a region.

The twenty-first century inevitably brings several new challenges to South Asian nations. On the one hand, we are in a new era of economic growth, following a path where Asia is going to become the center of major economic activities for the next several decades. On the other hand, Asia, including South Asia, is not yet mature enough to withstand the pressure of changes and the uncertainty around us. Poverty in South Asia is already a major handicap for our economies. High population density, low resource bases for energy and mineral resources, and natural disasters will continue to complicate South Asian plans to deal with its social deprivation. It will be difficult for policymakers to continue along the path of high economic growth without adequately addressing poverty in South Asia. However, ensuring the basic necessities for people living at the margins of their lives and society is a must. Unfortunately, we have not been able to identify measures based on solid research to deal with poverty yet. While we cannot find foolproof solutions to these problems, keeping a large percent of the population without basic needs, beyond just food, will remain a major risk in the regional pursuit for economic growth.

Experiments such as providing free education, health, housing and clothes for the poor at the state level have been tried and remain popular but they are devoid of sound thinking: such strategies are unsustainable and carry the risk of creating perverse incentives that might jeopardize the competitive edge of South Asia. These programs alienate local institutions, and limit communities' capacity to help each other thus increase the burden on the state. Furthermore, the process produces a new group of rent seekers (i.e. promotes corruption) who use the pretext of "poverty of our people" to increase their own wealth. Thousands of NGOs working in South Asia have been able to increase their own asset values while their impact on poverty reduction has lagged far behind their own successes in increasing their wealth. Some of these NGOs have successfully used the term poverty to encroach into the territory of business and politics, thereby, further distorting the overall social and institutional setup. In countries like Bangladesh, despite many good efforts and examples set by a qualified number of NGOs, as a group, they often tend to behave like an alternative government. This in itself is a threat to democracy.

Because of a high degree of poverty and illiteracy, South Asian nations face a classic dilemma between economic growth and equity. It is always popular for the policymakers to pledge establishment of a society "equal" in terms of income as such socialistic values have greater appeal to the masses. In a society with a large percent of people being illiterate and also poor, policies are often driven by whims and gut feeling rather than by thorough analysis and knowledge – getting out of this situation will be a challenge for all South Asian countries. Moreover, literacy, as we measure it, hardly provides any information on the actual number of people who can read and write well. For South Asians to be truly productive and for us to have a true measure of just how we are faring in terms of making our people capable of performing in modern economies, the concept of literacy needs to be modified to include people active in reading and writing. At the same time, health literacy, ecological literacy and historical literacy are very important for all nations since they reduce the cost of development and economic growth. Literacy helps in reducing resource waste, which is crucial for South Asia. In the next 50 years, each and every country in South Asia must proceed to improve their degree of literacy – not the index on literacy. This requires changes in the curriculum. A curriculum based on a sound understanding of South Asian ecology and history will help us understand each other and reduce conflicts. It will help us build tolerance amongst us, create brotherhood and develop friendships.

Corruption has become endemic in many parts of the world, including South Asia. This is also another major challenge for the region. The ideal approach to deal with corruption has not been fully analyzed but the traditional Western system of using anticorruption institutions has also failed to produce the desired results. In each country the society is a small network of people and as a consequence, institutions involved in taking anticorruption measures face a moral dilemma because they cannot rise beyond the interest of the network to which they belong. A high level of illiteracy and unequal access to public goods like education, health and government institutions eventually reduces competition and cannot break the cycle of the network that feeds off corruption.

Intermittent measures to deal with corruption will not be sufficient to reduce its extent. Neither will current institutional measures be sufficient to deal with the problem. This problem does, however, need to be addressed in a systematic fashion and with compassion and regularity to ensure a stable South Asia. Indeed, an anticorruption body comprising of members of all South Asian countries as a moral watchdog might help reduce corruption at the upper echelon of each society. On certain issues, South Asia needs to go beyond national boundaries and I believe corruption is one of them – the region must use its legal institutions jointly to deal with this menace.

As already mentioned, despite the long history of close cooperation, South Asia today is not well integrated. Trade within South Asian countries is far less than that with Western countries. South Asia inherited the common law system because of its colonial past and as such South Asian legal institutions cross-recognize interpretations of these laws in their respective courts; this is an advantage for South Asia. Despite this, trade within South Asia has not grown significantly, mainly because all South Asian countries were deficient in capital products and products with intellectual content. This is why most of the imports to the region were from Western nations. The recent trend, however, is changing as India and China are substituting many of the imports from Europe and America, and because these countries have been able to elevate their status from being producers of primary products to producers of manufactured goods and services.

Efforts to increase trade within South Asia are ongoing through two distinct windows: the South Asian Association for Regional Cooperation (SAARC) and the Bay of Bengal Initiative for Multi-Sectoral Technical and Economic Cooperation (BIMSTEC). Moreover, there are also steps taken to create subregional groups with one in the east comprising of Bangladesh, India, Sri Lanka, Nepal and Bhutan and one in the west comprising of Iran, Afghanistan, Pakistan and India. Furthermore, after the signing of trade agreements between Sri Lanka and India, and between Pakistan and Sri Lanka, it is now understood that trade could be a win–win game even if it is within South Asia. This might prompt others to participate in establishing an effective South Asian Free Trade Area.

Beyond trade, South Asian countries need to integrate themselves in terms of travel, education, healthcare and agriculture. At the same time, South Asian countries need to develop strategies to integrate their banking and insurance sector in order to benefit from each other.

To me, the shape of South Asia in the next 50 years will largely depend on how we, the South Asian nations, deal with poverty, illiteracy, corruption and economic integration. At the same time, it is also evident that we have to prepare ourselves for a more hostile environment in the future. Climate change is likely to put pressure on our economic activities as it will affect the livelihood of millions of people who are not "ready" to either adapt or cope with it. Coping or adaptation by a large number of illiterate masses is going to be a new challenge for South Asians because these would entail a change in the behavior of productions and also consumptions. Consequently, dealing with climate change will be very difficult for these nations. Our governments and other social and public institutions are not ready to deal with frequent disasters of larger scales. For instance, millions of Bangladeshis and Indians, affected by cyclone Aila in 2008 and 2009 respectively, continued to live in knee-deep water even a few years after the event. The overall preparedness of South Asia against climate change-related disasters like cyclones, floods, melting glaciers, flash flooding and drought is still very low. Yet, there is no option but to prepare to deal with these new challenges. One practical step could be to begin sharing information on rainfall, water level and other weather-related phenomenon in real time to prepare us to reduce the impacts of such catastrophes.

Despite these problems, it is my hope that by 2060 South Asia will emerge as a major hub of economic activity in the world economy – as a center of development with a mind full of compassion for the poor and as a region living in harmony with nature.

Chapter 18

SOUTH ASIA IN THE ASIAN ECONOMY: STRUGGLING TO OVERCOME HISTORY

Amitendu Palit

South Asia has remained economically backward compared to most of Asia. Despite comprising India – the world's twelfth largest and one of the fastest growing emerging market economies – the region suffers from low per capita incomes, poor connectivity, inadequate human development and pervasive poverty. The Indian economy reflects these traits conspicuously mirroring what most of the region typifies. The economic potential of the region is enormous given its abundant natural and human resources and strategic geography. Yet, it fails to give a better life to vast numbers of its people.

South Asia's current and future economic outlooks, have been, and will be shaped by three "P"s: people, potential and politics. Being one of the world's most populous regions, *people* will be critical in determining South Asia's economic prospects. Its *potential* for achieving high economic growth can hardly be overstated. Last, but not the least, *politics* is inseparable from regional economics. Much of the region's politics is inspired by varied concerns of its people articulated by diverse interest groups. The populism-laden politics is usually counterproductive to harnessing greater economic potential. It is hardly surprising that policies aiming at long-term economic benefits are time and again circumscribed in scope and scale for safeguarding short-term political interests. The regional political economy is distinct from the rest of Asia in its unabashed eagerness to maximize ad hoc political gains.

Population and Migration

Notwithstanding the political economy, economic policies influencing South Asia's interface with the world will be shaped significantly by issues concerning its people. From shares of 23.8 percent and 39.5 percent respectively in global and Asian populations in 2010, regional population is projected to increase to 25.3 percent and 44.3 percent of global and Asian populations in 2050. Higher shares will reflect the expansion in regional population from 1.6 billion to 2.3 billion during the period.

All countries in the region (except Sri Lanka) will add between 30–80 percent to their existing stocks of people over the next few decades.

The robust growth in population has interesting demographic implications. The United Nations (UN) projects South Asia outstripping East Asia as the world's most populous region within a couple of decades. The demographic "catch-up" between Asia's east and south is a natural corollary of the population trends expected to manifest in China and India. As China stops adding to its population and enters a phase of negative growth in population from 2030 onward, India's population will still keep growing at around 0.6 percent (Palit 2010). With more than 70 percent of the regional population, India's population trends will significantly determine South Asia's demography, much as China's will for East Asia.

East Asian population growth rates are expected to become increasingly similar to those of high-income mature economies in the West. In this respect, it will be an exception in Asia. Neither South, nor Central, West or Southeast Asia are projected to experience negative rates in population growth like East Asia. These parts of Asia, along with Africa, will be the main contributors to global population growth over the next few decades. East Asia's lower contribution to Asian population will be compensated mostly by South Asia. East Asia's share in Asian population is projected to reduce from 37.5 percent currently to 30.6 percent in 2050. This drop will be met primarily by South Asia (39.5 percent to 44.3 percent) and partially by West Asia (5.6 percent to 7.1 percent).

South Asian countries are expected to respond to future economic circumstances in a manner consistent with larger interests of their populations. High population implies enlargement of the domestic workforce. Working age cohorts (15–60 years) will dominate regional country populations with such people projected to occupy around 65 percent of India's population by 2040. Similar trends are expected elsewhere in the region as well. From the vantage point of interregional economic interfaces, South Asia's ample endowment of young workers will preserve its importance as a key source of labor for the relatively labor-scarce parts of Asia. Mature economies of East and Southeast Asia (Japan, Korea, Taiwan, Hong Kong, Singapore and China in the medium term) can look to South Asia for mitigating gaps in domestic labor supply. More trade deals between East Asia and South Asia should facilitate migration by making movements of both professional and semiskilled labor much easier.

Migration will be a major determinant of South Asia's economic prospects in the medium term. Outward migration will increase as workers from India, Bangladesh, Pakistan, Sri Lanka, Afghanistan and Nepal respond to opportunities outside the region. The process will be impacted by both "pull" and "push" factors. While the former will manifest as demand for cheaper labor from labor-scarce Asian economies, the latter will reflect eagerness of South Asian workers to respond to higher expected returns. Higher growth in population will imply that South Asian per capita incomes remain lower than those in most parts of Asia. These income gaps are unlikely to be bridged even if gross domestic product (GDP) growth in the region takes place at sustained double-digit rates for several years. India's current per capita income ($1017; World Bank 2009a) is

3.3 percent of Hong Kong ($30,863), 5.3 percent of Korea ($19,115) and 2.7 percent of Singapore ($37,597). The income is miniscule not only with respect to major economies of East and Southeast Asia, but also in relation to energy-rich West Asian economies such as Kuwait, Saudi Arabia and Jordan. The income difference and concomitant expectations of higher earnings from foreign locations will induce considerable outward migration from South Asia with the movements focusing on select higher income Asian economies. China is expected to figure among these destinations as it combines high economic growth with stabilizing population resulting in higher per capita incomes.

Asia's labor pool in the coming decades is expected to be dominated by South Asians provided the continent does not erect new barriers to interregional labor mobility. Success of East and Southeast Asian economies in generating technology-intensive productivity growth will be a key factor in this regard. If the more developed Asian economies are able to regularly produce labor-saving innovations, they may rely less on cheap labor and discourage import of the same. This will limit outward migration from South Asia and the consequences may not be entirely beneficial for the region. For several years to come, the region needs to encourage its people to move to jobs rather than the other way round, since its level of economic progress, despite quantum leaps, may not translate to creation of as many opportunities that will assure gainful employment of its workforce. At the same time, the quality of new jobs created may also turn out to be decidedly inferior.

Thus while "push" and "pull" factors will encourage outward migration from South Asia, the volume and quality of such migration will vary with changes in labor market conditions elsewhere in Asia. Migration will ensure that worker remittances remain major sources of foreign exchange for the region. Remittances have been a stabilizing influence for the region's balance of payments. India is the largest recipient of inward remittances having received $50 billion in 2008; Bangladesh and Pakistan rank 12th and 17th with $9 billion and $7 billion (World Bank 2009b) respectively. A gradual shift in the global economic momentum from North America and Europe to Asia will probably influence the source pattern of inward remittances with East Asia, and select Southeast and West Asian economies, becoming more significant sources.

Migration from South Asia will vary in skill content. Labor exports from the region include a relatively small, but skill-intensive category. Movement of skilled professionals from the region has increased with growth of new opportunities in a globalized world. At the same time, export of less-skilled labor for low-end occupations has also continued. Both these migrations are expected to continue in the foreseeable future. Lack of adequate opportunities – both in high-end specialized professions as well as low-end manual absorptions – will maintain impetus of migrations in the medium term. Indeed, pursuit of higher productivity in several Asian economies will sustain demand for skilled professionals from the South Asian region.

Regional Production Networks

Mobility of labor is expected to be facilitated by South Asia's increasing economic integration with other parts of Asia. The region is a late entrant to the flurry of formal trade agreements proliferating in Asia. Southeast and East Asia have particularly experienced dense growth of cross-regional trade networks. South Asia is gradually embedding into the more economically integrated regions of Asia largely through trade pacts forged by India with Southeast Asia, Singapore, Thailand, Japan and Korea. Southeast Asia is emerging as the "hub" in a "hub-and-spoke" format of Asian economic integration connecting South, Southeast and East Asia. The wheel can enlarge with South Asia entering into more economic agreements with West and Central Asia. Such possibilities are strong given large endowments of energy resources in the latter and the imperatives on part of the rest of Asia to access such resources. Trade negotiators across Asia are working overtime to deepen the "spaghetti bowl" (Bhagwati 1995). The possibility of South Asia becoming a core part of integrated trade networks both on its east and west appears distinct in the foreseeable future.

Economic integration has its own spin-offs, not the least of which is the ease with which goods and services can cross borders. As tariffs on South Asian exports come down with more trade agreements coming into force, the region will figure more prominently in Asian production networks. Industrial production in Asia has become spatially dispersed with various processes locating in different countries for reaping cost advantages. Manufactures of popular items such as Levis jeans, for example, are organized in activities handled by firms based in Taiwan, Cambodia, Bangladesh, US and Hong Kong at different levels of the supply chains. South Asian firms will feature more in such chains as the region integrates deeper into Asia's production system. Southeast Asia is expected to play a key role in this regard as its trade and investment links with South Asia can encourage more intraindustry trade involving South Asian, Southeast Asian and East Asian firms.

Will greater embedding of South Asian firms in Asian product chains help them "catch up" faster with their more developed counterparts in the rest of Asia? The "catch up" process will vary according to national technological capabilities. Asian countries can be broadly grouped into "leaders" (i.e., Hong Kong, Japan, Korea, Taiwan, Singapore), "potential leaders" (i.e., Bahrain, Kuwait, United Arab Emirates), "latecomers" (i.e., China, India, Indonesia, Jordan, Malaysia, Thailand, Turkey, Saudi Arabia, Sri Lanka, Vietnam) and "marginalized" (i.e., Bangladesh, Cambodia, Laos, Nepal, Pakistan) according to their capabilities for creating new technology, technological infrastructure and human skills (Archibuggi and Coco 2004). Though national technological trajectories do not necessarily reflect industry-specific R&D advances and innovative competencies, they do highlight degree of access to technologies (old and new) and effective application of the latter to economic development. Gaps across Asia are conspicuous in this respect. South Asia's extant capabilities, particularly in innovation and technological infrastructure, peg it way down in Asia's technological ladder. Most South Asian firms, irrespective of product lines, are likely to feature in relatively less technology-intensive lower-end functions in the regional chains over the next couple of decades. Till technology gaps narrow, most South Asian firms will contribute to Asian production more as suppliers of raw material and preliminary processers, rather than through high-end shop-floor practices. There will definitely be exceptions; Indian and Sri Lankan firms in knowledge-intensive service activities (information technology, communications, biotechnology) can feature at the higher end of the supply chains on account of their relatively advanced technological competencies. But such examples across industries will be few and far between.

Structural Imbalance

South Asia's unusual economic structure will influence the quality of its integration with the rest of Asia and its long-term economic outlook. Services are the most critical segments in South Asian economies. This is unusual since the normal evolution in economic development entails a progressively lower role of agriculture in the national economy to be matched by greater contribution from industry. Services become dominant at later and more advanced stages of structural development. South Asia has charted an odd course with lower shares of agriculture and primary sector in national GDPs being compensated by services rather than industry and manufacturing.

The unusual development has affected occupational patterns with agriculture and farming continuing to support maximum livelihoods despite contributing increasingly less to national GDPs. With manufacturing failing to become employment-intensive, the surplus labor from farming and rural occupations has not shifted to industry. Services, on the other hand, are catering more to nonfarming segments of the work force across the region given their requirements for different skills. South Asia's economic exchanges with the rest of Asia will be influenced by this structural distortion. Long-term prospects of services-oriented regional growth will result in South Asia's trade negotiations demanding greater market access for services. Such demands may encounter resistance, particularly on movement of qualified professionals, as other developing countries in Southeast and West Asia slowly build competencies in efficient service production. Cross-border labor movements then might involve encroaching into sensitive segments of domestic labor markets. But South Asia can hardly avoid future frictions with neighbors in this respect as is already visible from India's ongoing trade negotiations with the rest of Asia.

The foreseeable intraregional growth dynamics might crack South Asia into contrasting blocks of economic well-being. Some countries in the region may outperform others in the medium term. Regions within countries too might do better than others. India is the best example of such divergent trends. At a macro-level, the overwhelming size of the economy buoyed by double-digit growth might increase the economic distance between India and other regional economies. This may witness South Asia's gradual reorganization into two distinct economic entities: India and the non-Indian group. The eventuality can be avoided if intraregional economic cooperation proceeds more vigorously. Progress on South Asian Free Trade Area (SAFTA) has been constrained by lack of political will. Robust improvement in political climate with emphasis on intraregional trade and commerce can help the region acquire a more cohesive economic identity. India's role in this regard will be critical. It should encourage regional economic integration in order to avoid the negative externalities of coexisting in an economically subdued neighborhood.

Growth vs. Equity

What is unavoidable is the region's struggle to shake off chronic poverty and deprivation. Nearly half the world's poor live in South Asia. No other part of Asia harbors such magnitudes of income poverty. Adverse effects of the latter manifesting through limited access to basic needs and earning opportunities for poor households are accentuated by polarizations between incomes with the poorest quarter of the population accounting for barely a tenth of total income as against almost half by the richest. The region's development history, till now, offers little hope of income distribution becoming more egalitarian as poor governance impedes equitable growth. Governance will constrain India in its quest for growth with a "human face." Even if India races ahead of the rest of the region with higher GDP growth, it will probably continue to struggle with poverty and income inequality given its large additions to population – a phenomenon expected to be witnessed elsewhere in the region too. The contrast between better and worse-offs will presumably be sharper in South Asia compared to the East and Southeast, and most of West Asia.

Managing trade-offs between growth and equity will dominate policy agendas of South Asian economies as they proceed on their chaotic journeys to raise GDP growth. Absence of effective distributive mechanisms will handicap efforts for making economic growth inclusive and people-oriented. As more people fall off the growth bandwagon and social vulnerabilities increase, the political economy will become more active. History suggests that the political economy is more likely to revolve around agendas of specific interest groups rather than core concerns of people. Civil society activism in South Asia has occasionally assumed counterproductive postures by resisting development without advocating feasible alternatives. Industrialization resulting in displacement of marginal livelihoods based on forestry and primary resources has been heavily agitated against. Notwithstanding strong humanitarian foundations, the agitation has failed to suggest development strategies that industrialize without displacement. Over time, such agitations have become more agenda-driven than concern-driven. The interplay of interests between civil society, political community, business, judiciary and bureaucracy in South Asia, has created a complex web of responses that often overlook core concerns of people and restrain them from achieving their full economic potential.

Managing people, potential and politics in a harmonious manner will determine South Asia's economic outlook in the years to come. The challenges in this regard are substantive. Recent history does not offer much scope for optimism. Most complications, however, can be addressed if the region resorts to deployment of a fourth "P": pragmatism. Stakeholders must respond pragmatically to the region's concerns for securing gainful outcomes. Economic managements in East and Southeast Asia are good examples of such pragmatic approaches. Lessons picked up from the neighborhood can lead South Asia to a brighter economic future.

Chapter 19

GLOBALIZATION AND SOUTH ASIA

Sanjoy Chakravorty

South Asia has the highest density of futurists in the world – we call them astrologers. Their methodology for making predictions involves stars and planets and generous doses of credulity. Since I don't have access to their methods, I will have to attempt this exercise using what I know: some core principles and a theory about understanding long-term change.

First, if we begin from a limited understanding of globalization – that it is primarily an economic and cultural phenomenon, that too of recent vintage – then we won't get very far, certainly not to 2060. It is necessary, for sure, to pay attention to economics and culture, and I will do so in this essay. But, I believe, it is necessary to begin by thinking of globalization in terms of ideologies and institutions that create the framework of interactions at a global scale. In this sense, globalization has existed from the time global interaction has been possible; what has changed is the intensity and nature of the interactions, which in turn have been guided by ideologies and institutions.

Second, there is a serious problem with extrapolation. It assumes that the rate and direction of change follows a linear logic. This is similar to a core problem in evolution: is it incremental (an accumulation of minute changes over a very long time) or is it discontinuous (there are accumulated minute changes, no doubt, but there are periods of dramatic and large change)? I suggest that the latter (known as the "punctuated equilibrium" thesis) is the appropriate metaphor for history and social analysis. To put it simply, history (and the future) is not linear, but an accumulation of small changes interspersed periodically with "turning points."

Third, in looking for a theory of long-term historical change, I believe we should seriously consider the Hegelian possibility of thesis and antithesis (counterthesis in this essay), which argues that any dominant ideology or institution has unresolved contradictions, which over time, force adaptations to and perhaps replace the dominant ideology. One doesn't have to be a Marxian (or believe in the inevitable collapse of capitalism under the weight of its contradictions) to acknowledge the explanatory power of Hegelian dialectic. It is the bedrock principle of long-term theories that try to explain the rise and fall of great ideas and powers (in this context, Zakaria's 2009 work has special relevance to South Asia). In short, we are far from having reached the end of history (unlike Francis Fukuyama's famous proclamation at the end of the Cold War). So, let us begin by looking at history.

History and the Legacy of Ideologies

One hundred years ago, in 1910, South Asia was British territory – taxed and governed by them. India, Pakistan, Bangladesh, Sri Lanka… none of them existed, not even notionally. Colonization was the dominant global ideology and much of the world could be labeled thus: colonizer or colonized. South Asia was a significant node in that specific form of globalization. Readers of this article don't need reminding of what that meant – an economic system (production, trade, and revenue collection) designed to transfer surplus to the colonizing country. The counterthesis was anticolonial nationalism (the idea of the "nation" itself being borrowed from the colonizers), which was in germinal stage.

Fifty years later, in 1960, South Asia was a postcolonial region, the counterthesis having overwhelmed the contradictions of the colonial thesis. Bangladesh still did not have independent existence; it was called East Pakistan. Sri Lanka existed, but it was called Ceylon. Decolonization was one of the dominant global ideologies of the time and South Asia was its prominent node. The guiding principles were inward looking – nation building (giving organic meaning to the political units that had been created), modernization and industrialization (focused on support for public sector industry, protection from international competition for private industry, import substitution and a general indifference to exports). These were not renegade policies but the generally agreed-upon best principles among politicians, capital owners and intellectuals.

The other global ideology of the time was the Cold War, the battle for supremacy between the US and the USSR that was waged on Third World lands. The nations of South Asia became aligned into blocks that set the rules for global governance and traded internally (weapons and food primarily). The end game of the global Cold War was played out in South Asia. The story is well known. The USSR invaded Afghanistan, the US and Pakistan engineered a *mujahedeen* resistance, the USSR withdrew and the Soviet bloc fell apart, the Taliban took power in Afghanistan, sheltered Al-Qaeda, which carried out the 9/11 strikes in the US, leading to a Pakistan-assisted American invasion of Afghanistan, and so on. There is little doubt that right now, in this part of South Asia, the most fundamental influence of globalization works through violence and a chain of events set in motion by the global Cold War.

The counterthesis to the nationalist project may not have been obvious in 1960, but with the benefit of hindsight it is apparent today that it was beginning to be expressed through various forms of identity politics. Some politics have taken the form of ethno- or subnationalism; the formation of Bangladesh from East Pakistan, the 30-year Tamil-separatist civil war in Jaffna in Sri Lanka, the different insurgencies on India's borders (Kashmir, the northeastern region, Punjab), are all cases in point. This is not to suggest that the center holds while the borders fall apart. There are violent (not necessarily separatist) movements in the tribal belt of India running from Bengal to

Maharashtra, in Sindh, Baluchistan and the northwest frontier in Pakistan; radical Islamic movements in Bangladesh, and continued revolutionary guerilla activities in Nepal.

Economic and Cultural Globalization in South Asia

In fact, when we consider the various manifestations of globalization today, in 2010, it is clear that a major element is violence – abetted by global flows of actors, weapons and information using the very same technologies that aid the flow of legal goods and services. Insurgents, rebels and other nonstate purveyors of violence use the Internet, mobile phones, international networks of suppliers of arms and ammunition and international expertise in the use of lethal violence. This criminal world is a mirror image of the legal enterprises of globalization (see Castells 1996 for a good overview of globalization and networks, including criminal ones).

But the globalization of nonstate violence is not the reason why this term is the defining word of the new millennium. The fascination with globalization is largely due to the fact that normal or legal businesses involved in the production of goods and services, wherever they may be located, use inputs from very distant locations, often from countries that are thousands of miles away. This has become possible as a result of fundamental technological advances in transportation and communication. The cost of moving physical objects has been declining as a result of improvements in shipping technology (containerization, and bigger ships and trucks) and handling technology at ports. The cost of moving information has been declining precipitously as a result of the creation of a new technology (the Internet) and substantial investments in communication infrastructure (satellites, fiber optic cables).

Stan Shih's "Smile Curve" provides a good visual metaphor for these changes. Imagine the well-known smiley logo – a line that curves down and then up like a flattened letter "U." Now think of the various stages of production of any good (say a laptop). These include, in sequence, R&D, branding, design, manufacturing, distribution, marketing and sales and service. Value is added to the good at each of these steps. The closer to the origin or end of the curve (say R&D or sales) the higher the value added. The lowest point, with the least value added, is manufacturing. The improvements in transportation and communication technology have enabled this value chain to be sliced into ever smaller elements and the activities that add value to be dispersed over the globe. A laptop may be designed in California or Texas, its software inputs may be created in Bangalore or Hyderabad, branded using New York or London firms, manufactured or assembled in Shenzhen in China, distributed through large chains like Amazon or Walmart, and serviced through local entrepreneurs or phone handlers in Gurgaon or Dublin. A region's position on a value chain is the key to its prosperity, or lack of it. (A good exposition of this idea can be found in the writing of journalist James Fallows 2007.)

The cultural effects of globalization are manifested in two ways. First, there is the dominance of well-known brands (such as McDonalds and Coca-Cola, Nike and Benetton) and well-known clusters of production of cultural content (such as

Hollywood and Bollywood). Second, there is the spread of niche and "exotic" cultural products from distant or remote locations to all places that can afford to consume these products (Sufi music and Bhangra, yoga and tandoori, for example). There is an intense debate over the effects of these two forces – totalization by American big brand dominance and obliteration of local identities and products on the one hand, versus increasing diversity of consumer tastes and localization of global brands and products.

If we use the extrapolation method – that is, draw a straight line from now to 2060 – we would expect to see continuation and intensification of the key elements of economic and cultural globalization today: further lowering of the cost of transportation and communication led by technological improvements and investments in enabling infrastructure, continued slicing of value chains and intense competition by nations to move up different value chains, increasing dominance of big consumer brands simultaneously with the increasing emergence of niche products and increasing diversity of taste and preference (the best known work on value chains is by Gary Gereffi 2005 and his associates).

The nations of South Asia will necessarily have to be engaged in all three elements. The national states will have to keep tariffs low, allow the entry of products manufactured elsewhere and create or assist in the creation of infrastructure to enable ever more rapid transportation and communication. This will require massive investments in transportation corridors and hubs (road, rail, airports, ports) and telecommunication (satellites, cell phone towers, fiber optic cables). Private firms (often with the assistance of the state) will seek to embed themselves deeper into existing value chains and, at the same time, try to move up those chains. Textiles and garments is one large globalized sector where the South Asian presence is already significant (Bangladesh, India, Pakistan and Sri Lanka are all players) and is likely to remain so. Information technology (ICT) and related services is another large sector that is globalized but where India has a clear advantage among the South Asian nations. The others will try to enter this sector, possibly successfully, because other than market size (which may not create much of an advantage in ICT) there is little in India that the other nations do not possess – an English-educated and technology-literate class of young workers. India's market size advantage is likely to become useful in penetrating global markets for higher-end products like cars and televisions.

South Asians are as brand-conscious as any other people. Hence big global brands will continue to be successful in penetrating consumer markets all over the region. Clothing and accessories, personal grooming and hygiene, and consumer electronics are all sectors where global brands will become larger in South Asia. Global firms will continue to try to penetrate large service industries, especially banking and insurance, and increasingly health and education. They are more likely to be successful (as they already have been) in the former than the latter. South Asian firms will, at the same time, try to penetrate developed nation markets for products that require a human touch – food, artisanal and crafted material, and low technology manufacturing – to best utilize their comparative advantage in labor costs. They will also attempt to create overseas markets for unique local products (in food, art, music, clothing, etc.) by capitalizing on diversifying tastes, not only in the traditional markets of Western Europe and North America, but also perhaps in the emerging markets of East Asia and Central Europe.

How successful will the individual nations in the region be in integrating with the global market? That, of course, is the 64 crore rupee question. If present trends continue one would have to conclude that at least in the short term India has the pole position. Its economy has been growing rapidly in recent years and trade (especially in services) has been growing at two to three times that rate. Pakistan appears to be undergoing a serious crisis of governance and it is possible that right now economic and trade issues aren't of primary importance. Sri Lanka has a relatively small economy but it may be better positioned at the present moment to be a participant in economic globalization than Bangladesh and Nepal, both also with small economies and less stable politics.

But even if the rosiest economic globalization dreams work out – that is, each of these nations experiences strong and robust growth of trade and GDP – there are serious structural problems that will have to be dealt with. Some of these issues are independent of economic growth. The most pressing of these is demography. Though population growth rates have slowed across the region, the demographic momentum of a young population will lead to overall increases in the range of 40 to 50 percent by 2060. India's population, for example, is expected to reach 1.5 billion by 2040. It can be argued that economic globalization is necessary to generate sufficient economic growth to handle the basic needs of this enormous population growth – but the population growth is more or less guaranteed; globalization and economic growth aren't.

Another emergent issue that is more directly tied to globalization is the problem of regional inequality. There is sufficient evidence and there are good explanations for the evidence that globalization is not space-neutral either between or within nations. Some places – usually coastal and metropolitan regions – are heavily favored. Hence economic globalization is associated with large increases in inequality between subnational regions inside globalizing nations. We have seen this in China, where a "hard" state can manage discontent more effectively than the "soft" states of South Asia. It is difficult to imagine that any of these nations can "manage" a situation where the leading regions are 10 times richer on average than the lagging ones, a situation India appears to be headed toward in the next two decades.

Challenges Ahead

Finally, let us return to the framework I set up at the beginning of this piece. If globalization is the thesis, what, if any, is the counterthesis? Should we assume that because there is consensus among the leadership of the economic powers of the world that globalization and trade are good and desirable and global governance institutions (IMF, WTO) are geared primarily toward the promotion of trade and globalization, there is no resistance, or that the resistance is so ineffective (students throwing coffee cups in Seattle) as to be laughable? Has history ended because the Soviet system collapsed and therefore there is no possible challenge to the prevailing order of markets and trade? Is this form of globalization "natural," inevitable, and unstoppable?

I have identified some of the challenges in the earlier sections: nonstate actors who are globalized themselves, violent subnationalism or ethnonationalism as an organizing principle for disaffected "others," demographic forces, regional inequality and other forms of inequality I have not been able to discuss. These are significant challenges, but primarily at the regional level. These are unlikely to challenge globalization in the nations that are most globalized and that therefore are the leaders of globalization – that is, the most developed nations of North America and Western Europe.

No, the fundamental challenge to globalization is embedded within its own ideology of market based, energy-intensive production, consumption and trade. That challenge is climate change. The economic model at the heart of globalization is based on productivity growth, which in turn is based on technological change and increasing energy use. It is now clear that this model has generated environmental externalities that have not been priced appropriately. Fossil fuels have been and continue to be overconsumed. If the challenge of climate change is to be met then the economic model we all take for granted will also have to change.

Let us remember that economic globalization is fundamentally caused by improved (energy-intensive) transportation and communication technologies. This is what has shrunk the globe and made more interactions and trade possible between distant places. Among the many things this has enabled is the transfer of polluting production processes from the First to the Third World. That has certainly improved the local environments in the First World, but, to the extent that global production has increased, global pollution has also increased.

The official position of South Asian nations is, to put it crudely, an assertion of a right to pollute. That may be understandable from the perspective of historic injustices and exploitations and the current standards of low average development. But if the Himalayan glaciers are truly melting, and if the river system that is the life source of the Subcontinent is endangered, if the ocean levels are truly rising and vast coastal regions are in danger of being inundated, it is difficult to see how long that official position can be maintained. (For a good brief discussion of the possible water-related problems associated with climate change see Schell 2010.)

Ultimately, however, the contours of climate change will not be determined by official policy in South Asia, but by some combination of technological change in energy production (the "magic bullet" that may not exist) and reduced energy consumption. And those changes will determine the contours of economic globalization, working, as now, through institutions of global governance. I believe those contours are going to be very different from what we take for granted today. In one scenario, the new "low-carbon" global system will be achieved through technological change; in a second scenario it will be achieved through large reductions in consumption; and in a third scenario it will not be achieved at all. Whichever scenario unfolds, I have little doubt that the counterthesis to today's model of globalization will have become the new thesis in 2060, and South Asia, for better or worse, will have to play by the rules of that new thesis.

Chapter 20

TRADE RELATIONS: SOME PREDICTIONS AND LESSONS

Pradeep S. Mehta and Niru Yadav

While home to about 20 percent of the world's population and 40 percent of the world's poor, South Asia accounts for only about 3 percent of both global gross domestic product (GDP) and total world trade. The states of the region have followed a long history of protectionism with inward looking polices that curtailed the region's economic growth as well as its trade flows, both within and outside the region. Unilateral liberalization initiatives started in the 1990s and worked towards accelerating growth – raising trade and investment flows in the region and as a result South Asia's growth rate over the last decade has exceeded the average in developing countries. Likewise, the region's export and import growth has been quite robust at 9.1 and 4.1 percent respectively in 2012 against 7.0 and 6.2 percent in developing countries (UNCTAD 2012).

At the outset, references to regional trade in South Asia need to account for the diversity and varied priorities of the different member states of the South Asian Association for Regional Cooperation (SAARC): India is a major emerging economy with substantial economic and political clout not only in South Asia but also in the world; Pakistan, Sri Lanka, Bhutan and Maldives are developing nations, while Afghanistan, Bangladesh and Nepal are least developed member states. Additionally, while Sri Lanka and the Maldives are small island states, Afghanistan, Bhutan and Nepal are landlocked nations. Evidence on trade complementarities among South Asian countries is rather mixed. Given that the members are on different rungs on the development ladder, their structural composition and trade baskets do not completely overlap. Exploiting this diversity and seeking complementarities in trading structures would be the key to increasing intraregional trade. Above all, addressing political challenges and nontariff barriers are crucial for increasing regional integration through trade.

This piece seeks to provide an overview on current trends in regional trade, identify major challenges to regional integration through trade and suggest possible ways forward. The first section of the paper looks at trade flow trends in South Asia, while the second section provides an overview of existing trade agreements. The third section discusses the challenges faced by the region in realizing higher trade flows and the possible way forward.

Trends in South Asian Trade

In 2011, the total trade of South Asian countries amounted to $928.17 billion, with only $28.23 billion exchanging hands through regional trade. This indicates that only less than 4 percent of South Asian trade is intraregional, making it one of the least integrated regional blocs in the world and contrasts the much higher levels of intraregional trade in East Asia (32 percent) and Southeast Asia (25 percent; ADB 2009). From 1975 to 2005, the exports to GDP ratio in South Asia rose from 5 to 13 percent, while the corresponding rise in East Asia was from 10 to 39 percent (World Bank 2007). Intraregional trade in South Asia as a proportion of total trade has increased from 3.3 percent from 1980–84 to 4.2 percent in 2008 with the corresponding movements in export shares going from 4.4 to 5.7 percent and import shares moving from 2.1 to 3.3 percent respectively. In absolute terms, regional exports rose from $556 million to $12.96 billion while regional imports rose from $523 million to $12.99 billion. Thus, while trade in the region has increased over time, it started from a very low base, as indicated in Table 1.

However, over the last decade, the share of intraregional trade in total trade has remained constant, with a rise in the corresponding export share from 4.3 percent in the time period from 1995–99 to 5.7 percent in 2008 and has been neutralized by a decrease in the import share from 4.0 percent to 3.3 percent. These depict shares in totals which have been experiencing decelerating growth: South Asian exports and imports grew at only 15.3 and 15.9 percent respectively in 2006–2008 as compared to 21.7 and 18.1 percent in 2000–2004 (see Table 1). This in turn implies a deceleration in the growth of South Asian intraregional trade as well.

South Asia's intraregional export orientation is higher than its import orientation, but in both cases the relative orientation is remarkably weak – the US, EU, China, UAE and Eastern Asia are major trading partners of South Asian countries. Since India accounts for about 80 percent of the region's output and trade, South Asia's trading patterns are largely reflective of Indian patterns. None of the South Asian countries feature among India's top trading partners, whereas India is a major importer from and exporter to all South Asian countries except Pakistan, maintaining a trade surplus with most of its South Asian neighbors. Over 60 percent of intraregional exports originate from India in contrast to the 16 percent of regional imports that the country takes in, showing India's important role in the supply, more so than demand, of regional trade (World Bank 2007a). This can be explained by India's higher and increasing competitiveness in manufacturing and agriculture vis-à-vis its South Asian neighbors, the much higher competitiveness of countries outside South Asia in producing items demanded by India for import, and finally the existence of noneconomic trade barriers in the region.

Table 1. Intraregional trade in South Asia

	1980–84	1985–89	1990–94	1995–99	2000–2004	2006–2008+	2011+
Exports to region ($ US mil.)	556	684	1,148	2,198	3,872	10,587	15,364
Imports from region ($ US mil.)	523	555	1,134	2,648	3,864	10,442	12,871
Growth of exports in region (%)	1.6	7.7	11.2	10.1	21.7	15.3	–
Growth of imports in region (%)	5.5	0.1	23.4	14.4	18.1	15.9	–
Share of region in region's exports to world (%)	4.4	3.8	3.6	4.3	5.0	5.7	4.2
Share of region in region's imports from world (%)	2.1	1.9	2.9	4.0	3.9	3.3	2.2
Share of total regional trade as % of region's world trade	3.3	2.9	3.2	4.2	4.4	4.2	3.25

Source: Figures from 1980–84 to 2000–2004 (Chaturvedi 2007, 5); + own calculations from ITC data for 2006–2008 and 2011. Last column provides data for the year 2011 only.

Even for South Asian countries other than India – Pakistan, Bangladesh and to a lesser extent Sri Lanka and Maldives – intraregional trade is not of great significance and is less than 30 percent of total country trade, though this is not true for the landlocked countries of the region – Afghanistan, Bhutan and Nepal. Additionally, the smaller countries are much more integrated into the region than the larger ones. Lastly, as hinted above, most of the intraregional trade in South Asia features India as a partner – a trend that is likely to continue. Given virtually stagnant intraregional trade shares as a percentage of total regional trade in the last three decades, projections imply that this share will still be less than 10 percent by 2060. Therefore, major export markets for the region will remain outside South Asia. In addition, based on current trends, the share of intraregional exports in the region's total exports will continue to be higher than intraregional imports as a percentage of total regional imports.

In terms of products, exports from the region are dominated by mineral fuels, oils and distillation products, textiles and apparel, pearls and precious stones, iron and steel, and cotton. Intraregional trade is also dominated by mineral fuels, oils and distillation products followed by cotton, cereals, iron and steel, and organic chemicals. Primary goods and low value added manufacturing products dominate trade flows in the region. Given that the region is relatively abundant in low-skilled labor, there is much potential for expansion of low-skilled labor-intensive industries based on the region's natural comparative advantage. A projected rise in the region's working age population along with a projected fall in the working age population of East Asia, particularly; China will further contribute to the region's relative factor abundance in the decades ahead. However, this natural comparative advantage can be productively utilized for trade expansion only if complementary support systems such as infrastructure development, flexible labor markets, upgrading of labor skills, removal of bureaucratic hurdles and necessary trade facilitation measures are implemented.

Critics have pointed out that South Asian countries may not be natural trading partners due to their limited complementarities, leading to a pessimistic outlook for future trading prospects within the region. The high volume of informal trade in South Asia indicates otherwise. Informal trade, according to some estimates, is more than that of formal trade, which negates the notion of limited trade complementarities. Informal trade flows mirror formal flows in the sense that much of these involve India as a partner. Major items of such trade are textiles, electronics, food items, automobile parts, spices, cosmetics and jewelry. The presence of high tariff and nontariff barriers, trade restricting regulations and significantly high border trading costs has perpetuated cross-border informal trade at the expense of formal trade.

Trade Agreements in Place

Initiatives for regional cooperation started with the formation of SAARC in 1985, which led to the establishment of SAARC Preferential Trading Arrangement (SAPTA) in 1995 for enhancing regional cooperation through trade. In order to deepen regional integration through increased trade flows, the South Asian Free Trade Agreement (SAFTA) came into force in 2006. SAFTA is confined only to trade in goods with quite restrictive modalities, such as lack of substantive tariff reduction offers, the exclusion of many items through negative lists, and long time frames for tariff liberalization. Indeed, the average applied agricultural tariff rate for trade within the SAARC region is 23.12 percent, as compared to 27.64 percent by SAARC countries towards non-SAARC countries. For nonagriculture, the corresponding figures are 12.14 percent versus 13.39 percent (Weerahewa 2009, 25). For both agriculture and nonagriculture, the preference for intraregional trade emanating from SAFTA through tariff differentials is small, showing that the agreement does not provide a significant impetus to intraregional trade.

Most of the goods appearing on SAFTA's negative list make their way across borders via informal channels. Slow progress in SAFTA has prompted many countries in the region to initiate and engage in bilateral free trade agreements, some of which are more liberal and progressive compared to SAFTA. The bilateral agreements in the region mostly feature India as a partner – for example the Indo–Sri Lanka Free Trade Agreement (ISFTA), Bhutan–India Free Trade Agreement, India–Afghanistan Preferential Trade Agreement, India–Bangladesh Bilateral Trade Agreement and India–Nepal Treaty of Trade. The only bilateral free trade agreement in the region to which India is not a party is that between Pakistan and Sri Lanka. Another disturbing trend is that Pakistan and India are not part of any subregional arrangement.

ISFTA is the most liberal trade agreement in the region as it includes service trade, an investment agreement, a shorter negative list and a shorter time frame for tariff liberalization. This agreement has facilitated a substantial rise in trade and investment flows between India and Sri Lanka with informal trade flows between these two countries also experiencing a drop as tariff levels in India declined. This illustrated that a similar substitution of formal trade for informal trade might take place with countries engaging in more liberal trade agreements in the region. The success of ISFTA should encourage the inclusion of service trade and investment issues in other bilateral trade agreements. However, other challenges facing intraregional trade pertain to high protectionism in the form of nontariff barriers and substantial impediments to trade facilitation.

The presence of overlapping free trade agreements not only has potential for the "spaghetti bowl" effect but also scope for trade diversion. A more desirable approach would be to strengthen and liberalize trade via SAFTA instead of multiple bilateral trade agreements However, with the proliferation of free trade agreements in recent years it is projected that nations from the region will be actively pursuing such agreements with countries from outside the region.

Major Challenges and the Way Forward

The region's historical orientation towards import substitution and inward looking policies has been reversed through unilateral, regional and multilateral trade liberalization channels. Traces of protectionism still remain, however, as evidenced by the rather restrictive trade agreements in place. Bilateral mistrust, conflict and lack of political will for cooperation at the regional level have been major obstacles to regional integration and trade.

One could argue that political conflicts are present among the Association of Southeast Asian Nations (ASEAN) members as well, yet their regional integration and trade has been driven by the private sector via the extensive vertical supply chain linkages. This bottom up approach has been complemented by liberalization, infrastructure investment and associated regulatory changes facilitated by respective governments in the ASEAN region. When market forces play a dominant role in driving regional integration, economic issues receive primacy, without allowing political differences to stand in the way. In order for this to happen, people-to-people and business-to-business contact is essential. Such connectivity and cross-border movements of people is relatively limited in South Asia, as reflected by the fact that only 7 percent of international phone calls of South Asia are regional in contrast to 71 percent for East Asia (World Bank 2007a, 1).

Trading across borders is one of the most costly businesses in South Asia. Hence, it is not surprising that cross-border informal trade is thriving in the region to get around the bureaucracy and cumbersome customs procedures. According to World Bank's *Doing Business 2010* report, South Asia ranks the lowest in terms of "trading across borders" as the number of documents required for export is the highest in the region. Indeed, improvements in trade facilitation measures are predicted to increase intraregional trade by about 60 percent in South Asia (World Bank 2007, 5). Though SAFTA includes trade facilitation measures such as paperless trading, a harmonization of standards, customs cooperation, document simplification and infrastructure improvement, these have not been adequately carried forward to be implemented on the ground. Unless trade facilitation measures are improved and other nontariff barriers addressed, regional integration through trade channels has limited scope.

One of the key trade facilitation measures that call for substantial improvement in South Asia is development of inland transport infrastructure. Transport infrastructure is essential in South Asia because most intraregional trade takes place via land routes through road corridors and the low quality of cross-border infrastructure has increased lead-times for exports. For example, the average time taken for an export transaction within South Asia is 32.4 days, roughly comparable to 33.6 days in Sub-Saharan Africa (World Bank 2009c). The absence of a fully-fledged regional transport and transit agreement for cross-border movement of goods and vehicles in South Asia is a major impediment to trade flows, for while provisions for transit facilities are covered in bilateral trade agreements, these transit policies lack harmonization (De et al. 2008). While revisions for transit facilities are covered in bilateral trade agreements; however, these transit policies lack harmonization.

Given the increasing share of South Asian GDPs coming from the service sectors, and the region's competence in the sector, an inclusion of services trade in regional trading agreements is likely to enhance welfare gains for the region and deepen regional integration. Doing so provides the capacity for changing South Asia's regional identity from a labor-intensive manufacturing region – particularly in textiles and apparel – into a thriving service-based region.

The power dynamics among countries in South Asia have been complex due to a legacy of political tensions among neighboring countries and South Asia's political problems have made regional economic integration difficult. While India is emerging as a leading power, countries such as Pakistan, Afghanistan and Nepal are mired in internal conflict, leading to rising inequality across different countries. In order for South Asia to strengthen its regional identity and grow as a region, it is necessary for all countries in the region to have political stability with a decent economic growth rate. The increasing inequality between nations in the region poses a threat to South Asia's regional identity as this divergence between countries will make it difficult to harmonize trade policies and facilitation measures, which could be a substantial setback to deepening regional integration. On the other hand, the fast growing Indian economy could play an important role in driving South Asia forward. The smaller South Asian members can capitalize on India's dynamic growth, however, it is essential for them to first strengthen their own supply capacities, improve infrastructure and remove the border impediments such that they are in a position to take advantage of the growing markets in the region.

In order to advance regional economic integration, South Asian member states have to act fast on achieving the targets of existing agreements on trade and commerce and frame new agreements under the SAARC framework. The short-run priority in this regard is to finish the establishment of free trade area envisaged under the SAFTA Agreement by 2020. This requires elimination of negative lists, allowing duty-free market access across all product categories and reduction of nontariff trade costs through appropriate regional trade policy reforms. In addition, South Asia should fast-track services trade negotiations under the South Asia Agreement on Trade in Services (SATIS) so as to achieve equally free and fair trade in services sectors as that of merchandise trade by 2020.

This would in turn pave the way for enactment of new regional agreements on trade-plus issues including IPR, competition, standards, public procurement, labor and capital mobility, etc. as well as establish regional institutions for technical cooperation, trade infrastructure and governance, helping the region to realize the goal of becoming a customs union by 2040 as well as to prepare for the next generation reforms for monetary and fiscal integration. Reaching these milestones will be crucial for the region's expectations for further broader cooperation in governance at both economic and political level in the post-2040 period. In this phase, more regional institutions with additional delegation of power, including a regional central bank and centralization of monetary policies with fiscal federalism, should be the cornerstones of an inbuilt agenda so to make South Asian Union a reality by 2060.

Conclusion

Over the last 50 years, South Asian countries have undergone substantial transformations and successfully integrated into the world economy. Regional dynamics have changed over time with an extraregional focus, while regional integration has not progressed successfully despite the presence of various institutional mechanisms. However, the damaging influences of internal conflicts in a number of South Asian countries, political mistrust between neighboring countries, and low connectivity amongst South Asian nationals on South Asia's regional integration as well as its identity as a region, have been found to be decreasing in recent times compared to the past. Regional integration in South Asia through trade largely hinges on how quickly and comprehensively trade barriers are reduced. The promotion of services trade and investment agreements will also be crucial in increasing intraregional trade. Above all, strong political will, increased business-to-business contact and a collective effort by all stakeholders will be essential for furthering trade and deepening regional integration in South Asia.

Chapter 21

URBAN POLICY FOR ENVIRONMENTAL QUALITY AND WELL-BEING

Madhav G. Badami and Murtaza Haider

Introduction: Population, Human Development and Environment

South Asia has made significant progress since independence from colonial rule in the late 1940s. In the face of dire predictions made in the 1960s and 1970s about food security, for example, cereal production has increased about threefold since that time (FAO 2003). Life expectancy has increased from a mere 39 years in 1950 to about 66 years, which is just three years below the global average (UN Population Division 2010). Despite these vast strides, significant challenges remain.

Seventy percent of the region's inhabitants live on less than $2, and about a third on less than $1.25, daily, on a purchasing power parity (PPP) basis (World Bank 2013). A fifth of South Asia's population is undernourished, and a third of its children below five years are underweight. South Asia performs worse than Sub-Saharan Africa in the latter respect, and accounts for more than half of the world's undernourished children. Mortality rates for infants below five years have reduced by over 40 percent relative to 1990, but are still considerably higher than the United Nations (UN) Millennium Development Goal (MDG) target for 2015. While the region has made considerable progress with regard to safe drinking water, it has the worst record with regard to sanitation. Sixty percent of its people lack access to even what the UN deems "improved," but hardly adequate, sanitation, with significant implications for the spread of various infectious diseases (United Nations 2012).

One in four people globally is a South Asian today, compared to one in five in 1950. South Asia's population, currently 1.6 billion, is expected not to stabilize before 2065, due in part to a low median age of 25 years, and a total fertility rate that, although considerably reduced from even 20 years ago, is a little under three children per woman. At that point, the region's population is expected to be around 2.4 billion. India is likely to overtake China as the world's most populous country, and is expected to have over 1.7 billion people, which is the current population of the region, and was the total global population in 1900. Meanwhile, Pakistan's population is expected to increase by 65 percent from its current population of 174 million (United Nations Population Division 2010). These population increases will undoubtedly severely test already stressed food and other natural and societal resources, and pose monumental challenges in sustaining progress toward poverty alleviation, nutrition and other development goals.

The hitherto impressive growth in cereal yields will likely be difficult to sustain. Besides, the area planted for cereals has plateaued since the 1980s (FAO 2003, 2013), due to soil degradation and conversion to nonagricultural uses. These effects are only worsened in a region in which a significant share of food production depends on irrigation, by rapid groundwater depletion, due to excessive withdrawals, and severely reduced river flows, as a result of diversions for power generation, industry and other sectors. The Indus, which irrigates 80 percent of Pakistan's agricultural land, is perhaps the most extreme example of this situation (Briscoe and Qamar 2005). Many of the region's major rivers, including the Indus, are fed by glaciers; the recent controversy regarding the Intergovernmental Panel on Climate Change (IPCC) predictions about glacial retreat notwithstanding, their loss, if and when it occurs, will likely have devastating consequences for food security and well-being in a region that will be home to a quarter of the world's population in 2065.

Rapid growth in energy consumption, coupled with inefficient energy conversion technologies and poor fuel quality is causing, among other impacts, some of the worst air pollution globally, resulting in respiratory illnesses that are one of South Asia's leading causes of death (WHO 2008). While the region accounts for a small share of global CO_2 emissions, despite its population and energy consumption growth, it accounts for a large share of global black carbon particulate emissions, which contribute to regional air pollution and climate change, whose effects include changes in rainfall, more intense droughts and crop yield reductions (Ramanathan et al. 2005). Climate change impacts will likely exacerbate water and agricultural resources in South Asia, where these resources are already stressed, nutritional deficiency and poverty levels are the highest, and the bulk of the prospective global population growth is likely to occur.

The Challenge of Rapid Urbanization

The last major trend in South Asia is rapid urbanization, which has important implications for poverty, food security, environmental quality, public health, and energy security. South Asia and Asia were merely 17 percent urban in 1950, when the corresponding rate in Western Europe and North America was 64 percent. Even now, the urban population accounts for only 33 percent in South Asia, as against 45 percent in Asia, and 80 percent in Western Europe and North America. However, urban growth has been occurring very rapidly in South Asia, with its urban population doubling every 20 or so years between 1950 and 2010 (United Nations Population Division 2011). Urban growth in the region has been driven by natural increase, as well as significant in-migration. These trends are due to rural poverty, fuelled by the declining state of rural agriculture, infrastructure and services, and the degradation of the natural resource base on which the poor depend for their survival, as well as the concentration of national investment, employment and other essential services such as education and health in cities, where the rural poor migrate to join the burgeoning ranks of the urban poor.

Urbanization in South Asia has been characterized by rapidly growing megacities. Whereas this region did not account for even one megacity in 1980, it did so for 5 (New Delhi, Dhaka, Karachi, Kolkata and Mumbai), out of a global total of 16, in 2000. Since 1980, these cities have been adding 200,000 to 400,000 people on average annually; and, excepting Kolkata, have more than doubled their population, with New Delhi and Dhaka quadrupling theirs, to 22 and 15 million respectively. All of these cities continue to grow, albeit at a slower rate. At the same time, the region has seven cities with populations of 5–10 million, and over 40 cities with populations of 1–5 million. The growth in these medium-sized cities is at least as rapid as in the regional megacities (United Nations Population Division 2011).

The rapid growth in the region's cities is causing high levels of environmental degradation, and associated health, welfare and socioeconomic impacts. Water pollution due to improper waste disposal, and highly inadequate sewage treatment, is perhaps the most widespread, and most serious, urban environmental and public health problem in the region. While access to "improved" sanitation in the cities is higher than in the rural areas, 40 percent of the urban population are not served in this regard (WHO and UNICEF 2010). Total coliform counts in major rivers are several orders of magnitude above acceptable levels in the vicinity of major cities. Due to water pollution, and excessive groundwater withdrawal, water supply is severely inadequate and unsafe. Air pollution levels are health threatening in many cities; for example, in New Delhi, the level of particulates below 10 microns diameter (PM_{10}), which are strongly linked with respiratory and cardiovascular illnesses and deaths, has exceeded World Health Organization (WHO) guideline limits almost daily for many years, at several sites (CPCB 2013). Poor air quality is responsible for pneumonia, tuberculosis and other respiratory infections, which account for the bulk of deaths due to infectious diseases, predominantly among children under five years. The other major cause of infant mortality is diarrhea, due to poor water quality and sanitation, coupled with inadequate and overcrowded housing, and poor waste disposal and drainage; these environmental offences also cause illnesses due to malaria, dengue and typhoid. In short, poor air and water quality, coupled with malnutrition, are responsible for millions of preventable mortalities and morbidities in the region (WHO 2008; United Nations 2012).

Superimposed on these unresolved "traditional" risks are modern risks, such as those due to industrial and motor vehicle activity. The release of methyl isocyanate at the Union Carbide plant in Bhopal in 1984, which resulted in thousands of deaths and illnesses, is an extreme example of the dangers of industrial activity in an urban area, but the region's cities are home to large numbers of poorly regulated industrial units, many of which handle hazardous materials, and pose serious health risks. Motor vehicle ownership and activity are growing, perhaps more rapidly in South (and East) Asia than elsewhere. In India, which accounts for over 80 percent of South Asia's motor vehicles, the fleet has been doubling every 6–7 years since 1980 (MORTH 2012). This trend is causing a wide range of serious impacts, even as it provides mobility to millions. Traffic congestion is increasing rapidly, causing significant time and productivity losses, and severely compromising accessibility, in particular for the majority, who do not own motor vehicles. Motor vehicle activity is an increasingly important contributor to urban air pollution. But of all its impacts, perhaps the most serious result from road traffic accidents. South Asia alone accounts for about a fifth of global road fatalities, with India vying with China for the world's worst road safety record (WHO 2009).

Because high pollution levels are imposed on very large populations in South Asian cities, significant exposures and health impacts result, which are exacerbated by high levels of poverty. Thirty-five percent of urban households in South Asia live in slums and squatter settlements; this proportion is higher only in Sub-Saharan Africa (United Nations 2012). The poor typically suffer the highest exposures to pollution and other hazards – they often live, without secure tenure, on the most vulnerable land, lack access to basic services such as water and sanitation and use poor-quality fuels. Further, because they are in marginal health, and lack adequate nutrition and medical care, they are also the most affected by, and least capable of coping with, the impacts of pollution. The synergistic effects of pollution, nutritional deficiency and inadequate healthcare increase the impacts of pollution, which further exacerbate poverty. Poverty and pollution thus feed on each other in a vicious circle.

Urban Policy and Planning – A Critical Need

The already massive urban population in South Asia continues to grow rapidly. In 2025, Dhaka, Karachi and Mumbai will join Delhi in having a population above 20 million; Delhi's population in that year – just over a decade from now – is projected to reach 33 million. Meanwhile, Bangalore, Chennai and Hyderabad (in India) and Lahore are expected to become megacities. Additionally, there are likely to be five cities with a population between 5 and 10 million (including Kabul in Afghanistan), and more than sixty cities with populations between 1 and 5 million. South Asia's urban population, which more than doubled in the last 30 years, is expected to double again in the next 30. By 2050, this population is expected to be around 1.2 billion, larger than the urban population of North America and Europe combined, and just a little under the total global population in 1900. Yet, only a little over 50 percent of South Asia's population will be urban then (United Nations Population Division 2011). Along with this massive urban growth, per capita consumption and activity levels, which have been low, are increasing, with profound implications for the already serious local environmental, health and welfare and socioeconomic impacts.

In the face of these trends, it is hard to see how the gains in urban water and sanitation, food security and poverty, and so on, can be sustained through to 2060 and beyond. In this regard, note that one of the important causes of the loss of cropland in the region is urban expansion, which is largely unregulated. Finally, the rapid urbanization (and rising per capita consumption) in South Asia, which has until recently accounted for a very small share of consumption of global resources and sinks, despite its population, will likely have serious consequences not only for local well-being, but also for global resource use and environmental impacts. For example, because of rapid motorization, transport energy consumption in the region could double by around 2030, with serious implications for energy security and climate change (IEA 2009).

It is for all of these reasons that rapid urbanization in South Asia, already a major challenge, will become even more so in the coming decades, and will need concerted policy attention. This is by no means to suggest that rural areas should be neglected; it is to a large extent rural neglect that has driven rapid urban growth (and environmental degradation) in the region. As importantly, poverty is increasingly concentrated in its urban areas; it is estimated that half of all poor households globally will be urban, mainly in South Asia. Further, just as poor environmental quality most affects the urban poor, and exacerbates their poverty, infrastructure and services to improve urban environmental quality can contribute significantly to poverty reduction and other development objectives. Lastly, while the concentration of human activity in cities causes serious environmental problems, these problems are easier to address, and services such as water and sanitation can be provided more cost effectively, in urban areas, because of economies of scale. Urban policy and planning in South Asia (as in other regions) will therefore be profoundly important, from the point of view of local well-being, as well as global impacts. The metropolitan centers are undoubtedly important, but particular attention needs to be paid to the medium-sized cities, in which a significant proportion of the urban population lives, and population growth is at least as rapid, the situation at least as serious, and resources are far more constrained.

While poverty alleviation ought to be a major focus, urban policy and planning in the region, far from being pro-poor, is at best indifferent to them, and at worst, is anti-poor. The poor are most affected by the lack of access to water and sanitation, for which they often have to pay exorbitant prices; meanwhile, these services are heavily subsidized for the wealthy. While urban transport policy increasingly accommodates, indeed promotes, motor vehicles, it not merely ignores but actively discriminates against the poor and the modes on which they depend. What facilities that do exist for the vast majority who have no choice but to walk and cycle are dismantled to make way for motor vehicles. While the poor benefit the least from motor vehicle activity, they are affected the most, in terms of loss of accessibility, and road traffic accidents, which kill pedestrians and cyclists disproportionately. Lastly, in the name of urban development and beautification, thousands of poor families have been evicted, and have suffered, with little or no compensation, loss of personal security, social networks, livelihoods and access to essential services. So, far from serving the needs of the poor, the poor are rendered, as a result of conscious policy, even more so (Badami 2009; Mahadevia 2006).

It is certainly the case that, while institutional, financial and administrative resources were highly inadequate even a couple of decades ago, demands on these resources have multiplied rapidly: London's population took 100 years to grow from 1 to 7 million, while New Delhi's and Dhaka's increased from about 0.7 to 13 million in a mere 40–50 years (United Nations Population Division 2011). While resource constraints are an important factor, this state of affairs is largely due to misplaced institutional and societal priorities; there is a general lack of concern for the poor among the middle classes, who are increasingly insulated from the worst of the urban deprivation and environmental degradation, even as they most contribute to it, because of their ability to purchase amenities and services such as quality education and healthcare, and motor vehicles and bottled water. This lack of concern is reflected, on the part of decision makers, in what in urban transport may be termed a "windshield view" – while those who do not walk and cycle have a say, those who do, have no say at all.

Urban Policy Priorities and Strategies in South Asia

So, the very first priority for urban policy and planning is to focus on the needs of the poor, and to work with them to find solutions to their problems. Relatedly, there is an important need, given the massive unfulfilled basic needs and highly constrained institutional resources, to prioritize action in those areas in which the largest gains in health and welfare may be achieved at relatively low cost and as quickly as possible (for example, clean water, sanitation and cleaner fuels and stoves to mitigate harmful indoor air pollution), even as efforts are made to provide services that are likely to involve greater outlays, and take more time. For the same reasons, there is also an important need for approaches that are problem avoiding; to the extent that technological solutions are used, they should be low cost, and capable of being easily operated and maintained, under local conditions, with local capacity, over the long term.

In the case of urban transport, for example, there is an important role for motor vehicles and infrastructure for them, but continuous road building is not only expensive, and compromises access for the majority who cannot afford motor vehicles, but an exercise in futility. Road building may ease congestion in the short term, but leads to ever more vehicle activity and congestion, and the need for even more roads. Given inadequate resources to accommodate even present levels of vehicle activity, and growing demands on those resources, the focus ought to be on minimizing motor vehicle activity and the need for it. In view of the high population densities and mixed land use, the low income and vehicle ownership levels, the fact that pedestrians and cyclists bear the brunt of road traffic fatalities and injuries, and the significant share of trips accounted for by these modes, accessibility, in particular for pedestrians, should be the foundation of urban transport policy and planning. This should be complemented by public transit that is reliable, convenient, affordable and widespread, pricing of road use that internalizes the social costs of urban transport and land use–transport integration. Making walking and cycling safer and easier would help reduce road traffic fatalities and injuries, contribute to congestion reduction, energy security, air quality and climate goals cost effectively, and reduce the need for road capacity addition and end-of-pipeline technological cures (Badami 2009).

While problem-avoiding solutions are to be preferred to technological-curative ones, given the realities of the context, many of the most serious problems facing

South Asian cities, such as the lack of clean water and sanitation, and the solid waste situation, do not predominantly depend on expensive technologies for their resolution; the most important barriers to progress are institutional (and sociocultural), not technological.

There are encouraging examples of initiatives, in which nongovernmental organizations (NGOs), with support from local governments, have provided water and sanitation services at low cost. In the western Indian city of Pune, community toilets that benefit several hundred thousand people have been built thanks to such partnerships; the city covered the capital costs, the NGOs designed the toilets in consultation with local communities, who in many instances constructed them; the communities manage maintenance, for which families are charged affordable fees. These efforts are based on the recognition that, while private toilets in each home would be preferable, they are often infeasible, given the difficulty, in high-density environments, of building and connecting them to sewer systems, where they exist, and the high costs of waste disposal, where they do not. In Pakistan, the Orangi Pilot Project's Research and Training Institute (OPP–RTI) has developed an innovative "internal-external" model for providing sanitation services in about three hundred informal settlements in Karachi and elsewhere. OPP–RTI has trained local communities to finance, plan, build and manage private sanitary latrines and connections to neighborhood collector sewers, and supports local governments in financing the "external" trunk sewers and treatment plants (Burra, Patel and Kerr 2003; Hasan 2008).

Because these initiatives are community driven, they allow for greater local control, they are better designed and built, and are more durable; and because they are low cost, they are more affordable, accessible to many more people and enable governments to focus on providing the "external" components that communities cannot, and on expanding coverage. Further, these community initiatives engender self-confidence, dignity and self-respect; help create local community skills and employment; and positively affect relationships within and between communities, and with local governments (Hasan, Patel and Satterthwaite 2006).

While community organizations and NGOs can provide local water points, shared toilets and community sewers, only governments can provide trunk sewer systems, water and sewage treatment plants, and other infrastructure and services, especially in the periphery, where the costs of provision are high. Besides, the ability of the poor to pay for services is very low, as a result of which there is little incentive for the private sector to make the large investments that are required. Land use and transport planning, which require coordination of multiple functions and sectors on a regional basis, can be done only by governments. Lastly, for water and sanitation, and transit, public regulation is essential, to ensure that these services are delivered with equity and justice. So, while there is much that community groups and NGOs can do, and have done, to effect positive change in individual communities, only governments can and must do so at the metropolitan and regional scales.

But the problem, as noted, is a severe lack of institutional resources in the face of massive, and rapidly growing, unfulfilled basic needs. Given the serious challenges of urbanization, local governments, in addition to being pro-poor, need to be empowered to have a large measure of fiscal and decision-making autonomy – to generate local tax revenues, and to develop and implement plans to provide local infrastructure and services. While legislative measures have been adopted to provide constitutional protections to local governments, and to devolve fiscal and decision-making powers to them, much remains to be done to make these powers a reality.

As for the viability of municipal finances, urban land markets need to be more effectively regulated, and the collection of property taxes made more rational and comprehensive. The costs of service delivery need to be recovered more effectively, from those able to pay, in order to expand coverage, and ensure affordable access for low-income users. Note that, while private development, which is occurring rapidly and haphazardly, especially in the periphery, places considerable demands on public utilities, the ability of municipal agencies to collect development charges is weak, further compromising their financial position and their ability to control land use. For the same reasons, subsidies need to be reduced and more carefully targeted; subsidies mainly benefit the better-off, and hurt the poor, since they hamper the ability to expand coverage to them. In urban transport, reducing fuel subsidies, and implementing parking control and pricing, would help curb motor vehicle use, reduce congestion, improve accessibility for low-income road users and the modes on which they rely, and make mass transit more effective and serve as a means of funding it. Innovative loan financing and repayment schemes need to be developed and implemented for the provision of services to the poor (Alm 2010; Roberts and Kanaley 2006).

In order to relieve the severely stressed situation in the metropolitan centers, while also rejuvenating small and medium cities, it is important to promote the development of regional centers, by shifting further urban growth to them. Efforts to this end need to be supported by policies to provide adequate levels of essential services such as water, sanitation, health and education in these centers, and to develop and empower metropolitan and regional planning bodies to take on functions such as industrial development, and land use and transport planning, on a regional basis (Government of Karnataka 2009). Also, over the coming decades policies need to be implemented to reduce vulnerability to climate change, which will likely, among other things, increase the incidence and intensity of extreme weather events such as droughts, tropical cyclones, and extreme rainfall (as in the case of Pakistan in 2010), and exacerbate pressures on already stressed urban infrastructure and systems due to flooding as a result of sea-level rise, and saline intrusion into ground water.

The urbanization challenge in South Asia is truly one of epic proportions – its urban population, already about 500 million, is expected to more than double, to around 1.2 billion by 2050, as noted. While this will be the largest concentration of urban dwellers of any region in the world, along with that in China and other East Asian countries, South Asia will still be urbanizing, with only a little over 50 percent of its population in cities at that point (United Nations Population Division 2011). The provision of infrastructure and services is essential, to merely fill the massive gap between supply and current demand, let alone future growth, and to achieve objectives such as improved urban environmental quality, health and well-being, regional development and reduced vulnerability to climate change. While achieving this task in an efficient, ecologically sustainable and equitable fashion over the coming decades will be a major policy challenge, urban policy and planning in the region should also, very importantly, focus on filling the shortfall in institutional capacity in a wide range of areas, which if anything is even greater than the gap in infrastructure and services, and will likely take a long time to do.

There is an urgent need to build local capacities for data collection and analysis (on land use, for example), and policy development and implementation; systems and mechanisms for sound, transparent and accountable management; genuine citizen participation and effective coordination across a wide range of sectors and functions. Lastly, there is an urgent need to educate new generations of planners and other professionals to meet the massive urban challenges in the coming decades.

Chapter 22

URBAN FUTURES, URBAN CHALLENGES

Syed Abu Hasnath

The Study of Urbanization

The beginning of the second half of the twentieth century witnessed – among other things – three spectacular developments in Asia's sociopolitical transition: the birth of new nations, population explosion and rapid urbanization. They are related to one another and point the way to a foreseeable future of urbanization. In the following decades, the period also witnessed a notable resurgence of academic interest in population and urbanization in South Asia, which continually redefined the public interest. Initiated by Bert Hoselitz, the study of urbanization in relation to economic development emphasized the role of cities in mobilizing manpower and material resources for industrialization. The urban view of economic development was gaining ground in the 1960s along with the negative hypotheses of *overurbanization* and *urban bias* in Third World development; the combination of the two processes generates slow and inequitable growth in developing countries. The large and growing urban population was disproportionately employed in the service sector relative to the manufacturing sector, characterizing urbanization in South Asia. This pattern was in contrast to the development "at comparable levels of urbanization," which accompanied structural transformation in rich industrialized countries. Since economic growth is associated with the reallocation of labor and capital away from the traditional, low-wage rural sector to modern, high-wage urban sector, the city becomes the locus of economic power. The spatial transformation of man, material and capital – which gives rise to urbanization – contributes to a higher rate of economic growth because households and firms benefit from agglomeration economies of scale through network, civic facilities, information, mobility and specialization in given locations of cities and their surroundings. With above in mind, the following pages are devoted to examine the present state and future prospects of urbanization in South Asia.

Urbanization in South Asia: Levels, Trends and Patterns

South Asia consists of eight countries: Afghanistan, Bangladesh, Bhutan, India, Maldives, Nepal, Pakistan and Sri Lanka. There are demographic, geographic and socioeconomic diversities in the region. Within South Asia lies one of the world's largest countries, India, and two of the world's smallest countries, Bhutan and Maldives. The second largest country in the region, in terms of population size, is Pakistan, followed by Bangladesh. Three other countries of the region – Afghanistan, Nepal and Sri Lanka – have a medium-sized population (between 20 million and 30 million). The region dominated by the Indian subcontinent, which is home to a fifth of mankind, is comprised of India, Pakistan and Bangladesh. South Asia as a whole – and individual countries of the Subcontinent – is characterized by a slow pace of economic growth and a low level of urbanization. Both are likely to be dynamic if urban and rural productivities are enhanced simultaneously. In the last two decades, India's economic growth has been highest in the world after China.

In 1950 only 16 percent of the total population of South Asia was living in urban areas; the comparable figures for the world and more developed countries were 30 percent and 60 percent, respectively. By 1970 and 1990 the urban population of South Asia had risen to 20 percent and 25 percent respectively (Figure 1). The current level (2010) of urbanization, 34 percent, is not high by global standards, but the rate of urban growth is substantially fed by high rates of natural population growth and through a higher rate of rural to urban migration. The level of urbanization will reach an estimated 42 percent and 52 percent in 2030 and 2050, respectively. The neighboring countries of Southeast Asia have already reached the milestone of 50 percent level of urban growth. In developed countries the level of urbanization reached the 50 percent mark more than half a century ago. The aggregate level of urbanization also disguises a variation in the level of urbanization across South Asia, ranging from only around 18 percent in Nepal to 30 percent in India, and 37 percent in Pakistan in 2010. This begs the question as to why South Asia continues to remain less urbanized compared to its neighboring region of Southeast Asia, and within South Asia why there is so much of difference between Pakistan and Nepal. A short answer would be that, for 30 years (1965–95) the seven Southeast and East Asian countries, including the "Four Tigers" – Hong Kong, South Korea, Singapore and Taiwan – and three newly industrialized countries (NICs), Indonesia, Malaysia and Thailand grew faster than all other regions of the world. So was the case with Pakistan, which grew economically faster, and has been more advanced, than Nepal. Looking into the future of urbanization in South Asia, what we get from a projection of conservative estimates is that about 52 percent level of urbanization in 2050 which means an estimated 1.2 billion people will be living in urban areas of South Asia. The number is equivalent to the total population of Europe, the USA, Canada, Australia and Brazil combined, while the total area of South Asia is only 60 percent of Brazil. In all probability, the pace of urbanization will continue to accelerate in the remainder of the century; the level of urbanization will touch 80 percent by the 2080s. The pace of urbanization will, however, depend on the net result of demographic transition, rural–urban migration and areal reclassification. An important dimension of this growth is a bias towards large cities, growing faster than other size classes of towns. Some of them will become megacities with populations in excess of 5 million where there is growing interaction

Figure 1. Level of urbanization in South Asia and its share of employment in agriculture

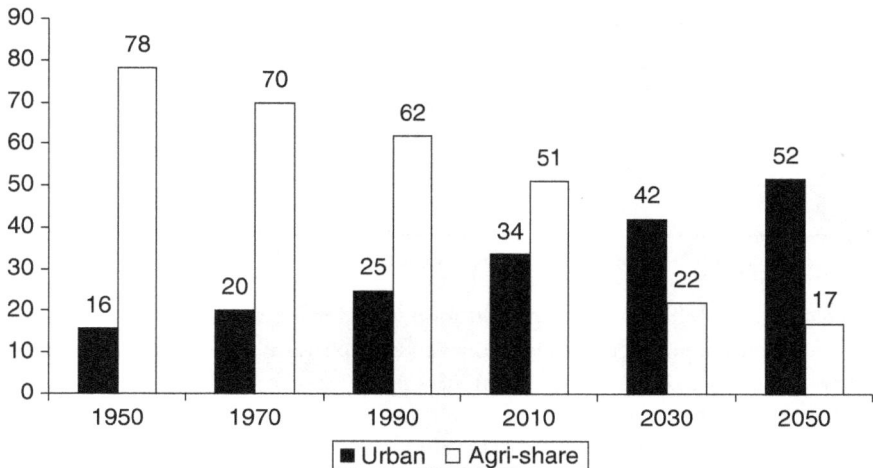

Source: CIA, *The World Factbook* (various years); UN, Economic Survey of Asia and Far East (various years); World Bank (2009).

between urbanization and globalization. Examples are: Dhaka, New Delhi, Mumbai, Kolkata, Chennai, Bangalore, Hyderabad (India), Karachi and Lahore.

Megacities have an important role in spearheading economic growth and social transformation as well as rendering many of the worst symptoms of underdevelopment which includes slums, congestion, pollution and crime. Currently, South Asia has nine megacities, housing 113 million people; in 2050 their population is projected to reach around 214 million, while many more large cities in South Asia are expected to reach the level of megacities at that time. Whether this unprecedented growth of urban agglomeration – along with the integration of the South Asian economy into the global economic system – has contributed to economic progress or given economic power and ownership to few is an ongoing debate. The fact remains: South Asia today is not only more urbanized but obviously richer than 50 years ago.

Economic Structural Change: Theory and Evidence

The underlying explanation for urbanization, in addition to population increase due to natural increase and migration, involves consequences of economic and technological change. Economic growth brings about complementary changes in the sector composition of output and employment. In an effort to grow faster, the economy moves from low-value-added agriculture to high-value-added manufacturing to higher-value-added services. The proposition of structural change includes two types of transformation: (a) industry and service share of national income increases, followed by (b) the higher share of employment in those sectors. The combination of the two contributes disproportionately highly to the nonagricultural sector productivity, and to the agriculture sector modestly. Two other positive effects of this process are

Table 1. Economic structure of South Asia by sectoral composition and employment share in GDP: 1970, 1990 and 2010

	GDP composition			Employment share		
	1970	1990	2010	1970	1990	2010
Agriculture	46	35	18	70	62	51
Industry	20	30	20	10	13	14
Service	34	35	62	20	25	35

Source: UN, Economic Survey of Asia and the Far East (various years).

(a) agglomeration effects – the concentration of enterprises in a locale – making the urban sector more productive, and (b) the demand for more skilled and knowledgeable workers. Another side effect of this process is the growing opportunities of gainful female employment in service sectors, including education, healthcare and information. The negative side of the process is that there is a gap between output growths and job creation; the situation is loosely defined as structural unemployment. This aspect of South Asia's economic structural change and urbanization is discussed next.

A review of two sets of data – economic structure of South Asia by sector composition and by employment share in gross domestic product (GDP) (Table 1) highlights a number of facts:

- The share of agriculture to GDP has fallen steadily from 46 percent in 1970 to 35 percent in 1990 and plunged further to 18 percent in 2010. The employment share in agriculture declined from 70 percent in 1970 to 51 percent in 2010, and is estimated to be around 17 percent in 2050. At the same time the yield per acre of all crops have been doubled and food crop close to tripled since the 1950s. This has been made possible by the introduction of the Green Revolution and other policies, including subsidies, pursued in the agriculture sector.
- In South Asia the growth of industries has been modest despite the region's immense potentialities in terms of low-wage and large market. With economic liberalization, the situation has considerably improved in India during the last two decades, moving from low-value-added textiles and garments to high-value-added steel, automobiles, pharmaceuticals and software industries. Nevertheless, the relative share of industries in South Asia has remained stationary. The industrial share of output in 1970 was about 20 percent, it rose to 30 percent in 1990 and then dropped to 20 percent in 2010, although the rate of absolute growth during the last four decades was around 6 percent. The share of employment in the industrial sector remained between 13 percent and 14 percent for the last two decades. The share of employment in industries for individual countries, including Bangladesh, Pakistan and Sri Lanka ranges between 20 percent and 30 percent, though their products constitute mostly low-value-added textiles and garments.
- Meanwhile, the share of service sector in South Asia's GDP has increased from 34 percent in 1970 to well above 60 percent in 2010. While the service sector's employment

share has grown at a less accelerated pace, it accounts for about 35 percent of national employment. Whether this leapfrogging over industrial sector, going straight from agriculture into services is equally effective – or significantly more or less effective – is a complex question. The empirical work of Ghani and Kharas (2009) shows that (a) there is a positive relation between services and overall growth, and between manufacturing and overall growth; and (b) comparing two sets of results, it is clear that the *slope is steeper* in the first set of relations. This means the service sector has a higher contribution to overall growth than the manufacturing sector. This may be good news for South Asia.

Issues of Urbanization, Development and Environment

The consequences of structural changes in South Asia can be described through dualism, the model of rural–urban labor transfer (first developed by Lewis and latter extended by Fei-Ranis). *Dualism* represents the chronic coexistence of two increasing divergence – superior and inferior – in a given situation that "push to develop its underdevelopment." Examples are the coexistence of traditional subsistence agriculture and modern commercial farming in rural areas, as well as formal sector organized economy and informal sector unorganized indigenous economy in urban areas. Below are two sets of selected issues that emanate from rural–urban migration to dualistic urban development in South Asia.

The first set of issues is *uneven development, urban sprawl and depletion of land and waterbodies.* Recent decades have witnessed substantial growth of industries and the dramatic rise of the service sector in South Asia. In 2010 the two sectors combined contributed more than 80 percent to GDP and close to 50 percent in employment; clearly, the GDP share is large, however, employment opportunity is, at best, modest. The condition is described as jobless economic growth. Within the service sector, nearly 40 percent of labor force is engaged in informal activities; they eke out a meager subsistence. There are also low-paid industrial workers such as garment girls, and underpaid office workers such as night guards who are formal sector employees but hardworking, poor people living in slums and squatters. They are the outflow of the rural poor who are landless, unemployed and often displaced by environmental disasters. The outcome of this endless stream of rural-to-urban migration is recognized as "urbanization of poverty," meaning the locus of poverty is moving from rural areas to cities. The UN Habitat Global Report 2003 gives the following explanation of this issue: Slums and squatters are linked to economic phases of urbanization, trends in national income distribution and to national economic development policies. The nature of structural change in the process of development demands more educated and skilled labor than unskilled rural labor and the negative effects of globalization – that ratchet up inequality and distribute new wealth unevenly – contribute to enormous growth of slums under the shadow of apartment complexes. The high-rise and slums are the juxtaposition of the formal–informal dichotomy in urban geographic space.

The accelerating pace of urbanization is also creating enormous pressure on agricultural land, which is already in short supply. Each year between 0.5 percent and 1 percent of cultivable land and waterbodies are being used for urban development.

If the situation is left unabated, the Bangladesh Bureau of Statistics reports that, by 2070, there will be no land available for agriculture in Bangladesh, which is an alarming scenario, indeed. The cities are spreading outward with negative connotation of urban sprawl to make room for industries (including brickfield), housing estates and peri-urban settlement. In the absence of well-thought-out urban plans and effective control of land use, the urban land and waterbodies have become developers' empire.

The second set of issues are *dysfunctional urbanization and environmental degradation*: While urbanization brings a unique set of growth advantages, including large-scale production of goods and services with higher productivity due to a structural change in the economy, the impacts of urbanization on physical environment and social polarization are seriously negative; therefore, the process of urbanization is unsustainable. The combined effects of the two opposite forces may be defined as dysfunctional urbanization. There exists a substantial gap between urban growth and urban development. That means there is growth of urban population, area, functions and wealth on the one hand, and the progressive decline of the distribution of wealth, opportunities and environment on the other. The gap has been increasing. It is hardly necessary to elaborate on issues of urban demand for housing, electricity, water, sanitation, health, education and clean environment. The demand will be double (or triple) by the middle of this century, as well as the rich–poor gap; the pollution will, however, clog the lungs of millionaires and their maids alike.

Future Prospects of Urbanization in South Asia

By 2050, over 1.3 billion people will live in South Asia's urban areas and the process of urbanization will be far from over. The way urbanization unfolds in coming decades will have profound implications for economic growth of metropolis, and sustainable urban environment. The growth will be accompanied by exploding demand for jobs, housing and infrastructure facilities, which are already short in supply with poor efficiency. The welfare of this billion plus people depends on how South Asia prepares for this inevitable growth.

There can be two ways of looking at the future: optimistic and pessimistic. The optimistic prediction is based on the favored view of *possibilism*, which believes that humans rather than the physical environment determine the development or underdevelopment of a nation; that human ingenuity can overcome the physical constraints. The pessimistic view suggests that physical environment is the dominant force in shaping the present and future of a nation's development, including urban and regional development. A middle ground between the two views may be more realistic, though surrendering to physical constraints cannot be an option. South Asia must:

- Constantly strive for excellence in the realm of technological innovation.
- Stress to discover and harness new resources, including energy from renewable and nonrenewable sources.
- Provide faster means of transportation and communication.

- Chart a rational course of energy use, abetting pollution (carbon, particulates and sulfur).
- Ensure good metropolitan governance for new and better ways of urban living.
- Keep the relationship between growth and distribution fair, economic growth and environmental goals balanced, and development and urbanization stable.

Using evidence-based arguments, Martine et al. (2007) provides a useful but challenging way to look for the new global frontier of urbanization, poverty and environment in the twenty-first century's developing world. Their key arguments include:

- The changing face of urban demography is a prime factor of poverty reduction, by presenting new options for youth and female employment.
- The scale of urban poverty depends on urban policy and development strategies. Poverty and inequality are quintessentially an issue of social justice, not of urbanization.
- Urbanization is not – by itself – bad for the environment. Bad development investments, accompanied by weak municipal governance, pose a major environmental challenge.

Billy Cobbett, a sustainable development expert, wrote the following words in praise of Martine's work: "well-managed urban growth has the potential to provide more solutions than problems" (see the 2010 reprint edition of Martine et al. 2008). In order to realize that potential, the following policy pointers may be considered a priority in a broader framework of future urbanization and development:

- *State capitalism and development pragmatism*: Given the limitations of availability of land for future urban and industrial development, the use of national land and waterbodies should be under almost total control of the state; it will direct the land use in the interest of the state. In this system, an individual owner of a piece of land – or a real-estate developer – is not the sole authority of determining the use of their land; although the private participation and their partnership with the government – along with the stakeholders – will be encouraged to augment limited public resources. This is in a sense, a functional master plan for the nation's whole geography – not part of it, urban or rural.
- *Metropolitan growth and secondary cities development*: From the above discussion, it is clear that the urban sector is more productive than the rural sector and the per capita GDP of metropolitan population is much higher – and growing faster – than the national average. It is also acknowledged that the metropolitan cities are experiencing worse problems with living environment than secondary cities and small towns. An alternative strategy of urban development may be the planned urbanization of secondary cities. They can counter primacy and produce a more balanced pattern of urban development. Studies suggest secondary cities can provide enough economies of scale, scope of employment in formal and informal sectors, and intervening opportunities for migrants by reducing attractiveness of long distance metropolis

(Rondinellie 1986). The secondary cities are by definition, not generative and developmental; they require an elaborate planning, municipal fund and appropriate policies for development. For metropolises, the basic requirements are: a large amount of investment, strict zoning regulations and political commitment.

- *Compact small towns*: The spatial pattern of urbanization in South Asia is dominated by large cities although small towns have the potential to assist in reducing migration to large cities and support growth of surrounding rural areas. With regard to Bangladesh, Rashid (2000) has developed the novel idea of developing compact townships (CT) to replace the existing, scattered villages with integrated settlements. CT is "an agglomeration of houses, hospitals, schools, markets, retail industries and local governmental units that provide all basic services to a population of 20,000. It is to be largely self-governing and self-financing." The compact township proposes an innovative way to solve manifold problems arising from fast population growth, adverse man–land ratio, unplanned rural–urban migration and riotous growth of metropolitan cities. The model can be implemented in Bangladesh and replicated in other countries of South Asia.

Conclusion

The future of South Asia's urbanization is bound with the nature of structural change and the level of prosperity that it will bring about in the respective countries. Several indicators of economic growth (such as output, income, trade and investment) and of social development (such as the alleviation of poverty, decline of infant mortality, higher rate of literacy and access to clean water and sanitation) appear to be positive and significant but not spectacular. South Asia accounts for nearly 25 percent of the world population – with no indications of a possible decline in the horizon – while the total share in global GDP is slightly higher than 2.5 percent; approximately 700 million people of this region live on less than \$2 a day. From an urban environmental perspective, the possibilities for sustainable urban growth due to the acute lack of economic prosperity for the greater population of this region would seem to be highly limited. Yet over the past five years, the level of pollution in Chennai, Colombo, Dhaka, New Delhi, Karachi, Kolkata and Mumbai has declined due to the conversion of all commercial vehicles from diesel to compressed natural gas (CNG), which produces lower amount of CO_2. Less pollution may be only half the battle; traffic congestion and increasing jam due to inadequate road and infrastructure facilities in South Asian metropolises is the other half of the battle yet to be won. Nevertheless, despite resource constraints, governance failure, housing and infrastructure deficiencies, and social tension, development has been taking place with the benefits of greater political democracy, public sector reform and an emerging sociopolitically powerful civil society in South Asia. Its economy appears to be more dynamic, prosperous, resilient and productive than 20 years ago. Therefore, South Asia's long-term economic prospect in urban areas appears promising. It is, however, important to remain cautious and acknowledge the limitations it faces.

Chapter 23

WATER SECURITY: RISKS AND RESPONSES

John Briscoe

Water and History in South Asia

Human civilization in South Asia is inextricably intertwined with water. It was along the banks of the great rivers that civilization developed, with this relationship enshrined in religious and cultural traditions and values. The development of contemporary South Asian economies, too, is deeply linked to water. Over the last 150 years massive investments were made to reduce the natural rhythms of rivers to better serve people's needs for food, water and safety from floods. The rewards from these investments is clear – in the massive growth of food supply, in the high correlation between irrigation and wealth, and in the production of cheap, clean hydropower. And as in ancient times, those who built such infrastructure have often been elevated by common people to the ranks of saints. Consider just one of many examples. Understanding that the barrage in the lower Krishna River transformed coastal areas of the state of Andhra Pradesh in India from a poverty-wrecked past to a prosperous agricultural present, people in this area have transformed Arthur Cotton, the builder of the barrage, into a saint, worshipped at countless shrines in the delta.

But the history of man's relationship with water – everywhere – shows that progress is never linear, and never static. In the words of Harvard historian David Blackbourn in his book *The Conquest of Nature* on water management and the state in Germany: "you find that each set of proposed new measures promises to turn the trick and finally overcome the ignorance, or engineering mistakes, or political constraints of earlier generations" and yet the overwhelming reality is that "the state of the art [of water management] is always provisional."

Consider just one of the many examples of this dialectic in South Asia: that of development in the Indus Basin.

Early Investments in a Platform of Water Infrastructure

In the mid-1800s the population in the Indus Basin was sparse. Present-day Punjab was a land of low-density pastoral farming; much of Sindh was sparsely populated because the Indus changed its course so frequently. The British saw potential – in the good land, abundant sunshine and abundant water resources. And so they built what is today the world's largest contiguous irrigation system, covering an area of over 20 million hectares. This required new infrastructure (the low barrages on the rivers, which diverted water into the vast network of canals), new institutions (the *warabandi* system, which gave farmers defined periods of irrigation water every seven days and the associated irrigation bureaucracy) and new social capital (including the "canal colonies" where migrant agriculturalists were settled). The system started in the north, extending only over time into the southern province of Sindh. In her autobiography, former Pakistani prime minister Benazir Bhutto (whose family home is in Larkana, near the Indus in Sindh) describes her grandfather's role in the construction of the Sukkur Barrage in Sindh in 1935, and how this transformed Sindh from a land so poor that it was part of the Bombay Presidency into a separate province by the revenue-sensitive British Raj.

In terms of the dialectic of water management, this intervention was a massive success, leading to large increases in food production and building the platform for the economy of a much-larger population in a once-largely empty land. But "water management is always provisional" and this success gave rise to a new set of challenges.

Challenges and Responses

A first derivative challenge was to find a formula for sharing what was now understood to be a very valuable resource. This meant sharing water within the Indus Valley between Punjab, the upper riparian, and Sindh, the lower riparian. And after 1947 it meant devising a water-sharing agreement between upper riparian India and lower-riparian Pakistan. This required human ingenuity in both the engineering and diplomatic realms. In terms of engineering, Pakistan had to chart unknown technical territory in building the then-largest earth and rockfill dam in the world at Tarbela. In terms of diplomacy, solutions (albeit "provisional" ones which face ongoing implementation and adaptation challenges) were found to the contentious issues of water sharing.

A second derivative challenge was a consequence of the technology – unlined canals – that had been adopted to distribute water in the basin. The vast network of unlined canals leaked, slowly filling the interstices of the alluvium in the Indus Valley. By the middle of the twentieth century the water table had risen to the surface of the ground in many places. Water always contains dissolved salts, sometimes, as in large parts of the Indus Basin, which were once covered by the sea, at high levels. When the water ponds on the surface, two bad things happen. First, most plants will not grow when their roots are in saturated soil. And second, the evaporating water leaves salt behind, forming a hard saline crust, which, too, seriously inhibits plant growth. This is why, by the middle of the twentieth century, large parts of the most fertile lands of Pakistan were being lost due to waterlogging and salinity. This constituted an existential threat to irrigated agriculture and to Pakistan as a country. Human ingenuity (and some good luck), however, came to the rescue once again. The ingenuity meant understanding that the "obvious" solution – "lining the leaky canals" – would be counterproductive, and that the solution involved more intensive use of groundwater by intensifying irrigation, in the process flushing salts out of the root zone, and drawing down the water table. A practical limitation was that the standard surface-mounted suction pump could not lift water by more than about seven meters. But good luck intervened in that around 1960 a simple but game-changing technology – the submersible pump – became widely available at a low cost. This meant that water could be pumped much more efficiently from substantial depths. These modest machines were, furthermore, exactly what was needed when the new generation of Green Revolution crops emerged a decade later, for farmers could use their tubewells to provide far more precise irrigation. Not only have these tubewells underpinned the massive increases in food production throughout South Asia – as much in Bangladesh and India as in Pakistan – over the last 40 years, but they have also meant a lowering of the groundwater and a dramatic reduction in the once-seemingly-insurmountable problem of waterlogging and salinity.

But, again, all water solutions are provisional, and now these granaries of South Asia – the Punjab in Pakistan, Haryana, Punjab and Maharashtra in India, and most of northwestern Bangladesh – are facing the problem of rapidly falling groundwater. Part of the current great challenge is to devise technical and institutional solutions to bringing abstraction of groundwater into balance with demand (that originates primarily from irrigation but also from rapidly growing cities and industry). Here are some promising signs of innovation, such as Gujarat's innovative program, which supplements groundwater recharge both through small and large-scale systems, and which simultaneously improves the quality of electricity supply for irrigation pumping and caps the number of hours that farmers can pump. Experiences in other parts of the world show that once farmers have incentives to use water efficiently and to reallocate water in times of scarcity, the results can be astonishing. The experience of the Murray–Darling Basin during a severe decade-long drought has shown that it is possible to have only very small economic impacts from 70 percent reductions in water availability.

In the area of major water infrastructure, as described earlier, Pakistan showed remarkable ingenuity and resilience in building the major infrastructure which was essential for the functioning of the Indus Waters Treaty. This was needed because the treaty allocated the waters of the eastern tributaries of the Indus (the Ravi, Beas and Sutlej) to India, leaving major irrigated lands in Pakistani Punjab cut off from their natural water sources. This meant that large-scale storage dams had to be built on two of the three rivers which were allocated to Pakistan – the Jhelum and the Indus itself – and massive "link canals," hundreds of meters wide, crossing on bridges over dry riverbeds had to transport water from the west to the east. In the 1960s it was well understood that Pakistan needed to build a new major dam about every decade in order to compensate for the buildup of silt and to give greater flexibility in meeting the competing needs of irrigation, hydropower and flood control. In part due to internal governance shortcomings and in part due to undue political correctness on behalf of Pakistan's bilateral and multilateral supporters, no new storage has been built in the past 40 years. This means that there is a capacity to store only 30 days of average flow on the Indus – compared to the 1,000 days which the United States can store on the Colorado River or Australia on the Murray–Darling River. This systematic underinvestment means that there is very little flexibility in the Pakistani system, and that the provision of always-needed irrigation and electricity take precedence over the not-as-common floods. The costs of living by this infrastructural shoestring (and the what-might-be alternative) are starkly illustrated by a comparison between the Yangtze and Indus floods of 2010. Infrastructure-rich China can afford to greatly reduce power production from the 20,000 mw installed at Three Gorges Dam during the flood season. The operating rule for Three Gorges is strict – priority is given to drawing down the reservoir in anticipation of the annual flood. This is exactly what was done in 2010. Inflows into Three Gorges were a record 70,000 cubic meters per second. But the drawn-down reservoir was, as designed, able to attenuate this shock, with releases never exceeding 40,000 cubic meters per second, and downstream communities spared the devastation that had been their historical lot. On the Indus the story was very different – facing endemic electricity shortfalls and always-threatening limitations on irrigation supplies, the operator of Tarbela stores every possible drop of water. As a result, Tarbela was almost full when the great flood of 2010 descended, and it was unable to play any dampening role.

Finally, in water nothing stays the same. Values, demography and demands change over time. And as we understand now, climate changes, too. And here the great question relates to the two drivers of the water systems of South Asia – the monsoon and glacial- and snowmelt in the Himalayas. In this context a few things are clear.

First, economies that have built infrastructure and institutions capable of dealing with known variability are well placed to deal with new sources of variability. And here it is clear that no country in the Subcontinent is well placed to deal with such challenges.

Second, climate science is a science that is in its infancy, but in which rapid advances are being made. This means that what is pronounced as "certain" one day, is likely to look very different in a few years time and that the press – and press-hungry advocates – are likely to be proven dramatically wrong in many cases – witness the claim in the Intergovernmental Panel on Climate Change (IPCC) report that the Himalayan glaciers would disappear by 2035.

Third, there seems – with the previous caveat in mind – to be an emerging convergence on the likelihood that monsoons will produce more rain in the Subcontinent (which sounds good when there is a drought, and sounds ominous when floods rage).

Fourth, the impact of change in rainfall, snow and glacial melt in the Himalayas matters for the great sweep of rivers – including the Indus, Ganges, Brahmaputra, Irrawaddy, Mekong, Yangtze and Yellow rivers – which arise near Mount Kailash, but matters much more for the Indus (which receives almost half of its flow from snow and glacial melt) than for, say, the Ganges and Brahmaputra, where 90 percent of flows are from monsoon rains.

Fifth, more multipurpose dam projects can play a major role both in mitigation (because hydropower projects in these low-vegetation environments generate very few greenhouse gases) and in adaptation (because all of the Himalayan South Asian countries, with the exception of small Bhutan) have made very little use of the energy and storage possibilities in the Himalayan foothills.

Sixth and finally, in building this infrastructure all South Asian countries have to do far better in ensuring that local people are the first beneficiaries (rather than the victims) of such projects, and that enhancement of downstream human and environmental uses is given priority in both design and operation phases.

How Context Matters (A Lot)

Just as every water "solution" is provisional, so is every single one of them context specific. Experience from Australia shows what is possible if good institutional arrangements are put in place for managing scarcity. And China shows how a strong platform of infrastructure is essential for water and energy security. But economic, demographic, cultural and political conditions are quite different in Australia and China from those prevailing in the South Asia. Water economies have a lot to learn from each other, but translation of lessons from one context to another requires political leadership and ingenuity, both of which need to be remobilized in the face of new existential challenges to water security in the region.

While it is possible to sketch a more water-secure future for the countries of South Asia, as former Harvard president Larry Summers has observed, the great distinction emerging in the world is between those who can implement and those who cannot. To move from vision to action is the great challenge of South Asian countries, in water and other matters.

The Challenges of the Future

The Harvard biologist Edward O. Wilson has recently described the challenges facing biotechnology. "Today," Wilson says, "we have god-like technologies, medieval institutions and paleolithic emotions." The same tensions and dimensions apply to water. South Asia is going to need technological innovation to provide a suite of technologies that enable farmers, cities, industries and people to produce more well-being with less water. Furthermore, South Asia is going to need an institutional revolution, which will include modernizing the ossified irrigation bureaucracies and devising practical ways of dealing with common property challenges of disappearing groundwater. And importantly, South Asia is going to need a new generation of leaders – in politics, government, business and civil society – who can understand the paleolithic emotions relating to water, and channel these into productive responses.

The particular challenges will be different in each country. The focus in Pakistan is on the Indus and the associated aquifers. In India there are many major river basins, each with their own natural and economic challenges. For Bangladesh the most obvious problem – flooding – is now being joined by endemic scarcity and challenges of groundwater management. Bhutan has done brilliantly in developing its resource of gravity and water, something for which similarly endowed Nepal has yet to find a solution. And everywhere challenges of adaptation to climate change, pollution and environmental sustainability loom large, as do the urgent need for new mechanisms for managing what former finance minister of India Palaniappan Chitambaram has described as "a growing set of little civil wars" – between head-ender and tail-ender, between agriculture and cities, and between provinces and between sovereign states in the region.

Finally, universities and other knowledge institutions have a role to play in generating a new set of hegemonic ideas in this technology/institution/emotion space. At Harvard University we are dipping our fingers in this stream with our dream being the development of a new set of "horizontal partnerships" with universities in South Asia (and other regions) and the development of a new generation of "specialized integrators" who will not only bring deep skills and perspectives of their own discipline, but will also engage with colleagues from other disciplines, equipped with a different perspective of the challenge of water security. It is with the spread of similar models of new thinking that we can be more optimistic for the future of water security in South Asia and beyond.

Chapter 24

AGRICULTURE AND FOOD SECURITY

M. E. Tusneem

South Asia, with a population of 1.7 billion, is the second most populated region of the world, after East Asia. Nearly half of the world's poor live in this region. It is one of the fastest growing regions, registering an average gross domestic product (GDP) growth rate of 6 percent per annum over the last two decades (1990–2010). Yet, it is also the least integrated region with high incidence of cross-border conflicts and vulnerability to internal and external shocks, climate change and natural disasters (e.g., floods, droughts, cyclones, etc.).

Agriculture (including crops, livestock, poultry and fisheries) continues to be a vital sector of the economies of the South Asian region despite significant structural change over the past two decades. Agriculture is still the main source of livelihood for 75 percent of its population that lives in the rural areas; it constitutes about 21 percent of the GDP and employs about 42 percent of the labor force of the region. The regional picture however masks the significant differences in the size and structure of the South Asian economies as reflected in Table 1.

For instance, India, Pakistan, Bangladesh and Sri Lanka with agriculture value added ranging between 12 to 38 percent of total GDP are transforming at a relatively rapid pace from agro-based to transforming economies, while Afghanistan, Bhutan, Maldives and Nepal with agriculture value added about 40 percent or more are still primarily agro-based. Nonetheless continued high growth of agriculture sector remains fundamental to achieving food security, poverty reduction, and economic transformation of all the South Asian economies.

Historically, South Asia has done remarkably well in achieving rapid growth of agriculture over the past four decades. It witnessed an unprecedented technological and economic transformation between the 1970s and 1990s. The transformation started in the late 1960s with the advent of high yielding varieties (HYV) of wheat and rice, and the ensuing Green Revolution. The elements of the revolution included combination of a seed-water-fertilizer technology package supported by improved agricultural policies and big investments in irrigation infrastructure, farm mechanization, research and extension. This led to doubling of food production during the period of 1970–90, taking the region out of a famine-like situation prevailing before 1965 when India and

Table 1. Key indicators of agriculture development for major South Asian countries

Key indicators	Afghanistan	Bangladesh	India	Nepal	Pakistan	Sri Lanka
Total population (million)[1] (estimated in July 2012)	30.42	161.08	1,205.07	29.89	190.29	21.48
Average annual population growth during 2012 (%)[1]	2.22	1.58	1.31	1.77	1.55	0.91
Rural population in 2010 (%)[1]	77.0	72.0	70.0	81.0	64.0	86.0
Rate of urbanization (%)[1] estimated for 2010–2015	4.7	3.1	2.4	4.7	3.1	1.1
Employment in agriculture (%)[1]	78.6 (2008–09)	45.0 (2008)	53.0 (2011)	75.0 (2010)	45.1 (2010)	31.8 (2012)
Agriculture share in GDP (%)[1] during 2012	20.0	17.3	17.0	38.1	20.1	12.0
Agriculture value added during 2012 (US$ billions)[1]	6.71	52.85	804.95	15.43	103.43	15.14
Average annual growth in real GDP during 2012 (%)[1]	11.00	6.10	5.40	4.60	3.70	6.80
Agriculture share in GDP during 2012 (%)[1]	20.0 (2011)	17.3 (2012)	17.0 (2011)	38.1 (2012)	20.1 (2012)	12.0 (2012)
Public R&D spending on agri. in 2009 (PPP US$ 2005; % of agri. value added)[3]	N/A	126 (0.32%)	2,276 (0.40%)	22 (0.23%)	172 (0.20)	38 (0.35%)
Permanent crop land (million ha)[1]	0.137	0.444	9.204	0.125	0.669	1.000
Cereal production in 2011 (kg/capita)[2]	144.48	349.32	230.02	282.18	204.39	192.25
Average annual growth in cereal production from 2001 to 2011 (%)[2]	6.61	3.63	2.18	1.42	3.32	4.60
Average cereals yield in 2011 (kg/ha)[2]	16,599	41,910	28,833	24,813	27,178	35,033
Meat production (kg/capita)[2]	10.28	4.11	5.02	10.77	15.68	6.67
Fruit production (kg/capita)[2]	3.33	11.41	6.15	26.04	3.06	3.49
Vegetable production (kg/capita)[2]	28.84	27.80	85.23	108.85	30.85	36.30

Source: (1) CIA, *The World Factbook*; (2) estimates made from FAOSTAT data from (http://www.fao.org); (3) Stads, Gert-Jan and M. Rahija (2012).

most other South Asian countries were depending heavily on food imports and/or food aid.

The experience of the Green Revolution has demonstrated that technology-driven transformation of agriculture was necessary not only to overcome large food deficits, but also to accelerate the overall growth process to a scale required for transformation of the economy to achieve broad-based economic growth, food security, and improved farm incomes.[1] More specifically, during the period of the Green Revolution (1975– 90s), the cereal production doubled primarily through productivity increases on the same area under wheat and rice as in the 1970s. Per capita food availability increased by 14 percent from 2,100 calories to 2,400 calories, despite 74 percent increase in South Asia's population with the addition of over 518 million people. From 1980 onwards, the GDP per capita increased by 190 percent, driven increasingly by the growth in urban, industrial and the rural nonfarm sectors. The incidence of poverty declined by 16 percent from 59 percent in 1975 to 43 percent in 1990s, but the absolute number of poor increased by 43 million (ADB 2000).

The momentum of Green Revolution–led growth, however, could not be sustained beyond the 1990s. The rising costs of Green Revolution technologies, negative impact on the environment and declining total factor productivity raised concern on the continued viability of these technologies for sustainable agriculture development. Further, the emergence of post–Green Revolution problems, especially pests and diseases, declining water resources and land degradation are continuously posing threats to sustained agriculture growth and food security in many developing countries. There is therefore a need for new research paradigms to generate more responsive technologies which help sustain and advance the contribution of the Green Revolution vis-à-vis the evolving challenges facing the sector.

Towards 2060: Six Challenges

At the turn of first decade into the twenty-first century, many countries of South Asia stand at a crossroads of economic transition from agro-based to transforming countries to decide the future growth strategies that not only sustain the high level of growth achieved during the past decades but also make it more inclusive and broad-based with greater impact on poverty reduction by tapping the potential of hitherto neglected sectors of the rural economy, i.e., livestock and off-farm rural enterprises. Livestock accounts for 20 to 40 percent of rural employment and is an important source of employment for women, landless dwellers and marginal farmers. It is essentially a social safety net of rural household. The Indian experience of smallholder livestock and dairy development in Gujarat and other parts of India demonstrates its impact on rural poverty and food security. To enhance growth of the nonfarm sector,

---

1 Studies on the links between agricultural growth and the rural nonfarm economy in Asia have estimated regional income multipliers between 1.5 and 2.0, i.e., for each dollar increase in agriculture value added, there is an additional $0.5 to $1.0 increase in the nonfarm sector (ADB 2000a).

governments must invest in rural infrastructure and institutions to promote vertical and horizontal integration of primary production in the agro-industrial system, which will in turn promote capital and knowledge-intensive commercial agriculture and related supply and value chains. Further, market-oriented policies and provision of rural financial services will be prerequisites for transformation of the economy. It is notable that India and Sri Lanka are increasingly becoming knowledge-based economies. They have managed to develop relatively robust institutional and physical infrastructure; whereas Bangladesh, Pakistan and Nepal continue to lag behind. In particular, Pakistan's market oriented high-growth strategy pursued since 2000–2001 got seriously disrupted in 2007–2008 with the change of government taking a heavy toll on the macroeconomic stability and process of institution building.

Looking ahead towards 2060, South Asian countries have the necessary human resources, natural resources and technology to sustain a high-growth trajectory and rapid socioeconomic transformation, notwithstanding the many challenges. They have the opportunity to emerge as a fast-developing region with a vision of shared prosperity by 2060 under an optimistic scenario, or continue to be a lagging region under a "business-as-usual" scenario. The final outcome will largely depend on how the political leadership of the South Asian countries in general and that of India in particular steer their national economies in an increasingly complex region endowed with abundant natural resources, but marred by lingering political conflicts and mistrust between India and its neighboring countries. The long-term vision of a "Fast-Developing and Prosperous South Asia" that is free from poverty, hunger and malnutrition by 2060 could serve as a common denominator for regional cooperation under South Asian Association for Regional Cooperation (SAARC). The major challenges and opportunities to achieve this vision in the area of agriculture development and food security are discussed below:

1.   *Demographic transition*: Managing early demographic transition is most critical to achieving rapid economic transformation and food security. South Asia's population is still growing at 1 to 2 percent per annum – an alarmingly high rate by international standards. Luckily, however, the region is well placed to take advantage of its favorable demographics by providing the youth access to education, health, technical and vocational training, and other employable skills that are most critical for achievement of Millennium Development Goals (MDGs) and transition to knowledge-based economy. This opportunity is time sensitive and available only for the next few decades. If lost, the region could face a serious demographic threat in terms of the multitude of uneducated or unemployable youth.

The degree of success in making agriculture growth pro-poor and environmentally sustainable would largely depend on success in demographic transition from "high fertility–high mortality" to "low fertility–low mortality" at a rapid pace. The high population growth exerts a downward pressure on wages, farm sizes and per capita income, hence worsening poverty and degradation of environment. Development of nonfarm, agro-based rural enterprises/trading activities can offset the negative impacts to some degree, but only if labor demand grows faster than the supply of rural labor force.

2. *Food security*: The challenge of achieving food security remains a real one notwithstanding the progress made in agriculture. Food availability, accessibility and affordability are three essential ingredients of food security. Long-term food security requires not only producing sufficient food to meet the market demand, but also ensuring its timely availability at affordable prices to the common man. By best estimates, nearly one-third of South Asia's population still suffers from hunger poverty and malnutrition. The most vulnerable are children, women and the elderly, especially among the lower-income groups. While the number of children suffering from severe malnutrition declined significantly over the past two decades, the prevalence of mild and moderate undernutrition, especially among those in the lower 30 percent income group, is still high. Prevalence of micronutrient deficiencies such as vitamin A, iron and iodine deficiency are becoming more common. As such, increasing food consumption alone is not a sufficient condition for overcoming malnutrition. The nutritional quality and food safety measures also need equal attention. It is also necessary to address the factors responsible for the high incidence of gastrointestinal infection. Assured provision of safe drinking water, improved healthcare and education are necessary elements of a comprehensive strategy to eliminate malnutrition and achieve the goal of food security for all before 2030. According to the latest report of the United Nations (UN) population prospects (medium variant), South Asia's population will grow from 1.7 billion in 2010 to 2.4 billion in 2060 – an increase of approximately 50 percent or an addition of nearly 700 million more people (UN Population Division 2011).

The recent Food and Agriculture Organization (FAO) study "How to Feed the World in 2050" (FAO 2008) estimates that the future demand for food for 9.1 billion people in 2050 will require a 70 percent increase in cereal production (40 percent for food plus 30 percent for animal feed to produce additional meat, milk and dairy products). The future food demand and its composition will largely depend on the pace of urbanization (which is expected to reach about 70 percent of the population), income growth and the resultant shift in the composition of food baskets. The projected increases in the consumption of milk/dairy products and meat are given in Table 2.

The caloric intake per capita per day will increase from 2,800 kilocalories (kcal) in year 2003/05 to 3,050 calories in 2050 at a global level and from 2,400 to 3,000 in South Asia as a region. According to FAO, the overall food production system of the world and that of South Asia has the ability to ensure food security on a sustainable basis by producing 70 percent more cereals in 2060 of which about 80 percent will come from productivity improvement on the same land. These estimates, however, do not include the cereal demand for biofuel, which is difficult to predict at this stage.

Livestock production, neglected in the past relative to crops, will acquire greater emphasis and appropriate adjustments in policies and investments to improve livestock productivity through research and extension aimed at improved genetic stock, nutrition and health. Livestock development offers the potential to become the engine of more

Table 2. Asia projected changes in the composition of major food commodities in South Asia

Commodity (kg/person/year)	1999–2001	2030	2050
Cereals	157	167	169
Milk and dairy, excl. butter (fresh milk eq.)	68	106	129
Meat (carcass weight)	6	12	18
Sugar (raw sugar eq.)	26	30	32
Pulses, dry	10	8	7
Vegetable oils, oilseeds and products (oil eq.)	10	15	18

Source: FAO (2006).

inclusive and broad based growth through improved productivity of milk and meat per animal, value addition and development of supply chain linking livestock holders with milk processors. It is noteworthy that unlike crops, the growth in livestock sector is more egalitarian, pro-poor and pro-women. It also serves as a safety net for the poor and landless as well as an insurance for household food security and child nutrition.

3. *Natural resources*: Managing the natural resources, particularly land and water against competing demands from agriculture and other sectors of the economy, poses a major challenge to the sustainability of the natural resource base. The available long-term studies suggest that while land resources are manageable, increasing water scarcity poses a serious threat. Water is the lifeblood of agriculture in the arid and semi-arid parts of South Asia where access to water and irrigation is a major determinant of agricultural productivity. The core issues are inefficient use of irrigation water and conflicts over cross-border allocation of water resources among the riparian countries bordering India. These are further complicated by climate change leading to increased uncertainties in the intensity and timing of rainfall and glacier melt. There are opportunities to address these issues at a bilateral/regional level in line with existing treaties and established international protocols. At the national level urgent reforms are needed in each of the regional countries to upgrade the existing institutional and legal framework for equitable water allocation, distribution and pricing to achieve high water use efficiency and productivity. The current water use efficiency under irrigated agriculture of South Asia – covering more than one-third of the total cropped area – ranges between 30 to 40 percent versus 60 to 90 percent being achievable through improved water management practices such as laser land-leveling, furrow irrigation, bed planting, and high-efficiency sprinkler and drip irrigation systems. In addition, there is a large potential for rainwater harvesting and storage.

4. *Productivity and competitiveness*: The fourth challenge is making agriculture production systems more productive, profitable, competitive and sustainable. In other words "producing more with less" by increasing the productivity per unit of land, water and

energy through research and innovations. The research on improving productivity through the application of agriculture biotechnology is well advanced. It has enabled the development of crop varieties with resistance to herbicide, insect pests, bacterial and viral diseases and tolerance to drought, salinity, and extreme temperatures. The production of HYV of cotton, maize, soybean and canola with genetic resistance to common insects and or herbicides – the so-called genetically modified (GM) crops – have increased at a rapid rate since their introduction in 1996. According to a recent report, the area under GM crops increased from 1.7 million hectare (Ha) in 6 countries to 134 million Ha in 25 countries in 2009 (James 2009). These technologies have led to substantial increases in the yield and production of GM crops with lower cost of production, lesser use of agrochemicals and higher profitability and competitiveness. More recently a US government–led initiative "Feed the Future" has been launched in collaboration with leading private companies in agriculture. It aims at doubling the yield levels of major crops by using one-third of the resources (land, water, energy) employing "systems approaches" that begin with improved seeds, access to fertilizer and extension services, and end with functioning markets. Beyond applications to the crop sector to increase production of food, feed and fiber, biotechnology is also being increasingly used in the livestock sector for genetic improvement of animals for milk or meat production, disease resistance, detection and prevention of diseases, vaccine and drug production, etc.

The biggest challenge faced by South Asia in this area is that hardly any biotechnology research is being undertaken on basic food crops or on the problem of small farmers. If successfully tapped, the biotechnology revolution could make an extremely important contribution to future agriculture growth, natural resource management and sustainable food security in the region. At present, most of the current agrobiotechnology research is being undertaken by a few multilateral companies that cater to the interests of farmers in developed countries. Unlike the Green Revolution technology, the GM seed and related technology package is a private good duly protected under the intellectual property rights. To access or develop these technologies, the public sector research system in South Asia will need to have a joint stance on managing this cutting-edge research to the best interest of its South Asian farmers. This would require collaborative research programs under public–public and public–private partnership at the national, regional and international levels to make its benefits available to farmers at affordable cost.

5. *Marketing and trade*: Agriculture growth will be sustained only if the markets work better. This will be achieved through market-oriented policies and investments in value-added products, and supply chain infrastructures that link farmers with markets and promote rapid commercialization and diversification of agriculture into high-value products in progressively transforming economies of South Asia (Bangladesh, India, Pakistan and Sri Lanka). The experience of East Asia indicates that better functioning of markets and trade is fundamental to commercialization of agriculture and export competitiveness. Strengthening of markets will require major investments

in supply chain infrastructure and institutions for improved governance, regulations and market information. Most of such investments should come from private sector with government providing the enabling environment in the form of market-oriented policies and institutions to provide incentives for foreign direct investments, joint ventures, technology and innovations in production systems such as cooperative/corporate farming, and provision of public goods (electricity, gas, water supply, sanitation, etc.). For agriculture to be profitable and competitive, the producers, processors and exporters of agriculture commodities must comply with World Trade Organization (WTO) requirements and protocols such as Intellectual Property Rights, Good Agricultural Practices (GAP) and Good Manufacturing Practices (GMP).

6.   *Climate change*: Climate change poses a major threat to agriculture production systems and long-term food sustainability. Climate change, especially in biophysical environment, is impacting the lives of all inhabitants in the region. The impact of global warming is leading to disastrous consequences in the form of hurricanes, heavy floods, severe droughts, extreme temperatures and forest fires. Recent data reveals that the 1990s was the warmest decade, and 1998 was the warmest year. Unprecedented heat waves, droughts, floods and cyclones are becoming more frequent in South Asia. The monsoon season has been shifting both in intensity and timing resulting in heavy losses to national economies. Region-wide joint research studies are needed in South Asia to understand the nature and extent of this climatic change and develop adaptation and mitigation strategies.

Regional Cooperation: Solution, If Not a Panacea

In the face of challenges discussed above, the regional cooperation is a necessity, not an option for South Asia. Addressing many of these challenges will require massive investments in: (i) agriculture institutions and infrastructure including agriculture research and innovations, water resources management and development, farm mechanization, marketing, trade and supply chain infrastructure; (ii) strategic food reserves; (iii) policy reforms and institutions; and (iv) collective action and political goodwill on the part of South Asian countries concerned. The challenges such as water sharing and management issues, disaster management, climate change and environmental issues, regional food security, cross border transit and trade and cutting edge agriculture research and innovations need to be handled on a priority basis. Regional cooperation will help synergize resources, reduce transaction costs, mitigate negative externalities and foster political goodwill for fast-track implementation and monitoring of regional projects and programs. This will require strong leadership at and capacity building of SAARC and mobilization of external resources in collaboration with the Asian Development Bank (ADB) and World Bank.

     In conclusion, if South Asia manages to achieve early demographic transitions, foster effective regional cooperation similar to East Asia and mobilize the necessary human and financial resources to address aforementioned challenges, the future food security of the region will be ensured and goal of poverty reduction substantially achieved. The region has the necessary human and social capital, technology and natural resource base to achieve broad-based economic growth and food security for all. By 2060, it has the potential to emerge as a fast-developing region and a strong trading block in Asia. Needless to say, the realization of this goal would require mobilization of substantial additional financial resources, strong political will and commitment of its leaders to move forward as a region to achieve the long-term vision of a prosperous South Asia free of poverty, hunger and malnutrition. On the other hand, if the status quo continues, the trust deficit between India and its bordering countries persists, and SAARC fails to foster regional cooperation/integration in key areas, the region will lag further behind other fast-growing regions in the world, in particular East Asia.

Chapter 25

MEETING ELECTRIC POWER DEMAND IN SOUTH ASIA

Rajan Gupta and Harihar Shankar

There are a number of reasons for focusing on what will propel development in South Asian countries (SACs). The most compelling is the intersection of demographics and poverty. The SACs considered here (Afghanistan, Pakistan, India, Nepal, Bangladesh, Bhutan, Myanmar and Sri Lanka)[1] are home to about 24 percent of the world population, and this fraction is predicted to grow to 26.5 percent by 2050. Most monitoring agencies estimate that about 70 percent of the total population of SACs (1,150 out of about 1,640 million in 2009) lives below the poverty line (on less than 2_{ppp}/day). Demographically, SACs consist of a number of ethnic communities that are widely distributed and, in many cases, ethnic and religious affiliations remain stronger than even national identity. While there is significant emigration to developed countries, especially of highly trained people, the total numbers compared to the total population are small. Mass migration out of the Subcontinent is an unlikely scenario as there are no new frontiers beckoning nor are there enough other countries that need hundreds of millions of untrained immigrants.

Power and Development in the SACs

Contemplating about the future of this large population, and whether the region possesses adequate resources to develop, as well as what development means to each of these countries, therefore, remain very timely issues. Without a doubt, governance will play a pivotal role at every level of the development process and determine the outcomes. There are large variations in governance within SACs, ranging from repressive to dysfunctional to barely functional. Each of the eight countries has a

---

1 Maldives is not included in the discussion here as it is geographically isolated and has multiple standalone grids on major islands that are dependent on imported oil for all their energy needs. Its needs are, however, small (about 60 MW for 400,000 people) and it is in the process of installing wind and solar systems, with batteries and LNG-driven gas turbines for backup, to become the first net carbon-free country by 2020.

different political system, and all SACs except Bhutan are facing issues of civil and political unrest with multiple insurgencies. Nevertheless, faced with widespread poverty and inadequate resources in the larger nations, their best option forward is cooperation and trade so that all their resources can be devoted to development.

This paper concentrates on electric power generation. We examine long-term and sustainable options for each of the eight countries to provide adequate (0.5 kW per capita will be used as the development goal) electric power to its citizens, opportunities for collaboration and the challenges involved.

To make the discussion of opportunities, options and challenges concrete, some of the key indicators of development as well as a 2008/2009 summary of energy resources relevant to this study are given in Table 1. Before examining individual countries, it is useful to state a number of common features:

- The current estimates of fossil fuel resources show that none of the SACs is rich in fossil fuels. SACs already import 75 percent of oil to meet demand from their transportation and other oil-based sectors. Myanmar has adequate gas reserves to fuel its own development, however, most of its production for the foreseeable future is earmarked for export. India has adequate reserves of domestic coal to develop up to about 300 GW of coal-fired generation but indigenous coal would increasingly need to be supplemented by imports. In the most likely scenario, if India develops 300 GW coal-fired capacity by 2040, it will need to import over 50 percent of coal consumed. As discussed later, Pakistan can develop using indigenous energy resources.
- All eight countries are facing severe power shortages and there are daily power cuts that persist for hours. All industries, and individuals who can afford them, have therefore installed diesel generator sets (more costly and with larger CO_2 footprint) to overcome the daily load shedding.
- Large fractions of the populations and geographical regions are without electric connections. There is dire need for developing the generating capacity to meet growing demand and for equal (if not more) investment in the associated transmission and distribution infrastructure to reach the entire population.
- Transmission and distribution losses are high – typically in the 20–30 percent range – compared to less than10 percent in developed countries. The infrastructure is old and in constant need of repair.
- The power demand in all SACs is growing at 7–10 percent. This is faster than the economic growth and accelerates the demand–supply gap.
- To provide adequate electric power (0.5 kW per capita) to all their citizens, all SACs require a factor of 5–20 increase in generating capacity and energy delivered.
- Bhutan can be energy independent based on its hydroelectric resources alone. The same is true of Nepal and Myanmar if their populations stabilize below the 2050 projections in Table 1. To develop these resources, they are forging strong collaborations with neighboring countries and international companies – Nepal and Bhutan predominantly with India, and Myanmar with China. For long-term

planning, however, they must take into account large seasonal and annual fluctuations in water flow, possible impacts of climate change on precipitation and impacts of erosion and silting of water reservoirs due to deforestation.

Before moving to a discussion of the electric power generation picture in SACs, a quick glance at the transportation sector in the region, one of the most crucial factors in shaping energy policies, will be helpful. The path forward in the transportation sector is relatively unclear since all SACs import oil and have very limited reserves. They have yet to develop sustainable transportation options and find the balance between individual owned and public transport. Most of these countries are beginning their phase of rapid urbanization, so they have the opportunity to develop cities planned around efficient and effective transportation systems. Unfortunately, current growth of cities is organic rather than planned and development of public transport systems are responding to the demand rather than driving the planning. There are no significant collaboration opportunities for oil trade as all SACs except Myanmar (44 percent) already meet 80–100 percent of their demand through imports. The supply for Nepal and Bhutan goes through India, while Afghanistan and Pakistan have yet to benefit from trade with their oil and gas rich neighbor Iran. In short, if oil remains the long-term energy source for personal and public transport, all eight countries have no option but to import it and pay the market price.

The Regional Picture: Opportunities Missed, Challenges to be Met

India, by strength of its large population, land area and economy, is the largest energy market in South Asia. If its gross domestic product (GDP) (and energy demand) continues to grow at over 8 percent, it will need about 4,000 TWh per year by 2032 (Government of India, Planning Commission 2006). Exploiting up to 80 GW of hydroelectric potential will provide only 280 TWh annually assuming the current realized 40 percent plant load factor (PLF). The only large fossil fuel reserve it has is coal. Assuming 50 billion tons of coal can be extracted in total, coal plants would generate 75,000 TWh at 0.6 kg/kWh and 85 percent PLF, i.e., a 20-year supply at 4,000 TWh per year. In addition to impacts of coal-fired generation on the environment and the climate, and consequent international pressure to reduce CO_2 emissions, India faces major impediments to mining the required volumes of coal – the almost total erosion of infrastructure and human resource needed for underground mining that is necessary to extract the majority of the reserves, and growing public opposition to surface mining. Development of new conventional fossil fuel based generation, therefore, cannot be sustained for much more than twenty years and during this time supply will continue to lag behind demand. For the long term, India's planners are banking on the success of its three stage nuclear program with the goal of installing 500–600 GW of nuclear capacity by 2060 (Bhabha Atomic Research Centre n.d.). Until that happens India can absorb, and will bid for, all surplus energy resources in the region.

Table 1. Energy and development indicator figures[2]

	Afghanistan	Pakistan	India	Nepal	Bangladesh	Bhutan	Burma	Sri Lanka
Population 2009 (million)	28.4	181	1171	27.5	162.2	0.7	50	20.5
Population per sq. km	44	227	356	187	1127	15	74	312
Rate of increase (%)	2.1%	2.3%	1.6%	2.1%	1.6%	1.7%	1.1%	1.2%
Population 2025 (million)	39.4	246	1,445	36	195	0.9	58	23
Population 2050 (million)	53.4	335	1,748	46	222.5	1.0	63	25
Literacy (%) M/F	43.1/12.6	63/36	73.4/47.8	62.7/34.9	54/41.4	60/34	93.9/86.4	92/89.1
Life expectancy years M/F	44/44	66/67	63/65	63/64	64/66	67/68	59/63	67/75
GDP (billion US$)	14	166	1,235	12.6	95	1.27	28	41
GDP PPP (billion US$)	21.3	440	3,526	32	225	3.4	68	92
GDP per capita (US$)	493	917	1,055	458	586	1,814	560	2,000
Real GDP growth rate (%)	3.4%	2.7%	8.5%	4.7%	6.4%	5%	1%	3.5%
% population living on less than US2_{PPP}$/day		60%	76%	78%	81%	50%		40%
Oil – proven reserves million barrels	0	289	5,625	0	28	0	50	100
Oil production million barrels/yr	0	21.6	321		2.09	0	6.72	0
Oil consumption million barrels/yr	1.66	136.2	1,088	6.44	35.7	0.476	15.2	32.72
Coal reserves MT (short)	73	2,185	62,278	0.013				
Coal production MTA/yr	0.039	3.8	568	0.454	0.772	0.108	1.455	0.101
Coal consumption MTA/yr	0.039	12.174	637.5			0.090	0.302	
Gas reserves (BCM)	50	885	1,075	0	141.5	0	283	0
Gas production BCM/yr	0.03	37.5	32.2	0	17.9	0	12.4	0
Gas consumption BCM/yr	0.03	37.5	43	0	17.9	0	3.85	
Generation capacity GW	0.489	19.44	159	0.617	5.245	1.486	2.5	3.0
Hydro resource tapped GW	0.26/0.75	6.7/53	40/80	0.6/43	0.23/0.75	1.5/23	1.4/39	1.25/9
Electricity generated TWh	0.825	90.43	787.5	2.78	23	4.475	6.286	9.507
Electricity consumed TWh	1.01	72.2	568	2.243	21.38	0.529	4.403	7.95
% population connected	26%	60%	56%	40%	32%	40%	27%	73.4%

2 For population data see Population Reference Bureau. For literacy, life expectancy and GDP data see CIA, *The World Factbook*. Oil, coal, gas and electricity data are from: US EIA; CIA, *The World Factbook*; BP Statistical Review (2010); and individual country statistics. Estimates of population living below poverty line, literacy and percentage of population connected to the grid have large uncertainties. Also, the criteria used to measure these often hide the full extent of the deficit. Blanks indicate data not available.

Given India's large energy market, the question is which SACs can profit from it? We examine four of India's neighbors, Pakistan, Nepal, Bhutan and Myanmar that possess excellent hydroelectric resources. Two of them, Bhutan and Nepal, are landlocked and can only export power to India and Bangladesh (another energy deficient country). Pakistan is unlikely to export its resources to India and is also the key transit route for transport of oil and gas from Iran and Central Asian countries. A status report on opportunities and obstacles to energy trade and cooperation between SACs is as follows:

Bhutan–India cooperation: The Government of India is funding the development of hydroelectric power projects in Bhutan that will provide revenue to Bhutan and much-needed power to India. There are three operating plants, Chukha (336 MW), Kurichhu (60 MW) and Tala (1020 MW) (for data on individual power plants see Global Energy Observatory n.d.), and seven more under development with design capacity of 10.616 GW as part of the "10 GW by 2020" Bhutan–India plan. Bhutan has 30 GW of hydro potential of which, it is estimated, 23 GW is technically and economically feasible. Once the full 23 GW is developed Bhutan can export the output of 20 GW (about 80 TWh of energy per year assuming 50 percent PLF) to India and Bangladesh and keep the remaining 3 GW to meet domestic demand. This export would provide an annual income of about $4 billion (about $4,000 per capita) at the current tariff rate of $0.05 per kWh. Thus, export of hydropower can fund the development of Bhutan, and provide long-term revenue.

Nepal also possesses excellent hydroelectric resources with an estimated 43 GW of technically and economically realizable capacity (Independent Power Producers of Nepal (IPPAN) and Confederation of Indian Industry (CII) 2006). The current total generating capacity is small (690 MW) but about 22 GW of hydropower is in planning or proposed stages, most of it in the western part of the country near the Indo–Nepal border and demand centers in India. Its own long-term needs are, however, much larger than Bhutan's (40 times the population) so it is targeting only large projects (over 500 MW) for export of power to India. The micro-, small- and medium-scale resources are distributed across the country and exploiting them for domestic consumption requires less investment in transmission and distribution infrastructure. Thus, Nepal's policy of promoting independent power producers (IPP) and working with multiple international organizations for developing its hydroelectric sector is prudent as it balances internal growth with export of power to India in the near term. In addition to its vested interest in the large plants, India should facilitate Nepal's development in order to build and sustain better relations. In the long term, assuming the population stabilizes at 50 million, Nepal would need 50 GW of hydroelectric capacity operating at 50 percent PLF to provide 0.5 kW per capita. Thus, as it develops, export of hydroelectric power will need to decrease and eventually a developed domestic market will demand the full resource as it has no known fossil fuel reserves.

Pakistan can fuel its development from indigenous resources. In addition to hydro, it has significant unexploited reserves of coal and gas as shown in Table 1. If all 2 billion tons of coal reserves in the Thar region (mostly lignite) are used for power, it would generate about 2,000 TWh. Similarly, the 800 BCM (billion cubic meters) of gas reserves could generate about 3,000 TWh, but gas has many other critical uses such as fertilizers and petrochemicals. These resources, about forty years' supply at current rate of generation, reduce to 25 years if Pakistan's demand and capacity continues to grow at over 7 percent. By simultaneously developing the estimated 53 GW of hydroelectric potential this window of opportunity can be stretched to 50 years. Pakistan can further extend this window by importing oil and gas from Iran via pipelines. The challenges Pakistan faces are (i) governance and security, (ii) generating revenues to fund this development and (iii) the rate of growth of its population. Solving the first problem would pave the way for exports to energy-hungry India, and help address the second. Development would help address the second and third challenges. Our conclusion is that, unless China's investments in Pakistan change the landscape, political instability, social unrest, security deficit, the Kashmir issue and lack of financial resources will prevent Pakistan from developing its resources sufficiently fast to meet demand and grow at over 7 percent, resulting in much less export power to India.

The poorest country in the region, Afghanistan, lacks any significant resources of fossil fuels or hydropower and is landlocked. In a perfect world it could, nevertheless, meet all its energy needs by importing oil and gas via pipelines from Iran and/or Turkmenistan, and electric energy from Uzbekistan and Tajikistan. This trade is unlikely to happen (even though donor countries have almost completed building the North East Power System transmission lines) until the political and security situation improves dramatically. Compounding this problem is the larger reality that Afghanistan has no revenue generating potential to pay for these imports, at least not until the recently announced enormous mineral wealth is tapped. Afghanistan will need very significant international help to develop.

Bangladesh lacks significant hydroelectric or coal potential and estimates of gas reserves vary widely between 150–600 BCM. Note that 150 BCM of gas generates 750 TWh, which is one year's energy demand of Bangladesh at 0.5 kW per capita, and thus not sufficient to power development of the anticipated population of 200 million people. The reality is worse: Bangladesh's gas fields and transmission infrastructure are highly underdeveloped and gas exploration and foreign investment has stalled. Its power plants are facing gas shortages and electric supply is not keeping up with the 10 percent growth in demand. It is also unlikely that it will be able to import significant electric energy from either Nepal or Bhutan given India's needs and India's role in developing those resources. Its neighbor to the east, Myanmar, is going with the highest bidder for its gas resources and its military junta has established a very disturbing but mutually beneficial relationship with China against which cash poor Bangladesh cannot compete, not to mention the lack of clout vis-à-vis China to protect Myanmar's military junta. Bangladesh's best hope is that its gas reserves are much larger than estimated.

Sri Lanka aims to double its generation capacity to about 6 GW by 2020 and has a long-term target of 15 GW. With the completion of Upper Kotmale hydroelectric project, Sri Lanka will have exploited 1.355 GW of the easy-to-develop 2 GW hydroelectric resource; therefore, in the short term the government-owned Ceylon Electricity Board (CEB) is mainly rehabilitating existing hydro plants. Ongoing and future development targets coal and LNG and fuel oil based gas turbine power plants, in which both CEB and private power producers (PPP) will participate. To realize this growth, CEB is working with CMC (China) and Mitsubishi Corporation (Japan) for respectively developing the coal and LNG handling infrastructure. It is unlikely to import any significant power from India by building the proposed Madurai (in Tamil Nadu, India) to Anuradhapura (in central Sri Lanka) HVDC link of up to 1,000 MW capacity at least until India develops excess capacity in its southern regional grid, presumably nuclear power. The current strategy increases Sri Lanka's reliance on fossil fuels for power generation and it will need to import all the fossil fuels it consumes.

The missed opportunities to construct three proposed international gas pipelines in the region provide clear examples of the lack of cooperation and inaction, even when they would have benefited all countries involved:

Iran–Pakistan–India (IPI) gas pipeline (Lall and Lodhi 2007): The 2,775 km long and 1.22 m diameter dual pipeline would carry 55 BCM of natural gas per year from the South Pars Field in Iran to both Pakistan and India. The expected price tag, $7.5 billion, is financially viable. The three major challenges to its construction have been (i) guaranteeing security through Pakistan; (ii) Pakistan's share of gas, and transit fee paid by India; and (iii) pressure on India and Pakistan to support international sanctions against Iran. The first two can be resolved by bilateral negotiations between India and Pakistan; the third is a larger issue given the international standoff vis-à-vis Iran's nuclear ambitions. In June 2010, an agreement to build the Iran–Pakistan section of the pipeline was reached but security issues in Baluchistan are delaying construction.

The Turkmenistan–Afghanistan–Pakistan–India (TAPI) pipeline (Tynan 2010): The 1,680 km long 1.42 m diameter pipeline would transport 27 BCM (eventually 33 BCM) annually from Dauletabad gas field in Turkmenistan to Afghanistan (2 BCM), Pakistan (12.5BCM) and India (12.5 BCM). This $7.6 billion pipeline requires guarantees of security from both Afghanistan and Pakistan, certification of reserves from Turkmenistan, and has the geopolitical consequences of providing an alternate evacuation route for Caspian resources that does not go through Russia, isolating Iran and providing much-needed revenue to Afghanistan. Unfortunately, the lack of security in Afghanistan, and failed tariff negotiations between Pakistan and India, continue to prevent this pipeline from being built.

Myanmar–Bangladesh–India (MBI) pipeline (Imam 2009): This 900 km long $1 billion pipeline was to carry gas from Shwe gas fields off the coast of Arakan in Myanmar to Bangladesh and India. The main hurdles pre-2008 were the conditions put forward by Bangladesh to India regarding trade tariffs and free trade corridors to Nepal and Bhutan. In June 2008, China National Petroleum Corporation (CNPC) negotiated with the Myanmar government to purchase all the gas and build an 1,800 km pipeline (12 BCM per year capacity) from Kyauk Phyu in Arakan to Kunming, China. Subsequently, Bangladesh came back to the negotiating table, especially since it is now facing a growing need for gas supplies as its production declines and demand soars. With the continued delay in reaching an agreement, it is now no longer clear whether the MBI pipeline is an attractive option for India since China has secured exclusive rights on all known export capacity of the Arakan belt and is already constructing the pipeline to evacuate it.

Projections and Outlook for the Future

Accepting the likely scenario that there will not be significant trade of electric power between most SACs, could they at least plan to integrate their grids to enhance overall stability? Based on the trends of the last decade, civil unrest, political differences and power demands varying by orders of magnitude between India and its neighbors, the most probable scenario is that each country will remain focused on its own development. Major interconnect sites for exporting power from Nepal and Bhutan to India will be the regional test-beds for grid synchronization, but the function of these few substations will most likely be limited to power transfer. There will be some small regional interconnects but nothing significant is anticipated. Developing these would, nevertheless, serve as a valuable demonstration of friendship and cooperation.

The above discussion makes it clear that, except for Afghanistan, the planning for the development of electric power is constrained but remains economically reasonable within each country and is proceeding at a rate the economy and the overall infrastructure can bear. Issues of governance, security and corruption, however, are undermining the rate at which this development could be realized. Only Bhutan and Nepal have credible paths to development based on hydroelectric power. Myanmar too will develop adequate hydroelectric generation capacity, mostly with China's help, but 85 percent of the electric output is targeted for export and the revenues are unlikely to be utilized by the military junta to achieve national development. A stable Pakistan can develop using indigenous resources and collect transit royalty on oil and gas export via pipelines from Iran/Central Asia to India. India, Bangladesh and Sri Lanka will be increasingly dependent on imports of fossil fuels for sustaining development. Export of power from Nepal and Bhutan will be significant and very beneficial but not adequate to meet the growing demand of Bangladesh and India.

This discussion has not considered impacts on the environment and climate change of such a business-as-usual, albeit efficient, fossil fuel–based development. The reason is that until CO_2 emissions are priced and/or taxed the development of renewable and conventional systems are proceeding in parallel but at very different scales and with different drivers. Growth of solar and wind is mainly driven by incentives and subsidies and investors are waiting for technology maturation, development of supporting infrastructure, and experience based learning on integrating intermittent generation. What this article highlights is as follows. (i) Three countries, Nepal, Bhutan and Myanmar, can underwrite their development using hydroelectric power, which over the long term will be vulnerable to environmental and climate changes. (ii) The populations and needs of three countries, Pakistan, India and Bangladesh, are currently too large to plan around renewables, so their coal- and gas-based development will have very significant impacts globally. We also show that their fossil fuel reserves are inadequate to sustain development in the mid to long term, thus it is in their interest to develop the knowledge and experience to be able to quickly scale up deployment of renewable technologies as they become cost-effective. (iii) At this point India's only long-term option is accelerating the development of its nuclear power program. (iv) Creating and maintaining the right balance between short-term development and long-term sustainability and climate change mitigation goals requires maintaining high GDP growth rate for holistic development, political and financial stability, careful planning and enlightened leadership.

As discussed here, each country has options but which of the SACs will actually achieve the desired electric supply goal will depend on governance, implementation, financial stability and resources, and anticipating and resolving the social and political challenges. As these countries develop, people will demand more transparency and will be more vigilant of practices of both the government and private corporations that impact the commons (land acquisition, resource exploitation, emissions, etc.). Governments anticipating these challenges and willing to address them in a transparent and timely manner will meet fewer obstacles and develop faster.

The discussion raises many important questions that are not easy to quantify: What will be the cornerstones of the economies of these countries that will fund development and support 1.65 billion people (increasing to 2.5 billion by 2060) as they develop? Will it remain tourism for Bhutan and Nepal, and will they use their energy-export revenues for broad-based development? Will India's niche in software, the service sector and the recent rapid growth in the manufacturing sector, buffered by its large domestic market, persist? Will handicrafts, textiles and garments, the traditional export items from SACs, grow in scale or are they too fungible and are there too many countries competing to provide a lasting niche? Will Pakistan achieve stability and focus on development? Will Afghanistan achieve peace and unity to even contemplate development, and will the military junta of Myanmar use revenues from oil transport from its ports to China via pipelines, gas exports and hydroelectric energy sales to seed broad-based development or to mainly support itself? Will population stabilization occur faster than projected? Hopefully, the answer to many of these questions will be a definite "yes."

Chapter 26

E-SOUTH ASIA: A SOCIAL SCIENCE FICTION

Rohan Samarajiva

In the early twenty-first century, Indian firms controlled most of the undersea telecommunication cables in the world, yet Asia's ocean, the Indian Ocean, was the least well served by cables in the world. Unlike other continents, Asia also fell short on terrestrial connectivity. Bangladesh, then a nation of around 150 million people, got its first undersea cable connection in 2005 and took years to make full use of it. It connected to the world terrestrially only in 2012 when tensions with India were attenuated.

In the early twenty-first century, Asian telecommunication operators had to rely on undersea cables more than their counterparts did in Europe and in the Americas. Intra-Asian connectivity lagged, despite the vast size of the continent. For example, intra-Asian, lit-submarine cable capacity stood at 7 terabytes per second, about half the lit capacity on transatlantic routes, according to Telegeography Research. Like trade, most electronic communication occurred with places outside Asia. And trade over telecommunication links was only beginning. Where it existed, the bits ran mostly from Asia to Europe and North America, and little within the region. At the turn of the century, almost all Internet traffic went to or through the continental United States because that was where the servers were, and where even much Asian content was kept. But Asian traffic had started to shift away from North America by 2009 (Table 1).

But by the middle of the century, things had changed. The density of undersea cables crisscrossing the Indian Ocean exceeded both the Atlantic and the Pacific. Terrestrial cables that went around the Himalayas and along the railways and highways connected with undersea cables to form a Silk Road 2.0 (see Figure 1). High bandwidth was no longer a luxury available only to big cities and coastal areas. The world's largest concentration of server farms was now located on the southern slopes of the Himalayas, benefiting both from cheap hydroelectricity and from the political stability afforded by the robust democracy of India and most of its neighbors. Now most of the world's Internet traffic came to inland South Asia, not to North America.

Table 1. International Internet-backbone connections within region and outside, 2001 and 2009 compared

	2001	2009
Asia, intraregional	17%	30%
Asia, with US and Canada	80%	50%
Europe, intraregional	75%	76%
Europe, with US and Canada	25%	19%
Latin America, intraregional	12%	25%
Latin America, with US and Canada	88%	74%

Source: Telegeography Research (2010).

Figure 1. The historical Silk Road

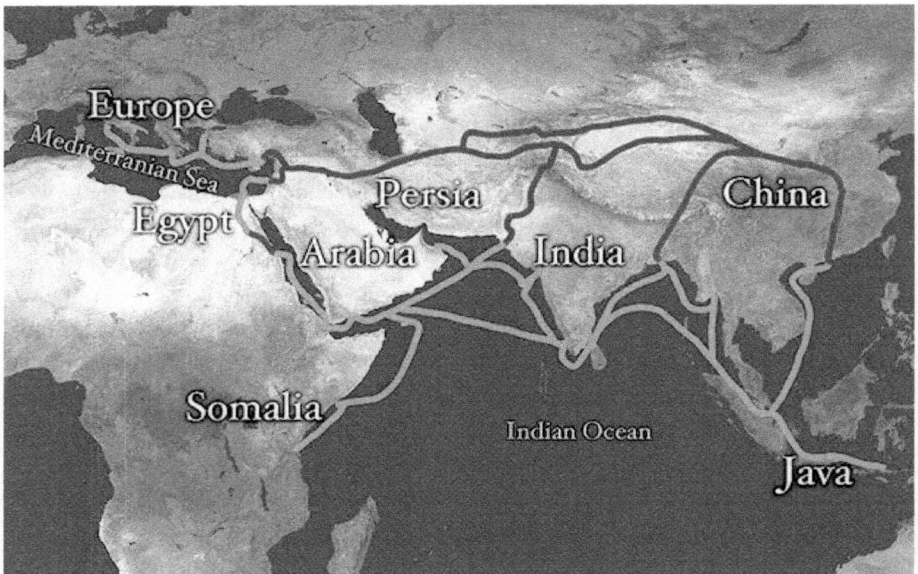

Source: NASA (2002).

Geopolitical Context

It was not that South Asia was free of turbulence, straddling boundaries on one side with militant Islam and on the other with China, it was jam-packed with nuclear weapons. The decrepit South Asian Association for Regional Cooperation (SAARC) had assumed a new role: that of safeguarding the peace in this fractious and nuclear-armed region that now encompasses the landmass stretching from the Persian Gulf to the Gulf of Thailand and south of the Himalayas. It was considering changing its name to Organization for Security and Cooperation in South Asia, evoking the

Organization for Security and Co-operation in Europe (OSCE) that served as a platform for keeping the peace in Europe in the waning days of the Cold War of the twentieth century. The Radcliff Line bifurcating British India had solidified over time. The generation with pre-Partition memories died off, leaving the problem unsolved. The new generations in India and Pakistan had imbibed too much propaganda to escape the endless, reinforcing cycles of recrimination and counter-recrimination. So growth occurred in the shadow of war, which posed the greatest threat to continued prosperity. Luckily, the Indian ruling classes abandoned the Mandala theory of foreign relations that counseled against trusting immediate neighbors and genuinely befriended those in the first circle. Sadly, this still excluded the Land of the Pure. The creation of two integrated economic regions, one stretching westward from the Radcliff Line to the Persian Gulf and the other stretching eastward from the Radcliff Line to the Gulf of Thailand, provided the people of each with a unifying "Hostile Other," thus alleviating fissiparous tendencies within each region. Multiple disputes ranging from riparian rights to moral nuances simmered within each region, but the South Asian ability to "adjust," exemplified by how more and more passengers could be squeezed into public transport in the bad old days, contained them in most instances.

The economic region formed by the states bordering the Bay of Bengal formed an economic powerhouse. As a bloc, they traded both with China and Russia-Europe around the Himalayas, connected through fiber-optic cables that first connected Silguri, at the intersection of Bangladesh, Bhutan and India, to Tibet through the Na Thula Pass in the first decade of the new century. By 2060, trade in services had merged with trade in goods for the most part, making physical transportation less important. What movement of goods that did exist, occurred over the now fully operational Asian Highway system and the extensive coastal shipping links, used more now for leisure than for movement of goods.

Economic integration did not lead to cultural integration, but to even greater cultural differentiation. Religions, sects and faiths proliferated with spiritual search reaching levels not very different from that in the time of the Buddha. Managing this cauldron of cultures was no easy task and politicians had short shelf lives. But the basics held, with economic integration and keeping the peace not subject to short-term political games.

Foundations of the New Economy

The second phase of the demographic dividend was critical to the emergence of the new economy. The first phase occurred in the southern part of the Subcontinent in the early part of the century and generated above-normal growth rates in the southern states of India and in Sri Lanka. By the time the second phase kicked in by around 2015 in the northern states of India, Bangladesh and Pakistan, the methods of channeling the massive energies of the first "boom" generations unencumbered by excessive child- and elder-dependency had been mastered to generate transformative growth of 10+ percent year after year. The wealth thus created had been used to create

Figure 2. Combined child- and elder-dependency in Bangladesh, 2006–2051

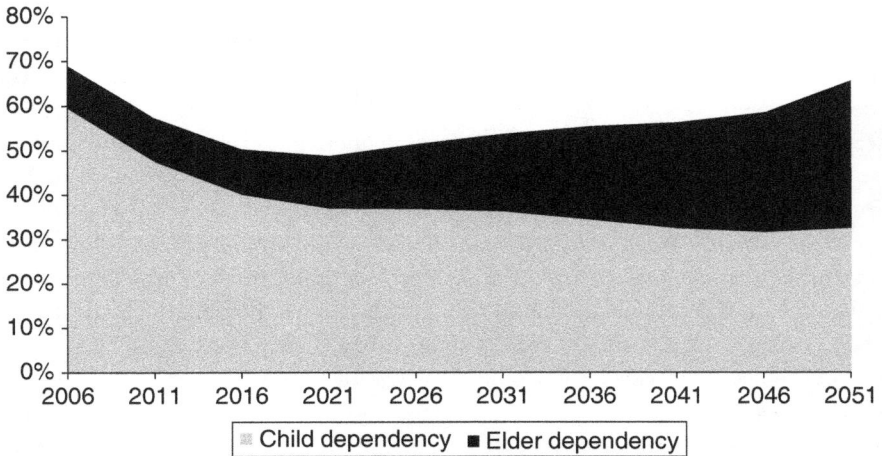

Source: Calculated using projections in Bangladesh Bureau of Statistics (2007).

effective social-safety nets that cushioned the effects of increasing elder dependency. The phenomenon is illustrated by the case of Bangladesh in Figure 2.

Investments in education had accelerated in the early part of the century since the lifting of the heavy hand of the state and the return to home during the first phase of the demographic dividend of those who had constituted the then lamented "brain drain" in the latter half of the previous century. The region's economic strength derived from knowledge-based industries. The body-shopping and low-end business process outsourcing firms that had initiated the export of knowledge services were displaced by high-end design and creative businesses. Machines endlessly talked to machines across gigabit networks, managing the articulated road trains that ran on the highways and balancing the flow of electrons on the vast energy grids fed by renewable energy sources as needed. Humans were important, but in most cases they did things machines could not do.

Learning was always valued in South Asian cultures, but in the low-trust, non-expanding-pie days of the twentieth century, education was more a means to get a piece of the limited pie in the form of a government job than about learning. Government schools were low in quality and people, including the poor, voted with their feet by preparing their children for the omnipresent examinations privately. But, sadly, private suppliers met the immediate demand by preparing students for credentials rather than for education. Government universities across the region were locked into downward spirals, with low-quality faculty producing and hiring even lower-quality faculty. The only private universities to succeed at the turn of the century were those offering quickly monetizable professional qualifications. The iron triangle of faculty wanting the quiet life, students who wanted to limit expansion of what they considered to be entry channels to the bureaucracy and to politics, and politicians wanting to avoid controversy held firm for many years.

The return to home of a critical mass of senior expatriate professionals, driven by the need to care for aging parents and attracted by the growth opportunities of the region, broke the iron triangle. Armed with nest eggs and international connections, they were unwilling to play the conventional university game. The increase of knowledge-process outsourcing activities created the need for interdisciplinary problem solvers as opposed to exam passers. Even the government began to demand different skill sets in the aftermath of widespread reengineering of government processes. Public–private partnerships of varying forms flourished. The greenfield educational institutions in the region were more nimble and efficient than their counterparts in the West, whose faculty had got mired in endless loops of self-referential theorizing. Supported by cheap and plentiful bandwidth and processing power, the new universities broke the mold of the conventional campus and escaped Baumol's Law of ever-increasing, per-unit costs of providing knowledge-intensive services.

Cheap and high-quality bandwidth and computing constituted the foundations of South Asian economies. The purchase of undersea cables by Indian firms at fire-sale prices in the *fin de siècle* dotcom crash and the location of server farms as a way to add value to Nepal and Bhutan's natural assets of gravity (cheap hydroelectricity) were not seen as consequential then, but in fact provided a key launch pad for South Asia's leap into the knowledge-based economy. But it was truly a knowledge-based economy, in that knowledge activities did not displace agriculture and manufacturing, but permeated them.

The New Economy

The move to a knowledge-based economy did not mean the end of agriculture, but the blending of agriculture and knowledge. The massive computing power agglomerated in the region enabled a solution to the water crisis that had threatened to turn the breadbasket of the Punjab into an arid desert and to start another war between Pakistan and India. The inefficient water-use practices on both sides of the border had driven down the water table and made the great Indus a mere trickle. Combining the brains of the region's scientists, cheap computing and ubiquitous connectivity, the region was able to do more with less water, also cutting down widespread fertilizer poisoning in the process. Gone were the days of free electricity endlessly pumping water from ever-receding groundwater pools. Science decided when the drip irrigation would be turned on and off. Previously flood-causing rains recharged groundwater pools. Life started returning to riverbanks as the region's rivers began flowing back to the Indian Ocean at fuller strength.

Food was one thing that still had to be transported because people continued to value the textures and the smells, but food never moved without its attendant cloud of data. Machines recorded every chemical that went anywhere near a crop or a farmed fish/animal and traceability of every agricultural product was routinely available. Price volatility, shortages and gluts were not absent, but were increasingly becoming rare. Access to weather and seed information changed cropping patterns. Returning to some of the region's traditional seed varieties not only restored diversity of flavors but also helped resist crop failures as the climate changed. No longer were farmers poor. But of course farming was now high tech and required considerable capital. The percentage of the population engaged in agriculture had greatly decreased.

Gone were the days of massive manufacturing plants that made lots of identical things that were then transported to far places at great cost and damage to the environment. Instead, goods were now produced through decentralized smart manufacturing processes that were controlled from central design centers at the nodes of massive data networks. Instead of making the same thing in millions of copies, the new manufacturing allowed customer input into the design process in ways that made supply follow demand, not vice versa. The relentless pressure to drive down transaction costs that emanated from the budget telecom network model that South Asia pioneered stood the region in good stead. Combined with the paradigm of design for extreme affordability that drove corporate strategy in the region in first few decades of the twentieth century, it gave South Asian tortoises an edge over the Chinese hares that had prematurely got locked in to old-style mass production.

Humans still needed a lot of tending and South Asia, endowed with millions upon millions of young people, did a lot of that. Doctors in South Asia remotely managed the care of a multitude of the extremely elderly all over the world. But spiritual quests, warm weather and the need for human touch brought a significant number of the wealthier and still mobile elderly to the many settlements dotted across the region, modeled on, and learning from, the United Nations Educational, Scientific and Cultural Organization (UNESCO)–sanctioned experimental settlement of Auroville in Southern India that was commenced in the 1960s. Caregivers in these settlements were high tech and highly paid. Thailand was still the place to go to for medical modification procedures, including for the increasingly commonplace sex-change operations. India was a center of artificial organ production, attracting hordes of medical tourists who wanted body parts replaced. There was fear that this form of tourism would wind down, since the surgeons were now perfecting the arts of remotely inserting replacement parts in patients. New body parts were beginning to be grown to order in vats on instructions that were communicated over distance.

People had more free time that they now used to be entertained, continuing the tradition of almost unhealthy indolence, exemplified by the South Asian habit of playing and watching cricket matches for five full days. Mostly, music and images came directly to the consumer, across fat pipes and then across wireless networks that directly reached the consumer, not the place they were normally associated with. Gone were the clumsy screens and ear phones; image and sound receptors were embedded in human bodies at birth and upgraded periodically through near-field techniques; batteries were obsolete because devices were capable of harvesting energy from radio waves. People did collectively entertain themselves in proximate social settings, but this either took the form of playing in holo decks or experiencing extreme thrills, in environments that were on the surface highly risky, but were in fact engineered to minimize death and dismemberment. All this required great bandwidth.

Status Quo Ante Restored

In sum, the South Asia of 2060 was quite different from the one that existed in 2010. The demographic structure that dragged down South Asia 100 years ago was now a key strength and advantage relative to the aged economies of Europe, Japan, and even China. Agriculture now employed far fewer people but those that it did lived very well. South Asia was no longer a periphery to the world system, but a core, balancing the other core in North America. Its core status derived from plentiful, low-cost and high-quality connectivity and computing power complemented by the brain power and energy of a youthful population supported by adequate infrastructure.

The brain drain of the twentieth century reversed direction and broke the educational logjam that had for too long stifled creativity in the region. The key to unleashing South Asia's potential was education. Nalanda in present-day Bihar, Taxila in present-day Pakistan and Abhayagiri in present-day Anuradhapura in Sri Lanka were preeminent knowledge centers of the world in the first millennium (CE). South Asia was reclaiming that heritage, building on a foundation of connectivity and computing. But, sadly, as was the case back then, prosperity did not come packaged with peace. A million mutinies continued, but now in the shadow of nukes.

Section IV

HUMAN WELL-BEING

Chapter 27

POPULATION DYNAMICS, ECONOMIC PROSPECTS AND REGIONAL COHERENCE

David E. Bloom and Larry Rosenberg

What do we foresee for South Asia in 2060, in light of the significant changes it has undergone in the past few decades? India has experienced rapid economic growth, but continues to suffer widespread, extreme poverty as well. Afghanistan, Nepal and Sri Lanka have seen major conflicts, with Pakistan always seeming on the verge of a major eruption. Nepal and Sri Lanka finally seem to have moved toward peace. As elsewhere, the region's many developments and crosscurrents make reliable predictions difficult, but one relatively neglected set of factors – demographic change – may shed some light on the region's future. Throughout the world, falling mortality rates and declining birth rates have been predictive of growing per capita incomes, and theoretical reasoning and related evidence are sufficiently compelling to think that the links may indeed be causal. In this vein, this essay explores South Asia's economic prospects through a demographic lens.

In addition, as we will see, there are some similar demographic trends across the countries of South Asia, but there are also a number of extreme differences. Regional heterogeneity bears on the question: "To what extent is South Asia a coherent region?"

The Current Demographic Scene

Demographically, South Asia is a diverse region of 1.64 billion people (24 percent of the world's population). The infant mortality rate (IMR: the number of children under age one who die in a given year out of 1,000 children born in that year) varies by an order of magnitude, from 152 in Afghanistan to 15 in Sri Lanka. The total fertility rate (TFR: the average number of children a woman of childbearing age will have assuming no change in current age-specific rates) ranges from a high of about 6.5 in Afghanistan to a low of 2.0 in Maldives. Life expectancy at birth (the average age at death of those born in a given year, assuming no change in age-specific mortality rates) is three decades higher in Sri Lanka (74.5) than in Afghanistan (44.5). The population growth rate also shows dramatic differences across countries: from 3.3 percent per year in Afghanistan (a doubling time of about twenty-one years) to 0.8 percent per year in Sri Lanka (a doubling time of nearly ninety years). And most obviously, the countries of South Asia vary by size from India (1.2 billion) to the Maldives (300,000), which is 1/4,000th as large.[1]

The demographic circumstances prevailing in South Asia today reflect the changes that have occurred as part of South Asia's demographic transition: the shift from high rates of mortality and fertility to low ones. These changes have been dramatic. For example, the regional average IMR fell from 168 per 1,000 in the early 1950s to 53 today. TFR began to decline soon after the onset of IMR decline, with the regional average going from 5.9 children per woman in the late 1960s to 2.8 today. Life expectancy, which averaged 39 years in the early 1950s, has risen to nearly 65 years today. The region's total population has more than tripled since 1950, when it stood at 481 million.

Many countries exhibit a similar pattern to that of South Asia, in which improvements in child survival (due for example to increased access to safe water, sanitation and healthcare), subsequently lead to lower fertility, as families begin to see that fewer children are needed to achieve target family size. (In addition, numerous other factors influence family size. For example, women's increased educational attainment has a powerful effect, as do women's increased opportunities in the labor market. Increased urbanization – which takes place as people move from rural to urban areas, as rural areas grow to become urban, and as urban areas expand to encompass formerly rural areas – brings greater economic opportunities for both men and women, and the consequent increased economic value of people's time leads to lower fertility.) The key point here, however, is that the initial mortality decline leads to a baby boom, since fewer babies die and because fertility has not yet fallen.

Historical and Current Economic Situation

Consistent with widespread poverty in South Asia, gross domestic product (GDP)/ capita in the region is low. At $2,484 in 2008 (in purchasing power parity (PPP) terms and constant 2005 international dollars), the region lies at almost exactly half the income per person of the World Bank's low- and middle-income countries. The economically best-off countries in the region are the Maldives ($5,169), Bhutan

---

1 All demographic data is from the United Nations (2009). Country-specific data, from which regional data is assembled, is available only to 2050. The UN Population Division uses a set of assumptions about changes in fertility and mortality to produce data for future years. These assumptions are subject to debate, and the resulting data reflects considerable uncertainty. United Nations 2009 offers three sets of future population indicators, based on low-, medium-, and high-fertility scenarios. This paper uses data from the medium-fertility scenario. Under all three scenarios, South Asia's population will increase by 2050: to 2 billion if fertility rates follow the low scenario, to 2.32 billion in the medium scenario, and to 2.68 billion in the high scenario. Where this chapter refers to current figures, the data is for 2010.

Figure 1. Average annual growth rate of GDP/capita

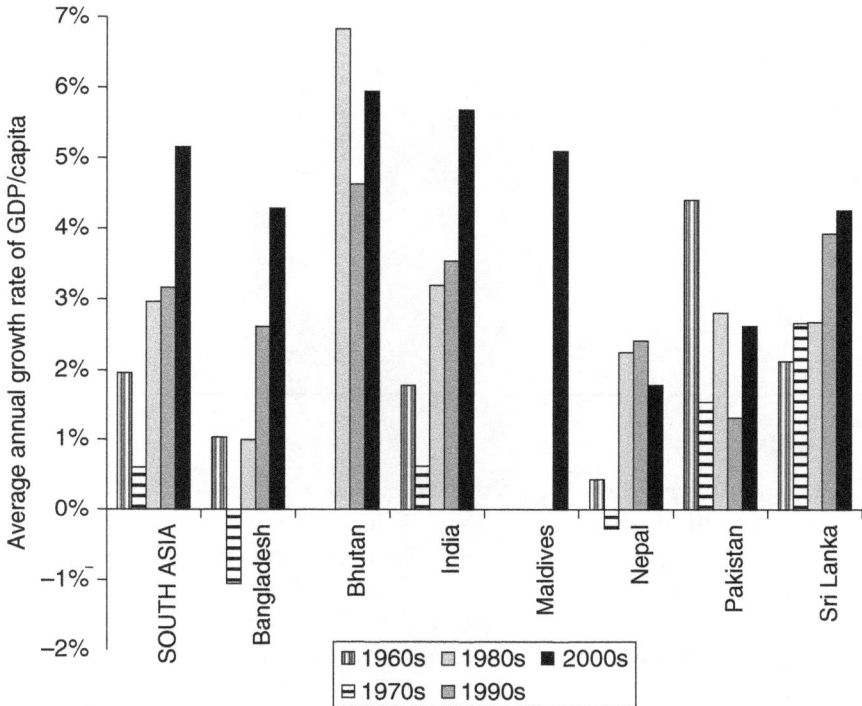

Source: World Bank (2013).
Note: Figures are exchange-rate based. A similar pattern appears if PPP figures are used, but the PPP data is not available before 1980. Data for Afghanistan is not sufficiently available to show changes over time.

($4,395) and Sri Lanka ($4,215). In the second tier lie India ($2,721) and Pakistan ($2,344). Bangladesh ($1,233), Nepal ($1,020) and Afghanistan ($1,019) are by far the poorest. Beyond this diversity of incomes, there are also wide ranges of economic well-being within the various countries.

Per capita income growth rates have varied dramatically across countries and over time. Figure 1 shows these growth rates for South Asia and individual countries. The region as a whole has been growing faster economically since the 1980s, a fact that is heavily affected by India's high share (74 percent in 2010) of South Asia's population, coupled with India's economic growth trajectory. South Asia's GDP per capita growth was low in the 1970s, higher in the 1980s and 1990s, and higher still in the 2000s.

Changing Age Structure

One consequence of the demographic transition is population growth, which (setting immigration aside) occurs when births exceed deaths. The region was growing at 1.8 percent annually in the early 1950s but sped up to a peak of 2.4 percent annually in the late 1970s. Since then, its annual growth rate has declined to its current level of 1.5 percent.

Table 1. Ratio of working-age to non-working-age population

	1970	2010	2050
SOUTH ASIA	1.24	1.74	2.08
Afghanistan	1.16	1.08	1.73
Bangladesh	1.10	1.87	2.02
Bhutan	1.24	1.88	1.98
India	1.26	1.80	2.13
Maldives	1.16	2.17	1.91
Nepal	1.23	1.50	2.13
Pakistan	1.16	1.46	2.02
Sri Lanka	1.31	2.12	1.57

Source: United Nations (2009).

But population growth is not the only consequence of South Asia's demographic transition. Another significant consequence is the change in the age structure of its population. This begins with the creation of the aforementioned baby boom, which quickly leads to a relatively large number of young people in the population. As fertility subsequently falls, the relative size of the "baby boom" generation is accentuated. With the passage of time, this cohort becomes a correspondingly large cohort of working-age adults.

For reasons that will become clear below, an especially salient change in demographic indicators is the increase in the ratio of working-age to non-working-age population. For South Asia as a whole, this ratio stood at 1.43 in 1950 and fell to 1.22 by 1965 as infant and child mortality rates fell. Since then, it has risen steadily to 1.74, as the baby boom generation has moved into working ages and as fertility rates continue to fall. The ratio is expected to reach a peak of 2.2 working-age individuals for every non-working-age person in 2040, before beginning to decline. Table 1 shows the historical and expected evolution of this ratio over time.

The countries of South Asia have, and will continue to experience, changes in age structure. Some countries in the region are very far along in their demographic transition: in Sri Lanka, for example, the working-age to non-working-age ratio reached its peak (2.2) in 2005. By contrast, Bangladesh is expected to peak at 2.3 in 2035, India at 2.3 in 2040 and Pakistan at 2.0 in 2045 (see Figure 2). At the opposite end of the spectrum, Afghanistan can expect its ratio to still be climbing in 2050, when it will be 1.7. Of course, all of these estimates depend on the actual path of fertility rates, mortality rates, and life expectancy – patterns that are often subject to a range of factors, including government policies.

Based on the demographic changes cited in the United Nations (UN) data, it is clear that the region will be very different demographically in 2050. With respect to age structure, our central measure of progress through the demographic transition,

Figure 2. Dramatically changing age structure

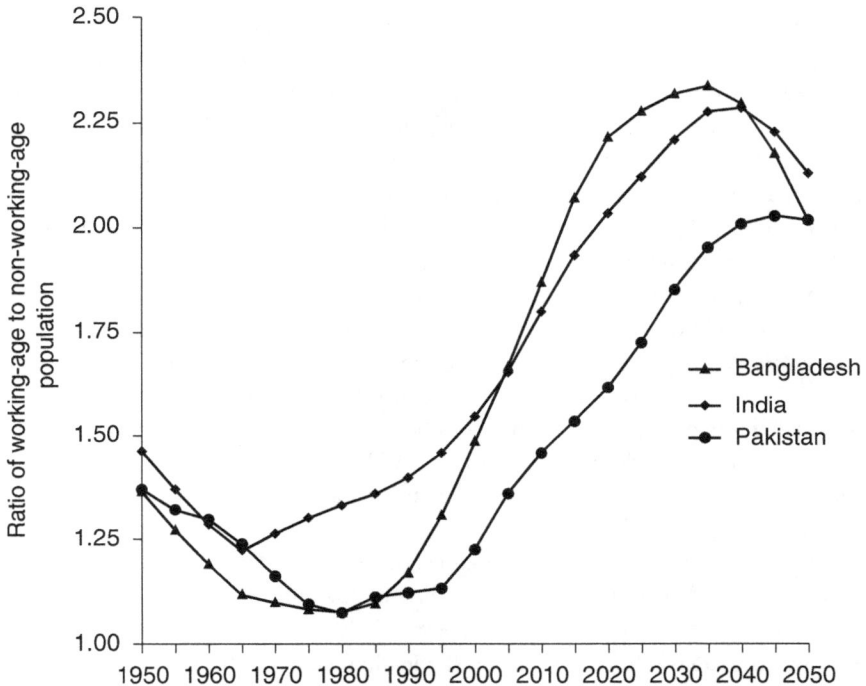

Source: United Nations (2009).

South Asia was quite homogeneous in 1970, with the ratio shown in Figure 2 ranging only from 1.10 to 1.31. Today this ratio ranges from 1.08 to 2.17. UN projections for 2050 show ratios ranging from 1.57 to 2.13. That is, there will be some convergence across the countries of the region, but this will occur slowly.

Linking Demographic Change and Economic Growth: The Demographic Dividend

Understanding the significance of these demographic changes requires an examination of the economic history of the region. In particular, the data shown above on the growth rate of GDP/capita is obviously relevant to a discussion of a possible interaction between demographic change and economic growth.

Two facts stand out from the previous discussion:

- The ratio of the working-age to non-working-age population in South Asia has been rising since 1965.
- The region's GDP per capita has been rising during the last 30 years of this period.

Is there a Connection?

For many years, rapid population growth was thought to be detrimental to economic growth. Thomas Malthus hypothesized that a rapidly growing population would inevitably outstrip any society's capacity to produce enough food, resulting in mass starvation and human misery. In the 1980s, a new idea, "population neutralism," came to the fore. Adherents of this view marshaled evidence to show that population growth was neither helpful nor detrimental to economic growth. More recent studies (Bloom and Canning 2008; Bloom, Canning and Sevilla 2002) have focused on the possible effects on economic growth of the age structure of a population. This body of research has found that, *ceteris paribus*, cross-country differences in age structure tend to translate into cross-country differences in macroeconomic performance. Specifically, a rise in the ratio of working-age to non-working-age population corresponds, in general, to increases in the rate of per capita economic growth. Roughly one-third of East Asia's economic "miracle" may have come about because of the rapid demographic changes that the region has undergone (Bloom and Williamson 1998). Propelled by similar demographic changes, Ireland also benefited economically, becoming the "Celtic tiger" (Bloom and Canning 2003).

This phenomenon has come to be known as the "demographic dividend." First, a baby boom cohort arises because of a decline in mortality rates that is followed, with a delay, by a decline in fertility rates. This relatively large cohort gradually enters the typical working ages – beginning when the leading edge of the baby boom enters its teens. A few decades later, the baby boom results in there being a disproportionately and historically large share of working-age individuals in a population – the pattern discussed above for South Asia. A rising, and relatively large, share of working-age people can be economically consequential because of the following factors:

- *Labor force size.* A rise in the share of working-age people means that a country's productive capacity is larger than it was in the past:
  - A higher share of people working, and a correspondingly lower share of children, allows a country to increase its per capita economic output.
  - The fact that there are fewer children per family allows more women to enter the workforce. Although women still bear a disproportionate burden of child raising, they are nevertheless more likely to enter the workforce when there are fewer children to take care of. Women's increased participation in the commercial economy can be highly significant in raising output per capita. Such participation is typically more possible and more remunerative than in the past because an increasing share of the population lives in urban areas, where earnings are higher than in rural areas.
- *Savings.* Savings may rise for two reasons, and increased savings may be channeled into increased investment via the financial system:
  - A preponderance of working-age people can lead to increased savings rates, because this age group saves more than the young or the old.

- o Because the demographic transition is accompanied by longer lifespans, workers also have an incentive to save more, in anticipation of longer periods of retirement.
- *Changed use of capital.* At both the family and the national level, resources can be redirected to spur economic growth:
  - o Families with fewer children can spend more on the health and education of each child without increasing their total expenses. Healthier children attend school more regularly, learn more while there and are poised to become more productive workers.
  - o At the national level, there are relatively fewer children to feed, clothe and educate. Even with continued construction of schools, a higher share of financial resources can be directed toward investments that yield returns in the short run via the creation of greater physical capital – factories, roads and other types of infrastructure.

Caveat Lector: Demography Is Not Destiny

Realization of a demographic dividend, via the mechanisms listed above, is far from automatic. A country's ability to capture the dividend depends on many factors and policies:

- Productive employment is the key. An economy can grow even if employment is stagnant, but inclusive economic growth, i.e., growth that benefits all sectors of society, requires the implementation of policies and practices that draw a large portion of the working-age population into the labor force. If large numbers of working-age people are unemployed, they will constitute an economic burden on those who do have jobs. Moreover, high unemployment or underemployment can become a major source of discontent.
- Particularly important is a country's ability to nurture its human capital. An educated labor force is much more likely to be able to work productively and to be able to adapt to the rapidly changing demands of an ever more global economy. Similarly, a healthy workforce will be more productive, and it may be better able to attract foreign direct investment.
- Carefully chosen and well-implemented policies and practices in other areas, such as governance, macroeconomic management, trade and social protection, are essential.
- Good relations with neighboring countries, trading partners and international institutions are important. Tense relations often lead to high military expenditures – and even wars – that detract from investments in physical or human capital that can more directly benefit the population at large.
- Internal peace is usually important for economic growth. Without it, a country will have a more difficult time ensuring a high level of employment.

To date, South Asia's economies have been improving, in response to many factors, quite possibly including the region's rising share of working-age people. Based on the

East Asian experience, the fact that South Asia is soon to see a further rise in the share of working-age people augurs well for increased per capita incomes in the coming decades. To be clear, this prediction is an "all-things-equal" statement. Demographic change may well operate as a significant factor in strengthening the region's economies, but (a) policies need to be in place to ensure widespread productive employment, and (b) factors completely apart from demographics may of course play a decisive role.

Two Potential Impediments to Realizing the Demographic Dividend

Within-country heterogeneity. Considerations similar to those discussed above apply within countries. The various states of India, for example, lie at very different points along the demographic transition (see Figure 3). The demographic heterogeneity of these states suggests that their future economic trajectories may differ significantly from each other. Thus, demographic heterogeneity may undermine the inclusivity of economic growth. In Indian states, as in the countries of the region, policies will need to be focused on specific measures that can promote productive employment.

Population aging. One further factor, population aging, is inherent to the demographic transition and potentially complicates the posited relationship between demographic change and economic growth. As the baby boom cohort reaches the upper end of the working ages, its leading edge begins to swell the ranks of the elderly. In conjunction with increased life expectancy, the end of this cohort's working years leads to there being an increasing share of the population that is elderly, not working, and dependent on the working-age population. Continued low fertility also contributes to the elderly representing a rising share of the population. The share of the region's population that is aged 60 or older stood at around 6 percent from 1950 through 1995. By 2010 it had reached 7 percent, and it is expected to reach nearly 19 percent by 2050. The countries of the region are aging at very different rates: Sri Lanka's 60+ population share is expected to increase from 12 percent to 28 percent over the next 40 years, Bangladesh's from 6 percent to 21 percent, India's from 8 percent to 20 percent, and Pakistan's from 6 percent to 15 percent. The share of those aged 80 or older is expected to rise from 0.6 percent in 2010 to 2.4 percent in 2050. This segment of the population is very unlikely to be working – and thus they are in general not contributing economically to the family or to the national economy. In general, their needs are much greater and more acute than those of the 60–79 group.

Population aging is a concern for various reasons. In South Asia, as elsewhere, traditional patterns of family care of the elderly are fraying – because of smaller families, more years between generations, women working more, movement to urban areas leaving the elderly behind and changes in social expectations. The elderly, who are often not able to support themselves and who most often have limited or no pensions, are financially dependent on others. Their contribution to economic output is greatly decreased. Although retirement policies have mostly so far been inapplicable to populations that are working primarily in the informal sector, countries will need to

Figure 3. Ratio, working-age to non-working-age population, by Indian state, 2001

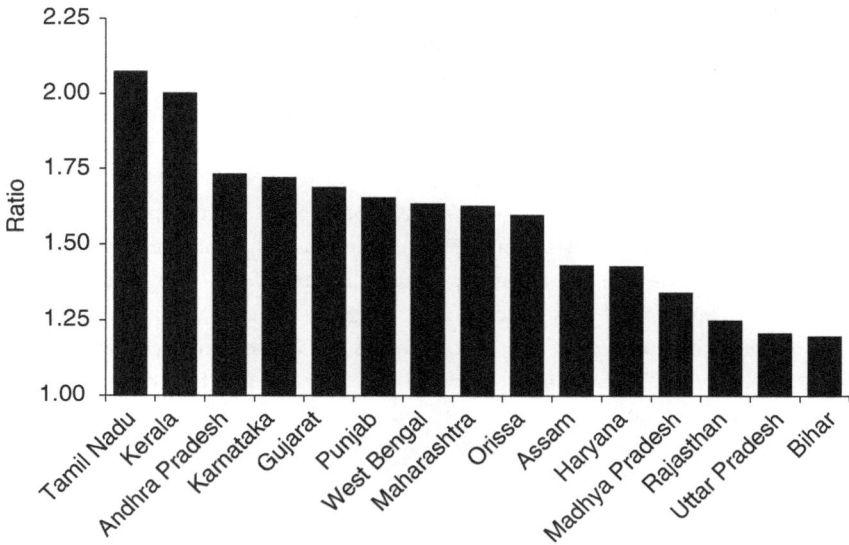

Source: Office of the Registrar General and Census Commissioner, Ministry of Home Affairs, India, 2001 (as shown in Bloom 2012).

rethink such policies, with a view to expanding pension coverage to a greater share of the population.

In addition, the elderly need greater access to healthcare, just at the time when their financial security is typically becoming worse. The strengthening of healthcare institutions and delivery that most countries need to accomplish is even more pressing in light of population aging. In the last few decades, several newly prominent factors have begun to affect population health, including the health of the elderly. Diets in many countries have become less healthy, as the availability of processed and packaged foods expands. Urban living, because of a combination of pollution, slums and in some instances an increase in sedentary jobs, is encouraging a significant increase in obesity and related chronic disease. Furthermore, the need to respond to chronic diseases comes while many developing countries are still dealing with the unfinished agenda of conquering infectious diseases.

Conclusion

Current demographic trends indicate that South Asia will be very different in the coming decades than it is today. Mortality and fertility rates will be lower, and life expectancy will be higher. Population growth will have slowed substantially. Of greatest note, the region's ratio of working-age to non-working-age population will have risen, peaked and begun to fall.

Economic predictions are much more difficult to make, as they depend on a much wider array of factors. But the coming demographic changes offer most of South Asia an opportunity to benefit from a demographic dividend. Policies that successfully promote productive employment are essential if this dividend is to be realized. Other factors are likely to play even larger roles in determining the region's economic future, but attempting to take advantage of the demographically driven opportunity is a wise move – especially because expanding work opportunities and enhancing the population's health and education are beneficial in their own right and would be good policy choices even in the absence of a demographic spur.

As the region's economies improve, the relationship between demographic change and economic growth suggests that the various countries' economic ranking within South Asia may change. Indeed, this has already happened. In 1980, India's GDP per capita, in PPP terms, was only 73 percent as large as Pakistan's. It stayed at roughly that level until the latter half of the 1990s, standing at 89 percent of Pakistan's level in 2000. By 2005, India had surpassed Pakistan by 2 percent, and in 2008, it was leading by 16 percent. The demographic comparison here is striking: India's TFR has fallen much faster than Pakistan's, and to a lower level (2.6 versus 3.8). Its working-age to non-working-age ratio began to rise earlier than did Pakistan's (1970 versus 1985), and it has reached a higher level (1.8 versus 1.5). More generally, the countries of South Asia are somewhat out of phase with respect to their demographic trajectories, which will create a tendency for their economic trajectories to be out of phase. This raises the possibility of other income crossovers and corresponding reordering of economic power.

It is apparent from this examination that there is considerable demographic and related economic heterogeneity both across countries and within them in South Asia. That heterogeneity has been and will continue to be a powerful driver of economic inequality. In addition, one might project that the lack of common circumstances suggests that South Asian leaders will continue to voice widely disparate interests. This poses a challenge to South Asia's coherence as an economic and political power.

Chapter 28

TOWARDS COOPERATION FOR POVERTY REDUCTION?

Safiya Aftab

Regional integration is a postcolonial process, the objectives of which are not always clear-cut. On the face of it, the process may be initiated as a means to foster economic cooperation, with trade facilitation being the major outcome. The underlying purpose of integration is, however, more often than not, for countries to forge links to safeguard their long-term political and security objectives, and to minimize the possibility of armed conflict. The most obviously successful example of regional integration in recent times is of course that of the European Union, which has effectively precluded armed conflict in Western Europe for the last 60 years. The broader objective of the South Asian Association for Regional Cooperation (SAARC) is to promote socioeconomic development in the region, but an offshoot of that stated strategy would be the maintenance of peace and security in the long term.

Cooperation in South Asia has, however, the added dimension of possibly being a catalyst for long-term poverty reduction in a region where one billion people (of a total of 1.5 billion), or 66 percent of the population, live on less than $2 a day (World Bank 2010a). The past decade's average annual regional growth, estimated at 6 percent, gives some cause for hope, but masks significant disparity in economic performance across the eight countries that comprise the region. Further, the link between gross domestic product (GDP) growth and poverty reduction is not always clear – the latter generally does not follow from the former unless redistribution of wealth and income is affected as part of a larger government policy of equitable development. So what is likely to happen to poverty incidence in South Asia in the long-term future? Can one dare to dream that there will be a significant improvement by 2060?

A Closer Look at Where We Are

It is difficult to get a uniform assessment of poverty incidence for the region, given that governments tend to use country-specific poverty lines for estimation, which are typically not comparable across different economies. The United Nations Development

Table 1. Country comparisons of poverty incidence

Country	$1.25 a day (PPP*) 2000–2009 %	National poverty line 2000–2009 %	Population in multidimensional poverty (head count %)
Bhutan	26.2	23.2	27.2
India	41.6	27.5	53.7
Pakistan	22.6	22.3	49.4
Nepal	55.1	30.9	64.7
Bangladesh	49.6	40.0	57.8
Sri Lanka	7.0	15.2	5.3
Maldives	1.5	16.0**	5.2
Afghanistan	NA	36.0	NA
Average	25.45	36	32.91

* PPP: purchasing power parity.
** This poverty line was equivalent to $1.17 in 2005.
Source: UNDP (2011), and ADB (2007) for Maldives national poverty lines.

Programme (UNDP)'s estimates of poverty incidence, as reported in its Human Development Report (HDR), which provide comparisons across standard measures such as the $1.25 a day and multidimensional poverty, as well as report on national poverty estimates, do however provide a starting point for the discussion.[1]

In general, the $1.25 a day cut-off should roughly correspond to a national poverty line, but as the data shows, this is not always the case. Bhutan, Pakistan and Bangladesh were three countries where the PPP estimate was close to the national poverty line, but in all other countries, the estimates varied significantly. For India, the $1.25 a day estimate of poverty incidence is 14 percentage points higher than the national poverty estimate, while for Sri Lanka the relationship between the two estimates is the other way round. The most glaring disparity is in Nepal, where the standardized estimate indicates that poverty incidence is over 55 percent, while the national poverty line estimates poverty incidence at less than a third of the population. The Maldives had a negligible incidence of poverty according to the PPP estimate, but the national poverty line estimated incidence at 16 percent. Afghanistan's national poverty estimate was second only to that of Bangladesh, but the country's poor security conditions presumably make data collection very difficult.

A more interesting measure is the relatively newly reported one of poverty, as measured through a multidimensional index, which accounts for deprivations in

---

1 The concept of multidimensional poverty indices is new for UNDP, and the first such indices were published in 2010. The indices identify multiple deprivations in health, education and standard of living, and classify households as poor or nonpoor depending on the number of deprivations the household is experiencing. Thus one or two deprivations may not cause a household to be classified as "poor," but if the weighted index of indicators in which the household is deprived adds up to 33 percent of the total weightage, the household is classified as poor.

Table 2. Country comparisons of key social indicators

Country	Gross national income (GNI) per capita in 2011 (PPP constant 2005 $)	Adult literacy rate percent aged 15+	Life expectancy at birth years	GNI per capita rank minus HDI rank *
Sri Lanka	4,943	90.6	74.9	12
India	3,468	62.8	65.4	−10
Pakistan	2,550	55.5	65.4	−7
Nepal	1,160	59.1	68.8	8
Bangladesh	1,529	55.9	68.9	11
Maldives	5,276	98.4	76.8	−3
Bhutan	5,293	52.8	67.2	−36
Afghanistan	1,416	NA	48.7	−13
Average	3,204.38	59.39	67.01	−4.75

*A positive figure indicates that the country is doing better on social indicators and human development than would be obvious from its per capita income. That is, its HDI ranking is better than its GNI ranking (given that for both GNI and HDI, a lower number represents a better ranking).
Source: UNDP (2011).

health, education and standards of living. For all countries except Sri Lanka and the Maldives, this measure estimates poverty incidence at a higher level than the income centered measures cited earlier. The most glaring disparity is for Pakistan, where the multidimensional index places poverty incidence at almost half of the population, compared to the quarter that national poverty estimates (albeit dated, given that they were calculated in 2005) would concede.

In spite of the inconsistencies, the data enables us to draw some broad conclusions. Even by conservative national estimates, approximately a third of South Asia's population, or close to 500 million people, live below the poverty line.

Poverty incidence does not appear to be correlated with overall population size (it is high in the populous states of India and Bangladesh, but also in the sparsely populated Nepal), or with conflict (Sri Lanka, which has faced an internecine civil war over a long period of time fares much better than average in terms of poverty and social development), or with physical features or terrain (the mountainous state of Nepal fares as badly or worse as does the delta which comprises Bangladesh). We can say, however, without indicating a causality that poverty occurs concomitantly with generally poor social indicators.[2] As Table 2 indicates, the average adult literacy rate for the South Asian region is 59.4 percent, while the average life expectancy is 67 years. The two island nations of Sri Lanka and the Maldives admittedly have social indicators that are on par with middle to high income nations. Other than that, South Asia has little to boast about.

---

2 Sri Lanka is probably the obvious exception to this rule, but its long-running civil war has skewed the country's development trajectory.

An interesting indicator of trends in development is given in the last column of the table. Countries whose gross national income (GNI) per capita rank is lower than the human development index (HDI) rank, and who thus have positive scores in this category, can be thought of as "investor" nations. In effect, their investment in human development is more than what would be expected from them given their level of per capita income. The reverse is true for those with negative scores. By this measure, South Asia seems to be moving in the wrong direction – the average score for the region is negative, indicating that in general, the region ranks better on GNI per capita than on HDI. Thus as a region, South Asia's human development appears to be lagging.

Individually, only three of the countries for whom scores were reported have an HDI rank which exceeds their ranking by GDP per capita. Not surprisingly, these include Sri Lanka and Bangladesh, both of whom have invested heavily in social sectors. Nepal also falls in this category. The glaring exceptions for South Asia are India and Pakistan, both of whom have not fared as well on human development as their income level would warrant. As the region's two biggest economies (although India's economy dwarfs that of Pakistan and all the rest of South Asia), their relatively low human development status has implications for the future development of the region.

Poverty Incidence and GDP

If GDP growth for the region as a whole remains on track at roughly 5 percent, South Asia's GDP will be close to $20 trillion by 2060, or roughly the level at which Europe is today. South Asia will still be playing catch-up, but given that the rate of growth in developed economies is far lower than the average for this region, the gap will have narrowed somewhat. But what would this mean for poverty in the region? To evaluate this, we have to get a sense of whether GDP growth does indeed coincide with poverty reduction in South Asia. Can we assume that a certain level of growth will indeed feed back positive effects in the economy such that there will be a reduction in poverty? Some back of the envelope calculations on elasticity of poverty incidence with respect to GDP, which show how poverty incidence is likely to change, given certain growth levels, give some indication.

Table 3 below gives poverty incidence and GDP in South Asia for two years, 1990 and 2004. The choice of these years for our estimation has been dictated by restrictions on data availability. The most recent and reliable data on poverty incidence in South Asia over two periods of time comes from a recently published report on the SAARC Development Goals or SDGs (ISACPA 2007). Data on GDP in South Asia for the same years was taken from the World Development Indicators 2009 published by the World Bank and is available online.

Essentially, this measure is used to deduce if change in one variable (in this case, GDP) is likely to be accompanied by change in another (in this case, poverty incidence). We do not imply causality here; we do not say that GDP growth causes poverty to decrease. All we are measuring is the degree of coincidence. The standard

Table 3. Poverty incidence and GDP in South Asia

Year	Poverty % below $1 a day (PPP values)	GDP Billion US $
1990	41.3	402.4
2004	31.3	890.6

Source: ISACPA (2007) and World Bank (2009).
Note: The elasticity of poverty incidence with respect to GDP can then be calculated as the percentage change in poverty incidence divided by the percentage change in GDP. Thus: *Elasticity of poverty incidence with respect to GDP = (change in poverty incidence/poverty incidence at time 0) / (change in GDP/GDP at time 0).*

interpretation of the elasticity measure is that if it is equal to 1, a percent change in one variable correlates with the same percent change in the other. An elasticity of more than 1 shows that change in one variable is associated with a greater than proportionate variability in the other and vice versa. Similarly the sign of the estimate shows whether the two variables are moving in the same direction or otherwise.

In this case, the measurement of the elasticity of poverty incidence with respect to GDP yields a value of −0.2. Thus it can be inferred that an increase in GDP is associated with a decrease in poverty incidence and vice versa, or the two variables are negatively associated. This corresponds to the conventional wisdom on growth and poverty. However, the absolute value of the elasticity measure is significantly less than one. This would indicate that while the negative relationship exists, there is relative inelasticity in the correlation. Thus while an increase in GDP is likely to be associated with a decrease in poverty incidence, the effect is not very strong. To translate this into more concrete terms, if the GDP is assumed to increase by 5 percent per annum, poverty will decrease by just about 1 percent per annum, by which measure, the poverty incidence in South Asia would still be close to 18 percent in 2060. This is hardly a welcome long-term prospect.

What can be done to improve South Asia's long-term prospects for poverty reduction? Broadly, if our elasticity measure is to be used as a yardstick, South Asian governments will either have to increase GDP growth rates significantly, and/or ensure that growth becomes more "inclusive" essentially effecting poverty reduction more strongly. Ideally both outcomes should occur simultaneously. If average annual growth in the region were to be in the region of 8 percent rather than 5 percent, poverty incidence would still be in the range of 14–16 percent in 2060. On the other hand, if the absolute value of the elasticity of poverty incidence with respect to growth were to increase to say 0.6, then an annual average rate of growth of 5 percent would result in poverty incidence coming down to about 6 percent by 2060. In a "best-case" scenario, where the annual average rate of growth is 8 percent per annum, and the elasticity of poverty incidence is −0.6, poverty incidence would fall to 2 percent by 2060. But what are the chances of South Asia experiencing high growth, while making sure that the benefits of that growth reach the poorest sections of the population?

Growth Projections and Poverty Reduction Policy

Growth forecasting is more an art than a science, and as per the dictates of human nature, tends to err on the optimistic side. The World Bank's recently published South Asia Economic Update 2010 provides a short-term snapshot, and postulates that South Asia has been least affected by the recent global slowdown of all the developing regions (World Bank 2010b). It puts regional growth at 7 percent in 2010 and 8 percent in 2011. Individual country projections are more diverse, as discussed below, but are generally on the high side.

To begin with the two largest economies in the region, India's medium-term growth projections place annual average GDP growth at 10 percent over the next five to seven years, compared to 7.4 percent in the last fiscal year. Pakistan's projections have necessarily been muted by the country's exceptionally poor economic performance in the last three years, but growth is still expected to average 5 percent over the next five years (2010 to 2015). In fact, the report of the Panel of Economists, which sets out the medium term growth policy, sounds confident that it may increase to almost 7 percent by 2015 (Government of Pakistan, Planning Commission 2010). Medium term growth forecasts for Bangladesh and Bhutan are similarly in the range of 5.5 to 6 percent according to the World Bank and the government, while Nepal and the Maldives are projected to grow at more modest levels of 3 to 4 percent.[3] Sri Lanka's government is newly confident of its ability to boost growth given its success in ending the decades old conflict that was devastating for the national economy, and projects that long-term growth in the country will average 8 percent. Afghanistan's growth, starting as it does from a very low base, was estimated at 22 percent in the last fiscal year, and is projected at over 8 percent for the medium term.

South Asia's projected growth is predicated on the growth of a labor-intensive manufacturing sector, the continued resilience of remittances, and on increases in foreign direct investment inflows among other things. In addition, the region's growing integration with East Asia (for example that of India with South Korea and Japan through the relocation of car manufacturing enterprises) is being cited as a positive trigger. At the same time, the costs of the continuing conflict in Afghanistan, which is threatening to engulf Pakistan can potentially derail at least part of the region, as can the continuing disturbance in Nepal and the Naxalite insurgency in India. In general, regional security can gain from economic integration, but such initiatives require national governments to take bold political decisions and develop a vision for the future that sees South Asia as an integrated regional market. At the moment, the chances of this happening are slim, mainly on account of the unresolved territorial dispute between India and Pakistan.

South Asia may well grow at 6 to 8 percent in the medium to long term, but effecting poverty reduction in the region is likely to remain an uphill task unless public

3 Based on the World Bank's "Country Economic Updates," available online at http://bit.ly/ 9IQYUT (accessed June 2013).

policy is specifically directed towards ensuring that the benefits of growth reach large sections of society. In some cases, this may mean something quite ambitious such as the need to effect asset redistribution, particularly improving access to land for the rural poor. In other cases, results may be achieved from improving farm and nonfarm linkages – essentially helping rural households to process agricultural commodities for value addition. In all cases, governments need to do more to ensure that all economic agents face a level playing field, whether this needs to be done by bringing in new regulation, improving enforcement, or in some cases by doing away with special treatment of specific interest groups. Again, another universal requirement is to keep up with efforts to improve social indicators, particularly in health and education, and to reduce the glaring income inequality and inequality of opportunity that continues to plague the society. South Asia is a young region: the dependency ratio is estimated at approximately 70 percent. There are conflicting theories on whether this is an advantage (the demographic dividend theory) or a potential source of social conflict (the youth bulge theory). Conventional wisdom and recent experiences with conflict zones in the region would suggest that the latter theory is more plausible for the region; social policy that reduces societal tensions is most likely to be an imperative.

Poverty reduction strategies in general and for South Asia in particular have been extensively discussed in the literature generated by international development agencies, the IFIs and by national governments and will not be repeated here. Suffice to say that governments know what to do, but in many cases seem to lack the will to do it.

Conclusion

So where do we see South Asia in 2060 when it comes to poverty and social development? Barring a serious escalation of regional conflict, South Asia seems set to grow at a relatively high rate. But without a serious realignment of government policy towards income redistribution and investment in human development; and in the absence of concerted efforts for regional integration, this growth will not translate into significant poverty reduction. In effect, poverty is likely to remain a feature of the economy of South Asia in the long term, if current trends continue.

This is, however, not an inescapable fate. The South Asian leadership needs to wake up to the fact that the region cannot fulfill its potential for growth and structural transformation without the resolution of regional political issues and unless the possibility of armed conflict abates significantly. Further, governments cannot become complacent about the region's apparent ability to weather global crises or rebound on a long-term high growth trajectory – this characteristic of the region may not result in poverty alleviation and in a worse-case scenario (if the benefits of growth continue to be divided unequally) may exacerbate social unrest.

South Asia needs a vision for the long-term future to ensure that the region emerges as a peaceful, prosperous part of the world, where jockeying for regional hegemony is less important than the well-being of its people. The region is currently at the center of the world's attention as its ongoing conflicts threaten to spill over beyond its boundaries. This may be an opportunity rather than a catastrophe, in that the region's leadership may consider using the good offices of the international community to forge peace and garner support for development efforts. The alternative is to remain mired in a low equilibrium stranglehold of poverty and underdevelopment.

Chapter 29

HEALTH CHALLENGES*

Gerald T. Keusch and Pramilla Senanayake

Introduction

Health disparities in South Asia are legendary, made even more apparent by the huge number of people in the region. The combined population of India, the giant of the region, Pakistan, Bangladesh, Sri Lanka, the Maldives, Afghanistan, Nepal and Bhutan is in excess of 2.25 billion, a third or more of whom toil at the very bottom of the economic ladder, earning no more than $1–2 per capita per day. While survival is possible, as the numbers demonstrate, development, a process of continuous improvement, is not. So many people living in abject poverty, suffering from ailments the wealthy are no longer exposed to, and having limited access to healthcare and preventive services, is a societal time bomb. It is the substrate for social disintegration and class struggle, for when the disparities are so great between the poor and the rich and life aspirations are so limited, those with nothing to lose may choose desperate ways to break out of the trap. Such struggles are commonplace in many poor developing countries, and are increasingly amplified by poor governance, corrupt leadership and extreme political views. This chapter will explore issues central to ensuring, by 2060, more equitable and optimal health for the people of the South Asian nations.

Health and Development

Health is now widely recognized to be an essential precondition for development. The evidence for this is well documented in the report of the Commission on Macroeconomics and Health (World Health Organization 2001), and it makes sense: healthy children learn better and healthier, better-educated adults are more productive and can generate greater individual and societal wealth. Rather than the traditional trickle-down concept that wealth creates health – it never adequately reaches down to the poor or the poorly educated – the operative concept is that health creates wealth,

* We thank Dr K. Mohandas, vice chancellor of Kerala University of Health and Allied Sciences, Thrissur, India, for his careful reading of this paper and for his thoughtful comments and suggestions.

Table 1. Country comparisons of key social indicators

Country	GDP billion US$ in 2010	GDP per capita (PPP) in US$	Poverty head count ratio at $1.25 a day (PPP) (% of population)	Population (in thousands)	Expenditure on health, public (% of GDP)	Life expectancy at birth years	Under five mortality (per 1,000 live births)	Human development index (HDI) rank minus GDP per capita rank*
Sri Lanka	**48.2**	**4,900**	**7.0**	**21,513**	**2.0**	**74**	**15**	**14**
India	**1430**	**3,400**	**41.6**	**1,173,108**	**1.1**	**63.4**	**69**	**-6**
Pakistan	174.8	2,400	22.6	184,404	0.8	66.2	89	-9
Nepal	15.1	1,200	55.1	28,951	2.0	66.3	51	21
Bangladesh	105.4	1,700	49.6	156,118	1.1	65.7	54	9
Maldives	1.4	4,500	1.5	395	6.4	71.1	28	9
Bhutan	1.3	5,000	26.2	699	3.3	66.8	81	NA
Average	–		25.45			67.8		

*A positive figure indicates that the country is doing better on social indicators and human development than would be obvious from its GDP per capita.

Note: The UNDP's HDR did not report on social indicators for Bhutan. Data on Afghanistan is not available.

Source: UNDP (2009, 2010); CIA, *The World Factbook*, World Bank, World Development Indicators.

from the bottom up to the top so that all derive benefit. Admittedly this may seem somewhat naïve, as we have witnessed the egregious rewards to those at the top of the financial and banking system who were responsible for the economic crisis of the past several years. Their apparent lack of concern for the poor and middle class, who bore the brunt of job and income losses, is a real-world example that provides little comfort that society will ever willingly make the necessary investments in health, especially for those at the bottom who can least afford it or afford to be without it.

The poor are often trapped in poverty because they lack access to education, the key to unlocking the barriers to a better life. They are also poorly educated because they are poor, and because they are poor they bear a burden of ill health unlike that of the wealthy. The gap is widened because they are also too poor to afford the food needed for optimum health. Ill health in early childhood, compounded by malnutrition – a consequence of poor diet and the adverse affects of repeated infection on nutritional status, a relationship aptly described some fifty years ago as synergistic – limits cognitive development and learning capacity, and the deficit is difficult to overcome because of continued entrapment in poverty. Malnourished adults cannot work to their full potential, thus limiting income. The result can only be described as a vicious cycle, and a true and ever-deepening trap. This is particularly prevalent in South Asia. See Table 1 for an overview of the region.

Recent Progress – India and Sri Lanka

At the same time, the picture is not entirely discouraging. Viewed through a lens focused on contrasting India and Sri Lanka, and persisting gender-based discrimination in access to healthcare, improvements in health status are apparent for many in South Asia, and, along with it, improvements in social status and wealth. In India, for example, over the past several decades the prevalence of severe malnutrition among children has significantly diminished; indeed India nowadays is alarmed by the increase in obesity rates. Many factors are involved in bringing about this improvement, including the Green Revolution, which has helped to meet basic food needs (but has also caused significant environmental consequences and may not be scalable at the level needed to address the added needs due to continuing population growth). In addition, organized campaigns to immunize children against common infectious diseases, programs to combat the impact of acute diarrheal and respiratory infections through the judicious use of oral rehydration therapy for the former and appropriate antibiotics for the latter, and through multiple efforts to prevent and effectively treat malaria closer to the scale needed, have reduced the burden of acute infectious illness. Although the HIV epidemic in India has not been as damaging as many thought it would be, or as it is in Sub-Saharan Africa, this is not necessarily due to the effectiveness of interventions by the government, but more likely linked to a combination of factors including social activism, culture and luck. Still, the overall burden of disease remains high among the poor, and among the wealthier the combination of genetic factors and lifestyle choices, such as diet, have resulted in a frightening "epidemic" of diabetes, cardiovascular disease, stroke and obesity. Similarly, despite near universal primary education and literacy amongst its youth, one in five adults in Sri Lanka is either diabetic or prediabetic, with all of its implications for cardiovascular disease and stroke. While some of these conditions can be managed by drugs, diet and exercise, there remains an excessive and increasing toll in morbidity, premature death and medical care costs throughout the region, even if the known interventions are applied fully and efficiently.

Measures of Health Status and Quality of Health Systems

There are a number of markers of a healthy society served by a robust healthcare system. Longevity – especially healthy years lived – is an overall measure of the health of a society. Sri Lanka currently ranks 85th in the world at 75.1 years, while India at 66.1 years is 161st. Looking at other countries in the region, Pakistan ranks 167th at 65.2 years, Nepal 165th at 65.4 years, Afghanistan 219th at 44.4 years, Bangladesh 184th at 60.2 years, Maldives 97th at 73.9 years and Bhutan 159th at 66.1 years. However, living longer means an added increment to population size, with increasing numbers of dependent old people adding to the already large and increasing proportion of the dependent young due to high birth rates. This will further stress the ability to feed people and to improve their health and living conditions, and new and effective means to reduce population growth are going to be critical in all countries of the region. Climate change will likely increase these concerns, as sea levels rise and severe weather, drought and flooding become more widespread. In the region, the Maldives and Bangladesh (already 50 percent covered with water) are at particular risk.

More specific metrics provide further insights into the functioning of a health system, such as maternal mortality rates, premature births, neonatal or under-5-year-old mortality, rates of immunization for vaccine preventable diseases, incidence of malaria or tuberculosis, HIV infection and, of course, access to treatment and/or prevention modalities. One measure of the effectiveness of current national efforts to improve health is the likelihood of achieving the health-related Millennium Development Goals (MDG) to eradicate extreme poverty and hunger, reduce child mortality, improve maternal health and combat HIV/AIDS, malaria and other infectious diseases. While it is predicted that most countries in South Asia are unlikely to achieve these goals by the target date of 2015, the picture in Sri Lanka is different and appears to be on track for most of the health-related MDGs. For example, regarding Goal 5 relating to maternal mortality targets, in 1990 the maternal mortality ratio per 100,000 live births was 0.92 and by 2001 was already halved to 0.47 and is expected to reach 0.36 by 2015. Efforts by the Institute for Health Metrics at the University of Washington in Seattle, and the World Health Organization, among others, will help define new and better measures of the health and disease burden of societies, and pave the way for more accurate assessment of progress and the efficacy of various interventions.

Where is India Today?

Nonetheless, for India, the future looks bright, even if clouds remain. The economy is growing at a near double-digit rate. Many fields directly relevant to improving health status look particularly exciting, such as information technology and the pharmaceutical industry. While the potential for further improvement has increased as India has become fully compliant with World Trade Organization regulations, is exploring free trade agreements with the West, and has adopted an intellectual property regime that invites foreign investment, it also carries with it the challenge to keep prices affordable and ensure access to new products. The country also has a large number of well-educated, highly intelligent citizens who have made many significant contributions to global science, medicine and the humanities. Many of them, however, have chosen to live abroad because of the perception of limited opportunities in India, a relatively inflexible social organization and a culture that often constrains innovation. While the trend of well-educated Indians settling abroad is reversing, the pace at which this is happening is currently inadequate for the needs at home. The number of Indians able to obtain quality public higher education in fields of their interest and passion is also limited by the capacity of existing universities to meet the demands, paving the way for new private-sector institutions of dubious quality to enter the market. The outcome cannot be satisfactory for either individual aspirations or the needs of society.

The public-sector health system remains limited, overstretched and underfunded to be able to provide consistent quality care for those who depend on it. Facilities are old, sometimes crumbling, and typically dingy and depressing. Just walk into the emergency department or ambulatory clinics of the best pubic institutions and you are impressed by the number of patients seeking care and become immediately aware of the overwhelming burden this places on even well-trained and well-intentioned medical and nursing staff. This is a formula for fatigue, if not ultimate burnout. As a result, the inevitable medical errors in such a setting are linked to the former and the loss to the system of the most clinically experienced staff due to the latter. To make it worse, in rural areas public clinics are limited in number, inconveniently located for many to access them or closed when there is need of emergency services.

With a rising middle class able to afford more personalized and accessible healthcare and willing to pay for it, a parallel private system catering to their needs has been growing. Although many private ambulatory clinics and small private hospitals dot the landscape, unless a system for evaluation of outcomes is developed, it is inevitable that many will remain subpar, generating increased revenues for themselves but not improved health for their patients. There are also clean, well-equipped, new private-sector hospitals, staffed by well-qualified physicians and other health professionals, with up-to-date laboratory and diagnostic capacities. The chains of specialty hospitals run by Apollo, Fortis and Max Healthcare attain a consistently higher standard and are therefore attractive to those able to afford the costs, providing services Indians previously had to travel internationally to obtain. They also attract foreigners seeking lower-cost interventions, and this business line, so-called medical tourism, is a significant part of the revenues generated by these openly for-profit institutions. However, unless such revenues are used to subsidize care to the less affluent, they will do little to improve the health of the poor.

Where is Sri Lanka Today?

Remarkable progress has been made by Sri Lanka in the social and health sectors since independence, including an extensive network of health services. This is in part, perhaps a large part, the consequence of Sri Lanka's outstanding national performance in primary education, the best in South Asia. The country is close to achieving universal primary education, with a net enrollment of over 98 percent of the eligible population in 2003, with nearly 98 percent of the children in primary school reaching grade five and youth literacy rates of 95.6 percent. Primary, secondary and tertiary education is free in Sri Lanka, and, since 1997, education for the 5–14 year age group has been mandatory and facilitated through an island wide network of 10,475 primary and secondary schools. However, dropouts before completing secondary schooling remain a concern. They are more commonly boys than girls, and among the poor in low-income urban neighborhoods, the tea plantation sector, remote deprived villages and the recent conflict areas of the north and east. Going forward, then, Sri Lanka needs to ensure that policies promoting the participation of poor, rural, street and other disadvantaged children are in place and applied.

This is not to say there are no other problems on the horizon. Since 1990, the country has achieved only a marginal decrease in the overall infant mortality rate. Maternal health and nutritional status during pregnancy and access to quality prenatal, at delivery and postnatal care remain contributing factors. Although contraceptive prevalence rates are high, with 70 percent of women reporting access to and use of birth control, the quality of family planning services and prevention of unwanted pregnancies is uneven, and unsafe illegal abortions continue to take place. Services must be improved in the former conflict areas and in the plantation sector, where health indicators lag behind the rest of the country. Nonetheless, the national infant mortality rate, which was 19.3 per 1,000 live births in 1990, was reduced to 12.2 by 2,000, exceeding the 2015 MDG target of 12.8. But, only 42 percent of mothers in the plantation sector are visited by health workers, and infant mortality was 1 in 20 in the 2000 Demographic and Health Survey, whereas in urban areas 90 percent of mothers receive home visits. Similarly, under-5 mortality was 22.2 per 1,000 live births in 1990, 18.8 in 2000, and by 2015 is predicted to reach the target of 12.0/1,000 live births. This is surely due to the provision of key services. For example, the proportion of the population with sustainable access to an improved water source, both urban and rural, was 72 percent in 1994, 82 percent in 2001 and is on track to reach 86 percent by 2015; the proportion with access to improved sanitation was 74 percent in 1994, 80 percent in 2001 and is on track to reach 93 percent by 2015; and the proportion of children immunized against measles by year one was 80 percent in 1990, increased to 88 percent in 2000 and by 2003 had reached the MDG target of 99 percent.

Challenges for the Future

Looking at the future, it is possible to observe a number of challenges for the region. India is at once an old civilization and a young modernizing country. It has been forged out of a past of royal city-states, a long colonial period, followed by 60 years of turbulent independence and intermittent war with Pakistan. In 2060 independent India will be just a decade over a century old. What needs to happen in the next 50 years if this country is to achieve the level of health and quality of life its politicians promise and its population craves? First, the public sector must invest seriously, significantly and sustainably in facilities, beginning with community-based clinics focused on prevention and treatment of the common illnesses that occur, all the way to secondary and tertiary facilities for more complex problems. Referral needs to be simple, seamless and secure.

Second, the number of quality medical schools needs to increase to meet demands. This too represents a significant investment, for the training of new physicians requires faculty who are able to teach the science and the art of medicine, appropriate facilities and the tools to provide quality care. It is expensive to build, and many of the new private medical schools are falling far short of the quality expected.

Third, a new workforce of physician and nonphysician public health workers is essential. The movement in India to open new schools of public health by the government and the Public Health Foundation of India is welcome, but the numbers and the current pace of development cannot match the need. It is presently unclear who will employ these new public health workers, without substantial commitment of resources from the government. The new workforce also needs to engage with traditional medical practitioners, who in turn must be informed by evidence-based evaluation of their practices.

Fourth, a new workforce of physician extenders is required, who are capable of providing care beyond the level of a well-trained nurse. Training of physician assistants or nurse practitioners requires capacities beyond the usual nursing program and is several steps closer to the level of physician education. At the same time, adequately trained, disciplined and supervised lower-level health workers will remain the bulwark of the healthcare system, meeting basic and sometimes targeted needs, e.g., immunization teams. It will not help if physicians actively work to limit the training of other professionals.

Fifth, a new generation of biomedical and bioengineering expertise is needed within academic medical institutions to develop innovative, effective but low-cost solutions to the major public health problems of the population. These must link to the private sector to produce these products, something neither academia nor government is particularly adept at.

Sixth, there must be a private-sector biotech and pharmaceutical capacity to move innovations into products that are effective, safe and both low-cost and highly cost effective. These are substantial challenges that will require exceptionally good planning, strong leadership and public-sector funding commitments at a scale not seen before. The Indian government cannot hope to achieve this while continuing to invest in military defenses on the India–Pakistan border. Improved health will surely be one of the dividends of peace in the region. Left to its own, the private sector will develop a market-based industry without the commitment to develop and deliver the products needed to improve public health in India – and worker productivity – at a cost affordable by government or lower-income individuals.

India must train and retain its best and brightest if it ever hopes to achieve these goals. The needs of Pakistan are similar, but Pakistan is smaller and lacks the economic-growth potential of India or the institutional capacity for innovation in health. The two giants of South Asia would better serve their own needs by working together to solve common problems.

Sri Lanka, too, is an ancient civilization that passed through a series of Buddhist monarchies, a long colonial period sequentially dominated by the Portuguese, the Dutch and the British, followed by independence in 1948. The past 50 years have been punctuated by rebellions by a far-left Sinhalese political minority and the prolonged rebellion of the Hindu Tamil Tigers, ending last year. The circumstances in Sri Lanka are different now that the country is, hopefully, firmly entering a post–civil war development phase, when it may become possible to invest in internal growth and development rather than military operations. There remain many challenges. If education is a key to development and improved health, Sri Lanka faces a shortage of qualified teachers, exacerbated by their uneven distribution across the country. Investments in facilities, curriculum and maintaining quality standards are all ongoing problems. Although poverty has declined since independence, the rate has slowed significantly and from 1990 to 2002 income inequality widened significantly, with the income of the poorest 20 percent increasing by about 36 percent while the income of the richest 20 percent increased by 49 percent. The disparity in income distribution is also apparent when comparing the consumption levels of the different segments of society. Over the same period of time, consumption of the poorest quintile increased by just 2.2 percent, while consumption expenditures of the richest quintile grew by 50 percent.

India, Sri Lanka and South Asia, 2060

Looking ahead to 2060, and taking into consideration the sheer size of the problem in just India alone, a lot of "out-of-the-box" thinking is needed for India to get out of the present poor education and indifferent health quagmire it is in. First, India has a long tradition of supporting multiple systems other than contemporary science-based medicine. Thus, practitioners of ayurveda, unani and homeopathy are out there, in the field, with a fair amount of public acceptance. It would be useful to devise mechanisms to effectively integrate them into the healthcare delivery machinery – not necessarily integration in "treatment" but in prevention of diseases and promotion of health. Roping them in as part of a systematic approach to improve the health of the people could more quickly help to overcome the predicted and increasing human resource scarcities. Second, huge sums are diverted towards achieving regional, religious and political stability and security. The "regional soil" is, unfortunately, ripe for the growth and perpetuation of this diversion, due largely to the inequitable distribution of opportunities and resources, and the consequent "loss of hope" among large sections of the public. Third, even where access to healthcare is not the problem, as in the Indian state of Kerala, there remains a preoccupation with curative medicine, continually driven by technology to be expensive and as a consequence limited in availability. This means medicine and public health must become equal partners in improving health, and together undergird discovery science and biomedical engineering initiatives that focus on high-quality and low-cost tools for disease prevention first, and secondarily to treat what cannot be prevented. Fourth, cultural traditions that limit the education of girls and the roles of women in society must radically change to ensure that the energies and capabilities of this critical half of the population is not lost, but can be captured to promote health of children and families. Finally inspired leadership is essential to ensure equity and probity in public life, to restore the hope and confidence of the young and to implement measures aimed at broadly improving education and health. Of course the nations of South Asia, most obviously India and Pakistan, must learn to live with each other and to collaborate and contribute to problem solving. If they do not, it is hard to see how the other South Asian nations can reach their own desired level of health.

For its part, Sri Lanka must reduce income inequalities and disparities in access to health services, vigorously pursue universal education though high school and open the opportunities for higher education for all, reduce the tensions between the majority Sinhalese and minority Hindu populations and promote economic development in order to keep well-trained professionals in the country and entice those who leave to return. According to the Institute for Policy Studies of the International Organization for Migration in 2009, Sri Lanka had the highest migration rate of doctors and the third highest of nurses to developed Organisation for Economic Co-operation and Development (OECD) countries. As a result there were only 800 specialty-trained doctors in the country to serve a population of 20 million people. To achieve its health targets Sri Lanka will also need a peace dividend, and be prepared to work collaboratively and effectively with all of the region's members.

It is also apparent that similar innovations are going to be required in the other countries of the region, with local modifications to address local priorities. Political instability in Pakistan and Afghanistan, countries with large numbers of tribal populations with high rates of illiteracy and isolation as well as current violence, are huge obstacles. Gains in health status across South Asia are most likely to occur if there is a regional approach, with individual countries contributing their competitive advantage in experience and capacity to the group, learning from and supporting one another in implementation strategies, driven further by the large regional market for low-cost products. Such regional approaches will require regional political and economic linkages, but it is altogether possible that the health benefits can serve as the leading edge to achieve these other, often more difficult, goals. It will be difficult to achieve the necessary regional cooperation if, for example, India and Pakistan continue to be expediently assigned to two different World Health Organization regional offices. Leadership will reside in the countries themselves, as well as with the international and multinational organizations. Surely 50 years should be sufficient lead-time to accomplish this.

Chapter 30

REGIONAL DISEASE DYNAMICS

Chalinda D. Weerasinghe

Introduction

South Asia has roughly about a fourth of the world's population. Nearly 50 percent live below the poverty line. Overall, South Asia is relatively more disease and disability prone along with Africa and the Eastern Mediterranean regions, with life expectancy at birth, healthy life expectancy at birth and neonatal mortality rate being second worst only to Africa. The region has significant variation in terms of disease susceptibility, prevalence, transmission and prevention. Nearly all countries show increasing vulnerability to noncommunicable diseases (NCDs), mostly due to lifestyle choices and pre-existing genetic dispositions. Rather surprisingly, NCDs cause about 60 percent of all deaths in the region and South Asia also accounts for nearly 50 percent of the global incidence of death due to such diseases. The susceptibility to communicable diseases (CDs), or infectious diseases, varies tremendously depending on environmental, public infrastructure and health constraints. CDs are responsible for the overwhelming majority (more than two-thirds) of deaths in children (aged under 5 years) in the region.

Many health officials and organizations expect these trends in CD prevalence and spread to continue and increase in the future. According to World Health Organization (WHO) projections the region will be one of two (the other being Africa) with marked increases in CDs; South Asia will surpass Africa in terms of mortality associated with certain diseases such as hepatitis B and C and dengue. More importantly, and in keeping with the extant literature, I will argue that death and disability due to NCDs would take an even larger toll on the residents in the region due to pre-existing genetic dispositions, environmental factors and increasingly sedentary lifestyles. WHO projections give a similar picture: the region is tipped to see a rise in NCD-related mortality. Unless drastic action is undertaken at both the regional and intrastate levels it is hard to envisage a future that is not plagued with widespread disease.

Current Disease Outlook

Table 1 gives a preview of the current disease profile in South Asia (details are discussed in the text). It is clear that even at present time NCDs account for more deaths in the region than CDs, although the latter causes far more deaths in children (less than 5 years of age) than the former. Environmental factors determine the bulk of NCDs, although underlying genetic predispositions play a crucial role in the major ones. The main reasons for the spread of infectious diseases are poverty induced living conditions, illiteracy, malnutrition, inadequate access to public health facilities, lack of clean water and unsanitary neighborhoods and toilet facilities.

In terms of NCDs, cardiovascular diseases such as coronary heart disease, stroke, rheumatic heart disease and hypertension are huge problems in the region since South Asians are more likely to have heart disease than people from other regions of the world. Many are unaware of this increased risk. Urban and higher economic class populations in the region show a significant increased predilection to developing and dying from these diseases compared to rural and poor populations. Obesity, diabetes, high blood pressure and dyslipidaemia are high in urban populations due to lifestyle choices and this explains a lot of the prevalence of cardiovascular disease compared to rural populations. Diabetes and hypertension are also beginning to be important factors in heart disease among these groups.

South Asia has seen the most rapid rise in diabetes rates compared to other parts of the world, with India at the moment having the highest diabetes incidence in the world. As in cardiovascular diseases, diabetes is more likely to affect higher socioeconomic groups and urban populations. More people from the region are aware of the propensity to develop diabetes than heart disease, even those with lower levels of body mass index, largely due to genetic inclinations. Recent studies have shown that South Asians are more prone to having metabolic syndrome (Ghaffar et al. 2004). Genetics and lifestyle patterns contribute to high blood lipid and fat levels, low high-density lipoprotein cholesterol (HDL) levels and glucose intolerance. Urban populations are showing more prevalence to this syndrome than rural ones. Males are more prone than females to the syndrome as well. Impaired fetal nutrition is a leading cause of diabetes and metabolic syndrome. The problem is accentuated due to high maternal and fetal malnutrition rates in the region.

South Asia is also experiencing rising cancer incidence rates. Cancer accounts for a large proportion of the disability-adjusted life years (DALYs) lost in the region. The most common forms of cancer are lung and oropharyngeal in males, and cervical, uterine and breast in women. Smoking causes lung cancer and is also linked to cervical cancer, while tobacco chewing causes oropharyngeal cancer. Emphysema, chronic bronchitis and asthma are the most common respiratory diseases found in the region. The main culprit is indoor and outdoor air pollution. These diseases are a major reason for the rise in disability rates in the region. Indoor air pollution in the region is mainly due to burning wood fuel in the house, while outdoor pollution is due to urbanization and industrialization.

Of the major CDs in South Asia, the most significant are those affecting children. Acute respiratory infections and diarrhea account for about 50 percent of all deaths of children in the region, although there are significant declines thanks to strong public health interventions. Neonatal infections also cause an unacceptable number of deaths.

Table 1. Current disease outlook for South Asia at a glance

Summary category	Communicable diseases	Noncommunicable diseases
Overall mortality burden	Accounts for approx. 40% of all deaths	Accounts for approx. 60% of all deaths
Division of burden	Responsible for almost 66% of child mortality More than 60% of all deaths due to CDs are among children	Almost 50% of all diseases affecting adults are NCDs
Main causes of disease spread	Poverty Illiteracy Malnutrition Lack of proper public health, clean water and toilet facilities Unsanitary neighborhoods	Environmental and lifestyle factors Genetic predispositions
Major death and disability causing diseases	Among children (age 5 and under): • Acute respiratory infections • Diarrhea • Neonatal infections Among other populations are: • HIV/AIDS • Tuberculosis • Malaria • Typhoid • Dengue • Hepatitis B and C	All populations: • Cardiovascular diseases • Diabetes • Cancer • Respiratory diseases The most common cardiovascular diseases are: • Coronary heart disease • Stroke • Rheumatic heart disease • Hypertension The most common forms of cancer are: • Lung • Oropharyngeal • Cervical • Uterine • Breast
Important disease facts	Second-largest AIDS/HIV population in the world in India Sri Lanka is the only country to bring death and disability caused by CDs under control	South Asians have genetic dispositions towards heart diseases, diabetes and metabolic syndrome India has the highest diabetes incidence in the world

Source: Ghaffar et al. (2004) and Zaidi et al. (2004).

The main causes of death and disability due to neonatal infections are lack of proper antenatal care, lack of tetanus immunization, low birthweights, unskilled birth attendants, unclean delivery practices and lack of breastfeeding among others.

The region is in the midst of an HIV/AIDS rise due to India being the country with the second-largest disease population after South Africa. Most of the disease spread is in the southern states in India. Disease prevalence rates are lower in other South Asian countries but they are rising fast in Nepal and Pakistan. The two main causes of HIV/AIDS spread in the region are heterosexual transmission and intravenous drug use. HIV/AIDS is emerging as an epidemic mostly due to sex trafficking into India.

South Asia has seen a rapid upsurge in tuberculosis (TB) cases, which is exacerbated by the rise in HIV/AIDS. Although attempts are being made to contain the spread of TB in the region under the auspices of the WHO, Afghanistan and Pakistan have largely been unsuccessful in controlling the spread of TB. Major obstacles to battling TB prevalence faced by countries in the region include public health infrastructure shortages, lack of awareness about the disease, lack of government funding for detection programs, the emergence of multi-drug resistant TB strains and lack of private practitioner awareness about TB prevention initiatives.

Malaria and typhoid are two of the most common reasons for febrile illness in children. Mosquito-borne diseases like dengue fever and dengue hemorrhagic disease have caused outbreaks recently along with encephalitis and chikungunya. Malaria is now not a major cause of death in the region although it continues to be a major cause of morbidity. Unsanitary environmental conditions are the leading cause of the spread of typhoid fever, and vector-borne diseases such as malaria and dengue in the region, especially in slum areas. Infection rates of children are alarmingly high.

Hepatitis B and C have also emerged as major CDs in the region. Hepatitis B is very prevalent in Bangladesh, India and Pakistan. The main reasons for their prevalence are unsafe blood supplies, reuse of contaminated syringes, lack of proper screening to prevent perinatal transmission and inadequate accessibility to the vaccine for hepatitis B, among others. Hepatitis C rates are rising along with chronic liver diseases. Contamination occurs at an early age for many in the region thanks to the widespread use of contaminated syringes.

Projected Regional Disease Outlook for 2060

These NCDs affect people in various socioeconomic groups differently within and across the countries. Urbanization is occurring at a rapid pace in the region. The gap between the rich and the poor is also widening. The changing structural economic milieus among the nations will bring about more service-oriented occupations that supersede labor-intensive agricultural and manufacturing jobs. All of these changes will lead to solidification and emulation of affluent and sedentary lifestyles in increasingly congested cities.

Although South Asia has seen marked improvements in terms of rise in per capita income, sustainable and equitable development has been elusive. These trends will only worsen in the future unless drastic course correction takes place. These socioeconomic changes will have varied effects on these diseases. For example, the poor will consume less fruit and vegetables, and the rich will have better access to education and healthcare facilities than the poor. These differences will figure prominently in disease contraction (Ghaffar et al. 2004).

Studies predict that given the rise in cardiovascular diseases from 1990 to 2010, we should expect continual increases in years to come. Obstacles to managing these diseases include sedentary lifestyles, extreme poverty and inadequate health systems. Lower socioeconomic groups, which have previously shown a relatively lower incidence of cardiovascular disease, are now adopting lifestyle patterns such as smoking, which will lead to increased risk for cardiovascular disease.

WHO projections show that South Asia will see a dramatic increase in diabetes rates with India leading the way with an almost 195 percent increase by 2025 compared to 1995. Existing genetic predispositions towards cardiovascular disease, diabetes and metabolic syndrome mean that these rates will rise naturally on average. Cancer rates will rise significantly due to increased smoking habits and outdoor air pollution, and respiratory diseases will also rise due to air pollution.

CDs will prove to be equally challenging to deal with in the future. Pneumonia, diarrhea and measles, the most common culprits causing child deaths, will increase since many in the region are suffering from poor nutrition and lack of micronutrients in their diet. About 50 percent of the children in the region are underweight or stunted in growth. Malnutrition causes about 55 percent of all deaths in children. The increasing poverty gap will worsen the situation.

In addition to lack of proper diet, countries in the region have not been able to adequately immunize their child populations. More effort and money needs to be spent on vaccine use and since even the basic vaccines are not available to many children in the region the immunization gap between them and children in the developed world who have access to newer, more effective, vaccines will grow at an increasing rate (Zaidi et al. 2004).

HIV/AIDS will be a major killer in the region. Many people in the region do not have access to antiretroviral therapy. Sex trafficking is now a major reason for the spread of HIV/AIDS in the region. Most of the trafficking at the moment is from Nepal to India. Governments have so far not done enough to curb infection rates. Those who are infected with HIV are more likely to have syphilis and hepatitis B than those who are not, especially among sex-trafficked women. This kind of co-infection will be an added problem in the future (Silverman et al. 2008).

Population growth will lead to increases in vector-borne diseases. These will be further complicated by the widespread emergence of drug resistant and untreatable infections. The emergence of drug resistance strains of pneumonia, dysentery, typhoid, malaria, among others, has already caused huge problems for the region. These drug resistant strains are immune to commonly used antimicrobial agents as well as drugs. Misuse of antibiotics and unsanitary living conditions will further compound the problem.

Finally, although there is a consensus that global warming will radically impact NCDs and CDs in the region, the effects are not clearly mapped out yet. Higher regional temperatures due to global warming will mean higher rates of heat related illnesses such as heat stroke that will further exacerbate existing NCDs. As temperature levels rise, food crops will be damaged leading to more such illnesses.

Rising global temperatures will cause infectious diseases to spread as was evidenced by the plague outbreak in Gujarat in 1994. A strong animal and human contact in the aftermath of a heavy monsoon that followed an intense heat wave caused this plague. Bhutan and Nepal both recently reported dengue for the first time due to the dengue-causing mosquito migrating to higher ground. With increasing ground global temperatures, previously inhospitable high altitudes become suitable conditions for mosquitoes to migrate. Likewise, warmer temperatures along with infrequent and disturbed rainfall patterns will enable animal vector-borne diseases such as chikungunya to have access to populations they previously did not reach (Narain 2008).

Averting Gloomy Future: The Way Forward

- Making critical lifestyle changes will be paramount if South Asians are to avoid the projected NCD burden. Most importantly, in terms of diet, people will have to switch from using ghee, currently by far the most widely used cooking oil in the region, which is high in both cholesterol and fat. They will have to start using olive oil or other similar low fat cooking oils. They will also have to incorporate more soluble and insoluble fibers into their diet. The former has been shown to reduce LDL cholesterol and increase HDL cholesterol, slow down the digestion of starch and reduce diabetes incidence, while also reducing the risk of heart attacks. Insoluble fiber has cancer-fighting properties because they target and reduce bile acid toxicity.
- Incorporating exercise into the daily routine will also be vital. Efforts to educate the population across the region will be vital here since many are ignorant of the level of physical exercise required per day especially to avoid heart attack and stroke. To combat these NCD crises there should be a dramatic shift in government expenditure towards disease awareness and prevention programs.
- The first step is disease monitoring. Currently, accurate data on mortality associated with NCDs is hard to come by due to reporting errors, differences in country specific and intracountry reporting practices, and institutional constraints within the countries. Death and disability due to CDs are more known, although there are inadequate reporting procedures for some of these diseases as well. Lack of proper monitoring currently complicates disease identification and treatment efforts. Proper monitoring, data gathering and reporting procedures need to be implemented as the first step in combating the spread of infectious diseases as well. There is a great need to establish sustainable and robust disease detection systems in the region. There needs to be a concerted effort by medical practitioners, epidemiologists, microbiologists and other health officials to gather and disseminate information to manage and prevent disease crises. These surveillance systems need not be expensive, as one

such notable example in Tamil Nadu that monitors commonly found preventable diseases shows (Zaidi et al. 2004). These kinds of public–private endeavors need to be fostered by governments and community activists.

- Maternal and child health need to be prioritized since this can significantly prevent death and disability as was shown above, and as some parts of the region have shown this can be done at little cost at the community level. Sri Lanka and the Indian state of Kerala have already demonstrated how this prioritization can be achieved, with the former doing so while waging a civil war until very recently. Most of the public health initiatives aimed at disease prevention are labor intensive so they can easily be replicated in poor areas of the region at very little cost.

- Family planning services are also invaluable in these efforts, as Sri Lanka has shown, whose population growth is currently at replacement levels. The reason for this success was the emphasis on, and investment in, public health and education. Sri Lanka has focused mainly on primary and rural healthcare while other countries in the region have focused on expensive tertiary care institutions and facilities. There is a larger return on investment in the former categories. Sri Lanka has also, until recently, been able to keep the gap between the rich and poor to manageable levels.

- Government regulation will also be important in combating NCDs like cancer and respiratory diseases. Tobacco and pharmaceutical industries need to be regulated and their harmful products controlled. Air quality standards need to be initiated and enforced. Health research and postgraduate education also needs to be emphasized. The region lags in surgery facilities and proper health facilities are still at inadequate levels in many parts of the region.

- Lab testing needs to be made more available to many parts of the region so that diseases like typhoid and dengue can be easily diagnosed. Immunization efforts need to be stepped up. With the exception of Sri Lanka, the other countries in the region have not been able to adequately immunize their child populations. Measles eradication is insufficiently addressed in the region. More effort and money needs to be spent on vaccine use. Vaccination efforts in India have significantly slowed down Japanese encephalitis rates, amply demonstrating the importance of concerted immunization efforts.

- Sex trafficking needs to be curbed immediately in order to control the spread of HIV/AIDS, other sexually transmitted infections (STIs) and TB. Programs need to be introduced and implemented to track the spread of the diseases by focusing on behavioral programs. At the moment a few NGOs are leading the way but this needs to change with more governmental and public/private sector involvement.

- Many people in the region do not have access to antiretroviral therapy. These life-saving drugs need to be available to the needy in the region. Screening for these multiple diseases among HIV patients should be implemented more widely. Comprehensive screening for all types of sexually transmitted infections will also decrease the spread of HIV/AIDS in the region.

- Simple steps to reducing deaths and disability caused by communicable diseases include promotion of exclusive breastfeeding, hand washing, better immunization, proper child and maternal care, and providing more information about easy methods to protect from disease contraction. Disease prevention activities such as those aimed at increasing awareness, especially among females, behavior modification, and the use of autodestruct syringes should be incorporated into public health programs. People in the region need to be empowered to help themselves; governments can achieve this objective by implementing community-based health initiatives.

Finally, the overall approach to combating diseases in South Asia needs to be moved from a country-specific one to a regional one. South Asian Association for Regional Cooperation (SAARC) will have to take the lead in combating regional diseases. Individual countries have led the fight against diseases thus far, but this needs to change in the future since most of the diseases are now highly mobile within the region and among the countries. SAARC as a regional body along with international organizations, NGOs, local community organizations and citizens of the region will need to join forces to battle both CDs and NCDs.

Chapter 31

EDUCATION: TIME BOMB OR SILVER BULLET?

Jamshed Bharucha

The future of a people is best predicted by the education of its youth. What South Asia looks like in 2060 will be determined by its ability to transform the educational profile of its people. A range of factors will influence what happens over the next 50 years, but education is a prerequisite for all of them. If there is one factor that could make the difference between catastrophic failure and breathtaking success, it is education.

The stakes are enormous. A poorly educated youth could despair at the lack of opportunity, sowing strife and violence. In contrast, the energy of a well-educated youth could make South Asia the cultural and economic dynamo of the world. This is a race against time: education versus the consequences of the lack thereof.

Because of the sheer numbers of young people entering adulthood today, South Asia will be both a potential flash point and an engine for the world. Half the population of India is under the age of 25. In Pakistan and Bangladesh, the median age is even lower. Compare this to China where the median is around 36. Each year that goes by without a quantum increase in educational opportunity for those under 25 means a new cohort of 30 million young people launching the next 50 years of their lives without the intellectual capital needed for success, if not survival.

Over the coming decades, China and Europe will be saddled with an aging workforce. The United States could maintain its dynamism in spite of its aging baby-boomer demographic by continuing to attract the best young talent from around the world. South Asia's challenge is to find ways to harness its young population – and that will require education.

The good news is that progress has been made in literacy, and the trend lines are in the right direction. The bad news is that this progress has not kept pace with population growth. Nor has it kept pace with seismic shifts in the global economy, the environment, technology, the political landscape and the nature of conflict. Only urgent and dramatic intervention in education can tip the balance decisively in favor of a bright prognosis for the region.

Literacy

The youth literacy rate (ages 15–24) in South Asia greatly exceeds the adult literacy rate (ages 15 and above), according to data from the Literacy Assessment and Monitoring Programme (LAMP) developed by the United Nations Educational, Scientific and Cultural Organization (UNESCO) Institute for Statistics. The recent rise in youth literacy has been most rapid in India, where it jumped from 62 percent in 1991 to 81 percent in 2006. The other nations are not doing badly overall. Pakistan is at 70 percent (2006) and Bangladesh is at 74 percent (2008). Sri Lanka enjoys virtually universal literacy. Bhutan is at 74 percent (2005) and Nepal at 81 percent (2008). By comparison, China is at 94 percent (2008).

The gender gap in youth literacy is also shrinking in most parts of South Asia, according to the United Nations Children's Fund (UNICEF) data. In an amazing development, Bangladesh appears to have achieved gender equity in youth literacy. In India, a 24-point spread in 1991 has been reduced to a 14-point spread in 2006. Pakistan lags with a gender spread of 21 points, but has nevertheless made progress in female youth literacy.

These literacy rates are heartening compared to 50 years ago, when only a fraction of South Asians were literate and gender imbalances were much greater.

But is it too little too late?

Increases in rates of literacy have been swamped by population growth. There are over 800 million people in the world who are not literate, of which 600 million live in South Asia. The illiterate population of South Asia today roughly equals the entire population of South Asia in 1960. Even low rates of illiteracy today translate into mind-numbing numbers. A staggering 323 million South Asians between the ages of 15 and 24 are not literate – and most of them are female, which is particularly unfortunate given the disproportionate impact of women's education on the next generation. Illiteracy always has been a ticking time bomb for South Asia. The sheer numbers coupled with the need to adapt to a rapidly changing world means that the clock is accelerating.

Secondary and Tertiary Education

Rising literacy rates also belie the fact that mere literacy – while infinitely better than illiteracy – is not a high enough threshold for jobs in the future. What, then, is the state of secondary and tertiary education?

According to UNESCO, in India, barely half of those in the appropriate age range are enrolled in secondary education. And only 13 percent are enrolled at the tertiary level. These are enrollment rates; graduation rates are much lower. In Pakistan, enrollment is 33 percent in secondary education and 5 percent at the tertiary level. In Bangladesh, secondary enrollment approximates India's, while postsecondary enrollment approximates Pakistan's. The secondary and tertiary enrollment rates, respectively, for other South Asian nations are as follows: Bhutan is at 56 percent and 7 percent, Nepal is at 42 percent and 5 percent and Sri Lanka is at 85 percent for secondary and UNESCO data are unavailable for tertiary education.

By comparison, China's numbers are 76 percent for secondary and 23 percent for tertiary education. Most developed countries have secondary enrollment rates well above 90 percent and tertiary enrollment rates above 40 percent. The United States is way up on the tertiary list with 83 percent, which is helped by the system of two-year community colleges and the ease of enrolling part-time and in nondegree programs.

For both South Asia and China, the critical bottleneck is at the tertiary level. Many more students are qualified and motivated to get into college or university than there are seats available. Competition for limited slots is fierce, and families go to extreme lengths to get admission. There simply aren't enough colleges and universities to go around. China has attacked this problem as only China can: tertiary enrollment has gone from 13 percent in 2002 (roughly India's current level) to 23 percent in 2008 – an astonishing achievement.

The Quality Pyramid

Even for the institutions that are already in existence, quality is a serious issue. While many of the top South Asian colleges and universities are of high quality, they are few in number and the quality pyramid is steep, dropping precipitously as one goes from the apex to the base. There are many more students worthy of being admitted to top-tier institutions than there are seats.

The entrance examination for the vaunted Indian Institute of Technology (IIT) serves as a massive selection filter in which only 3 percent make it. When they graduate they are snapped up by American graduate schools or elite corporations in India and abroad. But of the 97 percent who are rejected, many are strong enough academically to attend excellent institutions. However, once you get below IIT and a few other elite engineering colleges, the quality and reputation drops quickly, as do the job prospects.

The rate-limiting factor in improving quality is the shortage of qualified faculty. This is also the rate-liming factor in building more colleges and universities. Vacancies in faculty positions are widespread. This situation is the reverse of what it is in the United States, for example, where the number of highly trained PhDs seeking academic positions greatly outstrips the number of academic jobs.

The Shortage of Skilled Labor and Well-Trained Professionals

It is ironic that South Asia, despite its massive population, has labor shortages – but it does. Personnel in short supply include skilled laborers, school teachers, professors, engineers (including IT professionals), doctors and dentists – particularly at the highest levels of proficiency. Because of the steep quality pyramid in higher education, the raw numbers – as small as they are – overstate the true development of talent.

India currently enjoys a reputation in the West as a country awash with technically trained personnel. This is both true and false. It is true in terms of absolute numbers in some fields such as engineering and chemistry. But it is false in the sense that many do not have the proficiency or expertise to meet the demand. In much of the rest of South Asia there is neither the quantity nor the quality of trained professionals at the apex of the knowledge pyramid. And those few who do qualify are easily lured into international markets; this has led to a major outflow of knowledge workers from all of South Asia, especially doctors and engineers.

Anticipated shortages of doctors in the United States – a consequence of the aging of the baby-boom generation and the inability of medical schools to scale up their training of doctors – means that the United States will probably import more doctors from all over the world, including South Asia, which is already a major exporter of physicians (amongst other knowledge workers). This will put further pressure on the labor shortages.

India Rockets Forward

India looks like it may have gotten its act together – finally. One could argue that India's dazzling economic growth – if sustained – could lift all of its people, enable the country to dodge the looming economic and political costs of widespread illiteracy and arrive at 2060 with universal literacy assured, international standing at an all time high and its democracy intact. Indeed, all bets are on this strategy. Doing so may also lift other boats across the rest of South Asia.

After decades of neglect, the Indian government now has the wisdom, the will and the wherewithal to tackle education head-on. A lot of time has been lost and a lot of talent wasted. Hundreds of millions have lived their lives without having access to an education. And hundreds of millions will, over the next 50 years, have the same fate. But it's better late than never.

The objective is to expand educational opportunities at all levels, at the fastest possible pace – sparing no innovation. A spark has now been lit in the education sector, with the public and private sectors aligned. Central, state and local governments, private educators, corporations, philanthropists and entrepreneurs have leapt into the education space as never before.

The 86th Amendment to the Indian Constitution, passed in 2002, requires the state to provide free and compulsory education to all children aged 6 to 14, and stipulates this as a fundamental right. It also charges the state to provide early childhood care and education for all children until they complete the age of 6 years. To finance this, a 2 percent "cess" on taxes will be set aside. India's economic engine can only be sustained if it can produce large numbers of well-trained professionals who can innovate, compete with the West in the knowledge economy and supply the rising middle class with the professional services it demands.

To open the bottleneck in higher education, the government has set a goal of reaching 30 percent enrollment in tertiary education by 2020. This means more than doubling the current capacity in ten years, a daunting but necessary challenge. Speed is of the essence because of the opportunity cost of not developing the nation's talent. In order to fuel this growth, the government has liberalized higher education in bold ways. Because accrediting a university is a complex process, the University Grants Commission allows for a category called "Deemed Universities" – a deliciously bureaucratic way to get around the bureaucracy. Deemed Universities have considerable autonomy and many are for-profit. While a profit motive may be less than ideal for running a university, it has led to the swift creation of large numbers of new institutions with well-equipped campuses.

I mentioned earlier that the rate-limiting factor in building new universities in India is the shortage of qualified faculty. This is a much thornier problem than building new buildings, equipping them and recruiting students. There are three ways to address this conundrum. One is to increase the salaries of professors, improve the research infrastructure and provide incentives for the best students to get their doctorates and launch academic careers. Another is to import faculty. There are plenty of newly minted American PhDs languishing in the American recession who could be tempted to spend a few years teaching in Indian universities. A third solution is to innovate with technology; students in underserved areas can beam into classrooms far away and access coursework over the Internet.

The government is also moving to reduce entry barriers for foreign universities. This should strengthen areas that are weak in India (such as undergraduate liberal arts, doctoral education, professional education and advanced research) and drive domestic competition for quality. It will also catalyze global collaboration in teaching and research, student and faculty exchange, and curricular innovation. Finally, this will create international communities of students in India that bind together to form networked global cohorts.

The other South Asian nations should emulate this strategy if they are to forge hopeful futures. It is hard to imagine how one creates economic opportunity for hundreds of millions in the middle of the twenty-first century who cannot read. And it is hard to see how political upheaval can be contained when such large numbers of people lack opportunity while witnessing explosions of ostentatious wealth around them.

Sri Lanka has long been ahead of all other South Asia countries in terms of literacy and the provision of quality schooling. However, it has lagged in investments in tertiary education. One hopes that an end to civil conflict in the country will allow more resources to be diverted to higher education.

Pakistan and Bangladesh have both made sweeping changes to their higher education structures and seen massive growth in the creation of new universities. For example, Bangladesh in 1992 opened up the higher education sector to private institutions. It also has opened up the sector to foreign partnerships. Both measures have had the desired result of increasing the number of universities. In Pakistan, there has been a concerted effort by the Higher Education Commission since about 2000 to reform this sector, and many new universities have been created.

However, the pace of these changes needs to be quickened, and the quality remains varied. The availability of quality faculty as well as students will remain a problem until massive investments are also made in primary and secondary education. Even as all South Asian nations make educational improvements, they simultaneously look at India as an educational destination for their students. Creating a regional education market would be in the benefit of India as well as the rest of the region.

Physical vs. Intellectual Infrastructure

Physical infrastructure is not the strong suit of South Asian education. I recently visited Xhejiang University's massive, brand new campus in Hangzhou, China, built in the blink of an eye. I also visited some new Indian campuses built in record time. The quality of the physical infrastructure in India simply does not compare; buildings appear to be crumbling almost as soon as they are built.

However, what is astonishing about India's rise is how much can be accomplished with an abysmal physical infrastructure. If South Asia can build a world-class *intellectual* infrastructure, that could be a new model for education. Indeed, this could be South Asia's ace in the hole. Even if construction in South Asia has no chance of catching up with the physical infrastructure in China and the West by 2060, it may be possible to leapfrog in the development of intellectual infrastructure. This includes electronic communications and computing infrastructure, learning and knowledge infrastructure, human intellectual capital and financial infrastructure for leveraging these assets.

Cyberliteracy and access to cyberspace will help jump-start education in South Asia. With basic literacy and a minimum of guidance, children can figure out how to explore the Internet. For at least some motivated kids, this is a gateway to knowledge and opportunity. In some locations, expanding access to cyberspace may have more leveraging power than waiting to build brick-and-mortar schools staffed by hard-to-find teachers who are ill prepared. Software for learning languages and other subjects is getting better all the time. And at the advanced level, there are syllabi, lecture notes and reading materials that are freely accessible from universities around the world, as well as massive open online courses (MOOCs) that feature lectures from thought leaders.

A Regional Win–Win Strategy

The South Asian Association for Regional Cooperation (SAARC) has launched a new university, the South Asian University (SAU), that started operations in 2010. The Indian government has recently agreed to provide student visas to Pakistani students attending SAU on the same terms as they do to students from other South Asian nations. This is an important step, and the scope of this new policy should be broadened so that all South Asian applicants to Indian institutions be provided visas on the same basis.

Indeed, higher education cooperation in the region as a whole can be a stimulant for cooperation in other areas. There is clearly a need, as well as a demand, for higher education all across South Asia. Many of the countries in the region, however, are too small or mired in other deeper problems to afford the type of investments needed for higher education. India on the other hand has the ambition as well as the opportunity to become an international hub for higher education. Starting with its neighbors makes win–win sense for India as well as for South Asia as a region. A regional strategy would seek educational exchange amongst students and faculty between universities across South Asia. Consortiums of the top institutions in the region could be nurtured by SAARC.

The tension between India and Pakistan makes for one of the most volatile locations on the Earth. It is in the long-term interest of neither nation to escalate. As India pulls ahead in its development, it would be making a mistake to try to press its advantage. Quite the contrary, it is in India's economic and political interests for Pakistan to develop as well.

A major threat to the region's future is that Pakistan will not be able to focus on education – not with the daunting political and security challenges it faces. Lack of educational opportunity entails lack of economic opportunity, which implies an increased potential for civil strife and violence. This is all the more reason to focus on education; it may be the only way to break the cycle in the long run.

As India scales up the higher education sector, it should encourage Pakistani students, on the same basis as students elsewhere in South Asia and the rest of the world, to come to India to study. This could help create a new generation in the two countries that can think past, and help get past, the tensions that have weighed so heavily on both. I have a vision of Indian and Pakistani college students studying and living together, and emerging as networked leaders who can find ways for the two nations to resolve their differences and become cooperative neighbors. Idealistic though this may sound, the alternative is a perpetuation of distrust and – as weapons become more powerful and accessible – an escalation of conflict.

One of the many great successes of American colleges and universities is that they have been incubators for students from all over the world to get to know each other's cultures, to develop as global citizens and leaders, and to form relationships of trust that are leveraged in cooperative and mutually beneficial ways later in their careers. These global networks of college graduates create the platforms necessary for the resolution of global problems. India, as the obvious hub of higher education in the region, should strive for the same, producing new generations of leaders across South Asia who are comfortable working together on complex issues, integrating multiple perspectives, crossing cultural boundaries and who can provide a new and sorely needed brand of leadership.

Conclusion

To note some of the positive developments in the region, Sri Lanka has almost established universal education through the secondary level and India is finally taking education seriously at all levels, and thinking at the scale that it needs to.

The Indian government under Manmohan Singh launched an ambitious education revolution, and seeks nothing less than making India a global hub in higher education. Governments in other South Asian nations should also elevate the priority given to education at all levels. As India bursts forth, it should encourage students from other South Asian countries – including Pakistan – to avail themselves of India's expanding opportunities in higher education. An educated South Asia is in the best interests of an educated India. While the other nations are making significant progress, the pace needs to be accelerated. And India should take a benevolent view of the region, calculating that providing access to Indian higher education for the entire region is in everyone's best interest.

Even if South Asia succeeds in transforming its education, it will not be a panacea for the region. Education is not a sufficient condition for economic and political development. But it is surely a necessary condition. Education will not be a silver bullet for the region, but it could certainly help diffuse the time bomb that a chronic lack of education is and will be even more in the knowledge economy of tomorrow. While education does not guarantee a prosperous and peaceful future for all of South Asia, it is impossible to envision such a future anywhere in South Asia without it.

Chapter 32

SCHOLARSHIP IN AND ON SOUTH ASIA

Ali Riaz

The primary objective of this article is to outline scenario(s) of South Asian scholarship in the next half a century. It is a challenging task in many ways; two deserve special mention: first, forecasting is a perilous business, particularly on social and political issues. Secondly, my effort involves a region with eight countries, each of which is not only diverse on many counts but has also previously defied almost all predictions. There are several methods for forecasting, each has its own merits but none can be appropriate for all situations. However, in social sciences there is a proclivity towards quantitative method. When quantitative data is either unavailable or unreliable, and qualitative information can be gleaned from various sources to increase accuracy, relevance, or acceptability of forecasts, the preferred option among researchers has been to adopt the judgmental method (Makridakis, Wheelwright and Hyndman 1998; Adler and Ziglio 1996; Lawrence, Goodwin, O'Connor and Onkal 2006; and Surowiecki 2004). In this exercise, a simple trend-line extrapolation is neither expected nor helpful as scholarship is a precursor to imaginative innovation and by definition expected to influence trends in the future that are yet to exist. Inherent elements of the judgmental methods are based on certain assumptions and subjective bias. My approach in this paper is not devoid of these elements; I have adopted the subjective approach within the judgmental-qualitative method.

A Projection for the Region

In the coming decades South Asian scholarship will experience changes in an incremental manner, but at the end of the 50 years the result will be dramatic: it will be different in both contour and content. This claim, like any other subjective forecasting, is based on some assumptions, which need to be explained at the outset. One of the key assumptions relates to the social and political landscape of the next 50 years: the social, political and cartographic landscape of South Asia will change. A simple extrapolation of changes in the past century serves as a good indicator of the possibility of changes in the political map of the region, although it will not follow a linear path.

The region witnessed not only the partition of the Subcontinent, but also the emergence of Bangladesh as an independent country breaking away from Pakistan, all within a 25-year span between 1947 and 1971. A reconfiguration of the map of India – with more and more states within the federal structure, and the renaming of Pakistan's North West Frontier Province as Khyber Pakhtunkhwa and northern areas as Gilgit Baltistan in recent years also points to the possibility of further changes. The map of Jammu and Kashmir remained unchanged for most of the past century, but may not stay the same much longer. The failure of the Tamil secessionist movement may have prevented the dismemberment of Sri Lanka in the short run, but a political solution to the underlying causes of the one of the longest running regional insurgencies will likely have some geographical ramifications for the country in the future. The past three decades have been tumultuous for Afghanistan; yet the central issue – whether a centralized Afghanistan is possible – has not been resolved. Pakistan's struggle to define its *raison d'être* has not been successful in the past half-century and this will have to be resolved in the coming decades, possibly bringing about a seismic shift in the political and geographic landscape.

These changes will be prompted by political considerations, but two factors will be the driving force for social and economic change in the region: demographics and the environment. As far as demographic change, the population will continue to grow within the period under review and indeed South Asia will become the world's most populous region – by far – rapidly surpassing China. The population of all countries in the region, save Sri Lanka, will grow and grow rapidly. Afghanistan, for example, where the population is growing at 3.9 percent now, will witness a nearly threefold increase in its population by 2050. This growth is projected to end in the second half of the century as a gradual flattening of the total fertility rate (TFR) in the three most populous countries, India, Bangladesh and Pakistan, will bring an end to the dramatic population growth. Population growth will put strains on resources in the countries and have a deleterious effect on the environment, but will also provide an advantage to the region: a younger, productive population, often referred to as the "demographic driver of growth" (Dadush and Stancil 2010). Environmental challenges will be more pronounced however because of climate change and sea-level rises. The melting of glaciers in the Himalayas combined with environmental degradation throughout the region, especially in Nepal, India and Bangladesh, will cause significant changes in social relations, political actions and economic structures. Bangladesh has already become the frontline in the battle against climate change, but other countries such as India and Pakistan will face water scarcity and other environmental issues as well. These factors are bound to reshape the relationship between geographically contiguous countries.

Another key element that must be accounted for is the anticipated changes on the economic front. Overall the region will experience growth. India, due to its economic potential and size, will be the principal catalyst in economic growth, but smaller countries such as Bangladesh and Sri Lanka will follow suit and make significant headway (DFID 2007). South Asia could stumble on its way to prosperity, especially if the need for political stability and infrastructural development are overlooked. These changes will be incremental, but can be divided into two phases: the first from 2010–40 and the second from 2040–60). The first four decades will prepare the groundwork for the leap that will occur around 2040. Economic growth will engender a middle class throughout the region, however that does not mean an improvement in income distribution; instead, it will worsen the already problematic income equality in the region (Hillebrand 2008). Greater cooperation – economic and otherwise – will grow within the region, whether or not official policies reflect the changes. Cooperation will be required, in part, due to environmental changes and increased cross-border migration. At some levels, environmental changes will render the existing political borders ineffective. This will result in two conflicting responses in the near future, with more interactions among people of neighboring countries set against more belligerent posturing of the policymakers, with the need to cooperate to overcome the posturing in the long run.

Implications for Scholarship in and on South Asia

The snapshot of the most significant changes, presented above, will have snowball effects and engender various other changes within South Asia and these changes will have a serious impact on scholarship in and on South Asia. On one hand, scholarship in and about South Asia will reflect these changes while on the other, the changes will inspire more imaginative endeavors. The education scenario will have a direct influence on scholarship and in fact will be the critical determinant of scholarship in South Asia. In the past 50 years, generally speaking, literacy rates and access to education have increased with some countries performing better than others. This trend will continue and pick up speed in the second half of the period under review. South Asia currently has the world's highest illiteracy rate at 45 percent of the total population and thus is starting from a low base to achieve major progress. As primary education is the backbone of economic and social progress, it will receive the attention it deserves, but lack of investment and attention in tertiary education will be the key inhibiting force for scholarship and innovation. The extant weak infrastructure in tertiary education will be a serious road block to research and development (R&D) in science, and also to critical thinking. Only three percent of South Asians reach the tertiary education level in 2010, this share is projected to grow to 16 percent in 2060 (Revi 2007). Save any shift in policy regarding tertiary education, in the next decade, South Asia will lag behind in the adoption and adaptation of technology. Although India is leading the region, it is far behind other G-20 nations and not prepared to adopt newer technologies as "education, infrastructure and governance must be improved before broad-based and rapid technological advancement can occur in India" (Dadush and Stancil 2010).

The most visible change in scholarship will be the use of language, with South Asia becoming the region with the largest English-speaking population in the world. India, as a country, has already surpassed the United States in having the largest English-speaking population (Crystal 2004). The linguistic and cultural diversity of the region will also give rise to an attachment to regional languages, which will be reflected in the proliferation of media outlets in various languages. One key indication of this is the rise of electronic media broadcasting in local languages in the southern states of India and Bangladesh and across much of Pakistan. These conflicting tendencies, to be part of the "global citizenry" by adopting English as a means of communication and staying true to one's cultural roots by emphasizing cultural distinctiveness including language, will bring a new diversity to South Asian discourses. This will make the region unique in comparison to other parts of the world and we will thus see a proliferation of scholarship on both fronts – emphasizing local and regional heritage and adapting to globalization. Language use will be the point of departure, but the scope and nature of the debate will be far reaching, with affects on cultural products and lifestyles. Perhaps "glocalization" – a shift from a more territorialized learning process bound up with the nation-state society to one that is more fluid and translocal, as described by Gabardi – is one way to describe this transformation (2000).

The increased use of English will also reflect the influence of the South Asian diaspora. With significant numbers of South Asians living outside the region, including in English-speaking countries, they will tend to shape the use of language. In large measure, the new generations of South Asian descent will either demand the use of English as a *lingua franca* or will make it a de facto *lingua franca*. This does not mean that the culture of South Asian nations will lose their appeal to new generations; on the contrary, the new generation will be more in tune with the cultures of South Asia. Their interactions, however, will be mediated through a language that is not inherently of South Asian origin.

The interplay of the "local South Asian" and the "global South Asian" will engender shifts in scholarship on South Asian culture. This new stream is already emerging, however, one of the key weaknesses of these works – especially recent creative scholarship – is that they are elite based and tied-up with western ideologies and imageries. As their audience broadens, both in South Asia and among South Asians outside the region, these weaknesses will have to be addressed. This new stream of scholarship will come to the center stage within the next 25 years as we witness faster and more reliable modes of communication and further development of communication technologies.

Empiricist vs. Normative Scholarship: Implications for Security-Oriented Scholarship

The diaspora living in the largely English-speaking West will not be the only ones who will enjoy the privilege of influencing South Asia; those who lived and will be living in the Arabic-speaking Gulf region will be equally influential. While the economic power of these countries may be lessened by the middle of the century, their cultural and linguistic sway will increase, especially because of their sustained interactions with South Asia. The class and cultural differences amongst South Asian diasporas in the West and South Asian diasporas in the Gulf are already palpable and will further sharpen in the future, providing two different worldviews and civilizational perspectives. Additionally, the larger body of scholarship on South Asia will continue to follow the current trend by dividing broadly into two categories – policy-oriented scholarship and humanist endeavor, or empiricist versus normative. The second strand will gain greater prominence than at present for a number of reasons.

Policy-oriented scholarship will continue to address three areas: security, environment and the religion–secularism issue. While these topics are familiar because they are being debated now, in coming decades there will be a qualitative shift in terms of content. Focus of discussions on security will no longer be limited to conventional military aspects and the recent slow move to incorporate a nontraditional security dimension into security considerations will become mainstream. The paradigm shift in security studies in recent decades has not traveled outside academia even though South Asian policymakers may from time to time have provided lip service. However, there has not been any sustained effort to address this from an in-depth and long-term policy-oriented perspective. This scenario will come to fruition only if a new security architecture is developed and adhered to by the two regional arch rivals – India and Pakistan – in coming decades. The new architecture must address long-standing problems, but can only be developed if domestic developments in Pakistan allow it to tread a more peaceful path. If the domestic instability of Pakistan intensifies, scholarship on security will take a different turn and move away from the possible preeminence of nontraditional security. Scholars in the other countries of the region, in Bangladesh, Nepal, Sri Lanka, Maldives, have begun their journey to that end but whether Indian scholars and policymakers are willing to join and shape the contour is dependent upon the situation in Pakistan. Scholars and policymakers of all other South Asian nations are already willing to accept the merger of security and environment challenges. As opposed to securitization of issues such as the environment, health and migration, the new scholarship will redefine security to make it more people-centric. The current modes of securitizing environmental and related issues will dissipate after the next two decades, provided regional and international politics do not compel scholars to continue the current pattern of thinking.

The debate on interactions between religion and politics has occupied considerable space and time within South Asian scholarship in the past 50 years, especially in the past decade. The religious diversity of the region has been a critical factor in generating the debate, but the debate also came about because the legitimacy of nation-states in South Asia have faced questions from within. Global developments have intensified the debate both as a policy issue and a normative/philosophical concern and on many occasions, the two strands – policy and humanistic endeavor – of scholarship intersected. For policy-oriented scholarship, whether produced in South Asia or outside the region to formulate immediate responses, the primary objective was containment of religio-political forces. The humanist tradition has often questioned the dichotomy of religious and secular however, and thereby examined the role of religion in social space. In the coming decades this tradition will assume greater prominence as religion's role in South Asian society may pave the way for a reinterpretation of their mutual relationship.

Religion will reappear in scholarship on and within South Asia through a different door, particularly in humanist literature. Humanists will have to address the nature, scope and role of religion as they grapple with questions of identity. The issue of identity is nothing new and has remained an integral part of South Asian scholarship at least since the nineteenth century. What we are about to witness however, is a shift from the simple assertion of ethnic identities to a questioning of the rationalist modernist paradigm which has dominated the extant scholarship for long. South Asian scholarship has already undergone various stages of its interactions with the European/Western brand of modernity, including subscribing to the notion of nationalism(s) and "secularism." The mainstay of the emerging paradigm then will be the assertion of multiple modernities, and the relationship of South Asia with the dominant Western modernity. Building on critiques of the nation-state and its theoretical premise, and critiques of the West in terms of the failure of key capitalist institutions and human rights invocations, the new scholarship will inaugurate a counternarrative with an objective to radically displace the rational narrative of world events, ideas and institutions. Can there be an autonomous discourse outside the metropolitan, especially when I have suggested that South Asia will be a part of globalization? Can South Asia recover from the epistemic violence of colonialism and imperialism? Both questions are pertinent; because I argue that the new narrative(s) will not be a derivative discourse but a complete break from postcoloniality.

Emergence of Multiple, Alternative Paradigms

It is not simply a postmodernist critique but the construction of a counternarrative that reinvents and redefines "traditional" as "contemporary." It will question the past and engage in a rewriting of history avoiding causality. This critique of modernity and new constructions will be based on multiple sources. Religious identities and interpretations of religious texts and lived religious practices is one of the sources that will inform and enrich, but other marginalized voices, including subaltern and Dalit, will be an integral part of the mosaic of ideas and contestations feeding into the debate. The notions of secularism and religion, as we understand them now, will undergo a transformation. Two critical elements of this new paradigm will be a rethinking of the conception of home/belonging, and a changed engagement with history. The dichotomy of local and universal, both spatially and ideationally, will be blurred in the discourse of home/belonging and the contested nature of history will be more pronounced. Multivocality will be the defining characteristic of scholarship within this tradition and thus although I have referred to the changes as the emergence of a paradigm, it is better to acknowledge that multiple paradigms addressing similar issues will come into play, perhaps without any dominant one.

These changes, new discourses and new voices will shape the contour and content of social sciences in coming decades and eventually will influence political thought and actions; but they will primarily originate in the humanities in general, particularly in literature. It will be fiction, poetry and performing and fine arts which will lead the way to the new landscape. In some measure this is not unusual in South Asia as any examination of the past century of modernist discourse reveals that politicians and social science academia have been laggards. Political discourse did not shape the imagination but the collective imagination shaped political discourse as the works of Rabindranath Tagore and Muhammad Iqbal in the nineteenth century illustrate. This will continue to be true, perhaps even more so than in the past. What makes it different from the past however is the role of diaspora authors, who will play a significant role in reimagining history, reconfiguring the notion of present, defining self and blurring the local and translocal as they navigate the intersection of South Asia and the world.

In each interaction with Western ideas and subscription to modernist discourse, there have been changes in the form and style of South Asian creative arts. For example, the novel as a form of prose was borrowed from the Western tradition at one stage of interaction and painting too underwent transformation since the early twentieth century as forms from aestheticism to romanticism to realism to magical realism have all left their influences on creative fields. As new ideas germinate, newer art forms will be explored and invented and perhaps a revision of literary forms will occur – merging prose and poems, amalgamating reality and magical reality. Conversely, the "old" narrative form deeply embedded in various parts of South Asia and closely tied to linguistic traditions will be reinvented as well.

Is there a tipping moment for all of these changes? Is there a trigger factor which will drive towards the ultimate scenario? The answer to both is negative. There is no inevitability to the scenarios I have described and neither is there a single turning point to celebrate. What is important to note is that scholarship will not develop completely independently of the sociopolitical environment I laid out in my assumptions. This is not to contradict my earlier assertion that a different South Asia will emerge in scholarship even before the "reality" changes, but to reaffirm that I am not painting a path-dependent scenario. This is the challenge inherent in the nature of a forecasting exercise.

Chapter 33

RIGHTS AND JUSTICE:
A PROSPECTIVE VIEW

Balakrishnan Rajagopal

There are four broad trends across the diverse countries that comprise South Asia, which constitute severe challenges to the realization of human rights and justice in the medium- to long-term future, as compared to other regions of the world. The first challenge is that South Asia remains the weakest of any regional grouping in the world, especially revealed by the absence of any regional mechanism or even a set of robust principles affirming common commitment to human rights and justice or democracy. The second one is the rising tide of extremism and violence in intercommunal relations, mostly religious but also ethnic and caste, mainly along the fault lines of political mobilization, gender and class. The third challenge is the social stress produced by the appropriative politics of natural resources, especially that of land, housing and water, which exclude large segments of the population from the benefits of economic development through acts of violence and increasing levels of precarious existence under neoliberal economic policies. The fourth challenge is presented by the crumbling state of public institutions in countries across the region, especially the decreasingly democratic nature of elected bodies, the corrupt and biased nature of the bureaucracy and an increasing reliance on the judiciary as an organ of governance, producing conflicts with other branches and raising questions about the accountability of the judiciary in democracies.

The consequences of these trends can be seen in the terrible human rights conditions of many millions in South Asia, especially among women, children, low caste groups, religious minorities, those with insecure land and housing rights, the urban and rural poor and indigenous groups.

Countering these trends will be hard but not impossible. To begin, consider these shocking realities:

- more than half of the world's poor live in South Asia, often abused, ill treated, neglected and patronized, without dignity;
- there are more malnourished children in South Asia than anywhere else – in India alone, there are more malnourished children than in the entirety of Sub-Saharan Africa;

- gender discrimination and violence against girls and women is deep rooted and getting worse – according to a recent study in the British journal *Lancet* (Jaha et al. 2011), more than 12 million girl children may have been aborted in the last 30 years in India alone, honor killings sanctioned by the social and political structures in societies are rampant in India, Pakistan and Bangladesh (Human Rights Watch 1999, 104, 110) and so is a rising tide of violence and rape against women (on India see the report of the Committee on Amendments to Criminal Law (Justice Verma Committee), 23 January 2013);
- displacement due to conflict or development is more prevalent in South Asia than anywhere else: In India alone, between 16–38 million have been displaced since independence due to large dam construction alone, between 40–50 percent of which come from the country's small tribal population of roughly 8 percent of India's population – these numbers are much lower than the actual due to severe undercounting as well as exclusion of large categories of people from the official category of the displaced (World Commission on Dams 2000), resulting in massive violations of land and housing rights, including property rights and economic assets of people who are mostly poor to begin with;
- large-scale land expropriations for corporations, carried out by states, have targeted tribal areas predominantly, leading to violent resistance and armed retaliation, thus bringing almost 40 percent of India's territorial area under the control of Maoist groups (see Government of India 2008, 2–3, which estimates that the Maoists are now active in 125 districts over 12 states);
- the worsening state of minority rights as can be witnessed in the targeted killings of the Hazara/Shi'a ethnic group in Pakistan (also seen through the lens of increasing sectarian violence), the worrying situation of tribal communities and other minorities in India and the continuing oppression of ethnic Tamils in Sri Lanka even after the brutal end of the LTTE (for a recent overview of minority rights, see Rita Manchanda, "Living on the Margins: Minorities in South Asia" (2009))
- violations of humanitarian law by states and nonstate armed groups – systematic targeting of civilians, large-scale destruction of property, war crimes, ethnic cleansing, mass rapes and genocidal spurts of violence – have been committed on massive scales in virtually all South Asian countries during the recent past and are ongoing, in numbers and scale more intense than anywhere else with the exception of the conflict in Central Africa;[1]

---

1 The incidents of mass violence alone (not counting displacements as part of ethnic cleansing) include the following since independence: at least 500,000 died during the Partition riots in 1945–48; at least a million died in the 1971 genocide in Bangladesh, and between 200,000 and 400,000 women raped; more than 2,000 killed in Assam, India during the Nellie massacre in 1983; more than 5,000 Sikhs killed in Delhi in 1983 after the assassination of Indira Gandhi; close to 3,000 Tamils killed in Sri Lanka in 1983; an estimated 1–2 million Afghans died between 1978 and 1987 during the insurrection against the Soviets and more than half of the world's refugees in the 1980s were Afghans; between 9,000 to 27,000 deaths since 2001 in Afghanistan as a result of the armed conflict launched by the US and allies; more than 15,000 killed in Nepal during its civil war between 1996 and 2006; the pogrom against Muslims in Gujarat in 2002 killed 1,200–2,000 and witnessed a large number of brutal attacks against women. For a survey, see reports of Human Rights Watch at hrw.org.

- there is a notable shrinking of public space for freedom of expression, especially on matters of faith in Pakistan, and societal and state sanction for killings of journalists. Pakistan, where a large number of journalists have been killed by armed extremists and terrorists and also by police and intelligence operatives, was recently named as the world's most dangerous place for journalists by human rights groups (see Reporters Without Borders n.d.);
- consolidation of autocratic, militaristic antidemocratic regimes in the region, especially in Sri Lanka and the continued weakness of democratic political regimes.

It is clear that South Asia has become one of the world's most intractable regions in human rights terms. If there is a silver lining in all this, it can only be seen in the even-surprising level of civic capacity and democratic resistance from ordinary people in the region, challenging and holding states and private actors to account under very difficult circumstances. Nevertheless, it may well be the case that such civic capacity is not infinite and may fall victim to the larger trends and challenges outlined below.

Lack of a Regional Mechanism or Common Principles

Almost alone in the world, South Asia is a regional grouping that continues to lack a robust enough regional framework that can act as the basis for articulating common principles and pursue shared goals. Worse, in other international fora, such as the UN Human Rights Council, the South Asian Association for Regional Cooperation (SAARC) countries have emerged as a major part of an antihuman rights bloc, determined to prevent any meaningful action on human rights especially if it concerns one of their own. Witness the way in which any condemnation of Sri Lanka's murderous campaign against the LTTE, which saw widely acknowledged war crimes, was prevented by India and Pakistan (among others) initially, who seemed to find ways of coming together on something that they could finally agree on. Only after the compulsion of domestic coalition politics – when a coalition partner, the Dravia Munnetra Kazhagam (DMK) withdrew from the ruling coalition – did the ruling Congress Party–led Government of India change its stance to support a widespread demand for accountability for the atrocities committed in Sri Lanka during the war against the Liberation Tigers of Tamil Eelam (LTTE). Despite the establishment of SAARC, the region continues to suffer from a Westphalian mindset and a Hobbesian attitude, characterized by mutual suspicion, lack of trust and the absence of shared principles for economic, political and social cooperation. In areas as wide ranging as energy, water, climate change, trade and infrastructure, there is tremendous need and potential for regional planning and development, which can in turn lead to a sustainable basis for more trust building and understanding. That in turn can lead to the articulation of shared moral and political goals including in the form of human rights principles and commitment to democratic change. Other regions have seen such frameworks emerge for the mutual benefit of its members, such as in the Association of Southeast Asian Nations (ASEAN)

and Southern Common Market (MERCOSUR). They are now in search of regional
human rights mechanisms, such as the ASEAN Intergovernmental Human Rights
Commission, which they hope will prove to be effective. Almost twenty-five years after
its founding, SAARC remains without a viable set of principles that affirm human rights,
and without a mechanism for regional monitoring of national performance. In light
of the severe challenges to human rights, especially of minorities, women and others
outlined above, a regional commitment to human rights is an important device to improve
conditions on the ground.

SAARC has recently adopted a Charter of Democracy in 2011 (see SAARC n.d.),
at the initiative of Bangladesh, which has some encouraging features – it mentions
human rights and the Universal Declaration of Human Rights (UDHR) and rejects
"unequivocally" any unconstitutional change of an elected government. While these
are important commitments, the declaration remains far too weak, a paper tiger,
without teeth in the form of any enforcement or monitoring. The declaration is
overly solicitous of sovereignty and noninterference while being very tentative in
mentioning its commitment to human rights. Nevertheless, it is a first step in what
one hopes will be a more sincere attempt in designing a working regional human
rights system.

Rising Extremism

There has been a clear trend towards more violence and extremism in relations
between communities in South Asia during the last two decades. Relations between
religious communities, between Hindus and Muslims (see Brass 2003; Varshney 2003;
and Nussbaum 2009), and Shi'a and Sunni Muslims (see Ahmed 2011) – as well as
relations between ethnic and caste-based communities, such as tribal groups like the
Gonds in India, middle castes and the Dalits – have worsened during this time. While
violence between Hindus and Muslims was quite common in the Subcontinent even
before the Partition, there is a distinctive worsening of relations since the 1980s. Witness
the rising violence in the Kashmir Valley where there is now a virtual lockdown of the
entire people with an arbitrary and overly harsh suspension of virtually all civil and
political rights, the killing of Muslims and Hindus in Mumbai in 1993 and Gujarat in
2002, or the sectarian Shi'a–Sunni warfare in Pakistan within the majority community
with daily bomb blasts. In Pakistan, there is a rising tide of extremist groups, many
loosely affiliated with global jihadist groups, sharing a violent and intolerant ideology,
often reacting to and profiting from ill-conceived wars unleashed by the US and its
allies in the neighborhood. These groups have unleashed violence not only against
perceived enemies of Islam – India, the USA etc. – but they have also begun to erode
the foundation of the Pakistani state and civil society. Indeed, there is a veritable civil
war brewing between the Pakistani state and radical Islamic groups. The rising violence
and extremism has also resulted in frequent killings of journalists and leading political
figures, who incur the wrath of extremist groups and religious leaders. The inability
or unwillingness of the state to act more impartially and effectively in enforcing the

laws of the land, including elementary provisions of criminal law, is leading many to designate Pakistan, or parts of it, as a failed state but that begs the question of whether the state is itself now a terrain of contestation between larger tensions. In India, there is a distinctive coarsening of public discourse and political culture, especially in the form of a rising lumpenization of Hindu nationalist parties and an erosion of the secular character of the state and society. While these parties have suffered electoral defeat at the center, there are worrying signs that some extreme elements may be resorting to what has been referred to as "saffron terror," by engaging in terrorist acts while attempting to shift the blame to Islamic groups. This is not to belittle the very real violence inflicted on civilians in India by Islamist terrorists, but needs to be seen as part of a rising tide of extremist violence and weakening of the state by nonstate armed groups. The tragedy of Afghanistan continues, now in the form of continuing armed conflict between the US-led Afghan forces and the Taliban, threatening to end in stalemate and the return of the Taliban and its extremist politics to power. Accountability for war crimes committed during a very long war remain forever out of reach (for a recent report see Housing and Land Rights Network 2011), thus further undermining chances of reconciliation and peace. In Sri Lanka, the violence between the Tamils and Sinhalese worsened, and while it eventually crested in the form of a crushing military blow to the Liberation Tigers of Tamil Eelam (LTTE) leadership in 2009, no one would claim that the relations between the two communities has become better as a result. In particular, there is now ample evidence offered by the UN among others (United Nations 2011), that the Sri Lankan government and to a lesser extent the LTTE committed war crimes during the 2009 conflict, but the Sri Lankan government has reacted to these reports in a jingoistic and dismissive manner. Since 2009, it has also tightened political control over all avenues of potential opposition, such as an independent media, opposition parties and the Supreme Court, through violence, intimidation and unlawful dismissal of the chief justice of Sri Lanka. Nepal continues to simmer in a long-drawn process of peace making, where the unresolved issue of how to share power with the Maoists is exposing cracks in Nepalese society between the largely feudal, land-owning upper caste segment and the landless, lower caste and ethnically diverse constituency of the Maoists. Bangladesh and Bhutan have seen less violence during this period, but are by no means free of extremism. Bangladesh has, for instance, oscillated dangerously between religious extremism and military dictatorship.

In general, the entire region is much worse than what it was two decades ago as judged by rising extremism. Public institutions are too weak to prevent it or to deal with its consequences. For example, the Pakistan National Assembly would not even condemn the assassination of major political figures including the government's own minister of minorities in March 2011 or defend the rights of one of their own to speak on public issues, relating to the blasphemy law. Democratic structures such as political parties and the media also remain too weak or have become tools in the hands of violent extremists themselves. Judiciaries in Pakistan or Sri Lanka remain far too weak to take on the violence of the state and the extremism in society and are institutionally unable or unwilling to do more than occasionally attempt to enforce the rule of law. In India, the courts are strong but have proved themselves incapable of bringing the perpetrators of mass crimes to justice, when religious extremists, or state agents, commit them, whether in relation to the 1983 New Delhi violence against Sikhs or the 2002 Gujarat violence against Muslims.

Appropriative Neoliberalism

Since the 1980s, South Asia has seen the entrenchment of neoliberal economic policies in a range of fields from reductions in the role of the state, its gradual withdrawal from agriculture and rural income support, the withdrawal of subsidies to the poor, sale of public assets, privatization of public enterprises and the introduction of free market discipline in public services, agriculture, urban development and public finance. The result has been rural immiserization and mass poverty, accompanied by a rising tide of violence in the rural areas. While the details of this story vary from country to country, the broad trends are very similar across South Asia. To begin with, it must be noted that the majority of the people in South Asia continue to live in rural areas, employed in farming, fishing or other land-based livelihoods. In India, almost 70 percent of the population live in rural areas. Given this demographic reality, governments in the region leaned towards a proagriculture policy until the 1980s, through price-support mechanisms, subsidized agricultural inputs, rural credit and extension services and a strict limit on foreign competition in the food and farming sector. All this underwent a sea change during the 1980s, as governments signed up to a global shift towards neoliberalism, partly forced by their often weak macroeconomic situation, partly coerced by international financial institutions (IFIs) such as the World Bank and the IMF, and partly due to the rise of alternative political parties to power, which did not share the earlier commitment to prorural policies, which had led to a "Green Revolution" during the past decades. Added to the mix were the new obligations that governments had undertaken under the WTO such as Trade Related Aspects of International Property Rights (TRIPS), under which the monopoly profits of large corporations such as Monsanto were protected in the name of intellectual property rights, over seeds, as well as the new financial architecture of global equity markets, which saw the rapid inflow of vast capital into infrastructure, mining and real estate that led to rapid inflationary impacts on land and housing prices.

This shift to neoliberalism had a rapidly worsening impact on farmers, rural poor and landless, tribals, urban poor and those in the informal sector, even as production itself climbed in particular sectors such as textiles. The consequences could be seen in the rapidly climbing rates of rural suicides among farmers in India – in 2009 alone, there was one rural farmer suicide every 30 minutes, and since 1995, more than an estimated 250,000 have committed suicide (Center for Human Rights and Global Justice 2011) – rising rural Maoist insurgencies in Nepal and India, conflicts over land acquisition, anti-poor eviction drives in large cities and increasing levels of conflict over access to water. In all countries in the region, there has been a significant worsening of the right to food, right to water and land rights of the most vulnerable, which has had cascading political and security consequences. This message is hard to appreciate partly because the last decade is understood, in mainstream opinion, to have been a golden one in economic terms, especially for India, Bangladesh and, to a lesser extent, Sri Lanka. In economic terms, incomes have risen in pockets while human development has improved, on an aggregate basis. Yet, widespread violations of human rights are committed, violence and resistance are on the increase and precarious living conditions for the poor, whose numbers have not declined despite the impressive economic growth rates, have worsened. Indeed, the question of how to count the poor and what is poverty is far from settled, from estimates ranging widely from 300 million to over 800 million in India alone, thus ensuring a wide uncertainty about the vaunted positive effects of high economic growth. Adding to this has been the stress on natural systems produced by appropriate policies on the one hand, and disruptions induced by climate change on the other. Frequent failures due to monsoons, catastrophic floods and water scarcity have worsened the conditions of the rural poor in countries such as Pakistan during the last decade.

The governments in the region bear a responsibility to protect their populations, especially those whose rights are at risk, from further impoverishment by providing adequate access to food, water and shelter, and to ensure that their policies do not worsen their right to livelihood. Instead, what one senses is an anti-poor attitude in public culture, policymaking and even judicial rulings, which indicate that the problems could get worse. On the right to food, to take one example, there are vast numbers of people in India who suffer from malnutrition and hunger, while large, unused quantities of grain rot in government warehouses, despite judicial rulings that they be distributed, and the government is taking a position that subscribes to the idea that it is wrong to subsidize the poor. Earlier policies of universal public distribution systems are now sought to be converted to cash transfers to the poor, which in turn raises the question of whether the counting of the poor is accurate – not to mention the question of whether the poor themselves prefer it or not. On the whole, the broad shift since the 1980s to neoliberalism has seen the worsening of economic and social rights of the poor in South Asia, while leading to serious security challenges to the states, which in turn has led to massive human rights abuses on all sides.

The Worrying State of Public Institutions

Since the 1970s, public institutions – legislatures, executive agencies and courts – in South Asia have been in crisis, which has worsened (Kapur and Mehta 2005). The main causes of this crisis can be traced to two elements: the exhaustion of the legitimacy of the postcolonial state, with its logic of developmental nationalism; and the unsettling of the constitutional balance of power between the branches of government, in civil–military relations and the rise of judicial governance – or rule by experts. Both in India and Pakistan, the 1970s witnessed the rise of popular movements, which challenged the legitimacy of the state and the founding political party dynasties, suspension of constitution (in India) and the resumption of military rule (in Pakistan), and a political vacuum created by the weakening of the legislative branch. The crisis of postcolonial nationalism was evident in the challenge to dirigisme, rising corruption and the rise of new social movements around issues of environment, women's rights and human rights. Nepal and Sri Lanka also witnessed the beginnings of organized armed rebellions against state authority from the mid-1990s and the early 1980s, respectively, and a corresponding decline in trust in public institutions. The decline in the status and performance of public institutions has also been driven by causes internal and external to these institutions. Internally, parliaments in South Asia rarely, if ever, robustly discharge their duties to supervise the executive branch. Important bills originate solely from the executive branch, parliamentary supervision of the treaty-making process is a rubber stamp and committee-led supervision of the legislative process has been very weak. Studies have found that the meeting time of the parliament in India has been sharply declining, thus further contributing to the problem of its weakness.

Compounding this has been the delegation of rule making by the government to executive agencies with regulatory authority, under the pressure to deregulate during the neoliberal turn. External factors have also contributed to the decline of public institutions including the shift in law making to international bureaucracies such as the WTO and the pressure to conform to "best practices" in regulatory matters. Important treaties like the WTO do not receive the scrutiny of elected representatives, while executive agencies suffer from a serious accountability deficit. This deficit is exacerbated by weak judiciaries, which do not provide a fast and efficacious mechanism of remedy for violations of the law or hold the government accountable. The judiciary filled the political vacuum created by the weakening of other branches during the 1970s at first and emerged as an organ of governance, exercising policymaking functions in India. But the very act of expanding its domain into governance has made the judiciary share the vices of governance as well, including the backing of wrong-headed policies, shielding the powerful, cronyism, corruption and lack of accountability for itself. In Pakistan, the courts and the legal profession played a major role in ending the military regime of President Musharraf but have not been part of a wider social movement for sustainable political change towards bettering human rights. Court proceedings in virtually all South Asian countries take years to conclude, and judicial corruption has been on the rise, even in countries like India, which are known to have independent judges, compounded by the lack of judicial accountability mechanisms. Indeed, none of the South Asian countries have established even a judicial commission for appointment or complaints. The problem of corruption has emerged on a grand scale in South Asia, since the neoliberal reforms were introduced, and has severely eroded public confidence in state institutions. Despite some attempts to bring this problem under control – such as through the adoption of the Right to Information Act in 2005 in India – South Asia ranks very high in corruption and lack of transparency, as measured by Transparency International and other groups. The erosion of public institutions, as outlined above, poses a serious threat to human rights in South Asia, in the near to medium term.

Conclusion

The common future of South Asia depends crucially on the ability of governments and civil society to find ways of cooperating more actively. Regional links between countries remain very weak, almost inexcusably so. Regional trade between India and Pakistan, for example, remains miniscule – less than 1 percent of India's trade is with Pakistan while Pakistan trades less than 5 percent with India, in contrast to very high bilateral trade volume in the late 1940s, with 63 percent and 70 percent, respectively. This shows that there is always tremendous potential, and the only bottlenecks come from political barriers on both sides, exacerbated by frequent terrorist attacks, armed conflict and formal barriers such as the lack of most-favored-nation (MFN) treatment, etc. The fate of SAARC remains captive to the state of bilateral relations between India and Pakistan, the largest countries in the region, which remains negative. There is an extra burden on SAARC members to overcome these bottlenecks between India and Pakistan, and increase linkages, even if many other problems remain unsolved.

South Asia remains a powder keg in many ways. Increasing terrorism, ill-advised interventions by the US, lack of trust between communities, the nuclear menace, worsening human rights conditions for minorities, women, low castes, tribals and the poor, coupled with lack of economic linkages, worsening effects of climate change, natural disasters, the worsening state of public institutions and the lack of regional mechanisms for cooperation and accountability, all make South Asia one of the most challenging regions in the world from a rights and justice perspective. There is no single magic-bullet solution to these problems, which need to be tackled separately on their own, but there are many important steps that need to be taken simultaneously. They include – but are not limited to – the ending of impunity for massive human rights abuses such as the Gujarat violence in 2002 or the violations by Indian armed forces in Kashmir and the Northeast, the arrest and prosecution of terrorists implicated in the killing of civilians in India and Pakistan, the protection of minority rights including through the suspension of antiblasphemy laws and protection of freedom of speech in Pakistan, the prosecution of war crimes and need for accountability in Sri Lanka, the rejection of neoliberal economic policies and the protection of human rights of the poor, especially of housing and land, the improvement in the performance of public institutions including through effectiveness, transparency, accountability and anticorruption, and the establishment of a SAARC human rights mechanism that can monitor human rights throughout the region.

Chapter 34

PATRIARCHY, POWER AND PARADOX: DREAMING GENDER EQUALITY AND DEVELOPMENT*

Shahla Haeri and Brenda Gael McSweeney

"Just open the door and let the women out!"
Shahla Farid, Kabul University, 2006

"Can't you see, can't you *see*," said a Bengali village woman in 2003 when asked by Brenda McSweeney if an initiative for creative manual skills for self-reliant development made a difference in the community. "*Everything* has changed for us! Before, I myself and many other women *never left our courtyards*. Now, we are here together and our men are listening to us. Can't you *see*?"

Responding to the formulaic and age-old patriarchal justification for the unsuitability of women for manly professions due to their "nature," Shahla Farid, a law professor at Kabul University, Afghanistan, in a conversation with Shahla Haeri pointedly expressed the desire and desirability for mobility, and the unimpeded freedom of movement for women. Further implied in her statement, and in the story of the Bengali village women, is the multiplicity of meanings that are embedded in these poignant yet distressing narratives: it is not women's "nature" that has kept them underdeveloped, but rather the weight of political and cultural dominance and religious discrimination. Unless women are seen as "fully human" and heard by men in power, little will change. Women's energies and talents are wasted unless invested for the development of themselves, their families and societies. If given a chance, women can achieve excellence.

* We thank the contributors, including Kumkum Battacharya, Krishno Dey, Saraswathi Menon, Kalyani Menon-Sen, Asha Mukherjee, B. Murali, Jharna Panda, K. Seeta Prabhu, Anuradha Rajivan, Sanjit "Bunker" Roy, Pradeep Sharma, Lawrence S. Simon and Ramaswamy Sudarshan. Quotations in the text are taken from email communications with us by additional scholars and development specialists. We shall expand the discussion at http://www.unitwin. blogspot.com/

As we cast our eyes to the future, we remember these women from Bengal and Kabul with their emphasis on mobility and patriarchal dominance. To their voices we add those from flagship human development reporting as we try to imagine a mosaic that captures gender and people-centered development in the year 2060. Framing our "dreams of gender equality" tableau, and given the complex array of competing priorities, we appealed to social activists, policymakers and academics with fingers on the pulse of South Asia and known for leading-edge thinking and hands-on experience in this arena. With the key elements tallied and viewpoints expressed, we focus on the weight of dominance and legislative policy measures, followed by livelihoods and education concerns. We imagine a future for South Asia that has genuinely eradicated gender discrimination, for which we envisage the necessity of female mobility at the individual level, engendering local governance bodies like *panchayats* and *jirgas* as power-sharing institutions at the community level and devising a policy shift at the regional level borrowing successful gender equality strategies used in other regions of the world.

Allow us to go directly to the roots of gender injustice, indignities and unequal access to resources, rights and privileges in South Asia. Why, despite all the money and goodwill that has poured into developing and implementing projects to improve women's situation and living conditions globally (and with some successes), are South Asian women woefully underrepresented politically and economically? Many suffer malnutrition and low literacy, and are discriminated against with impunity. We do not have readymade answers, and are humbled by the enormity of the intractable problems facing South Asia. We dare to suggest, however, that the pervasively deep-rooted culture of patriarchy and religious ideology account for many of the social ills in the region, of which gender discrimination is the most debilitating example.

Current Trends and Trajectories

In much of South Asia today, the legacy of colonialism is still evident and archaic nineteenth-century legal codes form the foundation of the criminal justice systems in Bangladesh, India, Pakistan and Sri Lanka in varying degrees (UNDP 2010, 114). The inherited systems of "justice" have compounded the already existing gender inequality in these societies. Nowhere is this more evident than in the areas of marriage, divorce and family law that restrict women's mobility and activity in the public domain, leading to overlapping and binding forms of cultural discrimination and legal exclusion. Realizing that their girl children will face such discrimination all their lives, many women make the painful decision to abort the fetuses of girls rather than subject them to lives of hardship. Up and down the line, the network of invisibility, discrimination, exclusion and inequality is constantly reinforced (HDC 2000, 6).

We believe women's political voice is indispensable for development at the ground level, and agree with Indian economist Suraj Kumar that women's empowerment must be on the political and social reform agendas, and not only be correlated with domestic violence and family planning policies. Pakistani development specialist Atif Khurshid warns against "having laws" that come "under the quick fixes."

People should be educated to believe in the significance of egalitarian laws that are tied with "freedom and liberty that are essential factors of human development." Effective political voice and equitable legal rights are two most significant catalytic factors that can ensure gender justice now and in the future.

Stark inequalities face the marginalized and disenfranchised in South Asia who struggle to make ends meet daily. The scenario for men and children is bleak, yet as Nobel Laureate Amartya Sen puts it "if you're poor, lower caste *and female*, then you've really had it!"[1] Much of women's work in South Asia, like that around the globe, remains invisible, unacknowledged and seemingly unending. Some 85 percent of South Asian women are in unstable employment, typically in the informal sector (UNDP 2010). Even turning to the formal sector, a deplorable picture of female earnings compared to male earnings emerges across the region, ranging from lows in Pakistan (18 percent) and Afghanistan (24 percent) to high percentages in the Maldives (54 percent) and Nepal (61 percent) (UNDP 2009). While some South Asian Association for Regional Cooperation (SAARC) countries have shown leadership in corporate social responsibility, the bulk of the women of whom we are speaking scrape a living from the informal sector with little security, all the while shouldering the additional workloads of being a mother, wife, household manager and caregiver.

South Asia, as a region, has long been known as the epicenter of illiteracy. At present the region has a literacy and education mosaic not unlike that of Sub-Saharan Africa. Dramatically different female literacy rates characterize the SAARC countries, with the Maldives and Sri Lanka being the top performers and Afghanistan and Bhutan abysmally low on the scale. If one were to tackle successfully this challenge of illiteracy in just three countries of the region – India, China and Pakistan – one would resolve a major part of the Education for All goals set by United Nations Educational, Scientific and Cultural Organization's member states for 2015 (UNESCO 2012).

One of the few positive factors amidst the gloom, however, is the role of civil society in increasing women's participation in public life. Civil society initiatives have helped organize women and create awareness on a range of issues from people to people peace initiatives, to health, education and basic rights. A significant number of women work for civil society organizations, either on a voluntary basis or as paid employees. This means that development-oriented initiatives reach more women in both urban and rural areas, with widespread effects (HDC 2000, 6).

The Subcontinent also houses numerous striking examples of creative approaches by the civil society to boost women's self-esteem and livelihoods for themselves, their families and their communities. Best known of these is the work of Mohammed Yunus and his Grameen Bank, which now reaches the disadvantaged throughout Bangladesh and has been emulated around the world, including in industrialized countries like the United States. The mobility afforded to women who receive the micro-credit loans enables them to cross the threshold of their courtyard, to access existing opportunities, to earn a living

---

1 From a brainstorming meeting of Amartya Sen with the UN Resident Coordinator Brenda Gael McSweeney and the UN Country Team in New Delhi, 1999.

with dignity and to better support themselves and their families. Other programs that have made a visible difference for populations include those by the Aga Khan Foundation in Pakistan, and the Self-Employed Women's Association and Working Women's Forum in India, all of which reach impressive numbers of women and communities.

We wish to focus on the rural areas, and look at the Barefoot College that began in the Indian state of Rajasthan in the early 1970s. It captures a methodological approach that has been effective in India, in other South Asian countries, and beyond, involving ordinary, yet determined women and men who make decisions on priorities and integrate local leadership with traditional – and "modern" – knowledge. Empowerment and self-governance are at the heart of this method. It demonstrates the kind of revitalization that is desperately needed throughout South Asia at both the individual and community levels if gender equality is going to be achieved by 2060. Women and girl children take on crucial leadership roles at the Barefoot College. Girls are elected and assume key responsibilities in children's parliaments and in school committees and solar-lit night schools accommodate the workload realities in the part-time seasonal agricultural system.

The Barefoot College approach is now being employed in Afghanistan, a country with only an estimated 12 percent of females age 15 and older who are literate. The country went through a period of Taliban domination where, as a matter of policy, girls were not allowed to go to school. The weight of political and religious dominance is still keenly felt, not only by women and girls in Afghanistan, but also in parts of the neighboring Pakistan.

Most scholars agree that investing in girls' education is critical for the development of the entire region; however there are differing views about what kind of education provides real mobility that would facilitate women's equal access to opportunities and greater participation in the public domain. American scholar Martha Nussbaum notes that the key factor in shaping a positive future for South Asia is "improvement in access to quality primary education – meaning not just rote learning, but the empowerment of the student's mind to question, analyze and criticize." Sri Lankan economist Jehan Raheem champions shifting the analytical framework through which we think about gender equality and women's empowerment issues, for example, combining the use of modern science with women's traditional knowledge. A promising by-product of both these schools of thought is the Asian University for Women (AUW) established in Chittagong, Bangladesh in 2008. The university's mission is to provide an accessible educational environment for women from across Asia, particularly those from poor and rural populations. Mobile and empowered, the graduated women will then have the option to participate in various professions, including in civil society and to join the growing number of nongovernmental organizations.

Dreaming Women's Empowerment in South Asia

"How can a region, so rich in culture and tradition and with women leaders holding the highest political positions, be so cruel in its treatment of the vast majority of women?"

(HDC 2000, 2–3). Indeed how is one to explain these women's achievements and their promotion to such exalted positions in their highly patriarchal societies?

We propose looking into the tribal, feudal and patriarchal social structures that by and large form the patterns of social organization, human relations and inclusion and exclusion in South Asian societies. Power and authority are drawn from land ownership and control of wealth from which women have been historically deprived. Varying in terminology, yet similar in sociocultural intent, Haeri writes, are the dominant and deep-seated beliefs in the region that determine time honored practices and behavior: male control and ownership of land (*zamin*), wealth and gold (*zar*) and control of women (*zan*) – the three most sought after commodities in South Asia. In South Asia, patriarchal social structures and patrilineal patterns of power, prestige and privileges, accordingly, pass through fathers to sons (Haeri 2002, 36).

Perhaps the specificity of patriarchal caste and feudal systems that characterize much of South Asia – though serious attempts have been made to loosen the grip of feudalism in India – lies in their multiple capacity for extreme brutality and oppression of many women, and men, and for concentration of tremendous wealth, power and authority in the hands of a few. Some women, by inheriting land, are placed in a position to exercise feats of national greatness and authority. The enabling mechanism, however, is not the ownership of land alone; it is also the strong and special relationship between a lineage patriarch and his daughter. This cross-gender filial relationship, Haeri argues, is one of the prevailing, yet often invisible – to scholars – paradoxes of patriarchy (2002, 38). It is this benevolent aspect of patriarchy, we suggest, that has real potential of being utilized to initiate massive social transformations and to carry them out to full implementation.

The point we want to stress here is that "patriarchy" is not an unchanging monolith and does not work in a vacuum. Many potential and actual "patriarchs," such as fathers, husbands, brothers and sons care deeply for their women, and many "patriarchs" willingly and honestly want to advance the cause of their women. Indeed the origin of many women's movements, particularly in the Middle East and North Africa, as well as those of South Asia, can be traced to one or more such men, individually and informally, or formally and institutionally.

Rethinking the relationship within the context of women's development and empowerment in South Asia, we believe, father–daughter axis has the potential to be utilized toward legitimating women's mobility and public activity to achieve gender justice. It is the prospect for gender collaboration and male caring that needs to be tapped into and actively employed to explore approaches to gender equality, in mending abusive gender relations and in eliminating gender violence in South Asia – and indeed in much of the world. We believe that South Asian men – like men globally – have the potential to be educated about the collective benefits of caring and partnership, and learn of the profound values of women's mobility and productivity for gender relations, for their families and society; that their women's gain is not – and will not be – men's loss. Nepali development specialist, Sonam Yangchen Rana, argues that South Asian leaders, planners, and decision makers need to radically rethink issues of female empowerment, gender justice, human rights and social change; that "legal support must be backed by actions for social transformation by incubating and reinforcing the achievements related to gender issues thus far. Stronger demand among women and by men (and society in general) must be ensured to reach supportive norms and values for women's empowerment."

One dramatic example is the passage of the 73rd and 74th constitutional amendments in 1992 by the Indian government to the delight of many Indians, both women and men. The amendments enacted a major change to the *panchayat* and *nagar palika* system that historically was the exclusive bastion of male local control and governance. They envisaged a uniform three-tier system of local government, and mandated that "at least 33 percent of the total seats at the three tiers of local governments – both rural and urban areas" must be reserved for women. These amendments effectively changed the form and content of these traditional institutions, transforming them into modern entities. The seeds of gender justice and entitlement were thus sown in the minds of a vast majority of Indian women and men, though initially, many women may not have been aware of it and many men may have resented the power sharing – and some still do. The enthusiastic and active participation of women in local politics and decision making no doubt has wide repercussions for redressing gender discrimination and achieving equitable citizenship rights in India in years to come. Other South Asian countries, like Pakistan, have similar reserved representation for women.

Inspired by such grassroots democratic changes, we suggest that the prevailing local governance bodies, such as the *panchayats* and *jirgas*, be creatively reconceptualized for community development through educating and training men and women. We believe that these institutions have the real potential for social transformation, for socializing men and women into internalizing values of human equality and dignity, and for providing the channels to advance concepts of care and compassion in South Asian cultures (Haeri 2008). The more women that are involved in local and national governance, the more they are in a position to overcome male resistance to power sharing. Grassroots and civil society involvement is therefore essential. The South Asian paradox of the coexistence of a few exalted women political leaders and so many millions of poor women may thus become more comprehensible in light of the leaders' inability to institutionalize participatory political infrastructure for women – locally and nationally.

One need not be naïve regarding the intricate tapestry of the South Asian social fabric, and the entrenched complexity of its gender, class and caste systems. Nonetheless, with a representational number of women in the local and national parliaments, combined with the active work in grassroots political and social institutions, the SAARC member states can firmly put in place meaningful legal frameworks and procedures that work to support female-friendly laws and regulations, demand accountability and see to their implementation.

Making Dreams of Gender Equality Come True in 2060?

Strengthening civic initiatives to boost women's access to educational and livelihoods opportunities will complement the grassroots democratic changes and concepts of care mentioned above. Yet meaningful change is also needed at the national and regional levels. The present trend to increase women's political participation in several SAARC countries through the quota system is a welcome start, yet it needs to be gradually increased to 50 percent, and genuinely implemented if social transformation is to be achieved. It is encouraging to read of SAARC's regional plans and programs of action addressing women's concerns, the regional convention on trafficking in women and children, and the partnership with the United Nations Development Fund for Women (UNIFEM, now part of UN Women), including on a "gender info base" to map progress of the region's women. With political will in the SAARC countries will come – or should come – the elimination of gender gaps in education and literacy, the use of advocacy tools to combat harmful actions like sex-selection abortion, and the effective use of information and communication technologies to boost sustainable livelihoods and skills. There is also need to document the crucial role women have played as peacemakers and peace builders in the region and to learn from each others' efforts, since most local initiatives are not widely known across the region.

Yet a puzzling dichotomy exists between this substantial menu of important instruments and actions in the gender arena set out on SAARC's official website, and the absence of SAARC in the key "human development" works on gender. We propose a closing of the divide between the South Asia human development community on the one hand, and the regional political community on the other hand, by the time of SAARC's Golden (2035) and Diamond (2060) Jubilee years as stocktaking milestones. Should the SAARC political leadership focus on gender equality, and women's mobility and empowerment across the region, as the Nordic countries have done through the Nordic Council and Nordic Council of Ministers, we anticipate that our ambitious dream of a South Asian region free from gender discrimination and a culture of dominance may come closer to reality.

Chapter 35

WOMEN IN SOUTH ASIA

Anita M. Weiss

The myriad of economic, social and political transformations that are occurring throughout the South Asian subcontinent are reflected, to a considerable extent, in the kinds of changes women have been undergoing in the region and the challenges that lie ahead. The pervasive impact of the global economy throughout the region is forcing more women to need to earn an income, but there are few opportunities in the formal sector of South Asia's economies to incorporate them. Female literacy rates among young girls are rising today, but this doesn't help their mothers find jobs. What girls are learning in schools is also problematic: will this knowledge truly open economic and political doors for women in the future, or is it reinforcing stereotypes of maternal nurturing and submission? The entire region has implemented legal reforms to eliminate discrimination against women and to promote and protect their rights, but what is it that needs to occur to translate these new rights into common practices (e.g., allowing women actually to inherit land and reducing sexual harassment through legislation)? Finally, to change political agendas, women need to find their voices and be listened to; with the embedded patriarchy characteristic of most of South Asia, this may prove to be the hardest obstacle of all to surmount.

By the Numbers: Women in South Asia

The South Asian subcontinent is home to roughly 1.7 billion people (UNDESA 2011), less than half of whom (841 million) are women. It is the only region in the world to have such a marked inverse sex ratio: in the overall regional ratio women form 48 percent of the population. Areas of India, Pakistan and Bangladesh have even far lower sex ratios. While the masculinization of the region is the result of longstanding practices of "systemic differential treatment" that caused lower survival rates among women (e.g., poorer food intake, lesser access to medical treatment, and excess female mortality among infants and children), sex-selective abortions gaining popularity in the region in the past 30 years have exacerbated the problem (Guilmoto 2007, 2–6).

For example, we can see in Figure 1 the substantial rise in young male children in India since the 1980s when technological advances in prenatal sex determination

Figure 1. Sex ratio of children and overall population in India, 1951–2001

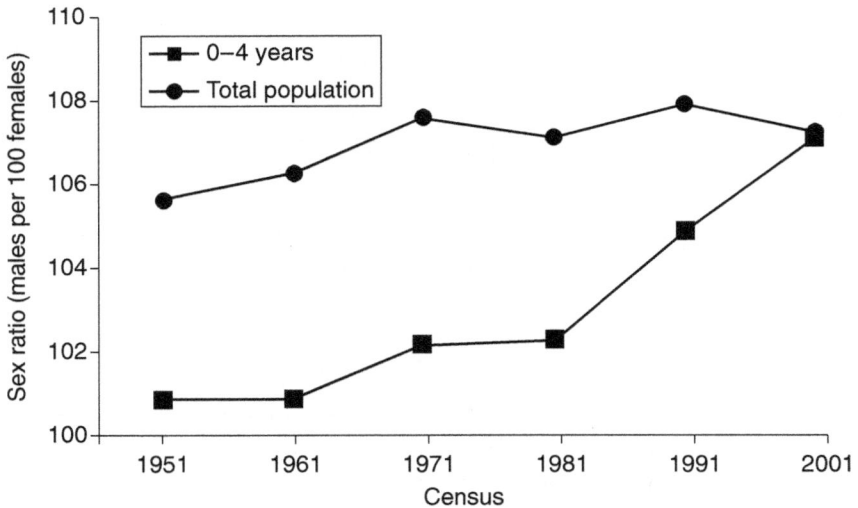

Source: Guilmoto (2007, 3); based on Indian Census data.

Figure 2. Sex ratio at birth by birth order, India, 1978–98

Year	India		Haryana		Punjab	
Date	1978–92	1984–98	1978–92	1984–98	1972–98	1984–98
All birth order	106	108	110	114	114	120
1st birth	105	107	109	110	109	101
2nd	107	108	100	114	111	123
3rd	107	108	114	129	117	136
4th +	106	108	116	108	122	134

Source: Guilmoto (2007, 6); based on NFHS data.

(e.g., amniocentesis and ultrasounds) resulted in greater numbers of sex-selective abortions and hence, greater numbers of male children, especially in urban areas. This is particularly true with "later pregnancies" when, despite accounting for less than a quarter of all pregnancies, the sex ratio at birth since the introduction of the new technology may jump to values of 130 or more, as seen in Figure 2.

Guilmoto (2007) surmises these sons have been born following one or more abortion attempts. While this discrete data is solely about India, similar trends exist in the region on the whole. The sociopolitical implications of these trends for women in the region are enormous as not only are men substantially outnumbering women, but the alarming trend in later pregnancies underscores a distinct prevailing gender bias. In the ominous words of the UNDP (2010a, 23), referring in particular to South Asia, "females cannot take survival for granted."

There is reason for cautious optimism in some arenas: the ratio of female/male life expectancy at birth is roughly equal; the ratio of girls to boys in primary and secondary education is narrowing (rose from 80 percent in 2000 to 90 percent in 2010 in the region overall, and to 93.6 percent in primary education alone); and literacy rates for females continue to rise, arriving at 52.1 percent in 2010 (UNDP 2010a, 41). The challenge that remains is how these greater numbers of better-educated women will be able to mobilize and translate this into greater opportunities and rights for women throughout the region.

Women and the Economy

Prior to South Asia's integration into the global economy through colonialism, women were still largely economically dependent on men, a phenomenon Ester Boserup (1970) characterized as a male farming system. In this plow-based economy, men were dominant in all spheres of food production with the exception of weeding and transplanting of seedlings. Women's economic dependence has been, therefore, deeply embedded in South Asian culture for centuries if not longer, and has been further exacerbated by land ownership traditions having been skewed towards men given the close association of land with economic and political power (UNDP 2010a, 49). This dependence was further reinforced through British colonialism, which concentrated on men in the institution-building process, not women. Men were encouraged to get involved in working and trading in the modern economic sector while women were relegated to the traditional markets. The ideological groundwork was set that men's labor was to be a part of the modern economy, but women's was not. In other words, men became involved in production for *exchange* while women's labor became more entrenched in production for *consumption*. Hence a critical challenge for women's economic empowerment throughout the Subcontinent has been the question of how to move into the formal sector of the economy in meaningful ways.

Today, women comprise 29 percent of the formal labor force in South Asia (World Bank 2010c) – more than in the past, but woefully short of women's economic force in other global regions. Such formal female workforce participation rates, however, hide the myriad nonremunerative tasks in which rural South Asian women engage, in addition to domestic responsibilities: weeding and transplanting in agriculture, caring for a family garden, animal husbandry, stuffing quilts and occasional domestic work for feudal elites. But as there is no cash exchanged, women who perform such tasks also gain no status or recognition for their economic contributions either.

Women's formal labor force participation rates throughout the region have changed dramatically in the past decade. We can see in Figure 3 that, surprisingly, adult female labor force participation rates in Bangladesh, India and Sri Lanka, in the 17 years between 1990 and 2007, have actually gone down, albeit by a statistically insignificant extent. This may be due, in part, to better methods of counting women's participation over the past two decades. In addition, while absolute numbers of women participating

Figure 3. Adult female labor force participation in South Asia, 1990/2008

(Percent of female population aged 15+)

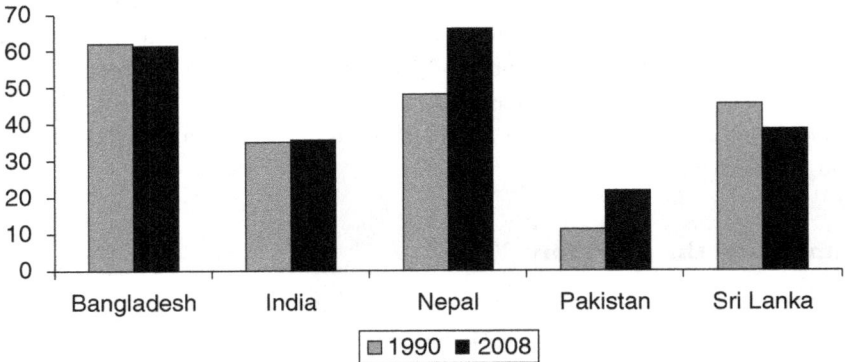

Source: UNDP (2010a; 2010b, 157–8).

in the economy have increased, it is the percentage that has declined as there are just not enough jobs for the larger numbers of women in these three countries today.

Despite this decline, the figures are far greater than those in Pakistan regardless of an absolute increase there. Female labor force participation rates in Sri Lanka have declined remarkably in just one year, from 42.8 percent in 2007 to 38.5 percent in 2008, perhaps due to civil strife in that country, or perhaps due to the impact of the global recession on jobs.

To rectify women's economic situation, four distinct kinds of strategies have been implemented with varying success throughout the region: organizing self-employed women toiling in the informal sector (e.g., Self-Employed Women's Association of India (SEWA)), providing women with micro-credit based on using their respectability as collateral (pioneered by the Grameen Bank in Bangladesh), women's nongovernmental organizations (NGOs) giving visibility to unpaid domestic work, and creation of new, culturally appropriate opportunities in the formal sector (e.g., call centers and other endeavors using information technology throughout the Subcontinent), whereby gender segregation can be maintained, at least to some extent.

Being Able to Avail of New Economic Opportunities: Getting Educated

A century ago, the concept of educating women was highly contested in most parts of South Asia. The demand to educate girls emerged from Western-educated men who desired educated marital companions. Prior to 1947, only a very small minority of South Asian women were literate and nearly all of those were elites. Understanding this baseline is important in appreciating how far female literacy has progressed in South Asia in the past 50 years, for looking at the figures otherwise would imply a very sorry state of affairs. Pakistan's female literacy is the lowest in the region at

39.6 percent, India stands at 54.5 percent, while Sri Lanka is the only success story at 89.1 percent (UNDP 2010b, 215).

What these rates fail to tell us are the efforts underway to improve women's literacy rates, how literacy is distributed throughout a given country, or the class breakdown for female literacy. Sri Lanka has an impressive 89.1 percent literacy rate among adult women. This relatively small island nation prioritized literacy at independence in 1948 in an unprecedented way for South Asia, underscoring the importance of starting such campaigns early.

Greater numbers of girls enrolled in primary and secondary school than ever before throughout South Asia provide a view of dynamic change regarding female educational attainment in South Asia. The desire to educate daughters as a survival strategy was shown to me over two decades ago while I was conducting field research in the Old City of Lahore, a working-class slum, when a widow with four daughters explained to me why she was making so many sacrifices for her daughters to be educated: because land and gold can always be taken away, but no one can take away a good education.[1] While being educated was not even imagined for most of their grandmothers, and an education was out of reach for most of their mothers, today the norm is to educate daughters nearly everywhere regardless of class, region or urban/rural location. What will the expectations of this population be for *their* daughters?

Women in South Asia have often feared change, a logical pragmatic response to a lack of a knowledge base of how things operate elsewhere and what possibilities exist. If a woman is not educated, why would she aspire to have fewer children when she knows she can rely only on them in her old age? An educated woman would be more likely to adapt to using environment-friendly equipment such as new kinds of stoves, sanitation and transportation than would a woman who is not connected to the global knowledge base and therefore does not see how her actions affect the atmosphere elsewhere. Importantly, once a woman is educated, she can read about her rights.

Women and Legal Reforms

Empowering women through legal reforms is an important step not only to make possible economic empowerment but also to promote women's engagement with political processes. South Asia has been riddled by the existence of customary laws, religious laws, British colonial laws and new versions of civil laws, many of which contradict each other. The lines become blurred, too, when considering customary practices and customary or religious laws.

While every constitution in the region forbids discrimination based on sex, the reality is far from that. The challenge has been to identify the most salient arenas for legal reform. For example, nearly everywhere, laws have been passed to ensure women's inheritance rights, to give women the right of divorce and to ensure penalties for perpetrating violence against women. Yet unfamiliarity with negotiating the legal

---

1 This was relayed to me while conducting research for Weiss (1992).

system perpetuates women's powerlessness throughout South Asia and women are still denied the right of inheritance or still give up land to their brothers, are either denied the right to instigate a divorce or else denied the full support to which they should be entitled, and have little recourse when victimized by violence and families often seek to hush it up so as not to be shamed.

Politicized religious groups and parties throughout the region – although especially in Bangladesh and Pakistan – regard certain constitutional rights as a threat to religion. In Pakistan, for example, the nonmilitant Islamist political party Jama'at-i Islami, continues to advocate the repeal of the 1961 Muslim Family Laws Ordinance, which mandates the registration of all marriages and requires the written permission of a wife before a man can marry a second wife, on the basis that such registration and permission is not required in the Quran.

Women and Political Participation

In South Asia, similar to the situation in most postcolonial areas, women have historically enjoyed limited participation in the formal arena of politics, both in standing for election as well as voting for representatives, despite having enjoyed the right to vote for over fifty years throughout the region. While some areas in South Asia have witnessed remarkable progress in encouraging women's political voice, others have seen marked increases in women's voting either only in urban areas, or when men need their votes to secure their candidates' victories. In 2009, one-third of all seats in Nepal's parliament were held by women, followed by 22.1 percent in Pakistan, 18.6 percent in Bangladesh, 10.3 percent in India and 5.8 percent in Sri Lanka. (UNDP 2010b, 224). These figures can be explained by the existence of reserved seats (or quotas) for women in parliament in Nepal, Pakistan and Bangladesh. While some critics denigrate the value of women's parliamentary representation when they are there as a result of quotas – a percentage of all seats won by a given political party are to be allocated to women the party nominates – women holding these positions are often responsible for female and child-oriented portfolios (e.g., education, and health), have the opportunity to engage in the running of the state and, indeed, would unlikely be there as a result of winning in a regular election (as the case in India and Sri Lanka suggests).

When women do vote in many parts of the region, they often do so in line with the candidates the men in their family advise them to support. So for many, the act of voting has been inconsequential thus far. However, this is changing as women become more literate and seek out information independently on which candidates to support. Indeed, when they have higher degrees of economic participation (to give them the sense of being stakeholders in the outcome), higher literacy rates (to fully understand the process) and the legal right to act independently in all arenas of life, women's political participation will not only be quantitatively greater but qualitatively more meaningful to them. Presumably too, as we witness more women in the region being elected to political office, they will likely prioritize those issues of greater interest to women (e.g., education, healthcare and childcare), as has been common elsewhere in the world.

What the Future May Hold

The world for many South Asian women today is substantively different from that lived by their mothers and grandmothers, but it is unclear if this translates into having greater control over decision making in their lives. The average age at marriage is 20; merely two generations ago it was just after puberty. Most women in the past met their husbands on their wedding day, products of arranged marriages; today that is changing and greater numbers of women, especially better-educated women in urban areas, are having some say in the selection of their husbands. Yet, does having a say in the selection of a husband empower a woman, or is it but a slight modification within the prevailing hegemonic system of patriarchy?

While we can pose that question today, it will be less compelling for the daughters and granddaughters of today's South Asian women in 50 years. The abstraction of empowerment will transform into concrete benefits through the actions of educated women. These women will be seeking employment in occupations previously unattainable for most women who lacked the education and skills for such jobs. Their actions will contribute to strengthening their country's economy, as well as the region overall, as the dependency ratio will surely decline. Given the viable employment options for such educated women, they will concomitantly wield greater power within the family. They will also, most likely, be able to convert their economic and social power into political opinions and actions, thereby engaging in political processes at a level akin to women today in industrialized countries, at least.

In South Asia, the single most important step that would facilitate a desirable future in 50 years – not just for women, but for everyone in the region – is for greater numbers of women to be educated. This education needs to be substantive, timely and rely on critical thinking, a true break from the kind of rote memorization that masquerades as education in far too many schools in South Asia today. We can see murmurings of this new order today in the actions of educated women throughout the region, and anticipate this will magnify a thousandfold 50 years from now.

Chapter 36

MEDIA: NEW TRENDS, OLD PROBLEMS

Beena Sarwar

"The open secret of the electronic media, the decisive political factor, which has been waiting, suppressed or crippled for its moment to come, is their mobilizing power," observed Paul Marris and Sue Thornham in *Media Studies: A Reader* (2000). That was when the electronic media was the main contender for such moving and shaking. Since then, the Internet, cell phones and social media (like Facebook and Twitter) have made massive inroads into the public domain, impacting public discourse in an unprecedented manner. The merging of these technologies and tools – Internet, cell phones, video, audio, web logs ("blogs"), and social networks – has led to a virtual (no pun intended) revolution that would once have been considered science fiction. So much so that the UN has declared Internet access as an indispensible human right, terming it "an indispensable tool for realizing a range of human rights, combating inequality and accelerating development and human progress."

The nations that form South Asia, home to about a fifth of the world's population, have much to gain by cooperating to combat common problems like poverty, illiteracy and high fertility rates, unplanned urbanization, gender violence, child labor, poor health services and lack of clean drinking water. The biggest single factor hindering such cooperation is the relationship between nuclear-armed India and Pakistan. Their tensions dominate all regional gatherings, including summits of the South Asian Association for Regional Cooperation (SAARC).

In this chapter I examine the media component of this problematic situation, focusing on efforts aimed at a better understanding across countries, including the media industry. Finally, I raise some questions regarding the future of a South Asian media amid a fast-changing global communications scene.

Regional Conflict and South Asian Media

The media's potential to fan as well as defuse tensions is well recognized. The high levels of illiteracy in much of the region lend radio and television more significance in terms of reaching the public than the print media or social media. But television channels, driven by the race for "ratings," often sensationalize news and information that can fan conflict – supporting the argument that the ongoing ban on each other's television shows in India and Pakistan is just as well, given that their chauvinistic programs would only increase tensions. But the increasing penetration of the Internet renders this ban irrelevant. All the top television channels are now online: in the post-9/11 world with its changed security paradigms and stricter border controls, the media crosses borders via the World Wide Web. However, these same channels also provide space for peacemongers.

Of the several cross-border media initiatives across the region over the past couple of decades, the most visible is the groundbreaking Aman ki Asha (a combination of Urdu and Hindi words that mean "hope for peace"), launched on 1 January 2010, by the Jang Group and The Times of India Group, the two largest media companies of Pakistan and India respectively. Although both are widely perceived as being "hawkish," the stated aim of the initiative is to create an "enabling environment for both governments to dialogue on all outstanding issues" (www.amankiasha.com). The identical front-page editorial published in all editions of their morning dailies *The News*, *Jang* and *The Times of India* on 1 January 2010 was a historic first, followed by several Aman ki Asha events and campaigns around literature, music, poetry, economic collaboration, media, health and strategic issues. The major difference between this, and previous cross-border peace efforts, is its huge visibility, with two mainstream media houses approaching like a corporate campaign, complete with a logo, an "anthem," and advertising and editorial campaigns built around events.

Given the centrality of Indo–Pak relations in the dynamics of South Asia, as mentioned above, the success of any bilateral program for peace between India and Pakistan will benefit the entire region, particularly trade and economy.

Beyond the geographical subregion of the Indo–Gangetic Plain, with its shared languages, heritage, music and food, India's entertainment industry ("Bollywood") cuts across regional boundaries, as do Pakistan's television drama serials and music to an extent. The 1990s spurt in the nongovernment sector included conferences that brought together Indian and Pakistani environmentalists, human rights and gender activists, development workers and others, including journalists. This, aided by the rise of the Internet, has facilitated cross-border contributions for each other's publications since the first Pakistan India People's Forum for Peace and Democracy convention of 1995. Today, practically every major newspaper in India and Pakistan has regular stringers and contributors across the border.

A "Southasian" Media?

An early attempt to bridge the regional media divide was the South Asia Media Association (SAMA) formed in 1991, spearheaded by Javed Jabbar, a prominent Pakistani writer, advertising executive and politician. SAMA conducted training workshops for journalists and organized seminars on regional issues. Its media agenda for South Asia, presented to SAARC governments in 1996, was even reflected in the

SAARC information ministers' agreement of 1998. SAMA led to the formation of the South Asian Editors' Forum (SAEF) in November 1999, focusing on indigenous language newspapers that reach over 80 percent of the regional readership.

As SAMA's activities tapered off, the South Asia Free Media Association (SAFMA) was formed in July 2000 at a South Asia media conference in Islamabad, barely a year after the "war-like situation" between India and Pakistan at Kargil. SAFMA founder Imtiaz Alam stressed the importance of "a regional body" for media professionals, although the conference was India/Pakistan-dominated in numbers and focus.

An ambitious attempt at regional journalism was South Asia Media Wise (SAMW) Online, which folded due to financial pressures (including bribery, the scourge of South Asia), despite an initial growth that resembled "a hockey stick on the graph" as its New York–based Pakistani founder Ibrahim Malick put it. Launched as a web portal on 1 May 2000, it obtained content from the independent South Asia Dispatch Agency (SADA), partly financed by venture capital, with its largest chunk of equity shares owned by journalists working there. SADA had a news exchange pact with the Indo-Asian News Service (IANS, formerly the India Abroad News Service), but tensions between India and Pakistan prevented joint marketing.

The Kathmandu-based *Himal Southasian*, launched by its editor Kanak Mani Dixit in 1996 with contributing editors in the South Asian capitals, has managed to struggle on over the years, thanks largely to grants and donations. *Himal* uses the term "Southasia" as one word in an effort "to restore some of the historical unity of our common living space – without wishing any violence on the existing nation states" and to inject "the aloof geographical term 'South Asia'… with some feeling." *Himal* organized the first competitive showcase of documentaries in the region: Film South Asia (FSA), a biennial festival in Kathmandu that has screened many films barred from the airwaves in their home countries. Responses to the films screened at FSA reinforce the sense that broadcasting them to larger audiences would substantially help to build bridges within the region.

India–Pakistan issues dominate regional information portals, like the South Asia Citizens Web (www.sacw.net, launched in 1996); the South Asian (www.thesouthasian.org/); and the South Asian Idea (www.thesouthasianidea.wordpress.com). The regional media organization Panos South Asia (http://www.panossouthasia.org/), launched in 1998 in Kathmandu has since 2002 included a series of Indo–Pak "media gatekeepers" meetings in its programming, in collaboration with *Himal Southasian*. The aim is to facilitate interaction and understanding between key players in Indian and Pakistani media.

During Aman ki Asha's "Talking Peace" editors' and anchors' conference in Karachi, April, 2010, Panos executive director A.S. Panneerselvan argued that these annual retreats have brought in "the question of Kashmir, not as a divisive issue but rather as a humanitarian crisis that the two countries need to address by keeping in mind the aspirations and political will of the people of Kashmir" (Panneerselvan 2010). He considers the increased contribution of Indians and Pakistanis in each other's media as "a new equation," and "a brave act of subverting the illiberal visa regime of the two countries."

Besides *Himal Southasian*, a few other media companies across South Asia also openly campaign on various issues – for example, education, public transport and corruption – like the Bangla daily *Prothomo Alo*, Bangladesh, English magazines *Tehelka* and *Mid-Day*, and the Urdu daily *Siasat*, India, and Geo TV, Pakistan. However, Aman ki Asha, the "Hope for Peace" between India and Pakistan, is the first initiative in which media companies from two countries are working together for a cause. Feedback from polls conducted in both countries a year after the launch suggests that this movement had already yielded dividends in terms of improving Indians and Pakistanis' perceptions about each other.

Privatization and Beyond

If the last two decades were defined by satellite channels and media privatization, this is the digital age. Satellite television had already exposed audiences across the region to cross-border news and entertainment, and consumer trends. The greater openness pushed governments to pay at least lip service to media freedoms and freedom of information.

The global trend towards private media has been echoed in South Asia too, where multiple private television channels operate with greater influence than ever before. In fact, many media owners are in it not just for financial gain (many run into huge losses) but for the social status and political protection that media ownership can provide.

The private media in the region largely propagates the "national agendas" as defined by the security apparatus of their respective states – except in Bangladesh, which is not embroiled in any major external security conflict. The security establishment's attempts to control information, particularly in conflict zones, have not changed much over the years, from Kashmir to India's troubled northeast, Balochistan to Pakistan's northwest, or the Sri Lankan state's war against the Tamil Tigers to the Maoist conflict in Nepal. The corporate sector also increasingly influences the media. The increasing trends towards consumerism and the push for "ratings" were apparent even a decade ago, as Page and Crawley documented (2000). More recently they noted: "In the rapid expansion of TV in Pakistan, which now boasts some seventy channels, journalistic training and editorial control have taken second place to commercial considerations. In many parts of the country, even in dangerous areas like Swat, news is often being provided to channels by young people with minimal training, inadequate contracts or no insurance" (Page and Crawley 2009).

The number of these young people is escalating. They are joining television broadcasting seemingly in droves, often without prior journalism experience. Many become overnight stars. In Pakistan, the number of journalists shot up from 2,000 in 2002 to 17,000 in 2010 while the average age of a reporter dropped from 47 to 23. As Adnan Rehmat, former executive director of Intermedia put it, "The lack of experience and increased competition ensures that the emphasis is not on investigation but on sensation and more opinion than fact" (Nakamura 2010).

Such trends make journalists in South Asia increasingly vulnerable to violence, kidnapping and murder. While individual reporters in smaller cities or in remote rural areas are more likely to be attacked if they step on powerful toes, journalists in big cities for major media companies are also targeted and killed, most notably in Pakistan and Sri Lanka. In 2012, Pakistan was ranked as the world's deadliest country for journalists for the second year running, according to Reporters without Borders (2011–12 Press Freedom Index). "There simply has been no one found guilty in any of the targeted or indirect killings of journalists in the past 10 years," comments Bob Dietz of the Committee to Protect Journalists (CPJ) (2013). In conflict situations, journalists are caught between security forces and nonstate militant actors, both of which try to prevent information from reaching the public, as the murder of investigative journalist Saleem Shehzad exemplified.

The proliferation of the Internet, the rise of the social media, particularly Facebook and Twitter, and camera-equipped, Internet-accessible cell phones and the marriage of these technologies, means that when information does emerge, it quickly goes "viral." Eyewitness accounts, photographs or video (often taken with cell phones) are uploaded instantly to blogs, Facebook and Twitter. This trend was dramatically evident in recent happenings in the Middle East. Major television networks like CNN and Al Jazeera highlighted tweets from the ground in Tahrir Square, besides interviewing "tweeps," as twitter users are called, providing viewers insights into the thinking of ordinary Egyptians.

Shoaib Athar (@reallyvirtual), an IT consultant in Abbottabad, Pakistan, tweeted real-time information about the US raid targeting the Al-Qaeda leader Osama Bin Laden, without realizing until much later the news-worthiness of his posts, starting with "Helicopter hovering above Abbottabad at 1:00 a.m. (is a rare event)," and ending with "Uh oh, now I'm the guy who live-blogged the Osama raid without knowing it."

Sri Lanka, with one of the highest Internet penetrations in the region, is where the Internet and mobile telephone revolution has had the "largest impact after Burma," with publications like the web-based Groundviews.org helping to further public discourse on democracy and pluralism, notes the media analyst A. S. Panneerselvan (2011).

In Pakistan, videos of army officers beating or executing suspected militants and Taliban flogging a woman made the rounds via cell phone and Internet before TV channels picked them up. The mainstream channels' broadcast of the "Swat flogging video" was a decisive factor in swinging public opinion in favor of the army's operation against militants. Channels are more circumspect about broadcasting videos that expose atrocities by soldiers but the circulation of such footage at least pushes the army into initiating inquiries – even if the results rarely reach the public. Videos apparently showing abuse by security forces against youth in Indian-administered Kashmir also testify to the increasing difficulty in hushing up unpleasant truths. Although police investigation into the Kashmir videos focused on the possibility of fraud, the fact that they took notice at all speaks for the impact of what can be termed the "paramedia" – a term coined by Bangladeshi journalist Afsan Chowdhury (2007) for the underground media of the 1990s.

Imagine if this technology had been around in the 1960s and during the 1971 war between then East and West Pakistan. Barred from addressing the discontent in East Pakistan, the Pakistani media presented the West Pakistan's military invasion of the eastern wing as a legitimate action necessitated by civil disturbances. The (admittedly few) protests in West Pakistan against the army action in East Pakistan never reached the public.

"Satellites over South Asia"

India began granting licenses to private television channels in the 1990s. The satellite dish brought the 1999 Kargil war into homes across the region. The media's reporting on Kargil featured a self-induced censorship, which "slanted public opinion to believe that war is inevitable and military force the only way" (Manchanda 2011). Private television clearly did not necessarily mean independent television; journalists tended to remain mired in their own nationalisms, as they still do, particularly in conflict situations.

NDTV's Barkha Dutt, in an essay for *Himal Southasian* later, recounted how a colonel showed her, behind the army's administrative offices, through a peephole: "[...] a head, the disembodied face of a slain soldier nailed onto a tree" (2001). She decided not to report about this "at least not while the war was still on." A Pakistani reporter may have made the same choice in that situation. Dutt's disclosure, in those pre–social media days, went unnoticed probably because it was published in a magazine that is not freely available in Pakistan. In contrast, reports of an Indian soldier being beheaded allegedly by Pakistanis in early January 2013 caused a huge public outcry in India and led to increased tensions between the two countries. There were very few journalists on either side who tried to transcend nationalistic outlooks and dispassionately examine the larger picture, actual facts and context of the incident.

The restrictive visa regime between India and Pakistan further hampers understanding, as does the "protocol" according to which each country allows only two full-time correspondents from the other country to work based in its capital city; the correspondent must obtain permissions to go anywhere else.

The Indian media's dominance during Kargil may have prompted then Pakistani president General Pervez Musharraf's much-lauded decision to "free the air waves," granting licenses to private channels in Pakistan in 2002 (which the previous government under Nawaz Sharif had strenuously resisted). This tied in with his "liberal" and "enlightened" image, but allowing private television channels in Pakistan also countered the media blitz from India. General Musharraf later clamped down on these channels when they became critical of him after he sacked the chief justice in 2007, leading to a tumultuous chain of events and his eventual ouster in which the independent media played a huge role. Geo TV, Pakistan's first 24-hour news channel, launched in 2002, was the third private satellite channel in the country (Pakistan now has nearly a hundred private television channels). Pakistan's first private radio station FM 100, launched in 1995, competes with over one hundred and thirty others. Bangladesh has recently started its first 24-hour news channel, ATN News, headed by the late Bangladeshi journalist Mishuk Munier, who was part of the starting team of The Real News, a web-based news and analyses channel launched in Canada in 2007 (now Washington-based).

New Politics, New Media, New Ethics?

As Page and Crawley (2009) observe, the state in South Asian countries, after being initially slow to respond to "the challenge of a multichannel universe," has since attempted "to claw back control – as a regulator if not as a broadcaster – through measures like the regulation of cable networks."

> In some fields, it has been aided in this process by technological and economic developments. In India, the tens of thousands of small cable networks gave way within a decade to more expensive, sophisticated systems controlled by a smaller number of players, which made the reassertion of effective regulatory control more achievable. Both Pakistan and India can now black out cross-border channels much more efficiently than they could ten years ago.

But these bans are meaningless today, with television and newspaper content easily available on the Internet. Additionally, the rise of the "paramedia" is chipping away at the carefully constructed edifices of nationalist or religious identities promoted by "big media" in much of the region. Blogs, text messages and social media are influencing public discourse despite their relatively low penetration in the region, making politicians and journalists more accessible and accountable.

The impact of the cross-border media initiative Aman ki Asha remains to be seen. The Times of India Group and Jang Group's editorial policies remain unchanged, as explained in the frequently asked questions (FAQs) link at the Aman ki Asha website: "Aman ki Asha has nothing to do with the editorial policies of either group. News coverage is determined and driven by actual on the ground events. However, we hope that Aman ki Asha will also result in media on both sides presenting a more complete and empathetic picture of 'the other side' – and also of injustices and inequities within their own countries."

A More "Democratic" Media Scene

As mentioned earlier, following the end of the Cold War, the 1990s were marked by a kind of media revival all over South Asia. In Bangladesh, for example, General Hussein Muhammed Ershad's civil–military conglomerate was under increasing attack not only by the media but by the "paramedia" – a "thriving underground press that in many ways has been left unstudied by media experts" (Chowdhury 2007).

The definition of paramedia can now be expanded to include Tweets, blogs and phone text messages. "We know now that when major events occur, the public can offer us as much new information as we are able to broadcast to them. From now on, news coverage is a partnership," acknowledged Richard Sambrook, director of the BBC's World Service and Global News division, following the 7 July terrorist attacks in London (2005).

Professional journalists no longer have a monopoly on news production. The significance of the media-related consumer technology that enables ordinary citizens to play a role in news reporting emerged on 11 September 2001. Amateur video and text messages played a critical role in major networks and newspapers' coverage of the World Trade Center attacks. This has since been evident during other disasters, like the tsunami in South East Asia in December 2004, the 2005 earthquake in Kashmir where the tremors destroyed the printing presses of local newspapers and the floods of 2010 in Sindh.

Websites and blogs initiated by expatriate South Asians politically and socially engaged with events "back home" also keep the attention on major issues, like an earthquake or floods. During the 2005 earthquake in Kashmir, expats set up www.saquake.org to coordinate relief efforts, and http://www.sarelief.com/ after the 2010 floods in Pakistan. The focus on "South Asia" in both efforts underlines the notion that disaster has no boundaries. Increasingly, posts on Twitter are helping to alert and engage mainstream journalists.

Initiatives like Maati.tv, a web-based television channel in Pakistan, are also breaking multiple barriers. Maati plans to work with rural women and college students, training them to document cases of abuse or harassment with cell phones and upload short reports to its website. The technology will become even more significant when 3G access becomes available, predicts Maati founder M. Waseem. "People will be able to view video wirelessly on their cell phones. This has real potential. The future is in that." The web channel is subsidized by the endowment fund of the Interactive Resource Centre, that started as an activist theatre group in Lahore in the 1980s (Waseem 2011).

South Asians are also investing in online media, like the Urdu language Mastmastradio.com, launched in May 2011. Financed by a US-based Pakistani, its target Pakistani audience may well spill over across the region given its cross-border Urdu/Hindustani music and entertainment focus.

Newspapers' websites in the region are increasingly targeting Internet-savvy readers, locals and expatriates. In Bangladesh, the online bilingual BDnews24.com is a relatively recent addition to Bangladesh's media landscape. Its Bangla language edition gets almost as many hits as the website of *Prothom Alo* site, which is the leading newspaper. In other words, there is "competition of the same product in different spaces" (Chowdhury 2011).

On the down side, the transformation of rural reportage enabled by the cheaper cell phone has led to newspapers slashing travel costs. In fact, many Hindi language papers in India now have subeditors to take care of call-ins that they base stories on (Panneerselvan 2011).

Some argue that blogs, text messages or Twitter updates are not reliable sources of information, as "citizen journalists" are not accountable to editorial policy or journalistic ethics, and don't necessarily double-check sources. However, the mainstream media is not free of disinformation or "planted stories" either. In the end, it is up to the public to decide how to take the information. More information, and multiple sources of it, will in the long run contribute to a greater openness and more accountability.

Looking Ahead

In conclusion, it would be safe to say that the rise in consumer-friendly and increasingly more affordable communication tools, combined with social media, is impacting the media landscape in an unprecedented manner. There is no going back to "the days when we had fewer channels, less frenzied competition and more meaningful work," as the prominent Indian television journalist Rajdeep Sardesai (@sardesairajdeep) wistfully tweeted.

Given the trajectory of the trends discussed above, the mainstream media in South Asia, as elsewhere in the world, may well be competing with what we've termed as the "paramedia" by the time 2060 rolls around. Or perhaps by then the paramedia will have emerged as the primary source of news so far as to be termed "mainstream."

Chapter 37

SPORTS: PASSION AND INDUSTRY

Saad Shafqat

Once you start thinking about it, it does not take long to appreciate that sports are essentially a vehicle for channeling primal urges – especially of competition and conflict – in a civilized manner. For that reason alone, South Asia as a region, with its long history of conflict and confrontation continuing into the present day, needs more sports.

Yet sports, today, are much more than that. They are a source of national identity and pride, a conduit for international exchange, a source of entertainment and of livelihood, an expression of self-esteem, a diversion and a distraction, and, ultimately, a major global industry and an integral part of national and global economies. Modern sports, collectively, are a behemoth.

The Legacy of Cricket

As with most things about South Asia, the region's relationship with sports has been heavily influenced by its colonial past. This is the primary reason one cannot talk very long about sports in South Asia without talking about cricket. Through the latter 1800s, as Englishmen posted in India began openly indulging in this most British of pastimes, native South Asians realized this was a game in which they could excel as well.

It is difficult to see Indians getting attracted to cricket as a leisure activity per se, for it is very much an acquired taste. Rather, a servant called upon to bowl at his English master in the nets would have discovered that if he cut the seam just so, and angled the delivery just so, and pitched the ball just so, then every now and then he would get past the edge of the master's bat to clip the off bail. Imagine the euphoria – you could go one-up on the otherwise invincible English *sahib*, even embarrass him in front of the *memsahib* if she happened to be out for a stroll, without the fear of coming to any real harm. If the master's mood was right and his disposition convivial, he could even find it endearing.

This ability to model the conflicts and competitions of life without the direst consequences is one of the magical features of sport, and over the course of the last century, in parallel with advances in media, marketing and technology, it has touched virtually the entire world population. Although a broad range of sports are played in South Asia, the region has experienced this magic through cricket more than any other sport. We may no longer be conscious of it, but in fact the paradigm of sports as a kind of equalizer has continued to exert itself. Modern international cricket offered South Asian countries a chance to defeat otherwise advanced nations such as England and Australia. It is no coincidence that even in India, an emerging superpower, cricket observers still agree that the marquee cricket contests are the ones against England and Australia – along with, of course, Pakistan, the perennial rival.

Why No Rivals to Cricket?

This South Asian facility with cricket does not yet extend to other sports – an asymmetry that is at least partly a function of resources. Many other sports require large social and individual expenditures before they can take on a national or regional profile. Games such as tennis or golf, which demand expensive equipment and sophisticated playing areas, cannot engage the South Asian mainstream in the absence of significant social and economic development that lifts individuals as well as governments with substantial material wealth. Likewise, developing international competitiveness in track and field, gymnastics or swimming, which are traditional centerpieces of the Olympics, requires huge investment in infrastructure and a concerted will at all levels of society. The examples of Japan, South Korea and China demonstrate the sacrifice and investment necessary for becoming a genuine sporting power in today's world. At present, it is difficult to see South Asian countries, which are overburdened by poverty and political strife, emulating this example. Even in India, which has enjoyed spectacular economic success after the liberalization of its economy two decades ago, a crushing poverty burden remains. The benefits of India's growing economic prowess will have to extend well beyond the privileged and the elite for there to be a meaningful impact on India's world standing in sports.

There is also the question of public interest and motivation. For a sport to take root a minimum of three conditions must be satisfied – there must be a public appetite for its consumption, there should be a pool of talent that excels at it and an administrative mechanism to oversee its organization and welfare. Cricket has succeeded in South Asia because all three elements have come together in a combustible mix to create a towering flame that dominates the cricket world as a whole. In doing so, it has also created a massive economic infrastructure that feeds off as well as adds to cricket's great success in this region. Cricket in South Asia is big. But the business of cricket in South Asia is even bigger. More importantly, the business of cricket in South Asia crosses national boundaries. Indeed, it is one of the very few – if not the only – areas of South Asian business where the dynamics are truly regional. Cricket advertising, revenue and even players (workers in an economic sense) are mobile across regional lines. Anyone who is skeptical about this need only look at the recruitment of Pakistani players into the domestic cricket extravaganza of the Indian Premier League (IPL), where the desire for talent has pushed political acrimony aside. And although this approach was suspended after the 2008 Mumbai attacks, we can be sure this is only a temporary setback. Even if players from Pakistan could not be included, Pakistani umpires have continued to cross the border to officiate in subsequent seasons of the IPL. Indeed, the tension-releasing effect of the India–Pakistan semifinal in Mohali during the 2011 World Cup, along with the feel-good aura from India's eventual lifting of the title, helped pave the way for Pakistan's tour to India in late 2012. Such contact promises to iron out not just sporting but also political kinks from the two countries' impossibly prickly relationship.

In fact, one could argue that the relationship – including economic, social and cultural interaction – between India, Pakistan, Sri Lanka and Bangladesh is better developed in sports than in just about any other area. These countries can usually not even hold the meetings of the South Asian Association for Regional Cooperation (SAARC) with any regularity, yet they have been able to host not one but three cricket World Cup tournaments jointly. This is far more than the transnational cooperation one sees in this region in other potential areas of cooperation. Given the prevailing political temperature of South Asia, it is quite remarkable.

Particularly surprising in the face of cricket's almost monolithic dominance in South Asia is the status of football, the planet's most ubiquitous sport, which is at best a stepchild in South Asian sports and at worst a nonentity. Here the issue appears to be not one of resources – even nations from Sub-Saharan Africa are getting through the arduous World Cup qualifiers – but one of taste and appetite. Despite football's enormous worldwide popularity, the great majority of South Asians would rather play and watch cricket than football. The disparity is so profound that, seen from today's vantage, it is difficult to foresee football mount a serious challenge to cricket in South Asia. Still, football's utter simplicity works in its favor, and the forces of globalization could well bring football into the South Asian sporting mainstream in the decades ahead. If that happens, football will most likely take its place alongside cricket, not displace it. Acquired tastes like cricket may be difficult to pick up, but they are also impossible to let go of.

Sports and Regional Dynamics: Politics, Business and Society

Even if South Asia's sporting destiny is to be monochromatic, this is not necessarily a bad thing. One of the secrets to success in life is to figure out what you're good at, and then stick to it. South Asia can consider itself fortunate to have found cricket. The region's relationship with cricket defies simplistic analysis. Certainly, South Asia has done a great deal for the game. Each of the three major teams – India, Pakistan and Sri Lanka – has produced players who could be counted among the best in the history of the sport. Cricketers from this region have also added depth to the game through innovation. Leg glance, leg flick, reverse sweep, reverse swing, the *doosra*, the carom ball – all these inventions have South Asian origins. In conceptualizing cricket as a business, the Indian Premier League, is threatening to reorder cricket's traditional international configuration. South Asia has also demonstrated the possibilities of cricket as an instrument of hero worship: the West has rock stars; South Asia has cricketers.

The IPL, especially, has emerged as a prominent showcase – not just for the possibilities of sports in South Asia, but also its perils. Formulated as a glamorous competition of privately franchised regional teams, this domestic Indian competition has attracted massive crowds in stadiums, and a gigantic television audience stretching throughout the world wherever cricket is followed. The aura of glitz and spectacle has attracted the world's best players, and all the cricket-playing countries have no choice but to arrange their schedules to accommodate a convenient spot for the IPL in the international calendar. The money figures are enormous, and unprecedented in South Asian sports. Top players fetch per-tournament salaries in excess of $1 million, and the league's net worth, including TV rights, sponsorships, franchise fees and gate receipts, approaches $1 billion, which is comparable to North American figures.

That the IPL eventually became mired in administrative (and more lately, spot-fixing) scandals demonstrates the treacherous fabric of South Asia's economy and society. Its former commissioner and founding figure has been accused of favoritism and financial mishandling. Suspended from authority, he remains locked in a legal confrontation with the Indian Cricket Board. It did not help matters that he had cultivated a rather grating persona of superior business acumen accented with fast cars and fast women. If there is a lesson for South Asian sporting initiatives in this, it is that they must be careful not to fly too close to the sun. Such hiccups notwithstanding, the IPL's future is bright. In a part of the world with so little regional trade, it offers an example of significant labor movement and potentially huge regional economic trade.

There are additional considerations. In political debate, cricket is sometimes promoted as a tincture for the ills of South Asia – and perhaps it is. To fully explore this possibility, you first have to get past the banalities and bromides ("it's only a game," "politics and sports shouldn't mix"). In South Asia, politics and cricket mix all the time, and mix well. India and Pakistan have used resumption of cricketing relations with each other as a kind of diplomatic icebreaker. There is the oft-cited example of Pakistani president Ziaul Haq, who traveled to see an India–Pakistan Test match in Jaipur in 1987 – at a time when the two countries were locked in an anxious border confrontation. This defused political tensions and may have averted a nuclear crisis. As mentioned earlier, the positive regional vibes following the 2011 World Cup, in which India, Pakistan and Sri Lanka all reached the last four, also offer great promise. This cricket diplomacy, however, has proved a double-edged sword. India and Pakistan have also deployed suspension of cricketing ties as a diplomatic weapon, which may not carry the physical hurt of military combat but leaves a psychological scar that diehard fans find no less damaging. This political dimension of cricket is unique to South Asia and may even hold the key to lasting peace in the region. Everyone knows that even in the middle of a communications breakdown, India and Pakistan will still be able to communicate through the language of cricket – either by actually playing the game, or by posturing around the idea of playing it.

Separate from the political arena, cricket in South Asia has also developed an interesting sociology. In a region with some of the world's most striking socioeconomic disparities, the game is equally distributed across all socioeconomic ranks. An industrial magnate in Mumbai will have the same love for the game as his driver; a feudal landowner in Sindh will enjoy a match with the same relish as his manservant. All of them will be able to discuss it with each other in a common bond, accepting equal status as fans in the eyes of the sport. The epidemic has also spread throughout the age spectrum and across genders, seducing old and young, men and women alike into a mass following. This is reflected in South Asia's international cricket teams: initially more accessible to the elite and the well connected, over the years they have become far more representative of the South Asian population as a whole. Even countries that don't have a major international cricketing presence have become involved, with the game being followed in all corners of the SAARC world, including Afghanistan, Bhutan, Nepal and Maldives. Indeed, Afghanistan has already been recognized as an international side and represents the first example of a team emerging on the world stage from a land that remained outside the former British Empire. Nepal, too, has won international cricketing laurels through its junior team. If you are searching for a pervasive, unifying, and even expanding democratic force in South Asia, look no further than cricket. No sport will be able to truly make a home for itself in South Asia unless it emulates this far-reaching example across all segments and ranks of society.

Futures of Sports, Futures of the Region

As we look ahead to the next 50 years, sports in South Asia can be anticipated from multiple different perspectives. One rather straightforward scale of measurement is in terms of competitive sporting achievement. It is hard to visualize that, in contrast to other Asian countries such as China, South Korea and Japan, the countries of South Asia will substantially increase their Olympic medal count or become world-class competitors in sports that do not already have a foothold in the region. The one exception might be tennis, in which South Asian players have just begun to have an intermittent presence in Grand Slam events, albeit in preliminary stages and in relatively peripheral fixtures such as men's doubles and mixed doubles. This may seem a depressing reality, but you have to appreciate that raw sporting success does not sit naturally within the South Asian ethos. Having said that, it is also important to acknowledge that 50 years is a long time, and world-class success in a diverse range of sports for South Asia is not inconceivable. A surge in the region's economic fortunes will be key. India appears most well positioned for this but, as the Far Eastern examples have shown, it will not come easy.

A more fitting appraisal would be in terms of how South Asia can use sports to make the region a better place, and what it can do for a sport like cricket, with which it has chosen to engage very deeply. In the rosiest scenario, South Asian countries will meet regularly in a range of sporting encounters on regional as well as bilateral platforms and this activity will become a catalyst for sustainable peace and the cultural articulation of a proud South Asian identity. Such a favorable outcome is predicated on economic advancement and political maturation within the region, and friendly global circumstances. At present, the South Asian games, initiated in 1984 and held in 2010 in its 11th edition, do provide a regional mechanism for sporting interaction and cooperation beyond cricket, but as a showcase occasion this event is still evolving its identity and status.

When envisioning the future, one is naturally inclined to be sanguine, but any hopefulness must be tempered by the realities of South Asia. This is a part of the world that has had more than its share of tragedy and strife, a region where war, terrorism and poverty continue to have an impact on daily life. The history of South Asia suggests that rosy scenarios are imagined at your own risk. Ideally, there should be peace and stability for South Asian countries to fully realize their sporting potential. Governments must be on good terms with each other, and the people must live without fear and have enough disposable income to enjoy the leisure of a sporting life. Cricket may appear to have thrived despite the drawbacks of South Asia – and there is no question it has done spectacularly well in the region – but a case can be made that it would have done far, far better had South Asia been a happier place. Inevitably, one is left to ask, do we need good regional relations to have a strong and successful sporting culture, or does a robust sporting culture lead to good relations? This may seem a catch-22 at first glance, but there is no getting around the fact that healthy relations are necessary, and sports are not the only means to obtain them. Good relations must come first; good sports will naturally follow.

One should also be careful not to let a vision of the future get too influenced by the heat of the present moment. Currently the outlook for South Asia may appear bleak in many ways, but conjuring up a vision is always something of a wild card, and the only thing certain is that nothing is certain. Half a century is a long time for things to change. In the middle of the Second World War when civilization was going up in smoke and life had been reduced to its bare essentials – even Test cricket stayed suspended for seven years – the future must have looked impossibly gloomy. Yet circumstances eventually improved. The great lesson of history is that the status quo is never indefinite.

It is worth noting that sports are ultimately an expression of human endeavor, and in that sense they have the power to inscribe romantic narratives even in the face of dismay and despair. We have already seen this quality of sports expressed brilliantly in South Asia, with a ravaged nation like Afghanistan finding dignity and glory in cricket when it landed a spot in the Twenty20 World Cup. Undoubtedly, there are many more such South Asian narratives waiting to emerge.

Regardless of whatever circumstances lie ahead – whether there is peace or no peace, and whether or not there is conspicuous prosperity and development – South Asia will almost certainly breathe its spirit into the fabric of cricket. In fact, the evolving nature of cricket could transform South Asia's association with the sport into an unexpectedly productive marriage. A sedate and esoteric temperament and a relatively marginal following have been traditional impediments to the international spread of cricket. That is certain to change because of two far-reaching developments – emergence of the thrill-packed Twenty20 format, and an overwhelming following that is concentrated not just in South Asia but also sprinkled across the world as a South Asian diaspora.

Not only does Twenty20 cricket follow a 3- to 4-hour convenient, TV-friendly format that approximates the winning formula of North American sports fixtures, it also compresses the game to a point where dull periods are eliminated and excitement simply overflows. Granted it lacks the subtlety demanded by purists, but it isn't really directed at the purist, for whom Test and One Day International (ODI) cricket already carry enough sex appeal. Rather, the aim of Twenty20 cricket is to bring new converts into the fold. Combined with South Asian media and diaspora making cricket a visible presence around the world, this might result in cricket becoming in the twenty-first century what football became in the twentieth.

The lynchpins in this process are the United States and China. In the case of China, cricket has already come under its ambitious sporting ambit, which calls for world supremacy in every sport that matters. China is on public record aiming to have an internationally competitive cricket team by 2025; their record with success in other sports newly picked up suggests this is not a long shot. Unlike China, the United States has so far been very insular with its sports, resisting even the entry of as permeable a game as soccer. America's cricket audience is estimated at around 15 million people, but there is no organized effort to properly market it and create a taste for it. Armed with the charisma of Twenty20, South Asian immigrants in the United States could be the spark that ignites cricket's American flame. There are immigrant communities in the United States from other cricket-playing nations too, but their numbers are smaller, and nor does cricket enjoy an overwhelming alpha status in those countries the way it does in South Asia. If cricket succeeds in America, the South Asian diaspora would have had a lot to do with it. Substantial benefits to South Asia will likely follow – a sense of pride and sporting excellence, business opportunities and greater international recognition. If Americans adopt an arcane and eccentric sport like cricket through South Asian persuasion, their views of South Asia as a backwater and South Asian countries like Afghanistan and Pakistan as nothing but trouble will begin to change.

Sports have the potential to shape the future of South Asia. As we look ahead to the next 50 years, there is good reason to anticipate a South Asian–engineered transformation of cricket into a truly global sport. There is also reason to hope that spreading economic prosperity will augment the international profile of South Asian countries in other sports. These developments could do a great deal for South Asia, not just in terms of regional cooperation, interaction and political relations, but also from the point of view of identity, self-respect and recognition on the world stage.

ABOUT THE AUTHORS

Editors

Adil Najam has served as vice chancellor of Lahore University of Management Sciences (LUMS) in Pakistan, the Frederick S. Pardee Professor of Global Public Policy and director of the Pardee Center for the Study of the Longer-Range Future at Boston University, and as associate professor of negotiation and diplomacy at the Fletcher School of Law and Diplomacy, Tufts University. Professor Najam holds a PhD and two master's degrees from the Massachusetts Institute of Technology (MIT). His research focuses on issues of global development, and particularly on climate change and environment.

Moeed Yusuf is the South Asia adviser at the United States Institute of Peace (USIP) in Washington, DC. He is responsible for managing the institute's Pakistan program. By training a political scientist, he has worked extensively on issues relating to South Asian politics, Pakistan's foreign policy, the US–Pakistan relationship, nuclear deterrence and nonproliferation and human security and development in South Asia. Before joining USIP, Yusuf was a fellow at the Frederick S. Pardee Center for the Study of the Longer-Range Future at Boston University, and concurrently a research fellow at the Mossavar–Rahmani Center at Harvard Kennedy School.

Contributors

Safiya Aftab has graduate degrees in economics (from Quaid-i-Azam University in Islamabad and the London School of Economics) and public administration (from Harvard University). She has had varied professional experiences, including permanent staff positions with multilateral development institutions, as well as in consulting and research. She has significant experience in primary data analysis, and has worked on a number of papers on economic policy and on political economy issues. She has also coauthored a book on Pakistan's economy.

Manan Ahmed Asif is currently an assistant professor of history at Columbia University. He received his PhD from the University of Chicago in 2008. His areas of specialization include the political and cultural history of Islam in South and Southeast Asia, frontier spaces and the city in medieval South Asia, imperial and colonial historiography, and philology. A collection of his essays has been published under the title *Where the Wild Frontiers Are: Pakistan and the American Imagination* (2011).

Jalal Alamgir is an assistant professor of political science at the University of Massachusetts Boston, and a fellow at the South Asia Initiative, Harvard University. His recent book *India's Open-Economy Policy: Globalism, Rivalry, Continuity* was selected by *Asia Policy* as a recommended book for its 2008 "Policymaker's Library." His research interests include political justice in Bangladesh, the foreign policy of Bangladesh, the representation of values in Indian foreign policy and the relationship between authoritarianism and globalization in Burma/Myanmar.

Madhav G. Badami has a joint appointment in the School of Urban Planning and the School of Environment at McGill University. After having studied mechanical engineering at the Indian Institute of Technology, Madras, he spent nine years in diesel engine development in the Indian truck and bus industry. His teaching and research interests are in the areas of environmental policy and planning, urban infrastructure and services in low-income countries, alternative transport fuels, urban transport and environment and development.

Jamshed Bharucha is president of the Cooper Union for the Advancement of Science and Art in New York City. He spent most of his academic career at Dartmouth College, where he was the John Wentworth Professor of Psychological and Brain Sciences and served in several leadership posts, most recently as dean of the faculty. He subsequently served as provost and senior vice president of Tufts University. He has served as editor of the interdisciplinary journal *Music Perception*, and was a fellow at the Center for Advanced Study in the Behavioral Sciences in 1993–94.

Manu Bhaskaran is a partner of the Centennial Group, a strategic advisory firm based in Washington, DC. Based in Singapore, he coordinates the Asian business of the group as head of its Economic Research Practice. Previously, Mr Bhaskaran supervised Asian economic and investment strategy analysis for Société Générale's Asian investment banking division. He is also an adjunct senior research fellow at the Institute of Policy Studies Singapore and a council member at the Singapore Institute of International Affairs (SIIA).

David E. Bloom is Clarence James Gamble Professor of Economics and Demography at the Harvard School of Public Health, former chair of its Department of Global Health and Population and director of Harvard University's Program on the Global Demography of Aging. He has worked extensively in the areas of health, labor, development economics and demography. Longstanding themes in his research include a focus on "healthier makes wealthier" and the potential positive economic impact of the demographic transition.

John Briscoe is Gordon McKay Professor of the Practice of Environmental Engineering at Harvard University. He was with the World Bank for 20 years, including as senior water advisor and country director for Brazil. His recent writings on water in South Asia include *India's Water Economy: Bracing for a Turbulent Future* (2006), and "Troubled Waters: Can a Bridge Be Built over the Indus?" (*Economic and Political Weekly* 2010).

Sanjoy Chakravorty is professor of geography and urban studies at Temple University in Philadelphia, USA. His recent books are *Made in India* and *Fragments of Inequality*. He has authored over fifty journal papers, book chapters, etc. in geography, economics, planning and urban journals. His research has been funded by the National Science Foundation (NSF), National Institute of Justice (NIJ), American Institute of Indian Studies (AIIS), the World Bank and the Indian government. In 2011 he was a fellow at the University of Pennsylvania, working on a book titled *The Price of Land* (published in 2013 by Oxford University Press).

Stephen P. Cohen joined the Brookings Institute in 1998 after a career at the University of Illinois, Urbana–Champaign. He has also taught in India, Singapore and Japan, and served on the Policy Planning Staff of the US State Department. In 2004, he was named as one of America's 500 most influential people in the area of foreign policy. Cohen is author or editor of numerous books on Asian security issues, and is the author of a book on India–Pakistan rivalries, *Shooting for a Century: The India-Paksitan Conundrum* (Washington, DC and New Delhi: Brookings and HarperCollins, 2013).

Kanak Mani Dixit is editor and publisher of *Himal Southasian*, a news and analysis magazine covering South Asia, and publisher of the Nepali-language *Himal Khabarpatrika* news magazine. Dixit holds graduate degrees from Columbia University and undergraduate degrees from Tri Chandra College in Kathmandu and Delhi University. He has been a human rights activist covering Nepal and the South Asian region at large. Dixit is also the chair of the widely recognized *Film South Asia* documentary festival.

Jacob Friedman is the 2010 Jeff Metcalf Summer Research Fellow at the Brookings Institution. A graduate of the University of Chicago, Friedman's areas of interest include the political nature of language policy in the Indian subcontinent and the linkages between language and political affiliation in India.

Rajan Gupta is an elementary particle physicist and a laboratory fellow at Los Alamos National Laboratory. He earned his PhD in theoretical physics from the California Institute of Technology in 1982 and has published over 125 research papers in prestigious refereed journals and is a fellow of the American Physical Society. He is using his scientific training to analyze global energy systems and to understand and accelerate development and education in the developing world.

Shahla Haeri is an associate professor of cultural anthropology, and a former director of the Women's, Gender, & Sexuality Studies Program at Boston University. Trained as a cultural anthropologist with specific focus on law and religion, she is the author of *Law of Desire: Temporary Marriage, Mut'a, in Iran* (1989) and *No Shame for the Sun: Lives of Professional Pakistani Women* (2002).

Murtaza Haider is professor of supply chain management and director of the Institute of Housing and Mobility at Ryerson University in Toronto, Canada. He is also an adjunct professor of engineering at McGill University and the University of Toronto. His research focuses on urban infrastructure development, transport and logistics management, and real-estate market analysis. He is also director of Regionomics Inc., a consultancy firm specializing in the analysis of urban systems.

A. K. Enamul Haque is professor of economics at the United International University in Dhaka, Bangladesh. Haque earned his PhD degree from the University of Guelph, Canada in 1991 in the field of environmental and resource economics. His research fields include issues in environmental economics (land degradation, water contamination, poverty and environment), energy economics, economics of climate change and evaluation of effectiveness, and impacts of foreign aid and grants.

Syed Abu Hasnath earned his MSc in economics from Wales University, and PhD in economic geography and environment from Boston University. Hasnath taught at Bangladesh University of Engineering and Technology, Dhaka for a decade, and at Boston University for another two decades. His papers have appeared in several international journals, including *Economic Geography*, *Annals of Regional Science* and *Technology Forecasting and Social Change*. Currently, he is an independent scholar, living in Boston.

Pervez A. Hoodbhoy received his PhD in nuclear physics from the Massachusetts Institute of Technology (MIT) in 1978. He currently teaches at Forman Christian College University in Lahore as well as at Quaid-i-Azam University in Islamabad. He is the recipient of the Baker Award for Electronics, the Abdus Salam Prize for Mathematics and United Nations Educational, Scientific and Cultural Organization (UNESCO)'s Kalinga Prize for Science Popularization. Dr Hoodbhoy has written and spoken extensively on topics ranging from science in Islam to education issues in Pakistan, and nuclear disarmament.

Ishrat Husain is currently the dean and director of the Institute of Business Administration (IBA), Karachi, and the Higher Education Commission (HEC) of Pakistan's Distinguished National Professor of Economics and Public Policy. Between 2006–2008 as chairman of the National Commission for Government Reforms he produced a comprehensive blueprint for governance reforms in Pakistan. As the governor of Pakistan's Central Bank (1999–2005) he successfully implemented a major restructuring of Pakistan's banking sector. For over two decades, he served the World Bank in Washington, DC in senior positions including as chief economist for the Africa and East Asia regions.

Najeeb Jung is the vice chancellor of National Islamic University, New Delhi, India since 2009. He holds master's degrees from St Stephen's College, Delhi and the London School of Economics. Jung joined the Indian Administrative Services (IAS) in 1973 and worked for 22 years in different capacities in the state government (Madhya Pradesh) and with the federal government (New Delhi). He has held senior research and administrative positions with the Asian Development Bank, Oxford Institute for Energy Studies and Observer Research Foundation, New Delhi. Jung is a regular columnist in national and international newspapers. An acknowledged international expert on energy issues, his latest book in Urdu (*Fikr-o-Aagahi*) on contemporary social issues was published in 2012. A volume on energy issues edited by him, dealing with energy issues in South Asia, is under publication.

Gerald Keusch is professor of medicine and public health, and special assistant for global health to the president of Boston University. He was previously the National Institutes of Health's associate director for international research and director of the Fogarty International Center. A graduate of Harvard Medical School, trained in internal medicine and infectious diseases, he has authored over two hundred publications and nearly one hundred book chapters. He has collaborated closely with government and academic medical institutions in India for nearly twenty-five years.

Maleeha Lodhi has twice served as Pakistan's ambassador to the United States and also as high commissioner to the United Kingdom. She is currently special adviser to the country's largest media group, Geo/Jang, and a member of the council of the London-based International Institute of Strategic Studies. Dr Lodhi served as a member of the United Nations (UN) Secretary General's Advisory Board on Disarmament Affairs from 2001 to 2005. She has been the editor of two of Pakistan's leading English dailies and has taught at the London School of Economics.

Amitabh Mattoo is director of the Australia–India Institute, professor of international relations at the University of Melbourne and professor of international studies at Jawaharlal Nehru University. Mattoo has been the vice chancellor of the University of Jammu, a member of the Indian National Security Council's advisory board and a member of the task force constituted by the prime minister of India on global strategic developments. Mattoo is also the current president of the Indian Association of International Studies (IAIS).

Brenda Gael McSweeney teaches gender and international development in Boston University's Women's, Gender, & Sexuality Studies Program, is a resident scholar of the Women's Studies Research Center at Brandeis University and a founding advisory board member of the Global Network of UNESCO Chairs on Gender. She is the editor of *Another Side of India: Gender, Culture and Development* (2008) and coeditor of *Gender Perspectives in Case Studies Across Continents* (2013).

Pradeep S. Mehta is the founding secretary general of Customer Unity and Trust Society (CUTS) International. Mehta serves or has served on several policymaking bodies of the Government of India relating to trade, environment and consumer affairs, including the National Advisory Committee on International Trade of the Ministry of Commerce and its working groups. He chairs the advisory board of the South Asia Network on Trade, Economics and Environment, Kathmandu.

Zia Mian, a physicist by training, directs the Project on Peace and Security in South Asia in Princeton University's Program on Science and Global Security. His research and teaching focuses on nuclear weapons and nuclear energy policy, especially in Pakistan and India, and on issues of global nuclear disarmament and peace. Previously, he has taught at Quaid-i-Azam University, Islamabad, and worked at the Sustainable Development Policy Institute, Islamabad.

William Milam is a senior policy scholar at the Woodrow Wilson International Center for Scholars in Washington, DC. He is the author of *Bangladesh and Pakistan: Flirting with Failure in South Asia*, and writes occasional articles for the Pakistani weekly *The Friday Times* as well as for various periodicals. Prior to joining the Wilson Center in 2003, he was US ambassador to Pakistan and Bangladesh, as well as chief of mission in civil war-torn Liberia.

Amitendu Palit is head (development and programs) and visiting senior research fellow at the Institute of South Asian Studies at the National University of Singapore. He is an economist specializing in trade, political economy, development and India–China comparative studies. He worked for several years in India's Ministry of Finance and is a columnist for *Financial Express*. His first book (coauthored) was on India's *Special Economic Zones* (2008), and his forthcoming book is on challenges, competition and collaboration in China–India Economics.

Balakrishnan Rajagopal is an associate professor of law and development at the Massachusetts Institute of Technology (MIT) and the director of MIT's Program on Human Rights and Justice. He received an interdisciplinary SJD (Doctor of Juridical Science) from Harvard Law School and formerly served with the United Nations High Commissioner for Human Rights in Cambodia between 1992 and 1997. He has consulted with the United Nations Development Programme (UNDP), the World Commission on Dams and with various civil society organizations. His research experience and interests are primarily in South and Southeast Asia, Brazil and South Africa.

Ali Riaz is professor and chair at the Department of Politics and Government at Illinois State University. He has also served as an assistant professor at the University of Dhaka in Bangladesh and as a broadcast journalist for the BBC World Service in London. His research interests include Islamist politics, South Asian politics, community development and the political economy of media. His most recent publication is *Political Islam and Governance in Bangladesh* (2011).

Nihal Rodrigo was honorary adviser (foreign relations) to the president of Sri Lanka (2007–10). He has served as Sri Lanka's foreign secretary, as secretary general of the South Asian Association for Regional Cooperation (SAARC), as ambassador to China, and as ambassador and permanent representative, respectively to the United Nations in New York and Geneva. His earlier postings were to Sri Lankan missions in Germany, India and Australia. He is currently a visiting lecturer on international relations.

Larry Rosenberg is a senior research associate at the Harvard School of Public Health. His research interests center on political and economic development in Latin America and Asia, focusing on steps developing countries can take that are distinct from those advocated by the international financial institutions. A graduate of Harvard's Kennedy School of Government, he has worked on projects relating to health, demographic change, economic growth, poverty alleviation, social protection, tax policy and the Israeli–Palestinian conflict.

Rohan Samarajiva is founding chair of LIRNEasia, a policy and regulation think tank active across emerging Asian and Pacific economies. He has written a regular column on public policy in *Lanka Business Online* since 2005, which was shortlisted for the Bastiat Prize for Online Journalism in 2009. He also writes for the *Daily Star* (Bangladesh), *Himal* (Nepal), and *Ravaya*, the *Daily Mirror* and the *Sunday Times* (Sri Lanka) on South Asian issues.

Beena Sarwar is a journalist, an artist and a documentary filmmaker with extensive experience working with television and print media in Pakistan and abroad. She was a Nieman Fellow at Harvard University (2005–2006), a research fellow at the Carr Center for Human Rights Policy at Harvard Kennedy School (2006–2007), and a fellow at the Ash Center for Democratic Governance at the Harvard Kennedy School (2012–13), and is currently working as editor of *Aman ki Asha*, a peace initiative between the Jang Group of Newspapers, Pakistan and *The Times of India*.

Pramilla Senanayake is the founder and chairperson of the Educate a Child Trust, an NGO based in Sri Lanka. She has 17 years of experience working for the International Planned Parenthood Federation, first as its medical director and then assistant director general. She also chairs the Geneva-based Foundation Council of Global Forum for Health Research.

Saad Shafqat is professor of neurology at Aga Khan University in Karachi, Pakistan. He also writes cricket opinion columns for ESPNCricinfo and *Dawn*, and is the coauthor of Pakistani cricketer Javed Miandad's autobiography *Cutting Edge* (Oxford University Press). His articles have also been published in *The Daily Telegraph* (UK), *The Telegraph Calcutta*, *Sports Illustrated India*, *The Wisden Cricketer*, and *The Nightwatchman*. His novel *Breath of Death* – a medical thriller set in Karachi and Boston – has been published by Chlorophyll (New Delhi). His cricket column *Reverse Swing* appears fortnightly in *Dawn* magazine.

Harihar Shankar obtained his master of science in computer engineering from the University of New Mexico in 2009 and is currently a research and development engineer in the research library at Los Alamos National Laboratory. He has been instrumental in the development of the Global Energy Observatory (GEO) and is working on open-collaborative tools to facilitate rapid dissemination of information and data management.

Hilary Synnott is a consulting senior fellow at the International Institute for Strategic Studies in London. A former Royal Navy submariner and British diplomat, he was deputy high commissioner in New Delhi and subsequently high commissioner in Islamabad, finishing his diplomatic career as the coalition provisional authority regional coordinator for southern Iraq in 2003–2004. He is author of *The Causes and Consequences of South Asia's Nuclear Tests* (1999) and *Transforming Pakistan, Ways Out of Instability* (2009).

Ramesh Thakur is professor of international relations, Australian National University and adjunct professor, Griffith University. He was formerly senior vice rector of the United Nations University (and assistant secretary general of the UN). His books include *The United Nations, Peace and Security: From Collective Security to the Responsibility to Protect* (2006), *Global Governance and the UN: An Unfinished Journey* (with Thomas G. Weiss, 2010), *The Responsibility to Protect: Norms, Laws and the Use of Force in International Politics* (2011) and *The Oxford Handbook of Modern Diplomacy* (2013).

John Thomson, a research affiliate at the Massachusetts Institute of Technology (MIT), served as the United Kingdom high commissioner to India and as the UK permanent representative at the United Nations. Amongst his previous posts he was head of policy planning and undersecretary for defense and disarmament in the Foreign Office and chief of the assessments staff in the Cabinet Office.

Lhaba Tshering is a deputy chief planning officer at the Gross National Happiness Commission of the Royal Government of Bhutan. He is a recipient of the Japanese government's Monbusho Scholarship and holds a master's degree in economics from the University of Wakayama. He is also a Hubert Humphrey Alumni from Boston University, under the Fulbright Hubert Humphrey Fellowship Program, and has participated in various international meetings and conferences representing his country. He was one of the keynote speakers at the 2nd International Conference on Sustainable Development and Happiness held in Costa Rica in 2012, along with the 42nd US president Bill Clinton and Ms Marina Silva of Brazil. In August 2012, he delivered a talk at the TEDx Cordoba, Argentina on "Happiness as a Global Development Goal."

M. E. Tusneem holds a PhD in agriculture and has wide-ranging experience in agriculture sector planning, policy formulation, and research and development in Asia and the Pacific region. He was member (food and agriculture) of the Planning Commission of Pakistan from 2008 to 2010, and chairman of the Pakistan Agriculture Research Council from 2005 to 2008. Tusneem previously worked with the Asian Development Bank for 25 years in various capacities, culminating in the position of director general for the East and Central Asia region, including China.

Chalinda D. Weerasinghe is completing his doctoral studies at the University of Maryland, College Park in government and politics and economics. His specializations are international relations, econometrics, political economy and development economics. He has master's degrees in economics and international relations from the Georgia Institute of Technology and a bachelor's degree in mathematics, economics, and history and political science from Shorter University in Rome, Georgia. He hails from Sri Lanka.

Anita M. Weiss is professor and head of the Department of International Studies at the University of Oregon. She has published extensively on social development, gender issues and political Islam in Pakistan. Her current research project analyzes how distinct constituencies in Pakistan, including the state, are grappling with articulating their views on women's rights. Professor Weiss is a member of the editorial boards of *Citizenship Studies* and *Globalizations*, and coordinates the American Institute of Pakistan Studies (AIPS)/Higher Education Commission (HEC) of Pakistan doctoral dissertation workshop project.

Niru Yadav is an assistant professor of economics at the School of International Studies, University of the Pacific, California, USA. She holds a PhD in economics from Indiana University, Bloomington with specialization in international trade, and was formerly senior research associate at Customer Unity and Trust Society (CUTS) International. Her research interest lies in the fields of international trade and development economics.

BIBLIOGRAPHY

Acharya, A. 2004. "How Ideas Spread: Whose Norms Matter? Norm Localization and Institutional Change in Asian Regionalism." *International Organization* 58: 239–75.

————. 2009. *Whose Ideas Matter: Agency and Power in Asian Regionalism.* Ithaca: Cornell University Press.

————. 2011. "Norm Subsidiarity and Regional Orders: Sovereignty, Regionalism and Rule-Making in the Third World." *International Studies Quarterly* 55.

Acharya, J. 2011. "Bhutanese Refugees: The Struggle in Exile." In *Minority Rights in South Asia,* edited by R. Hofmann and U. Caruso. Frankfurt: Deutsche Nationalbibliothek.

Alm, J. 2010. *Municipal Financing of Urban Infrastructure: Knowns and Unknowns.* Washington, DC: The Brookings Institution.

Asian Development Bank. 2000. *Rural Asia: Beyond the Green Revolution.* Manila: Asian Development Bank.

————. 2000a. *Transforming the Rural Asian Economy: The Unfinished Revolution.* New York: Asian Development Bank.

————. 2007. *Country Poverty Assessment: Maldives.* Manila: Asian Development Bank.

————. 2009. *Study on Intraregional Trade and Investment in South Asia.* Asian Development Bank.

Adler, M, and E. Ziglio. 1996. *Gazing into the Oracle: The Delphi Method and Its Application to Social Policy and Public Health.* London: Jessica Kingsley Publishers.

Agarwal, B., J. Humphries and I. Robeyns. 2006. *Capabilities, Freedom, and Equality: Amartya Sen's Work from a Gender Perspective.* New Delhi: Oxford University Press.

Ahmed, K. 2011. *Sectarian War: Pakistan's Sunni–Shia Violence and Its Links to the Middle East.* New York: Oxford University Press.

Ali, Agha Shahid. 1998. *The Country without a Post Office.* New York: W. W. Norton.

Amnesty International. 2004. "Protecting the Human Rights of Women and Girls Trafficked for Forced Prostitution in Kosovo." AI document EUR 70/010/2004.

Archibuggi, D. and A. Coco. 2004. "A New Indicator of Technological Capabilities for Developed and Developing Countries (ArCo)." *World Development* 32, no. 4: 629–54.

Avari, B. 2013. *Islamic Civilization in South Asia: A History of Muslim Power and Presence in the Indian Subcontinent.* New York: Routledge.

Badami, M. G. 2009. "Urban Transport Policy as if People and the Environment Mattered: Pedestrian Accessibility the First Step." *Economic and Political Weekly* 44, no. 33: 43–51.

Bangladesh Bureau of Statistics. 2007. *Population Census 2001: National Series, Volume 1 – Analytical Report.* Bangladesh Bureau of Statistics.

Barro, R. J. 1999. "Determinants of Democracy." *Journal of Political Economy* 107, no. 6, part 2: S158–83.

Bhabha Atomic Research Centre. n.d. http://bit.ly/gwSOh1 (accessed 22 July 2011).

Bhagwati, J. 1995. "US Trade Policy: The Infatuation with Free Trade Areas." In *The Dangerous Drift to Preferential Trade Agreements,* edited by J. Bhagwati and A. Krueger. Washington, DC: American Enterprise Institute for Public Policy Research.

Blackbourn, D. 2006. *The Conquest of Nature*. New York: W. W. Norton.

Bloom, D. E. 2012. "Population Dynamics in India and Implications for Economic Growth." In *The Handbook of the Indian Economy*, edited by C. Ghate. Oxford: Oxford University Press.

Bloom, D. E. and D. Canning. 2003. "Contraception and the Celtic Tiger." *Economic and Social Review* 34, no. 3: 229–47.

———. 2008. "Global Demographic Change: Dimensions and Economic Significance." *Population and Development Review* 33: 17–51.

Bloom, D. E., D. Canning and J. Sevilla. 2002. "The Demographic Dividend: A New Perspective on the Economic Consequences of Population Change." RAND, MR-1274.

Bloom, D. E. and J. Williamson. 1998. "Demographic Transitions and Economic Miracles in Emerging Asia." *World Bank Economic Review* 12, no. 3: 419–55.

Boserup, E. 1970. "Male and Female Farming Systems." In *Women's Role in Economic Development*, 15–35. New York: St Martin's Press.

BP Statistical Review. 2010. http://bit.ly/iopjO2. (accessed 22 July 2011).

Brass, P. 2003. *The Production of Hindu–Muslim Violence in Contemporary India*. Seattle: University of Washington Press.

Briscoe, J. and U. Qamar. 2005. *Pakistan's Water Economy: Running Dry*. New York: Oxford University Press.

Bruinsma, Jelle, ed. 2003. *World Agriculture: Towards 2015/30, an FAO Perspective*. Rome: United Nations Food and Agriculture Organization.

Burra, S., S. Patel and T. Kerr. 2003. "Community-Designed, Built and Managed Toilet Blocks in Indian Cities." *Environment and Urbanization* 15, no. 2: 11–32.

Castells, M. 2010. *Rise of the Network Society*. 2nd ed. Oxford: Wiley-Blackwell.

Center for Human Rights and Global Justice. 2011. *Every Thirty Minutes: Farmer Suicides, Human Rights and the Agrarian Crisis in India*. New York: New York University School of Law.

Central Pollution Control Board (CPCB). 2013. Ambient air quality data. New Delhi: Central Pollution Control Board. http://www.cpcb.nic.in/ (accessed April 2013).

Centre for the Study of Developing Societies. 2007. *State of Democracy in South Asia*. New Delhi: Oxford University Press.

Chaturvedi, S. 2007. "Trade Facilitation Measures in South Asian FTAs: An Overview of Initiatives and Policy Approaches." In UNESCAP, *Trade Facilitation beyond the Multilateral Trade Negotiations: Regional Practices, Customs Valuation and Other Emerging Issues – A Study by the Asia-Pacific Research and Training Network on Trade*, 83–115. New York: United Nations.

Chinese and Indian Special Representatives on the Boundary Question. 2009. "2009 Press Release." http://bit.ly/gEtu1P (accessed 18 June 2011).

Chowdhury, A. 2007. "A Critical Overview of the Growth of the Media Sector." In *Unbundling Governance, the Bangladesh Governance Report*, edited by H. Z. Rahman. Dhaka: Power and Participation Research Centre (PPRC).

———. 2011. Skype discussion with the author.

Central Intelligence Agency (CIA). n.d. *CIA – The World Factbook*. Washington, DC: CIA.

Clague, C., S. Gleason, and S. Knack. 2001. "Determinants of Lasting Democracy in Poor Countries: Culture, Development, and Institutions." *Annals of the American Academy of Political and Social Science* 573: 16–41.

Committee to Protect Journalists (CPJ). 2013. "From Islamabad to Hyderabad, Journalist Safety at Issue." CPJ. http://bit.ly/10aPSag (accessed 20 March 2013).

Coomaraswamy, R. 2005. "Human Security and Gender Violence." *Economic and Political Weekly*, 29 October, 4729–36.

Cooper, A. F., R. A. Higgott and K. R. Nossal. 1991. "Bound to Follow? Leadership and Followership in the Gulf Conflict." *Political Science Quarterly* 106: 391–410.

Crystal, D. 2004. "Subcontinent Raises Its Voice." *Guardian*, 19 November. http://bit.ly/g1f1nG (accessed 3 August 2011).

Dadush, U and B. Stancil. 2010. "The World Order in 2050." Carnegie Endowment for International Peace Policy Outlook, 21 April.

De, P., A. R. Khan and S. Chaturvedi. 2008. "Transit and Trade Barriers in Eastern South Asia: A Review of the Transit Regime and Performance of Strategic Border-Crossings." Asia-Pacific Research and Training Network on Trade, Working Paper Series no. 56.

deSouza, P. R., S. Palshikar, and Y. Yadav. 2008. "The Democracy Barometers: Surveying South Asia." *Journal of Democracy* 19, no. 1: 84–96.

Department for International Development. 2007. "Bangladesh in 2030: A DFID Horizon Scan."

Diamond, L. 1999. *Developing Democracy: Toward Consolidation*. Baltimore: Johns Hopkins University Press.

Dutt, B. 2011. "Confessions of a War Reporter." *Himal Southasian*, June. http://bit.ly/WyR3dw (accessed 20 March 2013).

Embassy of the People's Republic of China in India. 2008. "A Shared Vision for the 21st Century of the People's Republic of China and the Republic of India." http://bit.ly/ggo5Rb (accessed 3 August 2011).

Fallows, J. 2007. "China Makes, the World Takes." *Atlantic Monthly* 300, no. 1: 48–72.

Fernandez-Castilla, R., G. Martine, G. McGranahan and M. Montgomery, eds. 2008. *The New Global Frontier: Urbanization, Poverty and Environment in the 21st Century*. New York: Earthscan.

Fernando, L. and G. Gispert-Sauch. 2004. *Christianity in India: Two Thousand Years of Faith*. New Delhi: Viking.

Foroohar, R. 2009. "The Asian Century." *Newsweek*, 8 May. http://bit.ly/jcVHNn (accessed 22 July 2011).

Gabardi, W. 2000. *Negotiating Postmodernism*. Minneapolis: University of Minnesota Press.

Gasiorowski, M. J. and T. J. Power. 1998. "The Structural Determinants of Democratic Consolidation." *Comparative Political Studies* 31, no. 6: 740–71.

Gereffi, G. 2005. "The Global Economy: Organization, Governance, and Development." In *The Handbook of Economic Sociology*, edited by N. J. Smelser and R. Swedberg. Princeton: Princeton University Press.

Ghaffar, A., K. S. Reddy and M. Singhi. 2004. "Burden of Non-communicable Diseases in South Asia." *British Medical Journal* 328, no. 3: 807–10.

Ghani, E. and H. Kharas, eds. 2010. *The Service Revolution in South Asia*. Delhi: Oxford University Press.

Gilani, S. Y. R. 2008. "Address of the Prime Minister of Pakistan, Syed Yousuf Raza Gilani at the 15th SAARC Summit." http://bit.ly/itvI5O (accessed 18 June 2011).

Global Energy Observatory. n.d. "Current List of Nuclear Power Plants." http://bit.ly/igAn0Q (accessed 18 June 2011).

Goldman Sachs. 2007. "The N-11: More Than an Acronym." Goldman Sachs Global Research, Global Economics Paper no. 153.

———. 2007a. "India's Urbanization: Emerging Opportunities." Goldman Sachs Global Research, Asia Economics Analyst no. 07/13.

Gould, W. 2012. *Religion and Conflict in Modern South Asia*. Cambridge: Cambridge University Press.

Government of India. 2008. *Development Challenges in Extremist Affected Areas: Report of an Expert Group to Planning Commission*. New Delhi: Government of India.

Government of India, Planning Commission. 2006. *Integrated Energy Policy: Report of the Expert Committee*. New Delhi: Government of India.

Government of Karnataka. 2009. "Urban Development Policy 2009 Draft." Department of Urban Development.

Government of Pakistan, Planning Commission. 2010. "Final Report of the Panel of Economists: Medium Term Development Imperatives and Strategy for Pakistan."

Guilmoto, C. Z. 2007. "Characteristics of Sex-Ratio Imbalance in India, and Future Scenarios." United Nations Population Fund.

Haeri, S. 2002. *No Shame for the Sun: Lives of Professional Pakistani Women.* Syracuse: Syracuse University Press.

————. 2008. "Contested Terrains: Gender Justice and Violence against Women in South Asia." In *Another Side of India: Gender, Culture, and Development,* edited by B. G. McSweeney, 98–122. Paris: United Nations Educational, Scientific and Cultural Organization.

Hasan, A. 2008. "Financing the Sanitation Programme of the Orangi Pilot Project – Research and Training Institute in Pakistan." *Environment and Urbanization* 20, no. 1: 109–19.

Hasan, A., S. Patel, and D. Satterthwaite. 2005. "How to Meet the Millennium Development Goals (MDGs) in Urban Areas." *Environment and Urbanization* 17, no. 1: 3–19.

Hennessy, P. 2010. *The Secret State.* London: Penguin.

Hettne, B. et al., eds. 1999. *Globalism and the New Regionalism.* Basingstoke: Macmillan.

Hillebrand, E. 2008. "The Global Distribution of Income in 2050." *World Development* 36, no. 5: 727–40.

Hoodbhoy, P. 2009. "The Flight to Nowhere: Pakistan's Nuclear Trajectory." Heinrich-Böll-Stiftung.

————. 2011. "Pakistan Can't Handle Fukushima." *Express Tribune,* 22 March. http://bit.ly/hY5XLg (accessed 18 June 2011).

Housing and Land Rights Network. 2011. *Wikileaks, Housing Rights and Afghanistan: Documenting Gross Housing and Land Rights Violations as War Crimes.* Cairo: Housing and Land Rights Network.

Human Rights Watch. 1999. "Crime or Custom? Violence Against Women in Pakistan." http://bit.ly/pmFple (accessed 22 July 2011).

Humanitarian Futures Programme. 2010. "The Waters of the Third Pole: Sources of Threat, Sources of Survival."

Imam, B. 2009. "Myanmar Gas Bypasses India, Bangladesh." *Daily Star,* 17 December. http://bit.ly/eHimz5 (accessed 3 August 2011).

Independent Power Producers of Nepal (IPPAN) and Confederation of Indian Industry (CII). 2006. "Research on Nepal India Cooperation on Hydropower (NICOH)." January.

Independent South Asian Commission on Poverty Alleviation (ISACPA). 2007. "Taking the SDGs Forward." March.

International Energy Agency. 2009. *Energy Balances of Non-OECD Countries.* Paris: International Energy Agency.

Iyer, Ramaswamy R. 2012. "Dealing with Pakistan's Fears on Water." *The Hindu,* 28 January.

James, C. 2009. "Global Status of Commercialized Biotech/GM Crops: 2009." International Service for the Acquisition of Agri-Business Application, ISAAA Brief no. 41.

Jha, P. et al. 2011. "Trends in Selective Abortions of Girls in India: Analysis of Nationally Representative Birth Histories from 1990 to 2005 and Census Data from 1991 to 2011." *The Lancet* 377, no. 9781: 1921–8.

Joeck, N. *Maintaining Nuclear Stability in South Asia.* Adelphi Paper 312. Oxford: Oxford University Press, 1997.

Joshua, A. 2012. "Pakistan to Switch to Negative List for Trade with India." *The Hindu,* 29 February.

Kaminski, M. 2009. "India and the Future of South Asia." *Wall Street Journal,* 25 May.

Kapur, D. and P. B. Mehta. 2005. *Public Institutions in India: Performance and Design.* New Delhi: Oxford University Press.

Kerr, P. K. and M. B. Nikitin. 2010. "Pakistan's Nuclear Weapons: Proliferation and Security Issues." Congressional Research Service report, 19 March.

Krepon, M. 2003. "The Stability–Instability Paradox, Misperception and Escalation Control in South Asia." Henry L. Stimson Center paper.

Krishna, S. M. 2009. "Inaugural Address by EAM at Conference on South Asian Economic Integration." Ministry of External Affairs, India. http://bit.ly/jQnrgW (accessed 18 June 2011).

Lall, M. and I. Lodhi. 2007. "Political Economy of Iran–Pakistan–India (IPI) Gas Pipeline." ISAS Working Paper no. 26.

Lawrence, M., P. Goodwin, M. O'Connor and D. Onkal. 2006. "Judgmental Forecasting: A Review of Progress Over the Last 25 Years." *International Journal of Forecasting* 22: 493–518.

Lipset, S. M. 1959. "Some Social Requisites of Democracy: Economic Development and Political Legitimacy." *American Political Science Review* 53, no. 1: 69–105.

Maddison, A. 2003a. *The World Economy: Historical Statistics*. Paris: OECD Development Centre.

———. 2003b. Angus Maddison website. http://bit.ly/jRKBFO (accessed 22 July 2011).

Mahbub ul Haq Human Development Centre (HDC). 2000. *Human Development in South Asia 2000: The Gender Question*. New York: Oxford University Press.

Makhdum, S. Z. D. 2006. *Tuhfat ul-Mujahidin*. Translated by S. M. H. Nainar. Calicut: Other Books.

Makridakis, S. G., S. C. Wheelwright and R. J. Hyndman. 1998. *Forecasting: Methods and Applications*. 3rd ed. New York: John Wiley and Sons.

Manchanda, R., ed. 2009. *Living on the Margins: Minorities in South Asia*. Kathmandu: EurasiaNet.

———. 2011. "Kargil Conflict: War in a Media Society." In *Kargil and After: Challenges for Indian Policy*, edited by K. Bajpai, A. Karim and A. Mattoo. New Delhi: Har Anand.

Marris, P. and S. Thornham, eds. 2000. *Media Studies: A Reader*. 2nd ed. New York: New York University Press.

Martine, G., G. McGranahan, M. Montgomery, R. Fernández-Castilla, eds. 2008. *The New Global Frontier: Urbanization, Poverty and Environment in the 21st Century*. London: Earthscan.

McKinzie, M., Z. Mian, A. H. Nayyar and M. V. Ramana. 2001. "The Risks and Consequences of Nuclear War in South Asia." In *Out of the Nuclear Shadow*, edited by S. Kothari and Z. Mian. London and Delhi: Zed Books, Rainbow Press and Lokayan.

McSweeney, B. G., ed. 2008. *Another Side of India: Gender, Culture, and Development*. Paris: United Nations Educational, Scientific and Cultural Organization.

Menon-Sen, K. and A. K. Shiva Kumar. 2001. *Women in India: How Free? How Equal?* New Delhi: United Nations Resident Coordinator in India.

Mian, Z. and A. H. Nayyar. 1999. "Pakistan's Chashma Nuclear Power Plant: A Preliminary Study of Some Safety Issues and Estimates of the Consequences of a Severe Accident." In Center for Energy and Environmental Studies Report no. 321.

Ministry of Finance and Planning, Department of Census and Statistics (DCS) [Sri Lanka]. 2007. "Poverty in Sri Lanka (Based on Household Income and Expenditure Survey – 2006/07)."

Ministry of Road Transport and Highways (MORTH). 2012. *Road Transport Year Book* (2009–10 and 2010–11). Government of India, Ministry of Road Transport and Highways.

Misquita, S. 2009. "Defense Contractors Target Big Jump in India's Military Spending." *Wall Street Journal*, 17 July. http://on.wsj.com/hpBqMd (accessed 3 August 2011).

Misra, A. 2004. *Identity and Religion: Foundations of Anti-Islamism in India*. New Delhi: Sage.

Nakamura, D. 2010. "Pakistan's Press Piles on President." *Washington Post*, 21 October. . http://wapo.st/mLSVLL (accessed 3 August 2011).

NASA. 2002. "Visible Earth." NASA Goddard Space Flight Center, 11 February.

National Intelligence Council. 2008. *Global Trends 2025: A Transformed World*. Washington, DC: Government Printing Office.

Nayyar, A. H., M. V. Ramana, and Z. Mian. 2011. "Fukushima Lessons." *Dawn*, 27 March. http://bit.ly/fySZwq (accessed 3 August 2011).

Nussbaum, M. 2009. *The Clash Within: Democracy, Religious Violence and India's Future*. Cambridge, MA: Harvard University Press.

Obeyesekere, G. 2004. "Dutthagamani and the Buddhist Conscience." In *Religion and Political Conflict in South Asia: India, Pakistan and Sri Lanka*, edited by D. Allen. Westport: Greenwood Press.

Office of Technology Assessment. 1979. *The Effects of Nuclear War*. Washington, DC: Office of Technology Assessment.

Ohmae, K. 1993. "The Rise of the Region State." *Foreign Affairs* 72 (Spring): 78–87.

Page, D. and W. Crawley. 2000. *Satellites over South Asia: Broadcasting Culture, and the Public Interest*. New Delhi: Sage.

_____. 2009. "Diversity and Convergence: Indian and South Asian Approaches to Media Regulation." Paper presented at the 59th Annual Conference of the International Communication Association, Chicago, 21–5 May. http://bit.ly/j4WZiF (accessed 18 June 2011).

Palit, A. 2010. "Is China or India Ageing Better?" http://bit.ly/hXBB0f (accessed 18 June 2011).

Panneerselvan, A. S. 2010. "Re-imagining India–Pakistan Relations." *Aman ki Asha*, 15 April. http://bit.ly/iVDuCF (accessed 18 June 2011).

Population Reference Bureau (PRB). n.d. http://bit.ly/lxDhEK (accessed 22 July 2011).

Panneerselvan, A. S. 2011. Skype discussion with the writer.

Quinlan, M. 2009. *Thinking about Nuclear Weapons: Principles, Problems, Prospects*. New York: Oxford University Press.

Rajan, S. I. n.d. "Assessing the Economic Well-Being of Eldery Persons in South Asia." UN ESCAP Draft Background Paper. http://bit.ly/dESp1s (accessed 3 August 2011).

Ramana, M. V. 2009. "The Indian Nuclear Industry: Status and Prospects 2009." Centre for International Governance Innovation Nuclear Energy Futures Paper no. 9.

Ramanathan. V. et al. 2005. "Atmospheric Brown Clouds: Impacts on South Asian Climate and Hydrological Cycle." *Proceedings of the National Academy of Sciences of the USA* 105, no. 15: 5326–33.

Rantattani, H. 2007. *Mappila Muslims: A Study on Society and Anti Colonial Struggles*. Calicut: Other Books.

Rashid, A. 2012. "Pakistan on the brink: all crisis, no potential?" *The Globalist*, 23 March.

Rashid, S. 2000. "Compact Township as a Strategy for Economic Development." *Asian Affairs*. 22, no. 1: 7–24.

Reporters Without Borders. n.d. http://bit.ly/qgEtNK (accessed 22 July 2011).

Reuters. 2005. "US Unveils Plans to Make India 'Major World Power.'"

Revi. A. 2007. "Global & National Population-Education Trend Benchmarking." *International Futures* 5, no. 34. Denver: University of Denver.

Roberts, B. and T. Kanaley. 2006. "Lessons and Strategies for Sustainable Urban Futures." In *Urbanization and Sustainability in Asia: Case Studies of Good Practice*, edited by B. Roberts and T. Kanaley. Manila: Asian Development Bank.

Rondinelli, D. A. 1986. "Metropolitan Growth and Secondary Cities Development Policy." *Habitat International* 10, nos. 1–2: 263–71.

South Asian Association for Regional Cooperation (SAARC). 1985. *SAARC Charter*. Dhaka: SAARC. http://bit.ly/glBBgI (accessed 18 June 2011).

_____. n.d. *SAARC Charter of Democracy*. http://bit.ly/ppApt1 (accessed 18 June 2011).

Sabia, D. 1997. *Contradiction and Conflict: Popular Church in Nicaragua*. Tuscaloosa: University of Alabama Press.

Sambrook, R. 2005. "Citizen Journalism and the BBC." Nieman Reports, Winter. http://hvrd.me/lwQRoF (accessed 18 June 2011).

Schell, O. 2010. "The Message from the Glaciers." *New York Review of Books*, 27 May, 46–50.

Siddiqa, A. 2013. "The New Frontiers: Militancy and Radicalism in Punjab." Centre for International Strategic Analysis (SISA) Report no. 2. http://bit.ly/Xdh6K7 (accessed 23 February 2013).

Silverman, J. G., M. R. Decker, J. Gupta, A. Dharmadhikari, G. R. Seage III and A. Raj. 2008. "Syphilis and Hepatitis B Co-Infection Among HIV-Infected, Sex-Trafficked Women and Girls, Nepal." *Emerging Infectious Diseases* 14, no. 6: 932–4.

Singh, J. 1999. *Defending India*. New York: St Martin's Press.

Singh, M. 2008. "PM's Opening Remarks at the Press Conference in Srinagar." Prime Minister's Office. http://bit.ly/fhrw0v (accessed 18 June 2011).

———. 2009. "Prime Minister's Speech at 92nd Annual Conference of the Indian Economic Association." Press Information Bureau, Government of India. http://bit.ly/gfbTv4 (accessed 18 June 2011).

Stockholm International Peace Research Institute (SIPRI). 2011. "India World's Largest Arms Importer According to New SIPRI Data on International Arms Transfers." http://bit.ly/erUZv0 (accessed 22 July 2011).

Smith, C. 1991. *The Emergence of Liberation Theology: Radical Religion and Social Movement Theory*. Chicago: University of Chicago Press.

Söderbaum, F. and T. M. Shaw, eds. 2004. *Theories of New Regionalism: A Palgrave Reader*. Basingstoke: Palgrave.

Stads, G. J. and M. Rahija. 2012. "Public Agricultural R&D in South Asia." ASTI Synthesis Report, September.

Stern, R. W. 2003. *Changing India: Bourgeois Revolution on the Subcontinent*. Cambridge: Cambridge University Press.

Surowiecki, J. 2004. *The Wisdom of Crowds: Why the Many are Smarter Than the Few and How Collective Wisdom Shapes Business, Economies, Societies, and Nations*. 1st ed. New York: Doubleday.

Synnott, H. 1999. *The Causes and Consequences of South Asia's Nuclear Tests*. London: IIIS.

Telegeography Research 2010. Presentation at Telegeography International Telecom Trends Seminar, Pacific Telecommunication Council, Honolulu, HI, 17 January.

Thakur, R. 2012. "A Changing Chessboard: The New Great Game in Afghanistan." *Global Asia* 7, no. 4 (Winter): 87–91.

Thakur, R. and L. V. Langenhove. 2006. "Enhancing Global Governance through Regional Integration." *Global Governance* 12, no. 3: 233–40.

Times of India. 2009. "Army Reworks War Doctrine for Pakistan, China." 30 December. http://bit.ly/eboEuy (accessed 22 July 2011).

———. 2012. "Trade Dividend." 2 March. http://bit.ly/WTWQzg (accessed 19 March 2013).

Tynan, D. 2010. "The Turkmenistan–Afghanistan–Pakistan–India (TAPI) Pipeline Looks Set to Go Ahead." EurasiaNet. http://bit.ly/eJ1cQB (accessed 3 August 2011).

United Nations (UN). 2011. "Report of the Secretary-General's Panel Of Experts On Accountability in Sri Lanka."

———. 2012. *The Millennium Development Goals Report 2012*. New York: UN.

———. Various years. United Nations Economic Survey of Asia and Far East.

United Nations Conference on Trade and Development (UNCTAD). 2012. "Trade and Development Report, 2012."

United Nations Department of Economic Social Affairs (UNDESA). 2011. *World Urbanization Prospects 2011 Revision*. New York: UNDESA.

———. 2013. Population Division Data Bank. http://bit.ly/6bu54 (accessed 20 March 2013).

United Nations Development Programme (UNDP). 1995. *Human Development Report 1995: Gender and Human Development*. New York: Oxford University Press.

———. 2009. *Human Development Report 2009: Overcoming Barriers: Human Mobility and Development*. New York: Palgrave Macmillan.

_____. 2010. *Asia-Pacific Human Development Report: Power, Voice and Rights: A Turning Point for Gender Equality in Asia and the Pacific*. Delhi: Macmillan.

_____. 2010a. *Power, Voice and Rights: a Turning Point for Gender Equality in Asia and the Pacific*. New York: Macmillan.

_____. 2010b. *Human Development Report 2010 – The Real Wealth of Nations: Pathways to Human Development*. New York: Palgrave Macmillan.

_____. 2011. *Human Development Report – Sustainability and Equity: A Better Future for All*. New York: Palgrave Macmillan.

United Nations Educational, Scientific and Cultural Organization (UNESCO). 2010. *EFA (Education for All) Global Monitoring Report 2010: Reaching the Marginalized*. Oxford and Paris: Oxford University Press and UNESCO.

_____. 2012. *EFA (Education for All) Global Monitoring Report 2010 – Youth and Skills: Putting Education to Work*. Oxford and Paris: Oxford University Press and UNESCO.

United Nations Food and Agriculture Organization. 2006. *World Agriculture: Towards 2030/2050*. Rome: Food and Agriculture Organization. http://bit.ly/mEQeV5 (accessed 22 July 2011).

_____. 2008. "How to Feed the World in 2050." http://bit.ly/iBK0jY (accessed 22 July 2011).

_____. Various years. FAOSTAT data. Available via http://www.fao.org

United Nations Population Division. 2009. "World Population Prospects: The 2008 Revision." Working Paper no. ESA/P/WP.210.

_____. 2010. "World Population Prospects: The 2010 Revision." http://bit.ly/m1CdDS (accessed April 2013).

_____. 2011. *World Urbanization Prospects: The 2011 Revision*. New York: United Nations. http://esa.un.org/unup/unup/index_panel2.html (accessed April 2013).

United Nations Security Council. 2009. "Security Council Resolution 1887 [on Nuclear Non-proliferation and Nuclear Disarmament]." S/RES/1887, 24 September. http://bit.ly/oqG0ZS (accessed 3 August 2011).

United Nations Statistics Division (UNSTAT). 2009. UNSD Statistical Databases. http://bit.ly/jYQihR (accessed 22 July 2011).

US Department of Energy. n.d. "Energy Information Service." http://1.usa.gov/kdwjbx (accessed 22 July 2011).

US Department of State. 2010. "Country Reports on Terrorism 2009." 5 August, 147–63. http://1.usa.gov/kdwjbx (accessed 22 July 2011).

US Senate Committee on Foreign Relations. 2009. *Sri Lanka: Recharting US Strategy after the War*. Washington, DC: US Government Printing Office.

Varshney, A. 2003. *Ethnic Conflict and Civil Life: Hindus and Muslims in India*. New Haven: Yale University Press.

Waseem, M. 2011. Skype discussion with the writer.

Weerahewa, J. "Impact of Trade Facilitation Measures and Regional Trade Agreements on Food and Agricultural Trade in South Asia." Asia-Pacific Research and Training Network on Trade, Working Paper Series no. 69.

Weiss, A. M. 1992. *Walls within Walls: Life Histories of Working Women in the Old City of Lahore*. Boulder: Westview Press and Pak Books. [Republished by Oxford University Press, 2002.]

Wolfram Alpha Computational Knowledge Engine. 2009. Wolfram Alpha curated data 2009, retrieved 8 December 2009. http://bit.ly/j6P2nF (accessed 18 June 2011).

World Bank. 2007. *South Asia Growth and Regional Integration*. Washington, DC: World Bank.

_____. 2007a. *Fact Sheet: South Asia Growth and Regional Integration*. Washington, DC: World Bank.

_____. 2007b. *World Development Report 2008: Agriculture for Development*. Washington, DC: World Bank.

_____. 2009. World Development Indicators. http://bit.ly/gLzg6s (accessed 18 June 2011).

_____· 2009a. "GDP per capita (current US$)." World Development Indicators. http://bit.ly/i6Llen (accessed 18 June 2011).

_____· 2009b. "Workers' Remittances and Compensation of Employees, Received (current US$)." World Development Indicators. http://bit.ly/gIt3aW (accessed 18 June 2011).

_____· 2009c. *Doing Business 2010: Reforming through Difficult Times.* Washington, DC: World Bank.

_____· 2010. *World Development Indicators 2010.* Washington, DC: The World Bank.

_____· 2010a. "South Asia: Regional Strategy Update." http://bit.ly/icNN2m (accessed 18 June 2011).

_____· 2010b. *South Asia Economic Update: Moving Up – Looking East.* Washington, DC: World Bank, June.

_____· 2010c. "South Asia: Data, Projects and Research." http://bit.ly/eLht0Y (accessed 18 June 2011).

_____· Various years. World DataBank. Available from http://databank.worldbank.org/data/home.aspx

World Commission on Dams. 2000. *Dams and Development: A New Framework for Decision-Making.* London: Earthscan.

World Health Organization. 2001. *Macroeconomics and Health: Investing in Health for Economic Development.* Geneva: World Health Organization.

_____· 2008. *The Global Burden of Disease: 2004 Update.* Geneva: World Health Organization.

_____· 2009. *Global Status Report on Road Safety: Time for Action.* Geneva: World Health Organization.

World Health Organization and United Nation Children's Fund. 2010. *Progress on Sanitation and Drinking Water – 2010 Update.* Geneva: World Health Organization.

Zaidi, A. K., M. S. Awasthi and H. Janaka de Silva. 2004. "Burden of Infectious Diseases in South Asia." *British Medical Journal* 328, no. 3: 811–15.

Zakaria, F. 2009. *The Post-American World.* New York: W. W. Norton.

Zao, X. 2009. "South Asia in the Context of Global Financial Meltdown." Introductory remarks, 2nd South Asia Economic Summit, New Delhi. http://bit.ly/ld8PKx (accessed 18 June 2011).

Zardari, A. A. 2009. "Statement at the Sixty-Fourth Session of the UN General Assembly." New York: Pakistan Permanent Mission to the United Nations.

_____· 2009a. "How to Mend Fences with Pakistan." *New York Times.* http://nyti.ms/hER1Ma (accessed 3 August 2011).

INDEX

www.ingramcontent.com/pod-product-compliance
Lightning Source LLC
Chambersburg PA
CBHW021850020426
42334CB00013B/260